D0884341

When Prayer Fails

When Prayer Fails

Faith Healing, Children, and the Law

SHAWN FRANCIS PETERS

OXFORD
UNIVERSITY PRESS

2008

OXFORD
UNIVERSITY PRESS

Oxford University Press, Inc., publishes works that further
Oxford University's objective of excellence
in research, scholarship, and education.

Oxford   New York
Auckland   Cape Town   Dar es Salaam   Hong Kong   Karachi
Kuala Lumpur   Madrid   Melbourne   Mexico City   Nairobi
New Delhi   Shanghai   Taipei   Toronto

With offices in
Argentina   Austria   Brazil   Chile   Czech Republic   France   Greece
Guatemala   Hungary   Italy   Japan   Poland   Portugal   Singapore
South Korea   Switzerland   Thailand   Turkey   Ukraine   Vietnam

Copyright © 2008 by Oxford University Press, Inc.

Published by Oxford University Press, Inc.
198 Madison Avenue, New York, New York 10016

www.oup.com

Oxford is a registered trademark of Oxford University Press

Library of Congress Cataloging-in-Publication Data
Peters, Shawn Francis, 1966–
When prayer fails : faith healing, children, and the law / by Shawn Francis Peters.
    p. cm.
Includes bibliographical references and index.
ISBN 978-0-19-530635-4
1. Child health services—Law and legislation—United States.
2. Spiritual healing—Law and legislation—United States.
3. Freedom of religion—United States.   I. Title.
KF3826.C48P48 2007
342.7308'52—dc22   2006102014

9 8 7 6 5 4 3 2 1

Printed in the United States of America
on acid-free paper

For Maisie and Fred

Acknowledgments

I would not have been able to complete this book without the support of my family. My wife, Susan, provided both emotional ballast and stern editorial guidance. Maisie and Fred, my adorable kids, gave me a reason to get up in the morning. My brother, Michael Peters, offered suggestions and doggedly tracked down some crucial documents in Pennsylvania. (He was assisted in that endeavor by George Clay, who also gets my thanks.)

Several mentors and colleagues at the University of Wisconsin–Madison contributed to the success of this project. Time and again, Professor Ronald Numbers proved to be an indefatigable advocate for me and my scholarship; he also waded through my manuscript and provided firm but fair criticism. Professors John Milton Cooper, Judith Leavitt, John Sharpless, and Jeremi Suri furnished support and counsel on a wide variety of matters. I am also grateful for the friendship and good cheer of the students and staff in the TRIO Student Support Services Program.

Outside my immediate university community, scholars Jonathan Baer (Wabash College), Gary McGee (Assemblies of God Theological Seminary), Amanda Porterfield (Florida State University), Rennie Schoepflin (California State University–Los Angeles), Melvin Urofsky (Virginia Commonwealth University), and Grant Wacker (Duke University) either fielded inquiries or reviewed portions of the manuscript. Their input helped immensely.

Last but certainly not least, Cynthia Read at Oxford University Press capably shepherded the book toward publication.

Contents

When Prayer Fails

I

"Pointless and Preventable"

An Overview of Religion-Based Medical Neglect of Children

A happy, vibrant toddler, Dean Michael Heilman enjoyed playing outside his family's home in Lawndale, a middle-class section of Philadelphia. When the weather turned mild, Michael (as he was known to family and friends) darted about the yard, awkwardly tossing footballs in the air or rolling toy trucks over the grass. The twenty-two-month-old and his older sister also escaped the city's oppressive summertime heat by splashing about in a shallow plastic wading pool that their parents set up in the yard. The Heilmans were not a wealthy family—Dean, Michael's father, labored as a tile setter and brought home a modest paycheck, and his mother did not work outside the home—but the children never suffered from want of such playthings. Dean and his wife, Susan, were "devoted parents," according to one of their neighbors, and they always provided plenty of toys for the kids.[1]

One night in July 1997, Susan Heilman heard a shriek from the backyard, where Michael and his sister were playing. She quickly left the house and discovered Michael wincing in pain. He had step-ped on something sharp—a piece of glass or a jagged bucket han-dle, his mother surmised—and it had cut his right foot. The small wound bled freely, so Susan dashed a short distance down the street to find her husband, who had just begun walking toward the family's nearby church. Dean immediately returned home, cleaned his son's cut with some water, and wrapped it in a towel. When this failed to stanch the wound, the elder Heilman affixed some gauze to Michael's foot with some tape and then enclosed it in a disposable plastic diaper. Still the wound bled: the boy left a bloody trail in his wake as he hobbled around the house.[2]

With his cut still bleeding, Michael went to bed at 8:30 that evening. He slept only fitfully and cried at regular intervals throughout the night; he also vomited several times. Early the following morning, after Susan Heilman checked her son's bandage and found it saturated in blood, her husband dressed the wound in fresh gauze and then wrapped Michael's foot in a piece of fabric. It was clear by this point that the boy was in serious distress. But the Heilmans neither dialed 911 to summon emergency medical personnel nor rushed their son to the nearest hospital. Instead, they called Charles A. Reinert, the pastor of their church, the Faith Tabernacle. In keeping with the doctrines of their faith, they determined that the best way to prevent their son from bleeding to death was to have Reinert lead them in offering prayers for his recovery.[3]

To justify their repudiation of medicine, members of the Faith Tabernacle— a relatively small church with branches located mainly in Pennsylvania and New Jersey—cited passages from the scriptures suggesting that prayer, not the work of doctors, healed sickness. "We believe," the church's profession of faith stated, "that the Bible is opposed to all means of healing apart from God's way . . . and all medical and surgical practice whatever." The Epistle of James, for instance, seemed to contain very clear directions regarding the appropriate treatment for illness or injury. There, Christians are advised:

> Are any among you suffering? They should pray. Are any cheerful?
> They should sing songs of praise. Are any among you sick? They
> should call for the elders of the church and have them pray over
> them, anointing them with oil in the name of the Lord. The prayer
> of faith will save the sick, and the Lord will raise them up; and any-
> one who has committed sins will be forgiven. (5:13–15)[4]

As he lay bleeding from the cut on his foot, Michael Heilman's parents in- terpreted this passage literally, and quite narrowly. Following the text of James as closely as possible, they summoned their pastor, Reinert, who anointed the boy with oil and led a prayer session over the youngster's prostrate body. When police later asked Susan Heilman why she and her husband had chosen this form of treatment instead of calling 911, she seemed almost baffled by the question. "When you're sick, you pray and ask the Lord to help heal you," she said. "That's divine healing. If you're sick, you ask the pastor to come out and anoint you, and pray with you."[5]

In retrospect, it might seem surprising that the Heilmans trusted that prayer would heal Michael's cut, for it had not proven to be a particularly ef- fective means of treating the many ailments and injuries that seemed to have dogged him throughout his childhood. Michael had "bruised easily his whole life," as his father put it. According to one later account, "obvious contusions of the forehead, abdomen, back, flank, thigh, [and] shin" dotted the boy's body. And then there were Michael's knees, which had long suffered from extensive swelling. One physician later said that, in her sixteen years of medical practice, she never had seen a child with knees in such poor condition. (She surmised that they were so damaged that Michael must have had difficulty walking.) Michael also had suffered from an earlier bout of excessive bleeding: his aunt later told law enforcement authorities that the boy once had bled profusely after cutting his lip.[6]

Although prayer apparently had failed to heal these earlier injuries, the Heilmans did not hesitate to rely on it when Michael cut his foot. They beckoned their minister, but Reinert's efforts failed to restore Michael's health. More than twelve hours after it had been cut, his foot continued to bleed, and the boy's overall condition spiraled downward. As his parents took turns cradling him in their arms, the child occasionally cried out in agony. Weakened from an enormous loss of blood, Michael had difficulty keeping his eyes open. Then he simply stopped breathing. Michael's aunt participated in the prayer vigil, and she futilely checked his neck for a pulse. Finally, after bleeding for roughly nineteen hours, the boy died in his mother's arms.[7]

An autopsy later revealed that Michael Heilman had bled so copiously—he lost nearly half of his blood—because he had been a hemophiliac. Altered by genetic abnormalities, his blood had lacked the clotting factors necessary to stop the bleeding caused by the cut on his foot. About seventeen thousand Americans (an overwhelming majority of them men) currently suffer from the disorder, and when they experience uncontrolled bleeding, doctors typically treat them with an infusion of the clotting factors that their bodies have failed to produce naturally. The effectiveness of such treatments is beyond question: a hemophilia specialist at The Children's Hospital of Philadelphia, who had seen the infusions work on numerous occasions, said that she never previously had seen a hemophilic child die from a cut. This expert, along with several other physicians who reviewed the circumstances of Michael Heilman's death, suggested that the boy's life could have been saved relatively easily if his parents had taken him to a hospital for treatment. A straightforward and reliable procedure, they claimed, would have stopped the bleeding. "If proper medical attention had been given," said Dr. Catherine Manno, "this child would have survived."[8]

Even as they grieved over his passing, Michael Heilman's parents dismissed such pronouncements about the efficacy of medical science. When Philadelphia police opened an investigation into the circumstances of the boy's death, the Heilmans clung to the doctrines of their church and brushed aside accusations that their religious faith had played a role in his demise. Susan Heilman stated that she had not attempted to seek medical help for her son because "it's against my religious beliefs." These beliefs were so strong, she informed police, that she would have tried to restrain anyone who attempted to resuscitate Michael through medical treatment. She had few doubts that she and her husband had been justified in relying on prayer. "Your children are a gift from God," Susan Heilman told police. "They are angels on loan from heaven. If He decided to take my angel back, then I can't question Him why. I asked for Michael to be healed, and God took Michael."[9]

Both Philadelphia newspapers featured extensive coverage of Michael Heilman's death and his parents' apparent lack of remorse for their roles in it. One typical story about both Michael Heilman and Patrick Foster, another local Faith Tabernacle child who had fallen victim to religion-based medical neglect, carried a sensational headline calling them "tiny victims of blind faith." The newspapers' interest in the grim circumstances of Michael's death only intensified when legal observers began to weigh in on the possibility that his parents might be prosecuted for neglect or even manslaughter. For some, it was clear that the Heilmans had shirked their fundamental legal duties as parents by failing to obtain adequate medical treatment for their son. One former prosecutor stated that, whatever their religious beliefs, "Parents have a duty and obligation to care for their children. Parents don't let a 22-month-old child bleed to death . . . . It's their duty to get him medical help." But others wondered if a jury would convict the couple on criminal charges. A Temple University law professor pointed out that it was unclear if Dean and Susan Heilman actually had known that Michael was a hemophiliac. If they had been unaware that their son's blood disorder put him at risk of bleeding to death, the professor argued, prosecutors might have a difficult time proving that they had engaged in "outrageous and unreasonable" conduct.[10]

On August 15, 1997, the office of the Philadelphia county district attorney formally charged the Heilmans with involuntary manslaughter and endangering the welfare of a child. (A count of criminal conspiracy initially was filed against them as well, but prosecutors later dropped it.) The complaint filed against Dean Heilman mentioned not only the circumstances of his son's death but also earlier instances when the boy had been harmed by religion-based medical neglect:

> The defendant unlawfully endangered the welfare and caused the death of the decedent, Dean [Michael] Heilman, a hemophiliac, defendant's 22 month old son, by failing to obtain medical treatment when the child sustained a puncture wound to the foot, causing death by exsanguination [total blood loss], and defendant failed to obtain medical treatment for the child previously when he cut his lip or otherwise sustained bruising/injury.

The district attorney underscored the seriousness of the charges when he asked that the couple post ten thousand dollars in bail each. (Local authorities required them to post 10 percent of that amount, or one thousand dollars each, in cash.)[11]

The Heilmans' lawyers vehemently disputed the notion that, by choosing prayer over medicine, they knowingly had put their son's health at risk. Susan

Heilman's lawyer insisted that she had not known of Michael's hemophilia and asserted that both she and her husband "took extraordinary care of this child." Echoing these arguments, Dean Heilman's attorney characterized the couple as "good parents" who had violated no law. "You don't have criminality here," public defender Karl Schwartz said, because the Heilmans had made an earnest—if perhaps ultimately misguided—attempt to treat their son's injury through prayer.[12]

Not surprisingly, assistant district attorney Edward Cameron, whose office filed the criminal charges against the Heilmans, had a radically different view of the case. For Cameron, it mattered little that the couple had been following the doctrines of their church by treating Michael solely with prayer; their conduct amounted to child abuse. "Any reasonable person," he said at a preliminary hearing held before Municipal Judge Eric Lilian, would have rushed Michael to an emergency room for medical treatment after it had become apparent that prayer was not stanching the flow of blood from the cut on his foot. "What kind of parent looks at one of these diapers that are blood-soaked and [doesn't know] something is wrong?" Cameron added. By failing to take the obvious steps that would have saved their son's life, the couple had engaged in criminal wrongdoing, he argued.[13]

Lilian saw enough merit in this argument to order the couple to stand trial on the manslaughter and child endangerment charges. The judge respected the Heilmans' right to practice their religion freely, which both the commonwealth and federal constitutions protected. Yet there were clear limits to such rights, he held, when their exercise appeared to threaten the best interests of a child. "The parents' right to practice their religion ends where the child's welfare begins," Lilian said from the bench. "Young Dean Michael's life may have hung in the balance, but he had no voice because he was too young to speak on his own behalf." If convicted on all charges, the couple faced prison sentences ranging from eight and one half to seventeen years.[14]

In October 1998, both Dean and Susan Heilman pled "no contest" to the involuntary manslaughter and child endangerment charges. When it came time to sentence the couple, Court of Common Pleas Judge Carolyn Temin heard impassioned arguments from both sides of the case. Customarily blunt, prosecutor Edward Cameron asked that the members of the Faith Tabernacle receive a stiff penalty for having denied medical treatment to their dying son. Although Dean and Susan Heilman were devoutly religious and had acted on the basis of their sincere beliefs, they were, he said, "no different from anyone who kills a child anywhere in Pennsylvania" and thus deserved an appropriately severe punishment. Pulling no rhetorical punches, Cameron stated that jail sentences were warranted for the Heilmans because "they are murderers."[15]

The Heilmans' attorneys protested this withering characterization of their clients. In asking that the couple receive relatively lenient sentences— probation rather than imprisonment—both lawyers did their best to portray the couple as loving, concerned parents who never had intended to harm their child. Karl Schwartz called the Heilmans "ideal parents" and suggested that they already had been punished enough by the "devastating" loss of their beloved child. He also blasted the prosecutor's call for prison terms as a "reckless suggestion." Given the unique circumstances of the case and the unimpeachable character of the defendants, Schwartz maintained, probation represented a more appropriate punishment.[16]

The judge agreed. Temin sentenced the Heilmans to seventeen years of probation each and fined them two thousand dollars each. She also ordered them to attend parenting classes at a nearby hospital and to provide medical treatment to their two surviving children. As she imposed these penalties, Temin acknowledged the complexity of the sociolegal issues presented by the case. The judge said that she was "appalled" by the circumstances of this "hideous, tragic death," which "could have been totally prevented" by a trip to the hospital and appropriate medical treatment. She understood that the couple had been following the dictates of their faith, and she acknowledged that the courts had to "respect everyone's religion" and thereby safeguard individual rights. Nonetheless, it was clear to Temin that "the state requires certain standards" for the care of children and that the Heilmans, by denying medical treatment to their son, clearly had failed to meet them. Punishment thus was, in her assessment, warranted.[17]

Temin tempered her criticism for the Heilmans' conduct by praising their obvious devotion to Michael. The judge noted that the couple had loved their son deeply and that they never had intended to harm him. Their choice of prayer over medicine had proven to be a fatal mistake, but there had been "no malice in the treatment of [him] by his parents," she believed. Temin also acknowledged that the Heilmans themselves had suffered a great deal as a result of Michael's untimely death, suggesting that "the perpetrators are also the victims here." Taking into consideration all of these mitigating factors, she concluded that the couple deserved to be spared imprisonment.[18]

Harrowing incidents of religion-based medical neglect—in which devout parents, adhering to the doctrines of their faiths, refuse to furnish medical care to their ailing children—are not unique to a single church or a particular geographical area. Since the late nineteenth century, this phenomenon has imperiled the youngest and most vulnerable members of a variety of religious faiths in every region of the United States. From Massachusetts to California, hundreds of children have died as Michael Heilman did—in agony, and aided by little more than the ardent bedside prayers of their parents and fellow church members.

Many such deaths, as well as numerous nonfatal cases of neglect resulting from parents' exclusive reliance on spiritual-healing practices, have generated tangled criminal litigation. Indeed, cases similar to the prosecution of Dean and Susan Heilman have abounded in American courts for more than a century. The defendants in these cases typically have been intensely religious parents whose lives revolve around the doctrines and practices of small, close-knit Christian churches that ground their doctrines in narrowly literal interpretations of the Bible. As they have attempted to refute charges of manslaughter or neglect, these parents adamantly have claimed that the First Amendment safeguards their decision to adhere to their faiths' religious traditions and treat their ailing children solely by spiritual means, as they believe the scriptures mandate. They often have complemented these arguments with claims that they possess a fundamental right as parents to direct the upbringing of their children without interference from the state.

The prosecutors who have filed criminal charges against spiritual healers have taken a dramatically different view of the legal issues presented by cases of religion-based medical neglect of children. While respecting the right of individuals to freely practice their religious faiths, law enforcement authorities in these cases have balked at the notion that constitutional protections for religious liberty provide an absolute bar to state regulation of religious conduct, particularly when that behavior puts the safety of children at risk. They also have disputed the claim that the state has no right to limit the authority of parents to direct the upbringing of their children. Children have rights as well, prosecutors argue, and, in extraordinary circumstances, the state has a clear duty to intervene and safeguard them, even if it means abrogating the rights of their parents.

Instances of religion-based medical neglect of children frequently generated intense public interest in both the United States and Great Britain in the late nineteenth and early twentieth centuries. In England, for instance, members of a sect known as the Peculiar People became embroiled in a controversial series of neglect cases that began in the mid-1800s and lasted until the 1930s. Like many spiritual healers, members of this church took their cue from the Epistle of James and treated their children's illnesses exclusively with prayer and anointing. The results of this approach often were deadly: a host of ailments, including scarlet fever, diphtheria, and pneumonia, ravaged children in the church. In response, English authorities, in an effort that prefigured the later work of their American counterparts, mounted a succession of manslaughter and neglect prosecutions against church parents who had relied solely on spiritual-healing practices to treat their sick children. Not everyone approved of these legal endeavors; playwright George Bernard Shaw (hardly a religious zealot himself) wondered why the Peculiar People were targeted for prosecution more often than the physicians whose medical treatments routinely failed to heal patients. Nonetheless, the Peculiar People cases had widespread significance, establishing judicial precedent in England and influencing American courts' nascent approaches to the difficult legal and ethical issues raised by religion-based medical neglect.[19]

In the United States, cases such as the prosecution of a New York railroad clerk named J. Luther Pierson precipitated debates over the efficacy of medical science, the role of prayer in healing, and the obligations of both parents and the state to safeguard the physical well-being of children. Two of Pierson's children died in 1901 after he chose to treat their illnesses solely with prayer. "We believe that if we called a physician it might tend to the destruction of the child," Pierson said of the tenets of his faith, the Christian Catholic Church (which had been founded by the controversial healer John Alexander Dowie), "and that instead of the child being saved it would surely die. To avoid its death we adopted the mode and prayer of our creed and our belief and exerted ourselves for the child's protection and safety." Authorities charged Pierson with unlawfully withholding medical care from his infant daughter, who had succumbed to catarrhal pneumonia. A judge found him guilty, and the state's highest appellate court upheld the verdict, holding that parents could not shirk "the duty of caring for their young in sickness and in health, and of doing whatever may be necessary for their care, maintenance and preservation, including medical attendance if necessary." This benchmark ruling helped to bolster the emerging legal doctrine that parents, whatever their religious beliefs, had a legal duty to provide adequate medical treatment to their children.[20]

Locally, the *Pierson* precedent took an added significance when authorities mounted several other prosecutions of "faith-curists" (as the press dubbed them) who had failed to provide medical care to their sick children. Featuring innocent child victims and defendants who espoused apparently extreme beliefs about the curative power of prayer, cases such as the prosecution of Mr. and Mrs. John Quimby made compelling copy for journalists, and dozens of stories about them appeared in New York newspapers in the first decade of the twentieth century. The Quimbys—Christian Scientists from White Plains— were charged with manslaughter in 1902 after their seven-year-old daughter, Esther, died from a bout with diphtheria. The headline of a typical *New York Times* story on the Quimby case read, "Child Died without Medical Attendance; 'Diphtheria and Christian Science Neglect' the Causes."[21]

Ninety years later, cases similar to the prosecutions of Pierson and the Quimbys still were surprisingly common. In 1991, a measles outbreak in Philadelphia claimed the lives of five young members of the Heilman family's church, the Faith Tabernacle, after their parents spurned conventional medical treatment (including vaccinations) and attempted to cure their ailments by spiritual means alone. At the height of the measles outbreak, desperate public health authorities assembled a team of doctors to conduct hundreds of at-home visits to determine if young members of the church were at risk. The physicians were shocked by what they discovered in some Faith Tabernacle homes: one later said that he felt as if he had entered into a "time warp," while another bemoaned the "19th century conditions" he had observed. Their canvass prompted the city's district attorney to obtain court orders mandating medical treatment for several afflicted children and vaccinations for others who were at risk of contracting the virus.[22]

A number of factors make it difficult to determine precisely how many children have lost their lives in such tragic circumstances. Members of some faith-healing churches isolate themselves, living in insular communities and minimizing their contacts with law enforcement authorities and other representatives of the modern society that they consider to be spiritually bankrupt. (As a Faith Tabernacle minister put it, "We don't mix with the world.") The deaths of many children in these churches simply have not been divulged to law enforcement officials because their parents fear that such reporting would result in increased scrutiny—and perhaps suppression—of their religious practices. As a result, numerous young victims of religion-based medical neglect have been buried without anyone outside their close-knit church communities knowing the precise circumstances of their deaths.[23]

Even the limited evidence that has been compiled on religion-based medical neglect of children is unsettling. A wide-ranging study funded by the National Center on Child Abuse and Neglect investigated whether forms of religion-related child abuse, such as the faith-based medical neglect that proved so deadly in the case of Michael Heilman, posed a greater risk to children than other, more widely publicized threats, such as ritual satanic abuse. By surveying thousands of psychologists, psychiatrists, and social workers, the study's authors identified dozens of instances in which parents had withheld medical care from their children for religious reasons. (In a typical account of religion-based medical neglect, one physician reported, "Child's tumor was untreated. Needed amputation was not allowed. Father believed child was being punished for sins and could be cured only through prayer.") The prevalence of such cases led the authors of the study to conclude that "there are more children actually being abused in the name of God than in the name of Satan."[24]

In 1998, pediatrician Seth Asser and Rita Swan, director of the advocacy group Children's Healthcare Is a Legal Duty (CHILD), coauthored a pathbreaking study that likewise attempted to assess the pervasiveness of religion-based medical neglect of children. (Swan had painful first-hand experience with the phenomenon: a former Christian Scientist, she founded CHILD after losing her son to bacterial meningitis.) Published in the journal *Pediatrics*, the article documented a total of 172 child fatalities—the great majority of them attributable to religion-based neglect—in faith-healing churches over a twenty-year span. But even as they reported this substantial tally, the authors of the study realized that they probably only had skimmed the surface of a surprisingly deep problem. "We suspect that many more fatalities have occurred during the study period than the cases reported here," Asser and Swan wrote. As Asser later put it, "We felt that this study was the tip of the iceberg. I'm sure that there are other deaths out there and other churches that we don't know about."[25]

Events in Oregon bore out Asser's point. The *Pediatrics* article appeared in April 1998, just as myriad child deaths linked to the Followers of Christ Church were making headlines in the Pacific Northwest. Asser and Swan learned of the Followers' deaths in Oregon, as well as those linked to the church in Idaho and Oklahoma, too late to incorporate them into their landmark study. (In fact, they apparently did not even learn of the small church's existence until after they had completed their exhaustive research.) Had they been able to add the deaths of Followers children, their count of religion-based medical-neglect deaths would have increased by about one-third.

The findings of the *Pediatrics* study underscored Asser's later assertion that most faith-based medical-neglect deaths are "pointless and preventable." Of the 172 deaths reviewed, 140 "were from conditions for which survival rates with medical care would have exceeded 90 percent," and another 18 were from conditions for which typical survival rates surpassed 50 percent. The former group included ailments such as Rocky Mountain spotted fever, diabetes, and meningitis; the latter, Ewing's sarcoma, Wilms' tumor, and non-Hodgkins lymphoma. All told, all but three of the children whose deaths were reviewed "would likely have had some benefit from clinical help," according to Asser and Swan.[26]

In one of the many tragic examples of preventable fatalities cited in the *Pediatrics* study, a two-year-old slowly choked to death on a bite of banana while her parents, instead of endeavoring to dislodge it themselves or summoning an ambulance for help, attempted to organize a prayer session for her. Another case involved a father who had received extensive medical training before joining a church whose teachings proscribed medical care. When the child suffered through a prolonged and intense fever caused by bacterial meningitis, the father—who had completed a year of a medical residency—attempted to rebuke "the spirit of death," as he later put it, through prayer. The child expired after this effort failed.[27]

One typically agonizing portion of the study published by Asser and Swan involved prenatal and perinatal fatalities. Their research uncovered fifty-nine such deaths associated with religion-based medical neglect. Because of their faiths' proscription of medical treatment, the mothers in the bulk of these cases chose to forego prenatal care and then attempted to give birth at home without the assistance of a physician or a licensed midwife. The errors made in some of these home deliveries were extraordinary. In one instance, a mother who suffered through three days of painful labor was stricken by convulsions and discharged meconium, the tar-like substance that accumulates in the bowels of a fetus. The greenish discharge is a telltale sign of fetal distress, but a church elder present at the birth told the mother that it was a "good thing" that indicated prayers were in fact working. They were not, and the baby died. As they surveyed such incidents, Asser and Swan concluded that "all but one of the newborns would have had a good to excellent outcome with medical care."

The *Pediatrics* study also noted that mothers themselves sometimes suffered from religion-based medical neglect: the authors discovered numerous maternal deaths resulting from complications related to delivery.[28]

Asser and Swan reported that in the Faith Assembly, a small Midwestern church that encourages its members to forsake medical treatment in favor of prayer, nearly thirty children died because of botched deliveries or inadequate postnatal care. One case involved a stillbirth in Indianapolis, Indiana. When police investigators examined the child's corpse, they found a sizable disfigurement on its left temple. An obstetrician who later reviewed the case surmised that "the baby's skull was most likely crushed by an inexperienced person performing the delivery," according to a newspaper account. Many of the Faith Assembly stillbirths resulted from failed breech deliveries. One father who lost a child in such circumstances reportedly told police that the death was "a chastisement from God" rather than a product of his own negligence.[29]

Asser and Swan documented fatalities among twenty-three religious denominations in thirty-four states. Many of the churches were small, and some of their names were unfamiliar to most mainstream Christians. The obscure Faith Assembly had the dubious honor of recording the greatest number of neglect-related fatalities among members of any church—sixty-four. The more widely known Church of Christ, Scientist (commonly known as the Christian Science Church) came in second place in this bleak race with a total of twenty-eight deaths. Of these fatalities, the death of Ashley King was among the most "bizarre and horrifying," as one observer put it. When the twelve-year-old became ill in 1987, her parents chose to treat her at home in accordance with Christian Science practice. After Ashley's parents withdrew her from school, a succession of local authorities appeared at the Kings' home in Phoenix, Arizona, in order to determine if the girl had fallen victim to neglect. A police detective eventually gained entry to the house and discovered a ghostly looking Ashley confined to bed by a tumor on her right leg. The tumor was, according to a local deputy county attorney who later reviewed Ashley's case, "absolutely humungous, the size of a watermelon." (This was not hyperbole: the tumor had ballooned to a circumference of 41 inches.) Acting under a court order, the state's child welfare agency obtained temporary custody of the girl and had her admitted to Phoenix General Hospital, where she was diagnosed with bone cancer. There, in the words of another observer of the case, "the stench from [Ashley's] decaying flesh was so bad, it permeated the entire floor of the hospital." She lost her battle with the cancer in the summer of 1988.[30]

Investigating deaths like Ashley King's transformed pediatrician Seth Asser into a passionate campaigner against religion-based medical neglect of children. As he battled the phenomenon, Asser expressed frustration over the relative lack of public attention that faith-based medical neglect received—a function, he suspected, of the deaths happening sequentially rather than en masse. "Kids die from accidental deployment of air bags, and you get hearings in Congress," he said. "But this goes on, and dozens die, and people think there's no problem because the deaths happen one at a time. Yet the kids who die suffer horribly." Referring to the site of the People's Temple tragedy (where hundreds of followers of Jim Jones, including scores of children, died after ingesting poisoned Kool Aid in 1978), Asser lamented that the ongoing abuse of children from religion-based medical neglect was "like Jonestown in slow motion."[31]

Both Rita Swan and Seth Asser concluded that there are relatively simple ways to protect children from religion-based medical neglect. Like many close observers of the phenomenon, they insisted that dozens of lives would be saved every year if local authorities zealously and consistently enforced criminal neglect, manslaughter, and criminally negligent homicide statutes against spiritual healers. The prospect of severe criminal sanctions, they reasoned, would force many intensely religious parents to break with the spiritual healing practices of their churches and seek medical treatment for their sick or injured children.

But this seemingly straightforward approach may not provide a sufficient deterrent. First, such cases can be difficult to prosecute. Out of deference to grieving parents—or because they are wary of being perceived as insensitive of those parents' constitutional rights—law enforcement authorities often perform only cursory investigations of religion-based medical neglect. Even when police carefully scrutinize the circumstances of spiritual-healing-related deaths, some prosecutors are reluctant to vigorously pursue criminal charges. They conclude that such charges are unlikely to result in convictions, given how sympathetic the potential defendants—misguided but sincere parents who were genuinely trying to heal their children—would appear to jurors. "You bring in these parents, sobbing and upset that their child died, and they say that is what God told them to do," one Oregon prosecutor noted. "If they truly believe that and a jury believes they are sincere, you are not going to convict them of any crime." In still other cases, prosecutors decline to file charges because they sense that a conviction would do little to deter zealously religious parents from continuing to endanger their surviving children by treating them through spiritual means.[32]

And then there are the murky manslaughter and child-neglect statutes on which the prosecutors' charges might be based. Many such laws contain exemptions that provide a ready defense for practitioners of religious healing. Currently, the criminal codes in a clear majority of states (thirty-nine) provide religious exemptions to child-abuse or neglect charges, and nineteen states permit religion-based defenses to felony crimes against children. Wisconsin's laws governing child abuse are typical: a subsection entitled "Treatment Through Prayer" states that a person cannot be found guilty of a crime "solely because he or she provides a child with treatment by spiritual means alone for healing in accordance with [a bona fide] religious method of healing . . . in lieu of medical or surgical treatment." The presence of these caveats in state criminal codes has scuttled some prosecutions of parents who have failed to provide adequate medical treatment for their children. Many times, the law simply has been neither strong nor clear enough for prosecutors to obtain a conviction at trial or sustain a guilty verdict on appeal.[33]

Groups ranging from the United Methodist Church to the National District Attorneys Association have called for the repeal of religious exemptions to child-abuse and neglect laws. Several prominent medical organizations— among them the American Medical Association (AMA) and the Bioethics Committee of the American Academy of Pediatrics—have echoed those calls. In 1988, the latter body issued a statement declaring that "all child abuse, neglect, and medical neglect statutes should be applied without potential or actual exemption for [the] religious beliefs" of parents. Deeply committed to "the basic moral principles of justice and of protection of children as vulnerable citizens," the members of the bioethics committee called upon state legislatures to remove religious exemption clauses and thereby ensure "equal treatment for all abusive parents." Smaller but equally zealous groups such as Massachusetts Citizens for Children (MCC) issued similar calls for action. MCC maintained that religious exemptions should be repealed because they "lead to the cruel and unnecessary deaths of helpless children."[34]

No organization has been more vocal in lobbying for the repeal of religious exemptions than CHILD. Rita Swan has argued that these stipulations, while safeguarding the religious liberty of parents, endanger the health of children and violate several different interrelated constitutional standards. "Such exemptions discriminate against a class of children," she has written, "depriving them of their Fourteenth Amendment right to equal protection under the laws, and give a preference and an endorsement to a religious practice, violating the establishment clause of the First Amendment."[35]

Legal scholars studying the phenomenon of religion-based medical neglect have been no more kind to what one has lamented as the "haphazard array of faith healing exemptions [that fail] to protect children who are provided faith healing instead of medical care." Scholarly analyses have criticized the faith-healing provisions as being legally untenable on a variety of constitutional grounds. James Dwyer, an expert on children's rights at the William and Mary School of Law, has been especially forceful in making such claims. Maintaining that the provisions effectively deny a class of children equal protection under the law, Dwyer has asserted that "the invidious discrimination among groups of children that these exemptions represent is clear on the face of the statutes. . . . These exemptions cause harm to children who have neither the state nor any set of caretakers advocating for their temporal interests."[36]

As their critics often argue, these broad and sometimes contradictory religious-immunity provisions can derail even the most determined efforts by states to bring perpetrators of religion-based medical neglect to justice. Confusion over the scope of religious exemptions apparently reigned in Indiana until newspaper reports highlighted the problem. In 1983, the *Fort Wayne News-Sentinel* documented nearly three dozen apparently preventable deaths among infants and children whose parents belonged to the Faith Assembly. The circumstances of some of these deaths—which dated back to 1973, according to the paper—were nothing short of gruesome. A one-year-old girl named Eva Swanson died of blood poisoning and pneumonia in 1981 after she accidentally dumped a small pot of scalding tea on herself. The *News-Sentinel* reported that a fifteen-month-old named Dustin Gilmore "was deafened, blinded and killed" by a virulent form of meningitis. Because of their parents' religious beliefs, none of the Faith Assembly children received medical care. Said one Faith Assembly mother who lost an infant to pneumonia, "Jesus was his doctor."[37]

The case of Natali Joy Mudd, a four-year-old Faith Assembly child who died in 1980, was especially horrific. A fast-growing, highly malignant tumor called rhabdomyosarcoma sprouted from near the girl's right eye and, left untreated by medical science, "eventually grew to the size of her head," according to one press account. When Natali's parents called police to report the girl's death, investigators discovered trails of blood along the walls of their home. They surmised that the crimson stains had been left where the nearly blind Natali, groping her way through the house, had dragged her grotesquely disfigured head. "It's hard to comprehend a little toddler going through all that because of religion, with all the treatments available," one of the investigators later said. (For rhabdomyosarcoma, these treatments include surgery, chemotherapy, and radiation.) Natali's death was perhaps doubly tragic because her sister, who also initially was denied medical treatment, later died of the same kind of tumor.[38]

Although prosecutions had been mounted in other states, the *News-Sentinel*'s review of deaths of Faith Assembly children revealed that none of the parents in the church in Indiana—not even the parents of Natali Joy Mudd—had been charged with manslaughter or neglect. "Today," one state legislator lamented, "we're allowing the Faith Assembly to withhold medical treatment [from children] without being prosecuted." Explaining why he had failed to file criminal charges against parents implicated in more than a dozen religion-based neglect cases in his county, one prosecutor asserted that state law "specifically excludes [from prosecution] people who provide spiritual treatment" to their children in lieu of medical care. But Indiana's chief law enforcement officer, Attorney General Linley Pearson, suggested that this was perhaps too broad a reading of the statute and that prosecutors could move forward with charges and let juries determine if the measure applied in cases involving Faith Assembly parents. The state of the law in Indiana was so muddled that the two state legislators who had introduced the spiritual-healing measure disagreed as to whether it provided an absolute defense to parents implicated in cases of religion-based medical neglect.[39]

Their backbones stiffened by public outrage over their inaction in cases involving the Faith Assembly's healing practices, authorities in Indiana eventually took a harder line against members of the church, acting under existing statutes to mount several successful criminal prosecutions of parents and ministers who had been implicated in cases of religion-based medical neglect of children. One of their targets was church leader Hobart Freeman. Shortly before his death in 1984, a grand jury indicted Freeman for aiding and inducing reckless homicide for his role in the death of a fifteen-year-old girl. But religious exemptions continued to hamstring the efforts of law enforcement authorities in other states. Rita Swan has pointed to the prosecution of Jon Lybarger as a textbook example of how such provisions complicated prosecutions of parents who were apparently responsible for their children's deaths. Late in the winter of 1982, Lybarger's five-week-old daughter, Jessica, contracted a severe case of pneumonia. As the girl's condition worsened, several of Lybarger's friends and fellow church members urged him to seek medical treatment for her, but he chose to treat her condition solely with prayer and anointment. "I want the best help for my baby," he explained, "and God is the best help for [her]." Even an inquiry from two sheriff's deputies—they appeared at his home after learning from an anonymous caller of Jessica's dire condition—could not convince Lybarger to take his daughter to a hospital. She failed to respond to his spiritual treatment and died on March 15, 1982. Soon thereafter, Lybarger faced charges of criminal child abuse.[40]

The tortuous course of Lybarger's case—it wound its way through the courts in Colorado for nearly a decade—demonstrated how defendants in cases of religion-based medical neglect could exploit religious exemptions to state child-neglect laws. His first trial resulted in a guilty verdict and a sentence of six months' probation. Lybarger appealed, claiming that the trial court had erred in barring him from raising a defense based on language in the Colorado code stating that a child "who in good faith is under treatment solely by spiritual means through prayer" could not be deemed neglected. (The trial court had ruled that the First Amendment's establishment clause would be violated if Lybarger were permitted to raise a defense based on that spiritual-healing exemption.) The Colorado Supreme Court granted Lybarger a new trial in 1985, holding that the trial court had exceeded its authority in limiting his defense. Lybarger's second trial for felony child abuse also resulted in a guilty verdict, and he appealed once more, arguing this time that the trial court had blundered in its instructions to the jury regarding the panel's discretion in interpreting the meaning of the phrase "treatment by spiritual means." In 1991, the state's highest court sided with Lybarger, reversing his conviction a second time. After ten years, two trials, and numerous appeals, prosecutors found themselves back at square one. (When their third effort to prosecute Lybarger ended in a mistrial, they apparently gave up and dropped the case.)[41]

In response to cases like *People v. Lybarger*, several states attempted to reform their criminal codes and clarify or simply eliminate spiritual-healing exemptions. This legislative solution proved to be anything but straightforward, thanks in large part to the adroit lobbying of the Christian Science Church, the largest and most politically savvy religious body dedicated to spiritual healing. (Christian Scientists do not practice faith healing per se but rather believe that the "right thinking" described by Mary Baker Eddy, the faith's founder, can remove what they characterize as the illusion of illness.) In public testimony and behind-the-scenes lobbying, Christian Scientists repeatedly insisted that repealing religious-healing exemptions would imperil their religious practices. Their vocal resistance impeded the pace of legislative reform in many states and complicated efforts to prosecute parents involved in faith-based neglect cases. Change occurred, but usually after a widely publicized series of child deaths and fruitless prosecutions of parents had generated a groundswell of public support for reform.

Religion-based medical neglect is a pervasive phenomenon that continues to jeopardize the welfare of children throughout the United States. The victims in these cases are the youngest members of a wide array of Christian churches. Some of these churches exist on the fringes of American culture, in isolated, rural areas where time seems to have stopped somewhere in the middle of the nineteenth century. But others are closer to the mainstream, both physically and figuratively. Christian Scientists and Pentecostals are long-standing and familiar presences in most communities. (And with the explosive, worldwide growth of their faith, Pentecostals are becoming more familiar by the moment.) What is more, their affinity for spiritual-healing practices—grounded in an earnest belief in prayer's power to restore both spirit and body—is shared by many of their neighbors who belong to more long-established denominations. As two recent surveys have shown, millions of Americans regularly turn to prayer when they fall sick or experience a physical injury. Although it remains unclear how many people rely exclusively on prayer for healing, a study published in the magazine *American Demographics* suggested that more than 40 percent of the general public actually practices some form of faith healing on a regular basis, making it the most popular alternative health remedy in the country. A massive survey of more than thirty thousand adults, conducted by researchers working for the federal Centers for Disease Control (CDC), reached a similar conclusion. The CDC study of complementary and alternative-medicine use found that nearly half of all adults (45 percent) had prayed for their own health within the previous year. A similarly sizable percentage (43 percent) reported that someone else had prayed for their health during the same period.[42]

The CDC study also revealed the surprising popularity of prayer-based healing rituals—religious ceremonies that include the healing rites prescribed by the Epistle of James—in the United States. Nearly 5 percent of the adults surveyed by the CDC had participated in some kind of prayer-based healing ritual in their lifetimes, and 2 percent had taken part in such a ritual in the previous year. While these percentages might seem modest, they were comparable to those for such widely known forms of treatment as acupuncture (which was used by 4 percent of the survey respondents in their lifetimes and 1 percent in the preceding year) and homeopathy (3.6 and 1.7 percent). Prayer-based healing rituals were even slightly more popular than the much-ballyhooed Atkins diet, which was near the height of its popularity when the study was conducted in 2002. The results of the CDC survey suggest that, every year, several million Americans respond to illness by summoning their fellow church members and participating in religious-healing rites to harness the purported healing power of prayer.[43]

These devotees to spiritual healing often are stereotyped as being "poor, uneducated, [and] rural," as the sociologist Meredith McGuire has noted. But many of those who rely on prayer for healing are, according McGuire, "economically comfortable" and "consistently middle-class" people who reside, work, and worship in suburban communities. The CDC's findings appeared to support McGuire's claims. Although respondents earning less than twenty thousand dollars evidenced the greatest reliance on prayer for healing, it was surprisingly pervasive among all income levels. Almost 30 percent of the respondents with household incomes of more than seventy-five thousand dollars per year, for instance, reported that they had turned to prayer for healing at some point in their lifetimes.[44]

Studies of spiritual-healing practices conducted in three cities have further reinforced these findings. More than 14 percent of respondents to a survey in Richmond, Virginia, claimed to have experienced "healing of a serious disease or physical condition" as a result of prayer. (The ailments reportedly conquered there ranged from cancer to the common cold.) In Akron, Ohio, nearly a third of those responding to a survey reported that they had "experienced a healing as a result of prayer." About one in ten of all respondents in Akron asserted that their spiritual-healing practices had prevailed over a life-threatening medical condition. And in Fort Wayne, Indiana, a survey of alternative medical therapies found that a sizable number of respondents—almost 30 percent— relied on prayer to treat illness. According to one scholar, the results of these three surveys refuted the common assumption that faith healing is practiced primarily by the socioeconomically disadvantaged. "Rather," sociologist of religion Margaret Poloma wrote, "the belief in and practice of spiritual healing is widely diffused through a broad range of the general population."[45]

Spiritual-healing practices are so pervasive in the United States in part because they are so deeply rooted in the traditions of many Christian faiths. References to spiritual healing are common in the New Testament, which frequently depicts Jesus and the apostles healing the sick through prayer. Perhaps the most influential scriptural passage in this regard is James 5:13–15, which prescribes prayer and anointment as a cure for sickness. Taking their cue from this and similar passages, some Christians have continued to rely exclusively on spiritual-healing practices, despite advances in medical science. Their belief in the healing power of prayer alone has been strengthened by a recent pro-liferation of books, articles, and scientific studies touting the notion that, as one title put it, "prayer is good medicine."[46]

One striking characteristic of the women and men who cling to these traditions is their abiding sincerity. However irrational their thinking may appear to those outside their faiths, spiritual healers genuinely believe that prayer has the power to cure illness; they do not simply invoke that notion for expediency's sake during criminal proceedings. Spiritual healers typically at-tempt to counter the skepticism of nonbelievers by offering dramatic stories that illustrate the curative powers of prayer. Theirs is not a blind faith, they argue; it is based on long and profound experience.

To refute criticism of their religious beliefs and practices, Christian Sci-entists frequently refer to what one member of the faith has called "the reality of spiritual healing." Portions of the *Christian Science Sentinel*, a church peri-odical, regularly are devoted to first-person accounts from church members recounting their successes in using Christian Science to heal maladies ranging from eczema to polio. (One recent testament even described how prayer had cured a child's flat feet.) Tom Black, a contributing editor at the journal, fur-nished a typical account:

> [A] couple of years ago I fell while washing windows and injured one foot. I was unable to put any weight on it. Because I had always trusted God for healing, I didn't go to the hospital. Instead I bor-rowed some crutches from a friend of mine. However, I soon set them aside. It wasn't out of willful zeal, but because after a few days they were distracting me from placing my full reliance on God. As I prayed to strengthen my understanding of Him, I became con-scious of the startling fact that, as a spiritual idea of God, I never had fallen and could not have been injured. Within hours, every symp-tom was gone, and I could, in the words of the Bible, "run, and not be weary . . . walk, and not faint." I had drawn on the one, supreme source of power—and been healed.

Church spokesmen often use more far-reaching media outlets to trumpet the efficacy of Christian Science as a means of healing. "There are many cases of healings of blindness, epilepsy, [and] tuberculosis," one church representative said in an appearance on the *Today* show, "that have been healed through Christian Science treatment and have been verified by medical diagnosis."[47]

Members of less well-known faiths make similar claims, albeit often in more homespun language. A member of a Pentecostal group known at the Apt Full

Gospel Assembly, for instance, recounted how her brother, a minister in the church, had used prayer to heal her daughter after the little girl had fallen and "cut her lip terribly" with her teeth. After inspecting the girl's bloodied mouth and discovering that it "was so swollen that you just wouldn't believe it," the mother took her daughter to her brother's house for a prayer session. By the following morning, "the swelling was already starting to leave, and her mouth never got sore at all. I mean it was just—it wasn't sore at all. She ate everything she wanted." Although the Pentecostal mother was overjoyed by her daughter's recovery, she was hardly surprised that prayer had proven so effective. After all, she explained, "I've been healed myself many, many times."[48]

Such accounts commonly feature implicit and explicit indictments of conventional medicine. In recounting their successes in relying on prayer, spiritual healers often mention that a minister had succeeded where a physician had failed. Christian Scientists are particularly adept at pairing defenses of their healing practices with attacks on what one church member has called "the mixed record of medical practice." They concede that no form of healing is perfect and that children like Ashley King often perish despite their parents' adherence to Christian Science doctrine and practice. But, many Christian Scientists argue, is the track record of medical science any better? After all, tens of thousands of children die in hospitals every year while under the care of trained and licensed physicians. Angered by charges that Christian Science healing is ineffectual, one member of the church asserted that "medical practice itself could hardly survive the kind of scrutiny" directed at his faith.[49]

Outright mockery of doctors and hospitals has long been a rhetorical staple for spiritual healers. Late in the nineteenth century, John Alexander Dowie, the controversial spiritual healer who headed the Christian Catholic Church (to which J. Luther Pierson belonged), routinely lambasted practitioners of medical science as charlatans and butchers who swindled innocent people and imperiled their health. He went so far as to assert that the most lethal of all diseases was "*bacillus lunaticus medicus.*" It is worth noting that, at least in Dowie's era, such criticism was not completely unwarranted. Well into the nineteenth century, many physicians received spotty training and pursued many treatments that in retrospect seem misguided. But even as medical science has matured and proven its merits over the past 150 years (thanks to such advances as the advent of the germ theory of disease), spiritual healers have not much tempered their criticism of doctors. Most agree with the sentiments of the Church of the First Born member who asserted that God "cures more than they do in hospitals."[50]

Is there reliable evidence to back up these largely anecdotal claims? Relying on testimonies provided by church members, Christian Scientists issued an "empirical analysis of medical evidence" relating to 640 healings of children reported between 1969 and 1988. The study listed nearly ninety instances in which Christian Science treatments reportedly had helped children overcome potentially life-threatening illnesses, such as spinal meningitis and pneumonia. But, as the Massachusetts Coalition for Children insisted, some glaring methodological shortcomings marred this study, the most apparent being that it failed to make even a rudimentary comparison between the frequency or rates of successful and unsuccessful Christian Science treatments. More objective analyses largely have failed to demonstrate that Christian Science treatments are effectual. In their landmark study in *Pediatrics*, Rita Swan and Seth Asser pointed out that the purported "reality" of Christian Science healing seems to be largely illusory; the effectiveness of the church's healing practices has yet to be confirmed by "scientifically valid measures." In fact, two studies of the longevity of Christian Scientists have suggested that they have, on average, shorter life spans than the general public—an indication that their methods of healing might not be particularly effective.[51]

Several scholarly studies have indicated that successes attributed to spiritual healing practices might be best explained as the result of hypnotic or placebo effects. Sociologist James McClendon studied eighty-five accounts in which people described their experiences with various methods of spiritual healing. Subjects in McClendon's study recounted how ailments ranging from headaches and ear infections to severe burns and cancers had been alleviated through prayer or the intervention of a folk or religious healer. The author found that a sizable percentage of the symptoms described by his subjects were "often amenable to hypnotic treatment" and that much of the intervention of healers followed "a pattern of hypnotic processes."[52]

However, in her recent study *Healing in the History of Christianity*, historian of American religion Amanda Porterfield has highlighted the limitations of such approaches to religious healing. Recent challenges to the entire notion of the "placebo effect," she has cautioned, have underscored "just how difficult it is to isolate the therapeutic effects of religion from other factors." Porterfield has suggested that, in the context of physical healing, it might be most fruitful not to draw binary distinctions that privilege science over prayer. Rather, given the apparent interrelationships between mind and body, one might recognize "the confluence of biological, religious, and cultural factors" that can shape healing.[53]

Whatever their efficacy, age-old traditions of spiritual healing endure, and, much to the dismay of law enforcement and child welfare authorities, parents treat their sick children solely through such practices even when they know that it might result in criminal charges being leveled against them. Dennis Nixon's stubbornness on this score was typical. After Nixon, a member of the Faith Tabernacle, lost two of his children to treatable illnesses and found himself on trial for manslaughter, he said in court, "You are not going to change my religious beliefs." From the Peculiar People to the present day, numerous other parents who have been tried in religion-based medical neglect cases have made similarly defiant comments, insisting that the specter of temporal punishment cannot persuade them to forsake an essential religious tradition.[54]

In several poignant cases, however, parents' religious beliefs have been profoundly changed after they shunned medical science and treated their children's illness by prayer alone. Suzanne Shepard was raised a Christian Scientist and eventually gained a formidable reputation within the faith as a "practitioner" (someone who provides prayer and spiritual guidance for the sick). Shepard eventually repudiated her beliefs after her daughter Marilyn failed to respond to Christian Science treatment and nearly died from a ruptured appendix. "I still think about my loved ones who suffered needlessly, and I'm angry with myself for not doing anything for so long," she later wrote. "I grieve for the children of my Christian Science friends." Like Rita Swan, Shepard channeled her guilt and grief into action, becoming an outspoken critic of how the practices of her erstwhile faith jeopardized the health of children. In her case and numerous others, a personal awakening—and not the threat of criminal prosecution—led to a change in beliefs.[55]

Larry Parker also experienced a transformation after spiritual healing failed to cure his son's diabetes. Initially, Parker and his wife, Lucky, followed the advice of doctors and treated their child's ailment with insulin. But eventually they determined that prayer, not medicine, was the best way to cure young Wesley, and they discarded the drugs that had been keeping his ailment in check. "God *does* heal—I had seen it!" Parker later wrote. "Cancer, shattered bones, blasted minds, touched by the power of God." Unfortunately, the boy failed to respond to spiritual treatment, and his condition deteriorated. Despite mounting doubts about the course he had chosen, Parker pressed on; he was determined not to betray his religious faith. At one point, he led a prayer session at the child's bedside and fervently asked their Savior to let his "healing mercies flow upon Wesley." In a heartbreaking and somewhat ominous moment, the groggy child lifted his head and groused, "My head hurts; could you be quiet?" He died not long afterward.[56]

Even after Wesley's death, Larry and Lucky Parker clung to the idea that their intense religious faith would save their son. Like many other spiritual healers whose prayers have proven ineffective, they believed that their child would be resurrected, as the scriptures reported that Jesus Christ and Lazarus had been. When the coroner appeared at the family's home, Larry confidently informed him, "We believe Wesley is going to be raised from the dead." Incredulous, the official asked if the family wanted the body to be embalmed; Parker replied that it would not be necessary because Wesley's recovery was imminent. At the boy's funeral service, Parker remained so convinced that Wesley would be resurrected that he stood in front of a gathering of family and fellow church members and commanded the boy "to rise in Jesus' name." Citing the story of Lazarus (who had lain in a grave for four days before rising), the Parkers adhered to their beliefs even after the child had been buried.[57]

In time, though, the Parkers came to believe that they had made a grievous mistake in forsaking medical treatment for prayer. After the couple had been tried and convicted on charges of child abuse and involuntary manslaughter (a judge sentenced them both to five years of probation), Larry Parker penned *We Let Our Son Die*, a book in which he described his painful realization that his approach to spiritual healing had been the result of a faulty interpretation of the scriptures. "Wesley died needlessly, a victim of our imbalance and misuse of the Bible," Parker wrote. "We mistook presumption for faith, overstepping the proper bounds of God's sovereign plan for our son's life." Blinded by their insistence that prayer alone could heal Wesley, the couple had failed to realize that "God has many varieties of healing," including those involving medical science.[58]

Cases like the prosecution of Larry and Lucky Parker—a father and mother who struggled to reconcile the demands of their religious beliefs with their legal duties as parents—raise a welter of legal issues. Americans prize religious liberty, and protections for it are among the most treasured safeguards in the Bill of Rights. To many, the right of parents to direct the upbringing of their children, although it is not explicitly protected by the Constitution, is as sacrosanct as the right to worship freely. In cases of religion-based medical neglect, however, these long-cherished liberties run headlong into another important set of individual rights—those possessed by children—as well as the provision of the First Amendment that bars the establishment of religion by the state.

In cases dealing with faiths ranging from the Jehovah's Witnesses to the Amish, courts at all levels have tried to honor safeguards for religious principles while simultaneously upholding official efforts to limit religious practices that might disrupt public order or undermine civic institutions. This often has proven to be a precarious balancing act, at least in part because the conduct that troubles public authorities is typically a function of some individual's sincere religious beliefs. The Jehovah's Witnesses provided a classic example of this conundrum in the late 1930s and early 1940s. A series of prominent legal cases from the World War II era revolved around the question of whether public school authorities could expel Witness students who had refused to salute the American flag because the tenets of their religious faith prohibited the practice of idolatry. This clash between individual rights and state power confounded the U.S. Supreme Court: it ruled against the Witnesses in a flag-salute case in 1940 but then held in their favor in a similar case just three years later. Before they switched their votes, three justices even took the extraordinary step of publicly admitting that the first case had been "wrongly decided."[59]

Another prominent Jehovah's Witness case from the World War II era, *Prince v. Massachusetts* (1944), turned on the right of parents to direct the upbringing of their children. In two earlier cases, the U.S. Supreme Court had issued rulings that made it more difficult (at least in theory) for states to infringe on parents' rights in the realm of child rearing. In both *Meyer v. Nebraska* (1923) and *Pierce v. Society of Sisters* (1925), the Court had bolstered the rights of parents, in the latter case holding an Oregon law unconstitutional because it "unreasonably interferes with the liberty of parents and guardians to direct the upbringing and education of children under their control." But in his opinion for the Supreme Court in *Prince*, Justice Wiley Rutledge insisted that the First Amendment's protections for religious liberty did not give parents blanket authority to treat their children in any manner they deemed fit. After noting that "neither rights of religion nor rights of parenthood are beyond limitation," Rutledge delivered a now-famous maxim defining the limits of religious conduct: "Parents may be free to become martyrs themselves. But it does not follow they are free, in identical circumstances, to make martyrs of their children before they have reached the age of full and legal discretion when they can make that choice for themselves."[60]

Rutledge's admonition has been cited in numerous opinions in cases involving religion-based medical neglect. (Indeed, it is unusual to find a judicial opinion in such a case that does *not* refer to *Prince* somewhere.) His warning reflects the general consensus among judges and legal scholars that, despite the protections conferred on the free exercise of religion by the First Amendment, parents' spiritual-healing practices can be regulated when they jeopardize children's health. What often confounds the courts is that these parents are so transparently sincere and that state manslaughter and child-neglect statutes, with their myriad religious exemptions, do not always reflect the widespread view that the rights of children are paramount. The result often is protracted and Byzantine litigation that leaves prosecutors, lawmakers, and children's welfare advocates shaking their heads in frustration.

These already cloudy waters have been further muddied when other legal principles, such as women's reproductive rights, have been implicated in such cases. Some prosecutors seeking to prevent religion-based medical neglect of children have sought court orders to compel medical treatment for pregnant women who practice spiritual healing. In one noteworthy case in Massachusetts, authorities squared off in court against Rebecca Corneau, a pregnant woman belonging to The Body, a tiny church that had compiled a worrisome record of medical neglect of children. (One youngster in the church essentially had been starved to death, and Corneau herself had lost a child during a home delivery.) Asserting that Corneau's fetus would be in jeopardy from the moment its delivery began, prosecutors argued that the court should compel her to give birth while under state supervision. Critics of the state's action claimed that its intervention was premature—Corneau, after all, had not yet committed any crime—and threatened the hard-won reproductive rights of women of all faiths.[61]

The legal historian Lawrence Friedman has questioned the notion—advanced by countless observers of legal culture—that contemporary American society is in danger of being subsumed by a "litigation explosion" sparked by an unprecedented proliferation of lawyers. It is not so much the volume of litigation that has changed, he has asserted, but rather the expectations that shape Americans' views of their sprawling legal culture. Friedman has traced the development of a broad demand for "total justice," with the state acting as reconciler of divergent interests and guarantor of equitable treatment for all. Cases of religion-based medical neglect of children, bringing into conflict long-cherished notions of individual rights with emerging doctrines relating to the parameters of state power, have demonstrated how difficult it is for this grand expectation to be realized. Because they involve so many compelling but competing interests, these emotionally freighted legal clashes often have yielded results that more closely resemble Solomonic compromises than universally equitable judgments.[62]

The pursuit of justice in these cases—each of which presents not only a complex set of legal and cultural issues but also a profound human tragedy—is the story of this book.

2

"Are Any among You Sick?"

The Tradition of Spiritual Healing

"Healing," according to Lawrence Sullivan, director of the Center for the Study of World Religions at Harvard Divinity School, "occupies a singular and prominent place in religious experience throughout the world." Indeed, for millennia, the process of calling upon divine authority to vanquish disease or mend injuries has helped individuals in a broad array of religious traditions experience a profound spiritual rehabilitation that, by providing formidable evidence of divine power, has transcended mere physical recovery. These traditions have remained characteristically durable and pervasive in recent years, thanks in part to a torrent of books, newspaper and magazine articles, and scholarly studies purporting to establish, through precise scientific measurement, that prayer—Christian prayer in particular—can indeed combat illness. Whatever their merit (and many careful observers have called it dubious), these works have demonstrated that advances in scientific medicine have failed to weaken the long-standing conviction, present in societies both ancient and modern, that prayer can restore not only spiritual well-being but also physical health.[1]

A comprehensive, global history of religious healing is beyond the bounds of this relatively narrow study, which focuses primarily on the legal issues raised by cases of religion-based medical neglect of children. Yet even a cursory appraisal of prayer-based Christian spiritual-healing traditions—one emphasizing their emergence and development in the United States—can illustrate their deep roots and lasting influence. Briefly tracing the enduring vitality of these essential religious practices helps to explain not only why so many

Christians reject medical science–based treatments when their children fall sick but also why they so stubbornly resist state regulation of traditions they consider to be fundamental parts of religious experience.

Sickness and healing figure prominently in the sacred scriptures of Christianity. Reports of afflictions ranging from festering sores and boils to blindness and insanity are commonplace in the Old Testament. Such physical misfortunes often are described as resulting not from natural causes but rather from an individual's sinful behavior, and relief from them appears to come from but one source: God himself. (This point is made perhaps most directly in Exodus, in which God assures the Israelites that he is "the Lord who heals you" [15:22–27].) When physicians appear in the Old Testament, it is chiefly to demonstrate that, in terms of restoring health, they fail to match the prowess of the Almighty. Chronicles, for instance, refers to the error made by Asa when disease ravaged his feet: "He did not seek the Lord, but sought help from physicians," who ultimately failed him (2 Chronicles 16). Such jibes are aimed at both the practitioners of medicine and their patients, who have failed to exhibit sufficient faith in God's ability to affect physical healing.

Physicians in the New Testament seem similarly feeble. The infrequent references to them in the text generally highlight their ineffectiveness and avarice. Mark, for example, recounts the woeful story of a woman who had been hemorrhaging blood for a dozen years. This victim "had endured much under many physicians," he states, "and had spent all that she had; and she was no better, but rather grew worse" (5:25–34). The same story is told in a similar manner by Luke (who, ironically, was himself a physician). He reports that the woman could not be healed by anyone, including the physicians whose costly but futile treatments wound up bankrupting her (8:43–48).

The New Testament brims with accounts of healing, but these cures are effected by Jesus and his early followers rather than by physicians. Indeed, a substantial portion of the Gospels is devoted to descriptions of Jesus restoring individuals' physical health. Readers of these stories are told that he healed Bartimaeus of blindness, cured the ear of the slave Malchus (it had been lopped off completely), and relieved the suffering of ten lepers. The frequency and persuasiveness of such accounts make the Gospels a powerful depiction of Jesus' work as a healer. Surveying these abundant stories of physical renewal, one scholar has written that "above all . . . the Gospels highlight healing, for at the core of their narratives of Jesus' public ministry lies his activity as a healer."[2]

According to Mark, for instance, Jesus healed more than a dozen ailments. They included the aforementioned hemorrhage as well as fever, leprosy, paralysis, and blindness (twice). Although this work was not without risk for Jesus— when word spread that he had healed a withered hand, for instance, the Pharisees plotted his death—he persisted in his efforts to rid the afflicted of disease. This healing mission, as recounted in Luke, extended to people outside the faith, among them the slave of a gentile centurion "who was ill and close to death" (7:1–10). As the Gospels depict him, Jesus was such a potent healer that he could successfully overcome even death. The widow's son at Nain rose from a funeral bier after receiving a command from Jesus to do so. This remarkable healing electrified onlookers: Luke reports that witnesses "glorified God" and exclaimed, "God has looked favorably on his people!" (7:11–6).

John, in a lengthy description of Jesus raising Lazarus from the dead, provides perhaps the most dramatic account of Jesus' skills as a healer. The story begins with an exchange between Jesus and the apostles regarding the severity of Lazarus's affliction and the reception that might await them if they traveled to the sick man's home region. As John recalls, Jesus informed the disciples that they must accompany him to Judea, where he planned to awaken Lazarus from his sleep. Taking this explanation too literally, the disciples puzzled over the necessity of making a potentially dangerous journey—there were fears that Jesus would be stoned if he returned to Judea—simply to rouse a man from ordinary slumber. Jesus then informed his followers that he was looking forward to raising the dead man so that their faith might be strengthened. And, indeed, a remarkable manifestation of God's glory at Lazarus's tomb did bolster their belief. There, heeding Jesus' loud command to "come out," a bandaged Lazarus emerged after four days. In the words of John's account, this healing, like many others in Jesus' ministry, so astonished the public that many Jews "believed in him" (11:1–45).

Healing was, according to the Gospels, a transformative experience for those aided by Jesus. Whatever the nature or severity of their illnesses, he helped the afflicted emerge from a world suffused with sickness and sin and into the realm of salvation. It is intriguing to note that, in the Gospels, these healings were more a sign of Jesus' powers than of the beliefs of those whose health he restored. In only a handful of episodes described in the Gospels did Jesus respond to the faith of the sick themselves. Among them was blind Bartimaeus, to whom Jesus said, "Go your way; your faith has made you well." In a few other cases, he responded to the faith of people close to the sick, such as their friends or relatives. Mark recounts one such instance, in which an epileptic boy was healed after his father cried out, "I believe; help my unbelief!" Jesus intoned afterward, "This kind can come out only through prayer" (9:23–29). The relative rarity of such references in the Gospels seems to suggest that, for Jesus, an individual's demonstration of faith through prayer did not represent an essential part of the healing process.[3]

The Gospels indicate that, after receiving explicit instructions from Jesus, the apostles joined in his healing ministry. Luke recounts that Jesus "called the twelve together and gave them power and authority over all demons and to cure diseases, and he sent them out to preach the kingdom of God and to heal." This charge—the "great commission," as it is commonly called—is reiterated elsewhere, with Jesus instructing the disciples to heal the sick whenever they entered a town. "Bringing the good news and curing diseases everywhere," as Luke describes it, would herald the coming of God's kingdom (9:1–6).

Tales of healings effected by Jesus' early followers abound in the book of Acts. When Peter and John, for instance, encountered "a man lame from birth," they invoked Jesus' name and "immediately his feet and ankles were made strong" (3:1–11). Paul performed a similar healing of a man "who could not use his feet and had never walked, for he had been crippled from birth" (14:8–10). He accomplished a more spectacular feat at Troas, raising Eutychus from the dead after he had fallen from a window. (The text wryly notes that the people who took the boy away afterward "were not a little a comforted" by his return to life [20:9–12].) Also according to Acts, Peter had an analogous triumph at Joppa when he encountered the lifeless body of Tabitha: at his command, she rose from the dead (9:36–41).

The New Testament epistles, unlike the Gospels or Acts, mention sickness and healing relatively infrequently. One of their few references to healing occurs in James 5:13–15, which asks, "Are any among you sick?" and then prescribes prayer by elders and anointing with oil as treatment for bodily illness. This passage long has been the cornerstone of the argument made by faith-healers that the Christian scriptures contain specific guidance for healing—guidance that notably omits any role for either physicians or medicine.[4]

The entirety of the Epistle of James long has been the subject of vigorous debates among interpreters of the New Testament, and its reference to healing has occasioned particularly sharp disagreements. One recent commentator has asserted that the sickness referred to in the epistle is in fact spiritual weakness, not physical debility, and that the role of elders is to perform a kind of spiritual mending. In this reading, the text refers to strengthening those who are disheartened or even depressed. Other observers dispute this view, arguing that the passage clearly refers to bodily ailments and the use of prayer as a means of physical restoration. The latter interpretation reigns among members of a variety of faiths who insist that the language of James is to be read extraordinarily narrowly. Since James provides "no instruction . . . to go to a medical practitioner for healings," as one Pentecostal recently has put it, Christians should not rely on doctors for physical rehabilitation.[5]

Whether or not it amounts to a blanket proscription of medical treatment, James's reference to prayer and anointment as a means of physical and spiritual rehabilitation underscores the enormous importance of healing in the formative years of Christianity. Jesus and his early followers were renowned healers, and the acclaim they earned by tending to the sick allowed their embryonic faith to gain credibility. "Depictions of Jesus in the New Testament," according to scholar Amanda Porterfield, "support the argument that Christianity survived at least partly because of its radically simple and highly accessible rites of healing." This dimension of the faith—its promise to restore the body—has continued to attract adherents to Christianity throughout the centuries. Thus, from the start, a profound concern for healing has been one of the hallmarks of Christianity.[6]

However, Christianity's long-standing attention to healing has not always put it at odds with the work of physicians. Many early Christians embraced secular medicine and its practitioners, and several leaders in the church's formative years wrote approvingly of the work of doctors and physicians. Although Origen (ca. 185–ca. 254) touted the notion that Christ was "the Great Physician," he called medicine "beneficial and essential to mankind." Basil the Great (ca. 329–379) similarly concluded that "this medical art" could redound "to the glory of God." Both men suggested that medicine was one of God's many gifts, and that Christians should be grateful for it.[7]

In late antiquity, new forces influenced Christian approaches to healing. Among them were asceticism, which ascribed the causes of disease to demonic activity, and a burgeoning fascination with magic and superstition. With the latter came relics and magical charms believed to promote healing. However, these new trends did not displace prayer and sacramental anointing as methods of healing, nor did their advent completely marginalize physicians. When several Christian hospitals were founded in the fourth and fifth centuries, physicians often staffed them and offered secular treatments for illness. Thus, in the early and medieval church, a broad array of treatment options—including prayer, medicine and magic—"existed side by side among Christians" as avenues toward healing, according to one account of the period.[8]

Protestant reformers viewed healing somewhat differently. Appalled by excesses of the medieval church, they frowned upon the magical elements of some healing rituals. Reformers recognized the importance of miraculous healing in the early church, but they believed that it essentially had ceased after the apostolic age. Because God no longer endowed individuals with such extraordinary powers, John Calvin wrote, "The grace of healing has disappeared" and "has nothing to do with us." Downplaying the miraculous powers of individuals, reformers instead stressed "the redemptive power of Christ working within the hearts and souls of individual believers," according to Porterfield.[9]

Perhaps not surprisingly, many reformers struggled with the Epistle of James. Although he conceded that it was a "good book, because it sets up no doctrine of men but vigorously promulgates the law of God," Martin Luther unfavorably compared its many aphorisms and epigrams to the epistles authored by John and Paul, which he found far more substantive. Such works, he wrote, "are the books that show you Christ and teach you all that is necessary and salvatory for you to know, even if you were never to see or hear any other book or doctrine." In comparison, the Epistle of James "is really an epistle of straw . . . for it has nothing of the nature of the gospel about it." Asserting that the letter was not the work of an apostle, Luther suggested that its author "throws things together so chaotically that it seems to me he must have been some good, pious man, who took a few sayings from the disciples of the apostles and thus tossed them off on paper." But John Calvin, another titan among Protestant reformers, thought otherwise: he commented that the Epistle of James "contains nothing unworthy of an Apostle of Christ" and wrote an approving commentary on its passage relating to the performance of healing rites.[10]

While the fires of the Reformation flared, Christian spiritual-healing traditions made their way across the Atlantic and began influencing religious experience in North America. In the sixteenth century, European explorers stumbling their way through the American wilderness frequently invoked Jesus' prowess as a healer during their encounters with indigenous peoples. The results—if the explorers' later accounts are to be believed—often were startling. On its harrowing trek through the Southeast (which lasted from 1528 to 1536), the party led by Spanish adventurer Alvar Nunez Cabeza de Vaca sometimes found itself besieged by Native Americans eager to benefit from Christian healing rites. The Native Americans "brought us the sick people they had," the explorer later wrote of one such encounter, "begging us to make the sign of the cross over them." Further north, along the St. Lawrence River, Frenchman Jacques Cartier led so many Christian spiritual-healing ceremonies that, according to one account, he "became a virtual lay priest" on one of his excursions in the 1530s. (The irony here, of course, was that Europeans like Cabeza de Vaca and Cartier brought with them not only healing ceremonies but also the very diseases that necessitated such rites.)[11]

Healing figured prominently, if controversially, in the rise of several religious faiths in colonial America and the fledgling United States, among them the United Society of Believers (Shakers) and the Religious Society of Friends (Quakers). The numerous healings performed during the itinerant ministry of George Fox, for instance, were crucial to the growth of Quakerism. Fox claimed that, by laying hands on the afflicted and praying for them, he had effected more than 150 separate healings—each of them, in Fox's estimation, a testament to Jesus' considerable power. One typical success came in New Jersey in 1672, when Fox attended to a man named Jay, who had broken his neck after being thrown from a horse. Although the fall apparently had killed Jay, Fox believed he could be saved. As he later described it:

> [I] took him by the hair of the head, and his head turned like a cloth it was so loose, and I threw away my stick and gloves and took his head in both my hands, and set my knees against the tree; and raised his head and I did perceive it was not broken out that ways, and I put my hand under his chin, and behind his head, and raised his head 2 or 3 times with all my strength and brought it in, and I did perceive that his neck began to be stiff, and then he began to rattle, and after to breathe, and the people were amazed.

Like most spiritual healers, Fox refused to take personal credit for such cures. These healings were "done by the power of Christ," he once explained.[12]

Public debates over the validity and meaning of such claims to religious healing became particularly intense in the latter half of the nineteenth century and the early twentieth century, when the Holiness and Pentecostal movements roiled the waters of American Protestantism. Many Christians in this era of social and cultural upheaval addressed sickness by turning to prayer-based therapies that emerged from within their own churches. In the period after the Civil War, this impulse contributed to the emergence of a divine-healing movement that captivated tens of thousands of evangelical Protestants and occasioned a great deal of hand-wringing in the secular press. Spread through conventions, itinerant preachers, books and tracts, and the founding of hospitals and homes, faith healing became, according to one perceptive study, "not a concern for a small or unimportant subculture" but rather emerged as "an issue at the very center of middle-class Protestant life."[13]

Traditionally, Christians had enjoyed a fluid and unsettled relationship with physicians. While some had embraced medicine as a temporal manifestation of God's desire to conquer sickness, others had been more dismissive, perceiving it as a tepid substitute for prayer as a means of physical healing. But many of those involved in the Pentecostal and Holiness movements were not simply ambivalent about the practice of medicine; some viewed it as antithetical to the teachings of the scriptures and argued that Christians should repudiate it altogether in favor of exclusive reliance on prayer. As Grant Wacker, a leading scholar of Pentecostalism, has noted, this rejection fit into a broader pattern of "renunciative behavior" found among many evangelical Protestants. Some Pentecostals turned their backs on medicine in much the same way that they abandoned such other purportedly sinful practices as dancing, drinking, and smoking.[14]

Dynamic preachers such as Maria Woodworth-Etter, Charles Cullis, and Albert B. Simpson sparked fervent and widespread interest in spiritual healing. Woodworth-Etter began her healing ministry in the early 1880s after, as she later put it, "The Lord showed me . . . that I had the gift of healing, and of laying on of hands for the recovery of the sick." She often performed these healings at immense revival meetings that sometimes drew crowds numbering in the thousands. Ecstatic outbursts punctuated these gatherings. Attendees wailed and writhed as Woodworth-Etter helped the Holy Spirit to drive out the demons causing their illnesses, thereby restoring their health. Many of those healed in this manner appeared to lose consciousness, and their anxious relatives hovered over them until they could be revived.[15]

Like many leading spiritual healers before and since, Woodworth-Etter read the New Testament quite narrowly, and the Epistle of James, with its endorsement of prayer and anointment for healing, profoundly influenced her ministry. The text of James was particularly important, she maintained, because it represented a clear articulation of Christ's teachings relating to healing. "He delivered this doctrine of divine healing of the body to be taught and practiced in every church, that each member would know their privilege and duty to God," Woodworth-Etter wrote. "If he or she were sick . . . they should send at once for the elders and let God glorify Himself by manifesting the healing power in raising him up." She doubted that physicians, whom she regularly decried as "infidel doctors," could provide such true healing in accordance with God's word.[16]

Originally trained as a homeopathic physician, Charles Cullis earned the title of "apostle of spiritual healing in America" through preaching, publishing, and operating myriad healing facilities in the Boston area, the most prominent being the Home for Indigent and Incurable Consumptives. By the mid-1870s, Cullis had become a dynamic force in the healing revival, generating numerous publications through the Willard Tract Repository and organizing annual "faith conventions" held at various sites throughout New England. Healing services were central to these summer conclaves, and in them Cullis showed his fidelity to the Epistle of James by anointing hundreds of participants with oil. "It seems to me," he once explained, "that Christians are not living up to their gospel privileges when they fail to claim God's promises, not only for spiritual but for temporal blessings, and also for the healing of the body."[17]

Cullis published several volumes of testimony from individuals who claimed that he had healed them. The book *Faith Cures* contained numerous affidavits demonstrating that, as Cullis put it, "God promises to hear and to answer the prayers of His children when they call upon Him for [His] blessing." An unnamed man from the Boston area furnished a typical account, describing how he had battled consumption in the early 1870s. A doctor pronounced the victim's case hopeless, and doses of a patent medicine "seemed only to increase my disease," he reported. The turning point in his recovery came when he summoned Cullis and submitted to a healing rite modeled on the Epistle of James. "[Cullis] prayed, anointed me with oil, and in the name of the Lord Jesus commanded me to be healed," he later wrote. "Instantly my whole being was thrilled with an unknown power, from the top of my head to the soles of my feet." His lungs quickly cleared, and his health returned.[18]

Albert B. Simpson, a Presbyterian minister, cast aside his skepticism of spiritual healing after attending one of Cullis's faith conventions in the early 1880s. When he returned to his pulpit in New York City, Simpson incorporated what he called "divine healing" into his ministry and began conducting weekly healing services. These rites, according to one observer, soon "became a shrine for thousands of people connected with the churches of the city and its suburbs." Simpson further served these multitudes by operating a faith-cure institution known as Berachah House.[19]

Simpson asserted that members of his own family had benefited from divine healing. In his book *The Gospel of Healing*, he recounted the story of his daughter's battle with diphtheria. Against the counsel of his wife, who had insisted that he take the girl to a doctor, Simpson "simply took the little one to God and claimed her healing in the name of the Lord Jesus." Following the instructions laid out in the Epistle of James, he anointed her brow with oil and "cried out to God for speedy deliverance." The following morning, the girl's fever had abated and her throat had cleared, and she was able to run about and play.[20]

The story of Simpson's own healing was no less dramatic. He had suffered from a variety of physical and psychological ailments (including one episode that he delicately described as a bout of "nervous exhaustion") before turning to God for healing. Although his faith wavered—he admitted that he "floundered and stumbled for years," sometimes consulting with physicians—Simpson eventually committed himself to God and "His healing covenant." The results, he reported, were extraordinary. He possessed almost boundless physical energy, and his mental faculties were keen. "God has so helped me that my literary work has never been a labor," he wrote. "He has enabled me to think much more rapidly and to accomplish much more work and with greater facility than ever before."[21]

The doctrine of atonement played a central role in Simpson's spiritual-healing ministry. The notion has its roots in Matthew 8:16–17, which describes how Jesus "cured all who were sick. This was to fulfill what had been spoken through the prophet Isaiah, 'He took our infirmities and bore our diseases.'" Simpson and others read this passage to mean that Jesus, in suffering on the cross, had atoned not only for humankind's sins but also for its bodily diseases. Simpson termed this "atoning Sacrifice" the "fundamental principle of Divine Healing," and it undergirded the philosophies of many like-minded spiritual healers.[22]

Minister A. J. Gordon firmly believed in the atonement. Gordon wrote in his book *The Ministry of Healing* that this doctrine was nothing less than "the foundation laid for faith in bodily healing." To buttress this claim, Gordon published several lengthy testimonies meant to provide "evidences of God's immediate action in taking away the consequences of sin, as well as forgiving the sin itself." These accounts ranged from the healing of a daughter of a London clergyman to the miraculous recovery of Jennie Smith, a Philadelphia invalid whose story drew widespread interest in the late nineteenth century. After she had endured more than a dozen years of apparently excruciating pain, Smith's health returned after a prayer session attended by "a few Christian friends," as Gordon put it. "It seemed as if heaven were at that moment opened," she reported, "and I was conscious of a baptism of strength, as sensibly and as positively as if an electric shock had passed through my system. . . . My limbs and body seemed as if made new." Gordon reveled in providing such accounts because they seemed to offer further proof that "the Great Physician" offered the surest route to healing.[23]

Skeptics of these claims, and of the spiritual-healing movement that they buttressed, were legion. A mainstream Methodist journal termed the entire

movement an *"absurdity,"* and one perplexed minister concluded that its devotees were "silly." Of particular concern to many critics were the faith-cure
homes and "hospitals" operated by many spiritual-healing ministries. One
New York clergyman called for the city's board of health to investigate their operation and for upstanding Christians to repudiate "what has become a scandal
of common sense."[24]

Physicians, with whom spiritual healers were competing in an increasingly crowded and confusing marketplace for healing, offered especially sharp
criticism of the divine-healing movement. Motivated by both a genuine concern
for public health, as well as a somewhat less lofty desire to discredit potential
competitors, doctors routinely assailed healers like Maria Woodworth-Etter
as swindlers who preyed upon society's most vulnerable members. In 1891,
for instance, a prominent St. Louis physician, Dr. E. W. Saunders, accused
Woodworth-Etter of having induced "incurable insanity" in three city residents.
Stricken by "religious monomania" after attending the healer's revival meetings, all three had seen their lives completely fall apart. A young man suffered
from lurid hallucinations that featured howling dogs; a housewife became
so obsessed with Woodworth-Etter's teachings that she became "a sad wreck
of her former self," according to one press report. Saunders warned that if
Woodworth-Etter was not stopped immediately, the city would be so full of
such victims that it would have to erect more insane asylums to house all of
them.[25]

Several prominent figures in mainstream Protestant denominations disparaged the spiritual-healing movement in similarly blunt terms. One typically
caustic attack on it came in Benjamin Warfield's book *Counterfeit Miracles*, published in 1918. As the title of his work suggested, Warfield (a famously conser-
vative Presbyterian theologian who championed the notion of Biblical inerrancy) was deeply skeptical of the tales of religious healing told by the likes of
Simpson and Gordon, whose book *The Ministry of Healing* he subjected to
prolonged and withering scrutiny. Warfield suggested that there were straightforward temporal explanations for many of the miracles claimed by such
healers. "It seems to be the experience of every one who has made a serious
attempt to sift the evidence for miraculous healing," he wrote, "that this evidence melts away before his eyes." Warfield also assailed the scriptural basis
for the spiritual-healing movement, calling it "too precarious to bear . . .
weight." In making this claim, he went so far as to dismiss the oft-invoked
Epistle of James as "irrelevant."[26]

Warfield was among those who grounded their skepticism of the spiritual-
healing movement in a belief that the era of miraculous healing had long since
passed. He and other critics noted that miracles had been a defining feature
of the ministries of Jesus and the apostles. Jesus, of course, long had been depicted as the consummate healer; the Bible asserted that dozens of individuals
had benefited from the many healing miracles he had affected. Whatever their

minimal skills in mitigating the suffering of the sick, contemporary healers were pale imitations of these earlier miraculous healers, whose work had ceased in the apostolic age. "Jesus healed instantly, and everyone he pronounced healed was indeed healed," Robert Bruce Mullin has written in a summary of this line of argument. "No modern healer could make such claims."[27]

Such salvos failed to quiet the likes of Carrie Judd Montgomery, an early Pentecostal healer who routinely denigrated medical science as a totally inadequate substitute for prayer in bringing about physical healing. In her book *The Prayer of Faith*, published in 1880, Montgomery expressed a dim view of physicians' ability to heal. "Medicine is a most imperfect institution," she wrote, because it belongs to "this sin-stricken world." Ailing Christians would do far better to seek healing through "the prayer of faith," which was a "more perfect healing institution made ours by Christ's atonement" on the cross. Indeed, the power of the prayer of faith (or prevailing prayer) was central to Pentecostals' approach to healing. This notion was rooted in the idea that Jesus' atonement on the cross essentially guaranteed healing to those who surrendered themselves to God's word and prayed for physical restoration. F. F. Bosworth, a noted Pentecostal healer, likened prayer to engaging in a game of checkers with God: prayer prompted Him to act because "he always moves when it is His turn."[28]

Hundreds of Pentecostals offered testimonials in which they detailed the extraordinary results when God was moved to heal. "They detailed every conceivable form of restoration," Grant Wacker has asserted, "ranging from runny noses dried up to dead bodies raised to life—and everything in between." In accounts published in such organs as the weekly *Apostolic Light*, Pentecostals regularly reported how the Lord had responded to their stalwart faith by healing. A well digger from Spokane, Washington, furnished an almost comical narrative describing how he should have been brained by various pieces of falling debris and a heavy bucket. The victim endured a "very sore head" for several weeks, but it eventually fully healed after he attended a religious service. A Kansas schoolgirl named Eula Wilson had a somewhat more dramatic healing experience: she was resurrected from the dead. (This after being "borne to heaven in a white cloud attended by two [angels]," she reported.) Ecstatic over the girl's miraculous healing, her mother insisted that God had returned Eula to earth so that she would "spread his word."[29]

Individuals gained more than simple physical restoration from such incidents. For many of those cured, a healing was a kind of sacrament, and it represented a transcendent and transformative spiritual experience. God's conquest of an infirmity marked not only an exercise of his awesome power; it also demonstrated that the believer had earned His blessing by maintaining fidelity to the teachings of the scriptures. Healers benefited as well, gaining legitimacy each time they were used as instruments of divine will and provided temporal proof of the validity of broader theological dogmas. Their stature grew each time a healing demonstrated, in a tangible and quite often dramatic way, the continued potency of the lessons of the scriptures.[30]

The idea that God always responds to a genuine prayer of faith created a delicate problem for Pentecostals whose maladies failed to respond to spiritual treatment. As Grant Wacker has put it, "Given the premise that God always responds to genuine prayer of faith, the persistence of illness could be explained only two ways: Either one's life was impure or one's faith was shallow." In either case, Pentecostal doctrine held that the victims of illness, not God, bore responsibility—a potentially crushing burden that some prominent Pentecostals were loath to lighten. One asked, "Whose fault is it if you stay sick? Not the fault of the Lord. If we are not healed we must look for the cause of it in ourselves."[31]

F. F. Bosworth devoted one of his famous sermons to the question of "why some fail to receive healing from Christ." The remarkably thorough Bosworth—a Pentecostal minister who had trained under John Alexander Dowie, the controversial Chicago-area healer—outlined nearly two dozen specific reasons why so many of those afflicted by disease failed to achieve healing through prayer. Claiming that some sick individuals were hobbled by "insufficient instruction," he faulted the "ignorance concerning the healing power of the Gospel" shown by clergy who were woefully ill informed of the traditions established by the early church. Bosworth also assigned blame more broadly, asserting that the widespread repudiation of Christ's teachings made it less likely that he would bestow his healing gifts on particular individuals. They continued to suffer because contemporary society was a veritable "Nazareth of unbelief," he said.[32]

Bosworth collected and published numerous accounts of "souls saved and bodies healed," all of them attesting to the extraordinary benefits of religious healing. One woman, identified simply as "Miss Nix," claimed that she suffered through a crippling array of physical and psychological ailments: "cancer, sugar diabetes and enlargement of the heart, a twisted spine, almost total paralysis from the hips to the feet, the condition of being a nervous wreck and of almost total blindness." After a doctor—making the kind of misguided pronouncement that is often found in such testimonies—told her that she had less than two weeks to live, Nix read the Bible, prayed, and sang hymns with a woman who recently had conquered cancer through prayer. Soon thereafter, Nix herself experienced her own miraculous healing; her many ailments vanished, and she was able to resume an active life. "Do you wonder," she asked in a testimony published by Bosworth, "that I love God?"[33]

Pentecostals offered such accounts somewhat less frequently in the 1930s. Financial constraints created by the Great Depression made it more difficult for independent revivalists like Bosworth and Aimee Semple McPherson to mount tours and spread their message of divine healing. Factional disputes among Pentecostal sects—described by one worried evangelist as "divisions, splits and controversies"—also hindered the work of these spiritual healing advocates. In the years immediately following World War II, however, a healing revival swept through the Pentecostal movement. "The call for miracle revival came at once from every community," the historian David Edwin Harrell has written. "Hundreds of charismatic evangelists . . . rushed to answer the call."[34]

William Branham and Oral Roberts spearheaded the postwar Pentecostal healing revival. Branham told rapt audiences that his healing ministry began in earnest after he was visited by an angel who informed him that "God has sent you to take a gift of divine healing to the people of the world." He became a whirlwind after receiving this charge, crisscrossing the country and holding raucous revival meetings that drew crowds numbering in the thousands. (Branham was popular abroad as well: in 1950, more than seven thousand people filled an auditorium in Finland to hear him preach.) Roberts, although several years his junior, eventually supplanted Branham as the healing revival's acknowledged leader. Deft use of radio and television helped to foster the explosive growth of his healing ministry in the 1950s.[35]

Lesser-known evangelists like Jack Coe, who was purported to own a gospel tent even larger than Roberts's mammoth structure, also made their mark. Before his untimely death early in 1957, Coe had been among the many prominent healing evangelists who opposed medical treatment. He held particularly extreme views on the use of physicians: at one point he thundered that any Pentecostal who sought healing from a doctor would be seared with the "mark of the beast"—that is, the emblem of Satan. Other evangelists expressed more moderate opinions of medicine. One explained that while "doctors cannot heal," they were able to keep the sick alive long enough for them to turn to God and pray for Him to provide true healing. Such evangelists believed that physicians might complement their own healing ministries—if only to confirm that miraculous healings had indeed taken place.[36]

Kathryn Kuhlman seemed comfortable using physicians to help verify her successes as a healer. The ecumenical Kuhlman, who achieved widespread notoriety as a healer in the 1970s, presided over a small media empire: in addition to penning inspirational books such as *I Believe in Miracles* and *God Can Do It Again*, she produced religious broadcasts that aired on over fifty radio and sixty television stations. Kuhlman also appeared before packed crowds. Holding what *Time* magazine called "pointedly nondenominational" services, she discerned ailments and then healed the afflicted in a manner that was more serene than fiery. Sensitive to allegations that she was a con artist, Kuhlman claimed that a Johns Hopkins University physician regularly verified her purported triumphs over a broad range of illnesses, including cancer, blindness, and heart disease. Despite these successes, she rejected the label of "faith healer" and insisted, modestly, that she merely hauled "a water bucket for the Lord."[37]

Kuhlman's wild success as a healer failed to impress a Minnesota surgeon named William Nolen, who attended one her services in the early 1970s.

Skeptical of her claims, Nolen decided to conduct follow-up examinations and interviews with more than two dozen people who allegedly had been "miraculously healed" by the evangelist. The physician was appalled by what he discovered—or, rather, what he failed to discover. Nolen determined that none of those treated by Kuhlman actually had been healed. Reporting his findings in his book *Healing: A Doctor in Search of a Miracle*, he noted the heartbreaking story of a woman who had suffered from cancer of the spine. At the service Nolen had attended, this woman, listening to Kuhlman's entreaties, had thrown away her back brace and bounded across the stage. Nolen revealed that her joy had proven to be short-lived: her fragile backbone collapsed the day after the service. She died a short time later.[38]

James Randi did Nolen one better, making a career of exposing the foibles of purported frauds like Kuhlman. A magician and escape artist, Randi gained renown in the 1960s and 1970s by investigating and debunking a variety of pseudoscientific and paranormal claims (such as those made by Uri Geller, who contended he could bend metal spoons simply by wielding the formidable power of his mind). Randi dismissed faith healing as "fakery" because it could not withstand "straightforward, rational, scientific evaluation," and he mounted several prolonged investigations of its most prominent practitioners, whom he regarded as charlatans mainly concerned with lining their own pockets. In a typical attack, he savaged Leroy Jenkins by comprehensively documenting the prominent evangelist's many run-ins with law enforcement authorities (which involved such tawdry matters as his alleged participation in conspiracies to commit arson and assault). Jenkins attempted to fight fire with fire, brashly taking out a newspaper advertisement challenging Randi "to prove that I am a phony," but he eventually backed away from the confrontation and labeled his accuser a publicity hound.[39]

Randi was so confident in his ability to debunk the claims of faith healers that he challenged their dean, the venerable Oral Roberts. In 1987, after Roberts had publicly stated that donors to his ministry had a right to expect "signs and wonders" as proof that their money was well spent, Randi wrote to the evangelist and asked for "evidence for the performance of . . . miracles as a result of your ministry." Randi, unlike the millions of credulous people who had given money to Roberts over the years, was unwilling to take the evangelist's word for it; he asked for credible medical evidence proving that the minister had affected physical healings. Randi redoubled his efforts when Roberts claimed that "dozens and dozens" of individuals had been raised from the dead at his services. But Roberts never rose to the challenge: the most Randi ever received from him were some bland letters extolling the power of the scriptures and some samples of the minister's voluminous published writings.[40]

Not all participants in the healing revival achieved as much fame (or attracted as much scrutiny) as Oral Roberts. On a far less grand scale, yeoman healers like David Harrison, a preacher and medium who worked in Illinois and Indiana in the early 1970s, also tackled injuries and illnesses. Harrison's circumstances, unlike Roberts's, were decidedly modest: to support his preaching at the Golden Hour Spiritualist Church in Terre Haute, Indiana, he worked as a waiter in a restaurant. But Harrison's lack of temporal wealth in no way diminished his fervor for serving "as an instrument that God works through" to heal. Physically as well as spiritually, acting as a conduit for God's power was an extraordinary experience, he explained, "because it gives you a feeling of strength flowing through your body. And anyone who has this power or has the healing touch who put their hands upon an individual can feel the sensation almost instantly. This sensation is a warming that goes through your whole body, the vibrations you can feel wherever you are touched."[41]

Remarkable as they were, these physical sensations did not always produce instant results. God often restored individuals to health, Harrison explained, through "slow, divine healing" that took place over a period of days or even weeks. One such healing involved an elderly woman who had been told by doctors that she never would walk properly again. After God gradually wielded Harrison as his instrument of healing, "she don't drag those feet no more, [and] she walks as good as any eighty-four-year-old person you'd want to see," as Harrison put it. With God's powers working slowly but surely, another woman with a debilitated arm was restored to health in a similarly measured way, Harrison reported.[42]

Harrison never took credit for such healings. The "power that flows through my body" emanated from God, he said, not from man. Andy Rogers, another healer who was active in the Terre Haute area, also was quick to credit God for his successes in restoring the sick to health. "It is the gift of God and it is not the healer himself that does the healing," Rogers explained. "It has to come from without, from another source, and the healer is merely the channel or instrument through which the healing takes place." Rogers believed that anyone who made a sincere effort to understand the teachings of the Bible similarly could act as a channel for God's healing powers.[43]

Although it is easy to scoff at such claims, tens of thousands of people from all walks of life sincerely claimed to have been restored to health by healers like Rogers and his more famous colleagues in the healing revival. Whatever their credibility, their accounts speak volumes about the central place of healing in religious experience. For Reverend Robert Evans, the pastor of a small church in Danville, Illinois, healings provided unparalleled demonstrations of God's determination to vanquish sin. Evans had firsthand experience with such dramatic manifestations of God's power: he was spared from commitment to a tuberculosis sanatorium after "the ministers of the Gospel prayed for me and the Lord raised his hand and touched me and gave me a new lung," and both of his parents rose from their death beds after God responded to prayer and healed them. Evans rejoiced at these healings; he viewed them as indisputable evidence of the truth of the scriptures.[44]

A far different kind of healing revival flowered in the 1990s. Its leaders were not flamboyant and controversial evangelists but rather sober researchers and authors who, in an ironic twist, invoked the authority of medical science—the very thing that previously had been used to undercut the claims of spiritual healers—to argue that prayer did in fact cure illness. This new generation of champions of spiritual healing included the likes of Dr. Harold Koenig, director of Duke University's Center for Spirituality, Theology, and Health, and Dr. Herbert Benson, a professor at Harvard Medical School. Backing up their many books and articles with apparently solid research, these experts attempted to give spiritual healing a patina of scholarly respectability by demonstrating that "science tells us that prayer works," as the author Larry Dossey reported in his book *Prayer Is Good Medicine*. Their dogged efforts added a new and compelling—if not controversial—chapter to the history of a movement with origins dating back to the days of the earliest Christians.[45]

At the heart of these new claims regarding the efficacy of spiritual healing were dozens of scientific studies designed to gauge the impact of prayer on physical health and emotional well-being. Early on, at least, few of these studies bore positive results. In 1872, a prominent British scientist, Sir Francis Galton, conducted an early inquiry into the usefulness of prayer. Galton compared the longevity of "materialistic" professionals—doctors, lawyers, and the like—against members of two groups that presumably benefited from prayer: members of the clergy and sovereign heads of state (who were prayed for tens of thousands of times every day by loyal subjects). Galton found that "sovereigns are literally the shortest lived of all who have the advantage of affluence," a result that seemed to belie the notion that prayer produced salutary results. There was still no scientific proof, he concluded, conclusively demonstrating "the agency of prayer either on disease or on anything else."[46]

By his own admission, Galton's methodology was imperfect, but his results were not seriously challenged in the scientific community until the 1950s, when researchers at the University of Redlands in California conducted what became known as "the Prayer Experiment." Subjects in the experiment, all of whom suffered from varying degrees of psychological distress, were divided into three groups and offered different forms of therapy. The "Just-Plain-Psychology" group received standard psychotherapy; the "Just-Plain-Prayer" group received no psychotherapy but rather prayed for their well-being every evening; and the "Prayer-Therapy" group prayed together daily in two-hour sessions. At the experiment's conclusion, the final group showed the greatest improvement, besting even the psychotherapy group. These results provided the basis for a popular book—cowritten by the chief experimenter in the Redlands study, William Parker—entitled *Prayer Can Change Your Life*. Prayer, Parker wrote, "can heal your diseases. . . . I have proven this truth in my own personal experiences beyond the shadow of a doubt."[47]

Other studies followed, and some of the results seemed to back up the findings of the Redlands experiment. In one famous study, a cardiologist named Randolph Byrd tested the effects of prayer on patients in the coronary care unit at San Francisco General Hospital. One group of Byrd's subjects was prayed for by home prayer groups that he had organized outside the hospital; the other group received no such prayers. Byrd found that patients who were prayed for were significantly less likely to require antibiotics; less likely to develop a potentially fatal condition known as pulmonary edema; and less likely to require the creation of an artificial airway and the use of an artificial ventilator. According to Larry Dossey (who fell into this group himself), Byrd's work furnished believers in the curative power of prayer with "a careful study [that] finally demonstrated a profound effect of prayer."[48]

By the late 1990s, Duke University's Harold Koenig had emerged as perhaps the leading scholarly advocate of what he termed "the healing power of faith." Koenig oversaw numerous studies designed to measure how individuals' religious faith and practice affects their physical health and emotional well-being. According to Koenig, he and his colleagues at Duke did not "try to establish the validity of faith healing" per se but rather investigated "the therapeutic or healing power of people's religious faith." The results of these inquiries—all of which adhered to established techniques of medical and social science research, Koenig asserted—were startling. The Duke researchers discovered that churchgoers have lower blood pressure and are less likely to suffer from depression and that they tend to have stronger immune systems. "The results of our research," Koenig wrote, "suggest it would be beneficial to increase your religious practices if this is compatible with your personal faith."[49]

Koenig pointed out that his research demonstrated that a religious *lifestyle*—not necessarily prayer itself—is comparatively healthy. (Superior physical and emotional well-being, he noted, might result from adhering to religious beliefs that discourage potentially destructive personal habits such as smoking and drinking.) But not everyone who explored the relationship between religion and health shared Koenig's circumspection. "Prayer is back," Larry Dossey proclaimed. "After sitting on the sidelines for most of this century, prayer is moving toward center stage in modern medicine." In countless articles and books like *Prayer Is Good Medicine* and *Healing Words: The Power of Prayer and the Practice of Medicine,* Dossey touted the notion that prayer itself is beneficial to an individual's health. He could back up this claim with scientific research, Dossey said, because "it is possible to take prayer into the hospital and the clinic and the laboratory and test it pretty much like you would a new medication."[50]

Part of what distinguished these contemporary champions of "the healing power of prayer" from many of their forebears was their insistence that prayer can complement, rather than supplant, modern medicine. Indeed, Dossey and other like-minded physicians often expressed revulsion at the practices of faith healers, asserting that they took a sound idea to potentially deadly extremes. Dr. Dale Matthews, a professor at Georgetown University School of Medicine and author of the book *The Faith Factor*, criticized members of the Faith Assembly—an Indiana-based church with notoriously high infant mortality rates—for clinging to prayer as the sole path toward physical healing. Matthews argued that "our mental, physical, and spiritual health are best served when we enjoy the benefits of religious commitment *and* take advantage of the best that traditional medicine can offer us." Matthews made this point somewhat more cleverly in a later address: "The medicine of the future," he said, "is going to be prayer and Prozac."[51]

Although Matthews's relatively moderate position—essentially, that prayer can boost medicine's power to heal—was a far cry from John Alexander Dowie's vitriolic attacks on doctors, it too was savaged by skeptics. Numerous critics claimed that the likes of Byrd, Koenig, Dossey, and Matthews based their findings on inconclusive or simply faulty science. Dr. Richard Sloan of Columbia University Medical Center expressed reservations about research suggesting a strong link between prayer and health. In an article published in the British medical journal *Lancet*, Sloan called the scientific evidence regarding associations between religion, spirituality, and health "weak and inconsistent." Among the problems cited by Sloan is the failure of some of the studies on religion and health to adequately account for "confounders" such as the behavioral and genetic characteristics of subjects. (For instance, levels of morbidity and mortality among priests and monks might be affected by their adherence to codes of conduct which proscribe such potentially risky habits as smoking, drinking, or engaging in sexual activity.) The presence of such variables—along with an apparent lack of methodological consistency in published work in the field—led Sloan to caution against "suggestions that religious activity will promote health." Appearing on a television broadcast not long after his *Lancet* article appeared, Sloan was more blunt: "There's really no evidence whatsoever," he said, "that praying for others has any medical impact."[52]

Dr. Stephen Barrett, head of the anti–health fraud organization Quackwatch, was similarly unimpressed by recent studies of the efficacy of prayer in treating illness. Barrett noted that some of the studies purporting to show the benefits of prayer had in fact produced clinically inconclusive results. And the apparently conclusive outcomes of other investigations, such as Randolph Byrd's famous study of heart patients, appeared to have been shaped by researchers' biased handling of data. Barrett also worried that studies purporting to show the benefits of prayer might in fact be counterproductive in that they could lull some religiously devout individuals into a false sense of security regarding their physical well-being. "Prayer may help some people feel reassured when they are worried," he argued, "but to me it makes more sense to spend one's time and energy on more constructive health-promoting activities," such as exercise regimens.[53]

Hector Avalos, a professor of religious studies at Iowa State University, highlighted several potential practical and theoretical flaws in experiments designed to measure the effects of prayer. In a particularly caustic assessment of Randolph Byrd's research, Avalos argued that "there can be no such thing as a controlled experiment concerning prayer" because "there is no way to know that someone did not receive prayer. How would anyone know that some distant relative was not praying for a member of the group that Byrd identified as having received no prayer?" Avalos also wondered how Byrd's experiment might have been impacted by the millions upon millions of prayers offered by churchgoers for the sick throughout the world.[54]

Avalos went beyond examining the methodology of experiments designed to gauge the relationship between religion and health to address the thorny philosophical and theological issues they might raise. According to Avalos, although spiritual healers long have invoked the Bible to support their claims that prayer can affect physical rehabilitation, several passages in the scriptures "severely undermine the possibility of controlled experiments of prayer" because they suggest that God will ignore particular people's prayers if he is angry with them. In Isaiah 1:15, for instance, God cautions that "even though you make many prayers, I will not listen." Jeremiah 11:14 similarly quotes God warning individuals not to pray for particular people "for I will not listen when they call me in the time of their trouble." Avalos found it impossible to reconcile such passages—carrying with them the possibility that God might "listen to some prayers but not others"—with a truly scientific study of prayer's effectiveness. "Bible problems," as Avalos termed them, help "render any thought of a controlled scientific study of prayer absolutely meaningless."[55]

Other critics of efforts to quantify the effectiveness of prayer raised similar concerns. Censure came not only from scientists and scholars but also from religious leaders who questioned the value of attempting to quantify God's mercy. These skeptics asserted that "there's no way to put God to the test," as Rev. Raymond Lawrence, Jr., put it. As director of pastoral care at New York-Presbyterian Hospital/Columbia University Medical Center, Lawrence encouraged members of all faiths to turn to prayer and other religious traditions as a means of coping with illness. But he recoiled at the notion that science somehow could measure the temporal impact of such efforts. "This whole exercise cheapens religion," he said, "and promotes an infantile theology that God is out there ready to miraculously defy the laws of nature in answer to a prayer."[56]

In the spring of 2006, Lawrence and like-minded critics pointed to the results of a long-awaited study of the therapeutic effects of intercessory prayer. Conducted by a team of researchers led by Dr. Herbert Benson, a self-described "pioneer in mind/body medicine," the large and expensive study—it involved more than 1,800 patients in six hospitals and cost more than

$2 million—found that prayers offered by strangers had no effect on patients recovering from coronary bypass surgery. Lawrence expressed the hope that Benson's dismal results, which showed such prayers to be "medically ineffective," would dissuade researchers from further attempting to prove that "the ruler of the universe can be mechanically requisitioned to intervene in people's suffering or health."[57]

3

"Defended by Lord Jehovah"

The Peculiar People in the British Courts

In March 1899, a religious healer claiming to be Francis Schlatter drew a large audience to New York's Tammany Hall. Confidently promising to effect "healing by faith," the minister offered physical relief and spiritual fulfillment to victims of a variety of ailments, including epilepsy and rheumatism—provided, of course, that the afflicted demonstrated sufficient faith in the Lord's ability to restore health. Many of those summoned to the stage and treated by "Schlatter" claimed to have been healed immediately; others left the premises with nothing more than a promise from the minister that "if you are not cured now, you will be tomorrow." Some of the attendees failed to receive even this assurance: a skeptical newspaper reporter who observed the service noted that the healer ignored the entreaties of those suffering from such dire afflictions as blindness and that he conspicuously rebuffed a lame youngster who hoped to regain the use of his legs.[1]

The minister who addressed the throng assembled at Tammany Hall probably was not Francis Schlatter, the famed "New Mexico Messiah," but rather an imposter who was capitalizing on Schlatter's notoriety. Before he vanished under mysterious circumstances in Mexico in the mid-1890s, Schlatter had been one of the many spiritual healers to gain a measure of celebrity in the United States in the late nineteenth century. He reached the height of his fame over the course of two months in 1895, when crowds estimated in the thousands flocked to the healing services he held on a makeshift wooden platform in Denver. (Many audience members arrived in town on special trains chartered from New Mexico and Nebraska.) "The sensation of touching the hand of Schlatter," reported one of those healed, "is something like an electric current being turned on." That a fraud claiming Schlatter's mantle could attract attention in New York in 1899—several years and thousands of miles removed from the actual healer's greatest triumphs— testified to the burgeoning appeal of spiritual-healing practices in the United States in the late nineteenth century.[2]

In the very same month that New York newspapers were reporting on the healing ministry of the would-be Schlatter, they also gave prominent notice to methods of addressing illness that were purely secular. Only a few days after it reported on the faith-healer's efforts at Tammany Hall, the *New York Times* carried a glowing account of the recent activities of Robert Koch, the renowned German bacteriologist. The paper noted that Koch—who, among his many accomplishments, played a key role in advancing the germ theory of disease by demonstrating that specific microorganisms caused such maladies as anthrax, cholera, and tuberculosis—had received a generous grant from the German government in order to mount an expedition that would probe "the nature and origin of malaria." He hoped to build on the findings of an earlier expedition to Africa, a journey that had led him to conclude (correctly, as it turned out) that mosquitoes transmitted the malady between humans and that administering doses of quinine to victims could help break malarial fevers.[3]

That "Schlatter" and Koch could simultaneously command public attention in the same city for advocating antithetical approaches to curing illness speaks volumes about the profound conflict between medicine and religion that occurred in the late nineteenth century. While spiritual healers such as Schlatter (and his impersonators) took to the hustings and touted the power of religious faith to restore physical health, Koch and his colleagues in the scientific community made a succession of key theoretical and practical advances that demonstrated the growing capability of medical science, with its reliance on observation and experimentation, to successfully treat illnesses or prevent them altogether. Many accounts have described the results of these efforts as revolutionary. "The medical world of 1900 was . . . utterly different [from] that of 1800," one observer has written. "After millennia of wishful thinking and groping in the dark, medical science at last got it right." Although this is perhaps an overstatement—even today, medical treatments fail many patients— medical science clearly experienced a period of significant maturation over the course of the nineteenth century.[4]

The public took notice. Particularly among the educated elites who determined public policy in both the United States and abroad, "supernatural explanation of disease increasingly gave way to naturalistic ones, and the commonly shared values of medicine rather than distinctive religious beliefs more and more determined attitudes toward sickness and health," according to scholars Ronald Numbers and Darrel Amundson. These emerging attitudes not only bolstered the stature of medical science but also highlighted the apparent dangers posed by religious-healing practices and thereby made them prime targets for state regulation. This was especially true in England. There, while breakthroughs in fields such as bacteriology, immunology, and public health were saving thousands of lives every year, a succession of children in a faith-healing church known as the Peculiar People died after being treated exclusively by the methods prescribed in the Epistle of James: prayer and anointing. Occurring against the backdrop of dramatic advancements in medical science, their deaths lead to a series of unprecedented prosecutions of parents for manslaughter and neglect. These emotionally charged cases, which would have profound influence on both sides of the Atlantic, marked the first sustained effort by public officials in any country to fix legal responsibility on parents whose children died after receiving only spiritual treatment for their illnesses.[5]

Ironically, the prosecutions of the "Peculiars," as they sometimes were called, did not prove to be idiosyncratic. Indeed, their cases established a rough pattern that would be repeated in hundreds of subsequent cases of religion-based medical neglect on both sides of the Atlantic. The defendants were devoutly religious individuals who resisted preventive health measures (such as vaccinations and quarantines) and stubbornly clung to a narrowly literal interpretation of the Epistle of James whenever their children fell ill. When deaths resulted, authorities—who were increasingly confident that medical science could have saved the youngsters—asserted that the parents had violated legal standards designed to protect the health and welfare of children. Although this clash between individual rights and state authority sometimes confounded the courts, it had little apparent effect on the defendants, many of whom would lose multiple children to religion-based medical neglect. As would be the case with many subsequent spiritual healers, the prospect of temporal punishment failed to deter the Peculiar People from treating sickness in a manner consistent with their interpretation of the scriptures.

Founded by a minister named John Banyard, the Peculiar People appeared in Essex and nearby counties in England in the mid-1800s. (The group took its name from 1 Peter 2:9, which calls the Lord's followers "a royal priesthood, a holy nation, a peculiar people.") According to one history of the faith, these pious folk, taking their cue from the Epistle of James, "had no faith in medical aid, and trusted in God for healing." Sir William Osler, the renowned Canadian physician and medical educator, noted that the Peculiar People "carr[ied] out a consistent gospel of faith healing" grounded in "their belief in the plain saying of Scripture." The Peculiars thus were part of a religious healing tradition with deep roots, according to Osler: "This primitive Christian attitude toward disease has never lacked adherents in the Church, and medieval literature is full of illustrations of a practice identical with that of the Peculiar People."[6]

The Peculiar People's first reported success in spiritual healing involved a church member named William Perry. After physicians had failed to end his long bout with consumption, Perry asked Banyard to lead a session of prayer and anointing based directly on the Epistle of James. (Perry turned to the text of James, he later said, because God had quoted it directly to him as he prayed one morning.) Banyard overcame some initial reluctance and led the rite, and the results were extraordinary. As one of the church's publications reported, "the Lord sent the healing power upon them, which entered William Perry, chasing away all consumption, giving him a perfect deliverance." It was said that Perry recovered so immediately that the previously frail man walked more than twenty miles on the very day of his healing.[7]

Sect member Fred Jiggens grew up hearing stories of "much healing of the sick, and curing of all manner of diseases and infirmities" among the Peculiar People. One memorable tale involved Jiggens's own grandmother, who once fell gravely ill with smallpox. A doctor was summoned to her bedside, and after examining her he declared that he would be returning the following day with a death certificate, since she clearly would not survive the night. After the physician left, the ailing woman called for her father, a church elder. Refusing to accept the doctor's grim diagnosis, "he offered prayers, asking for God's help, more prayers, and laying on of hands," as Jiggens later described it. These efforts revived the woman's flagging health, and by the following morning she was feeling stout enough to leave her bed and perform some chores around her home. When the doctor—death certificate in hand—returned as promised, he was so flabbergasted to see the woman walking that he left the house without uttering so much as a word to her. The incident had a profound effect on Jiggens's grandmother: afterward, as he later reported, "both she and Grandfather gave up their lives to the Lord whom they worshipped and worked for."[8]

According to Jiggens, a succession of such incidents led the Peculiar People to question whether it might be best, both spiritually and temporally, if they simply rejected the services of doctors altogether. The breaking point came after an incompetent physician botched the surgery of a church member in Rochford. The surgeon's lancet slipped, and the devout man bled to death. "This upset and angered the Peculiar People," Jiggens wrote, "who were all of the same opinion, that in [the] future they would trust only in God, who would be their Divine healer, and [they] would have nothing to do with doctors at all." From that point forward, church members resolved to follow the Epistle of James whenever one of their number fell sick. Church elders would pray over the afflicted, lay hands on them, and anoint them with oil.[9]

In 1848, the faith's healing practices came under intense scrutiny by authorities and townsfolk in the village of Prittlewell, who were troubled by the death of a boy whose fatal illness had been treated solely with prayer. The village brimmed with hostility toward the boy's father, who was a member of Banyard's church: handbills excoriated him, "and a song was composed and sung in the streets, mocking the idea of healing the sick without a doctor," according to one account. The curate of a local church soon joined the fray, preaching a sermon that suggested Banyard and his followers held beliefs regarding healing that were contrary to the scriptures. Among the verses cited by the curate was Matthew 9:12, in which Jesus said that only those "who are well have no need of a physician." Banyard responded with an impassioned address of his own, and one of his followers later marveled at how effectively he had "turned the sword into the curate's own bosom" by using many of the same scriptural passages to make a persuasive case for the soundness of his church's spiritual-healing practices. (It was said that Banyard's response was so devastating that it contributed to the curate's death a short time later.) As these theological debates raged, local authorities mounted an inquest into the circumstances of the boy's death, but it apparently did not result in charges being filed against the father.[10]

As advances in medical science led the elites who guided public policy to regard spiritual-healing practices as more risky, the Peculiar People found it increasingly difficult to avoid the scrutiny of British law enforcement authorities. A turning point for the church—and, more broadly, for the courts' approach to spiritual healing—came in 1868 in a case known as *Queen v. Wagstaffe*. The defendants, Thomas and Mary Ann Wagstaffe, were Peculiar People charged with manslaughter after their daughter Lois died from inflammation of the lungs. During her illness, the Wagstaffes had treated Lois, a fourteen-month-old who had been in frail health since birth, in accordance with the Epistle of James, summoning their church's elders and allowing her to be anointed with oil. According to one account, they had supplemented this by furnishing the girl with "barley-water, new milk, corn flour, port wine, and gruel, and occasionally a little weak brandy and water" (presumably because they believed she had been suffering from nothing more serious than teething pains). These remedies all had proven ineffectual, and Lois had died after battling her illness for about two weeks—without having been seen by a physician. Aghast at this apparent neglect, a local official brought the manslaughter charges against the couple because "it was lamentable to think that there should be such a perversion of Scripture with respect to children, who were unable to take care of themselves, and were entirely dependent upon parents for their sustenance," as one press report summarized.[11]

At the Wagstaffes' trial, Fanny Hadley, a fellow member of their church, testified at length about the beliefs of the Peculiar People as they related to healing. She explained that they followed the guidelines established by the Epistle of James whenever a member of their church fell ill, choosing to rely on prayer and anointment rather than the aid of physicians "because we believe so much in the healing power of God, and have confidence that He will raise us up again." Doctors, Hadley continued, were "very well for those who do not put their trust in the Lord," but the Peculiar People firmly believed in the Almighty and his ability to heal, and they had seem him restore the sick to health on many occasions.[12]

Both Thomas and Mary Ann Wagstaffe offered similar testimony. The latter said she had done her best to provide nourishment and care for Lois during her illness. Addressing the issue of her legal responsibilities, she also said that she had "not [been] aware that she was breaking any law" by failing to summon a doctor, according to one account of the proceedings. Thomas Wagstaffe described himself as a law-abiding laborer who always did his best to remain at peace with his God and his fellow man. "The Lord had done much for him, and he put his trust in Him and tried to obey His word," one newspaper reported in its summary of Wagstaffe's testimony. "He was, besides, very kind to his children to the extent of his means."[13]

The judge's charge to the jury in *Wagstaffe* underscored the difficulties faced by the courts in cases of religion-based medical neglect of children. One problem for jurors to consider, the judge said, was the still-evolving field of medical science; its treatments might not have proven any more useful than prayer in saving Lois's life. The judge also addressed the obvious sincerity of the defendants and their determination to comfort and heal their daughter. According to one account, he stated his belief that the jury "would be of the opinion that [the Wagstaffes] did not act with any dishonesty in the matter. He thought, to the contrary, this was a case where affectionate parents had done what they thought the best for a child, and had given it the best of food."[14]

Indeed, had the couple done something as unreasonable as denying their daughter food, the judge said, the case would have been entirely different. In that case, the jury might have been able to "stamp the conduct with the imputation of gross and culpable negligence" because it clearly would have put the girl's health in jeopardy. But the Wagstaffes' decision to rely on prayer had not been so obviously irrational. After all, accepted treatments for the sick had varied over time, and it probably had not been unreasonable for the couple to have believed that prayer—a method of treatment in use since at least the dawn of organized religion—offered the surest route to Lois's recovery.[15]

And then there was common law. As one standard treatment published in the late nineteenth century described it, religion-based medical neglect of children apparently did not fit under the purview of common-law principles governing manslaughter:

> Under the common law no conviction of manslaughter predicated
> upon an omission to provide medical attendance upon conscientious
> motives has been reported, and none probably be had or sustained.
> Opinions have widely differed in all ages as to the proper mode of
> ministering to the sick, and, in the absence of a statute declaring it
> a positive duty upon a parent to call in a medical practitioner, the
> omission to do so can scarcely be considered negligence so gross and

wanton as to be criminal, when the fact is admitted that the defendant acted in all good faith, doing the best he could according to his lights.

However callous or careless they might have seemed to some observers, the Wagstaffes' actions did not appear to contravene established legal norms.[16]

Common-law doctrine prevailed in *Wagstaffe*, and the defendants were acquitted. But even as it set the couple free, the jury castigated them, offering in court "an expression of opinion that both the parents were liable to censure for not calling in medical advice" when Lois fell sick, as one press account put it. The jury's ambivalence about the verdict—and the attention it received in the press—prompted Parliament to change the Poor Law Amendment Act, the statute outlining parents' responsibilities in child rearing. Changes in the statute that took effect just six months after the *Wagstaffe* trial made it applicable in cases where parents chose to treat their ailing children with prayer rather than medicine. The new law stated that "when any parent shall willfully neglect to provide adequate food, clothing, medical aid, or lodging for his child . . . whereby the health of such child shall have been injured . . . he shall be guilty of an offense."[17]

Two subsequent Peculiar People cases from the early 1870s demonstrated that there were limits to the effects of changing neglect statutes and mounting vigorous prosecutions under them of parents who relied on spiritual healing. In May 1872, authorities prosecuted a church member named George Hurry for neglect after his daughter Cecelia died from smallpox. (Initially, Hurry also faced a manslaughter charge, but it was withdrawn before his case went to trial.) Hurry, like the Wagstaffes before him, followed the directions set forth in the Epistle of James. "When his child fell ill, he called in the elders, who anointed her with oil, laid hands on her, and prayed over her to the Lord," according to a newspaper account. "They trusted solely in the Lord, believing that He alone was able to save the child's life." The girl had been given arrowroot and brandy, but she never received treatment from a physician.[18]

In words that would echo in numerous subsequent cases of religion-based medical neglect, the grand jury that indicted Hurry rebuked both him and the other members of his faith for allowing their religious practices to endanger public health. Because she had fallen victim to a formidable contagious disease, Cecelia Hurry's bout with smallpox had imperiled not only herself but also other members of her community. Such cases usually were controlled after they were reported to public health authorities, who imposed quarantines that limited the victim's contacts with those not yet infected. But Peculiar People like George Hurry thwarted this scheme, according to the grand jury, because they neither sought medical treatment for the victim nor alerted public health authorities. The panel claimed that the Peculiar People, "even in cases of smallpox of a virulent kind, take no medical means either to stay the disease or to cure or mitigate the illness of the patient, and are practicing a doctrine dangerous to the community at large."[19]

At his trial, Hurry benefited from the vigorous arguments presented by his counsel, a barrister named Bateman. In dramatic tones, Bateman portrayed his client as a victim of religious persecution. The barrister compared Hurry to Roman Catholics and purported witches who had been burned at the stake— "judicially murdered," Bateman called it—for their religious beliefs. Although he did not face the prospect of a fiery death, Hurry's fate was similar to these other victims in that he was being tried simply for having followed the scriptures. This represented, the barrister suggested, another regrettable case of "religious despotism."[20]

Invoking a line of argument used in numerous cases of religion-based medical neglect, Bateman also implied that Hurry had fallen victim to "medical despotism." Although much had been made at the trial of the "alleged good effects of vaccination," a careful study of official statistics kept by public health authorities failed to demonstrate that it reduced smallpox mortality rates. Indeed, no one could say for certain if vaccination could have prevented Cecelia Hurry's illness, or if any particular medical treatment could have cured it. And, Bateman wondered, how were the Peculiar People supposed to know which of the "many and varied schools of medicine" they were obliged to follow in treating the sick? He repeatedly suggested that Hurry, in relying on a method of healing that had proven effective since the times of Jesus Christ, had chosen a reasonable course of action—one that held fewer risks than depending upon the well-documented vagaries of medical science.[21]

The ambiguous resolution of Hurry's prosecution typified the outcomes of many religion-based medical-neglect cases. The jury found Hurry guilty of neglect, but neither the prosecutor nor the judge seemed particularly eager to punish him. The former said, according to a newspaper account, that he had "no desire to press harshly" against the Peculiar People, at least in part because "they had never thus far been brought before a Court" (a statement that seemed to betray his ignorance of the *Wagstaffe* case just four years earlier). The judge was similarly disposed toward leniency because Hurry stated that he now understood his legal responsibilities and would pledge to fulfill them in the future. These assurances were good enough for the judge: he discharged Hurry without imposing a sentence, telling the defendant that "he would probably never be called upon [to return to court] if he did not misconduct himself in the future."[22]

This, unfortunately, proved to be wishful thinking. Just two years later, in 1874, another member of Hurry's church faced neglect charges, and Hurry was directly implicated in the case. Authorities charged Thomas Hines after his son Joseph died from what court documents described simply as "fits." At Hines's trial, Hurry disclosed that he was one of the church elders whom Hines had summoned to treat the ailing boy. "I laid my hands on it in the name of the Lord Jesus Christ, and prayed over it; and I believe I anointed it with oil in the name of the Lord Jesus," Hurry recounted. Neither he nor Hines had consulted with a physician to treat the boy, Hurry said, "because we have such belief in the efficacy of prayer that we thought he might be raised up again." Other members of the church offered similar testimony, all of them asserting that the Peculiar People's healing practices had proven effective in numerous other cases.[23]

Hines's case turned on the trial court judge's apparent ignorance of the changes made to the Poor Law Amendment Act after *Wagstaffe*. When, at the trial's close, the prosecutor asked if a parent in Hines's circumstances was "bound to call a medical man," the judge replied, "I answer that he was not unless the Legislature enacted that he was, which it have never done yet"—an answer that seemed clearly at odds with the amended Poor Law Amendment Act, which explicitly stated that parents were obliged to furnish sufficient "medical aid" to their children. The judge continued in this vein, stating that it would be difficult to find Hines guilty of neglect "without any enactment by the Legislature" that proscribed his conduct. As the law stood (or at least as he believed the law stood), there probably could not be a finding of neglect because Hines "appeared to have done everything for the good of the child according to his lights." With this misconception of the law guiding the jury's deliberations, it found Hines not guilty. He escaped with only an admonition from the judge to reconsider the "superstitious notions" that appeared to guide his attitudes toward healing.[24]

Not until the 1875 case *Queen v. Downes* did the British courts clarify the applicability of the Poor Law Amendment Act to the practices of the Peculiar People. John Robert Downes was a Banyardite father with a two-year-old son who had suffered through a lengthy illness. "I called in no medical aid or advice," Downes explained. "I am one of the Peculiar People, and do not believe in it. I trust to the Lord." Other members of Downes's church, including George Hurry (by then a courtroom veteran), reinforced the defendant's testimony about his beliefs. Hurry told the court that the Peculiar People approached healing as they did every facet of their lives—by following the mandates of the Bible, regardless of the temporal consequences. "It is laid down to us as the law of Scripture," he said of the healing practices outlined in the Epistle of James, "and we would be the last to break it." Like many other spiritual healers who have tried to win over skeptics, Hurry also stressed that members of his church had fared well without doctors, experiencing numerous healings after receiving prayer and anointment.[25]

In his charge to the jury, the judge presiding over Downes's manslaughter trial explained how the Poor Law Amendment Act should be applied to the case. According to the Court for Crown Cases Reserved, the appellate court that ultimately reviewed the case, the judge said that a parent had "a duty to provide according to his ability all that is reasonably necessary for the child, including, if the child is so ill as to require it, the advice of persons reasonably believed to have competent medical skill." If the parent neglected this duty and the child died, "it is manslaughter" even if the parent sincerely "believed that he was doing the best for the child" by relying on other methods of healing, such as prayer. With the case framed in this manner, the jury found Downes guilty of manslaughter, and the appellate court upheld the conviction. Several members of that panel mentioned that the conviction would not have been possible without the changes in the Poor Law Amendment Act that had followed *Wagstaffe*. The amended statute, one of them wrote, "imposes an absolute duty upon parents, whatever their conscientious scruples may be," to furnish adequate medical care to their sick children.[26]

Shortly after the jury convicted Downes, the *Times* of London devoted a lengthy editorial to the sociolegal issues raised by his case. Discerning lines of argument that would become common in cases of religion-based medical neglect among all faiths, this perceptive assessment recognized that the Peculiar People had two potent claims at their disposal. "They can insist on the undoubted rights of a father over his own offspring," the editorial stated, "and they can appeal, further, to the principle of religious toleration to exempt them from penalties for the consequences of a religious system which they have accepted from a conviction of its truth." However persuasive these arguments were, they failed to withstand serious scrutiny, for the courts in England long had recognized that neither parental rights nor religious liberty were "without limitation." American courts, thanks to a series of cases involving Mormons and practice of polygamy, were starting to come to a similar conclusion in the 1870s and 1880s, in part by drawing a distinction between religious beliefs (which were inviolable) and religious conduct (which could be subject to regulation by the state). Advocating that same approach, the *Times* was hopeful that the Peculiar People could be "compelled to change, not their opinions, but their actions." But the newspaper recognized that church members— convinced as they were that the scriptures sanctioned their customs—might not be particularly amenable to changing their behavior. When it came to persuading the Peculiar People to give up their healing practices, the rational arguments made by barristers and judges might not "have the slightest influence with the erratic minds to which [they] would have to be addressed."[27]

John Robert Downes himself confirmed the *Times*'s fears about the intransigence of the Peculiar People. In 1876, a little more than a year after he had been convicted of manslaughter, Downes once again faced charges stemming from the death of one of his children. This time the victim was his thirteen-month-old daughter, who succumbed to scarlet fever and a kidney ailment. At his trial, Downes argued that he had been unaware that the law required him to provide medical assistance to his daughter. Although the Court for Crown Cases Reserved had made precisely such a determination in Downes's own case just ten months earlier, the trial court judge seemed to believe that the defendant was sincere in claiming ignorance of the law. After the jury found Downes guilty, the judge imposed a relatively light sentence of three months' imprisonment without hard labor. As the *Times* reported, he hoped that such a sentence "would indicate to everybody in this great country that their first duty as citizens and men was to obey the laws under which they lived."[28]

This message apparently was lost on the Peculiar People. They continued to deny medical treatment to their children and to flout public health regulations. In 1882, Abraham Morby, the eight-year-old son of church member John Morby, died from smallpox in the village of Plumstead. When the coroner's inquest into the boy's death was held in the parish mortuary, many jury members were so wary of being exposed to contagion that they refused to enter the room where the body lay, opting instead to view it through an open door. Numerous Peculiar People, including the boy's parents, attended the proceedings, and their presence infuriated the jury foreman, who complained about coming into contact with people who had so recently left a house "reeking with infection." Rachel Morby, Abraham's mother, proved to be the star witness of the inquest. She told the coroner that both her husband and surviving son had been "out and about during" Abraham's fatal illness, thereby potentially exposing their neighbors to the disease. "Do you think," the coroner sputtered, "your creed authorizes you to murder a street full of people?" She downplayed the danger posed by the lack of quarantine, but the coroner continued to press by asking if the family at least had reported Abraham's illness to public health authorities. Even though members of her church had been instructed to do so on numerous occasions, she replied that "we did not know it was necessary" to inform authorities of the boy's illness.[29]

After the coroner's jury returned an indictment against John Morby, he went on trial for manslaughter. The proceedings followed a familiar pattern, with the defendant's attorney arguing that Morby could not have committed manslaughter because there was no conclusive evidence that medical treatment would have saved his son. To support this claim, he pointed to the testimony of a physician called by the prosecution: the doctor only could say that Abraham's life "might probably have been prolonged," as a newspaper report put it, by medical treatment. Citing the precedent established in the first *Downes* case, the prosecutor countered that Morby "had a legal obligation placed upon him as a father to call in medical assistance" and that failing to provide such care made him legally "responsible for the crime of manslaughter," regardless of his religious beliefs. The jury agreed and convicted Morby, and the trial judge sounded a familiar warning against the Peculiar People, cautioning that they could not "disobey the law and neglect their duty towards those who were helpless with impunity."[30]

Although it seemed that Morby's case paralleled *Downes*, the Court for Crown Cases Reserved vacated his manslaughter conviction. In its opinion in *Queen v. Morby*, the appellate panel seized on the testimony of the physician who had waffled on the question of whether conventional medical treatment would have saved Abraham Morby. "It was not enough, in order to sustain a conviction for manslaughter, to show a neglect of the legal duty; there must also be evidence to show that the neglect to take reasonable means to prolong life had the effect of shortening it," the panel held. The doctor's inconclusive testimony meant that no such evidence of causation had been presented, leaving the manslaughter charge unproven. Morby might have committed the lesser crime of simple neglect, the judges wrote, but his legal responsibility for manslaughter had been "left in doubt."[31]

Morby's somewhat narrow victory proved to be one of the last won in the courts by the Peculiar People. The resolution of *Queen v. Senior* typified subsequent manslaughter cases involving members of the church. In the fall of 1897, Thomas George Senior's fourteen-month-old son, Amos, fell sick with pneumonia, and he decided to treat the boy with prayer and anointment. Previously, Senior had failed to offer conventional medical treatment to five of his other children, and in each case the results had been disastrous: all of those children had died. Amos met a similar fate, and authorities charged his father with manslaughter. At his trial, Senior claimed that his actions had not contributed in any way to his son's death. "The Lord gave," he said, "and the Lord hath taken away." This blithe explanation failed to impress the jury, and it convicted him of manslaughter.[32]

Senior's appeal to the Court for Crown Cases Reserved turned on changes that had been made to the British statutes regulating child welfare. In 1894, the Prevention of Cruelty to Children Act had supplanted the measure that prosecutors had so frequently wielded against the Peculiar People, the Poor Law Amendment Act. Significantly for the case at hand, the words "medical aid" had been left out of the provisions of the new law that defined child neglect. This omission might have turned the clock back to the days of *Wagstaffe*, but the appellate court was unwilling to believe that Parliament had intended "to take what may be described as a retrograde step." The panel held that because Senior's failure to provide medical care to his son "clearly...amounted to willful neglect," as one of them wrote, the manslaughter conviction could stand.[33]

If the appellate court's ruling and the trial court verdict that had preceded it were meant to deter Senior and his coreligionists, they failed miserably. On December 15, 1898—just five days after the Court for Crown Cases Reserved had upheld his conviction in *Queen v. Senior*—he was tried yet again for manslaughter. The victim was Senior's eight-month-old son, Tansley, who had died from pneumonia. At his trial, the prosecutor confronted Senior with the fact that he had now lost seven of his twelve children to illness—a lamentable tally that seemed to provide incontrovertible proof that his reliance on prayer for healing was misguided. Senior pointed out that his children had died over a period of eighteen years and asserted that this mortality rate was comparable to that of a family relying on medical science for healing. Senior lost once more and received more than the customary slap on the wrist: the judge sentenced him to serve four months in prison with hard labor. But even as he imposed this punishment, the judge wearily acknowledged the futility of attempting to alter Senior's conduct. "He did not for a moment suppose," the *Times* reported, "that any punishment which he should think it right to inflict upon the defendant would make the smallest difference with regard to him or other people standing in the same position."[34]

Senior's conviction and sentence attracted criticism from a seemingly unlikely quarter. As one of England's leading "freethinkers," George William Foote waged "a relentless war against Superstition in general," as he once put it, "and against Christian Superstition in particular." Foote's secularist efforts included the publication in 1882 of several irreligious cartoons in his journal, the *Freethinker*. (Given Foote's provocative ways, it was perhaps not coincidental that the cartoons appeared in the journal's Christmas edition.) A judge declared the issue blasphemous and sentenced Foote to a year in prison, during which time the *Freethinker* was published with a banner headline proclaiming "Prosecuted for Blasphemy." Foote's imprisonment made him an icon among freethinkers, and he played a leading role among British secularists until his death in 1915.[35]

Perhaps the only thing that bothered Foote more than "Christian Superstition" was rank hypocrisy, and he felt that the prosecution and imprisonment of Senior reeked of it. England billed itself as a "Christian country," Foote wrote in a pamphlet on the Senior case, and who were more earnestly Christian than the Peculiar People? After all, they steadfastly adhered to the teachings of the Bible, following "the detailed prescription" for healing practices laid out in the Epistle of James. But authorities had chosen to prosecute Peculiar People like Senior for following that mandate, and the appellate court had upheld his conviction, thereby making it "a penal offence to act upon the religious teaching of the Bible, and especially upon the Christianity of the New Testament." In mock outrage, Foote declared it a "shocking blasphemy" for the courts to conclude that prayer was "not to be trusted absolutely."[36]

Foote's real goal, of course, was not to champion the cause of the Peculiar People. (He revealed his true colors in the conclusion to his pamphlet, when he thanked the appellate court for holding the New Testament "up to public scorn and derision.") Nevertheless, his pamphlet highlighted some complex theological questions that have long complicated cases of religion-based medical neglect. As Foote pointed out, Thomas George Senior merely had followed the teachings of the scriptures when he repeatedly (and unsuccessfully, as it turned out) chose to treat his children with prayer and anointment rather than conventional medicine. Was it hypocritical for societies that prided themselves on their purported fidelity to the lessons of the Bible to prosecute such intensely religious people when translating those teachings into practice proved ineffective? Were judges and juries irreligious when they essentially held that choosing prayer over medicine amounted to "willful neglect"? And did the tragic facts of such cases expose as foolhardy belief systems that included unsubstantiated and "superstitious" tenets? Such questions proved vexing in Foote's time—and well beyond it.[37]

Foote was not the only notable British freethinker to puzzle over the fate of the Peculiar People. The playwright George Bernard Shaw also had reservations about the courts' increasingly punitive treatment of them. Writing in 1911, Shaw recalled that in his youth "the Peculiars were usually acquitted" after child deaths resulted in authorities leveling manslaughter charges against them. But "today all is changed," he lamented: juries routinely convicted Banyardites and sent them off to prison. Shaw believed that the damning testimony of doctors—men who took the stand and confidently proclaimed that medical treatment was far more effective in treating illness than prayer—was crucial to the emergence of this trend. But what really was the value of this testimony, Shaw wondered, when the failures of doctors were legion? "A modern doctor thinks nothing of signing the death certificate of one of his own diphtheria patients," Shaw wrote, "and then going into the witness box and swearing a Peculiar into prison for six months by assuring the jury, on oath, that if the prisoner's child, dead of diphtheria, had been placed under his treatment instead of that of St. James, it would not have died." Making a claim that spiritual healers themselves often articulated, Shaw pointed out that "hundreds of children . . . die every day" in the care of doctors, yet few ever were charged with crimes after their treatments failed.[38]

Shaw also made a brief but telling reference to the Peculiar People in the preface to his play *Saint Joan*. The playwright saw clear parallels between Joan of Arc's trial and execution for religious heresy in 1431 and the prosecution of members of the spiritual-healing sect more than four hundred years later. Had Joan been prosecuted in contemporary London, Shaw argued, she would have been "treated with no more toleration than . . . the Peculiar People." Both were persecuted because they had chosen to "cross the line we have to draw, rightly or wrongly, between the tolerable and the intolerable."[39]

Unlike Foote and Shaw, legal observers generally had little sympathy for the Peculiar People. Among those who monitored the courts in both the United States and Great Britain, there was strident criticism—if not outright mockery—of defendants like Thomas George Senior. In an article that referred to parallels between the Peculiar People cases and analogous litigation in the United States, the *Green Bag*, an American law periodical, argued that lawmakers considering legislation to mandate vaccinations should not consider "the pig-headed and maudlin objection of ignorant cranks" who wanted to be exempted from its provisions, for doing so might broadly imperil public health.

To bolster its case, the journal approvingly quoted a London legal periodical that had addressed the potentially disastrous implications of the scripturally based arguments advanced by the Peculiar People when they were tried for manslaughter or neglect: "Here is obviously the germ of social disintegration. The whole theory of law is that the individual must bow to the expressed will of the community of which he is a member. Honesty of intention cannot justify anti-social perverseness." For both the *Green Bag* and its London counterpart, the healing practices of the Peculiar People merited legal suppression not only because they threatened the welfare of children within the sect but also because, more broadly, they endangered public order.[40]

At least one observer, however, was more reluctant to give the state free reign to regulate the religious practices of the Peculiar People. In 1876, Luke Owen Pike published the second volume of his expansive *History of Crime in England*. Pike drew a disturbing parallel between the contemporaneous prosecutions of British faith healers and earlier instances when the state had targeted religious nonconformists. "Our forefathers thought they burned heretics for the good of the Commonwealth and for the good of the heretics themselves, just as we think we ... send Peculiar People to prison ... for the good of the children and of the State in general," Pike wrote. "We believe we know what is expedient better than a small minority who look upon the same matters from a different point of view." A reviewer of Pike's work singled out this passage for praise, commending the author for rightly noting "a certain affectation of inerrancy, which is one of the tendencies of the Modern State."[41]

As children within the church continued to die from medical neglect, though, such words of caution became increasingly rare. More common were the sentiments published by an anonymous "correspondent" in the *Times* of London. This observer was familiar with the beliefs and practices of the Peculiar People's fifteen hundred or so members, and he felt that church members had many admirable qualities. In some ways, in fact, they were "remarkable exemplars of some of the primary social virtues." They frowned on the accumulation of material wealth and eagerly shared their meager resources with church members who were aged or infirm. There was only a single—but glaring—flaw with the church: its members held extraordinarily misguided views about the treatment of children's illnesses through prayer. "If they could only be persuaded to give up their one great fallacy," the correspondent wrote, "they would be deserving of nothing but esteem."[42]

The Peculiar People were doubly maddening because they clung so tenaciously to this "great and unhappy error," the correspondent pointed out. It seemed that nothing—not even prosecution and punishment—was likely to change the beliefs of these intransigent people. Recently, he commented, several members of the church had escaped manslaughter convictions because juries had taken pity on them:

It is to be regretted that the delinquents should escape as they have done; but it is doubtful whether the severest punishment would have any deterrent influence upon the Peculiar People. . . . Whenever they have appeared before the public they have been condemned with one voice; but they are confident in the truth of their own principle, and nothing will induce them to swerve from it for a moment. They listen quietly to all the arguments and remonstrances addressed to them, and they go on their way as before, ridiculing what they call the "absurd pretensions of doctors," and firmly believing in the direct interposition of Providence for the cure of their bodily ailments.

The writer surmised that the number of such obstinate people eventually would dwindle as "enlightenment advance[d]" and their thoroughly erroneous beliefs became indefensible.[43]

In the meantime, there were frequent reports expressing disgust over the "homicidal peculiarities" of sect members like James Cook, who was twice tried for manslaughter after children in his care died. Cook's first brush with the law started in the summer of 1898, when his twenty-month-old daughter, Ethel, died from pneumonia. At the coroner's inquest, Cook's wife testified that the family had treated the girl in accordance with the precepts outlined in the Epistle of James: "She was anointed twice with oil, and we prayed for her in the chapel." Neither Grace Cook nor her husband had summoned a physician, preferring instead to leave the girl's fate "entirely to the Lord." After finding "that the parents were guilty of criminal neglect in not providing medical assistance when they knew their child was so ill," the jury returned a manslaughter indictment against both James and Grace Cook.[44]

The Cooks' manslaughter trial, a grim proceeding that featured a recounting of their daughter's agonizing death, began on an unexpectedly light note. When the court clerk asked if the defendant was being assisted by counsel, he replied that he would be aided by the Almighty. "Gentlemen," the prosecutor said to the jury, "the defendants are defended by the Lord Jehovah." The trial soon turned to the life-and-death matter at hand—namely, the defendants' decision to treat their daughter solely with prayer and anointment. Despite strong instructions from the judge ("It was the duty of the parents to provide medical aid to their children," he said), the jury deadlocked and the Cooks had to be retried. The retrial resulted in guilty verdicts for both parents and the requisite stern lecture from the presiding judge, who, after declining to impose prison terms, said, "Go away and mend your ways and do better in the future."[45]

The judge's admonition to the Cooks included a more substantive discussion of how the Peculiar People might "do better" when children in the faith fell sick. Like many who puzzled over spiritual healers' distaste for medicine, the judge suggested that the defendants read the scriptures too literally and thereby failed to benefit from all of the Almighty's gifts. "Remember," the judge urged, "that He intended us to use the assistance which science and skill undoubtedly afford. They are sent by Him just as much as food is sent by Him—sent by Him to be used." The trial judge was, however, a realist: he conceded that his advice on this score probably would "have very little weight" with the Peculiar People. (And, indeed, James Cook was back before the same judge in 1906 after his six-year-old daughter, Dorothy, died from complications from measles and bronchitis.)[46]

Cook's twin failures in court typified the trend in such cases involving the Peculiar People. "In the early days, the parents in these cases usually were acquitted, proof that the same disease could be cured by medical means being lacking," one observer has written. "But as medicine grew into a more exact science, and doctors began to assume through their drugs and pills an almost divine infallibility, the number of convictions grew." Even as late as the 1920s and 1930s, British authorities occasionally hauled church members into court and charged them with manslaughter and neglect. A beefed-up statute outlining parents' legal duties in caring for their children aided the prosecutors who targeted the Peculiar People in these later cases. In the Children Act of 1908, Parliament declared that a parent or legal guardian "shall be deemed to have neglected [a child] in a manner likely to cause injury to his health if he fails to provide adequate food, clothing, medical aid, or lodging to the child." Church members Henry and Louisa Purkiss ran afoul of this measure in 1923 after their three-year-old son, Norman, died from diphtheria. At the inquest held shortly after the boy's death, the coroner zeroed in on the boy's suffering and the likelihood that he would have survived if he had been treated by a physician.

"Would medical assistance have prolonged the child's life?" he asked a surgeon named Angus Kennedy, who had participated in the autopsy.

"Yes, there is no doubt about it," Kennedy said.

"Did the child suffer much?"

"Yes, it is a death by slow strangulation. In all probability, had the child had a dose of diphtheria anti-toxin, it would have recovered."[47]

When the Purkisses later went on trial for manslaughter, the prosecutor made a point of explaining that adults were, in the words of one press report, "perfectly entitled" to choose prayer and anointment over medical treatment if they fell ill themselves. Such was not the case, though, for parents caring for sick children. Judicial precedent (much of it forged in earlier cases involving the Peculiar People) and the Children Act of 1908 made plain that parents in such circumstances had a clear legal obligation to seek out a doctor.[48]

Henry and Louisa Purkiss conducted their own defense, and it was vigorous. In an effort to justify their decision to treat Norman's illness solely with prayer and anointment, they called to the stand T. W. Moss, a Peculiar People elder who stoutly defended the church's approach to healing. Moss asserted that he knew of many cases, including several in his own family, in which prayer and anointment had proven successful in curing disease. Because he had adhered to the teachings articulated in the Epistle of James and elsewhere in the scriptures, Moss told the court, "God has brought me and my children many times from the jaws of death."[49]

The presiding judge—who had heard a doctor testify that Norman's life probably would have been spared if he had received timely medical treatment—seemed unable to fathom Moss's willingness to deny children, on religious grounds, the services of the trained physicians who likely would save their lives.

"We have to protect life," the judge said. "Suppose you had a child obviously dying from diphtheria. Would you call in a doctor?"

"No," Moss replied. "If a child dies, we are satisfied that it was beyond human skill to save it."

"You know that anti-toxin has cured 50 percent of cases of diphtheria?" the judge asked.

"And prayer, the laying on of hands, and anointing with oil has cured an even greater percentage," Moss insisted.[50]

Part of what confounded critics of the approach to healing of the Peculiar People—and members of other spiritual-healing faiths—was church members' apparent inconsistency when it came to spurning the services of medical professionals. Testimony elicited from several Peculiar People during various manslaughter and neglect trials revealed that, in certain circumstances, they would seek help from a doctor. At least some church members seem to have believed that it was permissible to have a physician reset broken bones: in trial testimony offered in 1899, one admitted that if her child's leg had been run over and broken, "I would take it to a doctor." At the Purkiss trial, Moss made a similar concession, telling the court that he would rely on a physician to treat a broken leg. He also said he would have a dentist extract a decaying tooth.[51]

Moss seemed untroubled by this apparent inconsistency—prayer could vanquish diphtheria, but it was powerless against an aching molar—because he discerned an obvious explanation for it. A broken or decaying bone, he said, was not a sickness, and therefore its treatment was not limited by the strictures of the scriptures. Many Christian Scientists would make analogous claims in their own trials for religion-based medical neglect of children. In those cases, as in the prosecutions of the Peculiar People, such assertions were greeted with no small amount of skepticism by prosecutors, judges, and juries. The judge presiding over the Purkiss trial seemed completely baffled by Moss's apparent hair-splitting. "Don't you recognize," he wondered, "that God uses human agency for His purposes?"[52]

The trial ended with guilty verdicts for both Henry and Louisa Purkiss. As had happened in numerous other cases involving Peculiar People, the jury recommended that the judge impose lenient punishments. He did spare Louisa Purkiss a jail sentence (she only had to pay a fine), but he dispatched her husband to prison for six months. When he imposed those sentences, the judge addressed the tragedy of religion-based medical neglect of children. The Purkiss couple obviously had adored their son, he said, and had given him everything—save for medical treatment, "the one thing which would in all probability have saved his life," as a newspaper report summarized. Although the defendants were devout and sincere in their religious beliefs, the judge believed that this kind of neglect had to be stopped in order to properly safeguard children's welfare. Whatever their motives, he added, they and their coreligionists "must not be allowed to break the law of the land and to send children to premature death by refusing to avail themselves of the intelligence and skill of medical science."[53]

Even in midcentury (not long before the declining sect renamed itself the Union of Evangelical Churches and apparently softened its opposition to medical treatment), Peculiar People still flouted the law of the land in England as it related to furnishing medical care to children. In 1935, church members Walter and Mahala Levett faced charges of manslaughter and neglect after their thirteen-year-old son, Cyril, died from a throat infection. A revealing exchange between the presiding judge and church elder William Copsey marked one of the highlights of their trial. It began when Copsey described how he had attended to the sick boy by following the practices described in the Epistle of James. "I tendered God's Word," he said, "by anointing with oil and by laying on of hands, which we have proved many times to be effective." Like many of those perplexed by religion-based medical neglect of children, the judge wondered why Copsey—and, by implication, the Levett parents—had chosen prayer and anointment over medical treatment, which God presumably had allowed to develop into an effective method of remedying sickness.

"You believe in Almighty God and His intervention in human affairs?" the judge asked.

"Yes," Copsey said.

"Do you believe that such gifts as man enjoys come from Almighty God?"

"Yes."

"If medical knowledge may be a gift from God, why not act on that as well as from the gift of prayer?"

"We look to God to have almighty power. We go there first."[54]

Prosecutors had a difficult time making the manslaughter charges against the Levetts stick because they could not conclusively prove that Cyril would have lived if he had received medical aid for his throat. (Doctors called in as expert witnesses equivocated on this point, informing jurors only that medical treatment might have saved the boy.) Although this uncertainty led the jury to acquit the couple on the manslaughter charges, the jury did find the parents guilty of neglect, and the judge sentenced them to a year of probation each. As he imposed that penalty, the judge cut to the core of the persistent conflict between the state and spiritual healers who, because of their ardent religious beliefs, flouted laws designed to protect the welfare of children:

> It cannot be too widely known that whatever belief people may choose to hold on the subject, while they are citizens of this country it is their duty to give obedience to the law of this country, and the law of this country says that parents shall be deemed to have neglected a child and to have offended against the law unless they provide adequate medical aid for the child when it needs it. It won't do for people to come and say that they hold this belief or that about medical aid when Parliament, representing the will of the people, has made it a law that if parents have the custody of a child and it needs medical aid, they will provide it.[55]

The judge's comments highlighted one of the central paradoxes of the Peculiar People cases and the neglect and manslaughter prosecutions in the United States that they foreshadowed. In both Britain and, somewhat later, America, statutes gradually evolved in response to changing cultural norms relating to the efficacy of medical science and the duty of parents to furnish its benefits to their children. Their provisions permitted authorities to criminally sanction parents who relied exclusively on prayer when their children fell ill. But the enactment and uneven enforcement of these measures did not necessarily mean that children were any safer. Even when they fully understood that their intransigence might land them in court, some parents still resisted the primacy of state authority and the web of temporal laws that undergirded it, honoring instead a narrowly literal interpretation of the scriptures. Authorities did prosecute these devout individuals for their stubborn allegiance to the Epistle of James, but usually after their children already had perished. The state's concern for children's welfare thus often manifested itself too late to do the children of spiritual healers much good.

4

"The Horriblest Thing
I Ever Saw"

*Early Religion-Based Medical-Neglect
Cases in the United States*

Children have fallen victim to neglect and outright violence since the
dawn of human civilization. Infanticide through exposure was so
common in ancient Greece that Euripides, the great tragedian, wrote
about it at length in several works (perhaps most famously in *The
Phoenician Women*, which recounts the saga of the abandoned Oedi-
pus). Children fared only marginally better in Rome. There, fathers
exercised absolute control over their children, who essentially were
considered chattel. The passage of legal reforms eventually criminal-
ized infanticide, but the father "had the power to sell his children,
[and] he had the power to mutilate them," according to George Henry
Payne's often gloomy history of childhood, *The Child in Human
Progress*.[1]

Although the Bible features numerous instances of healing, it
also is replete with references to the brutal mistreatment of children.
Indeed, such repellent practices as infanticide and abandonment
are critical to the stories of several key figures in the scriptures. The
Bible relates that the mother of Moses sent him floating down the
Nile in a basket and that Herod's efforts to slaughter all boys aged two
and younger nearly cut short Jesus' young life. A cursing Joshua
referred to another form of maltreatment, immurement (burial of the
living), when he cautioned that whoever rebuilt Jericho would have
to enclose his children within its foundation and gates. And, according to the scriptures, Hiel of Bethel made precisely this sacrifice when
he endeavored to rebuild the city.

Although the threats posed by immurement or wholesale slaughter eventually subsided over time, children remained vulnerable to

abuse and neglect. Even in the formative years of the United States, common law provided them relatively little protection; its safeguards did not yet extend to what later generations would recognize as the basic legal rights possessed by all children. Moreover, courts imposed relatively few strictures on parental authority, generally giving mothers and fathers free reign to discipline their children as they saw fit. Parents typically faced the prospect of criminal prosecution only when they had engaged in truly egregious conduct. In the words of one account of this era, "Parents were considered immune from criminal prosecution except when the punishment was grossly unreasonable in relation to the offense, when the parents inflicted cruel and merciless punishment, or when the punishment permanently injured the child."[2]

American children benefited, albeit sometimes only marginally, from the gradual emergence of legal principles relating to family governance. Among them were the ideas that parents possessed broad but not unlimited rights and that they bore primary responsibility for protecting the welfare of their children. While they had "a right to the exercise of such discipline as may be requisite to the discharge of their sacred trust," as the eminent New York jurist James Kent summarized in the 1820s in his celebrated *Commentaries on American Law*, parents also were "bound to maintain and educate their children."[3]

An 1840 criminal case from Tennessee demonstrated an early attempt by an American court to demarcate limits on parents' rights to discipline their children. As the state supreme court summarized, various witnesses had testified that two parents named Johnson had abused their daughter by striking her with their fists, banging her head against a wall, and whipping her with a cow skin (this after tying her to a bedpost). A jury convicted the parents for excessively punishing their child, but the state's highest court reversed the conviction because of an erroneous instruction given by the judge to the jurors. As it threw out the conviction, the court noted that while the right of parents to discipline their children was unquestioned, they were not free to "exceed the bounds of moderation and inflict cruel and merciless punishment."[4]

As the nineteenth century progressed, children benefited from more concerted and forceful efforts by public authorities and private charitable organizations to protect them from exploitation and abuse. Although they sometimes lacked teeth, laws prohibiting child labor were in place in most industrial states by 1900. During the same period, reformers dedicated to "child-saving" established institutions and aid societies designed to protect youngsters whose parents were unwilling or unable to provide them with food, clothing, or shelter. By 1870, New York City alone boasted more than two dozen organizations that endeavored to help needy children. Their efforts intensified in 1874 after the widely publicized case of Mary Ellen Wilson dramatized the plight of abused children. Sensational newspaper accounts indicated that the youngster had been routinely abused—both physically and psychologically—by her foster mother, Mary Connolly. In court, the girl reported that "Mama," as she called Connolly, had "been in the habit of whipping and beating me almost every day" with such implements as a rawhide whip and scissors. Connolly was convicted on multiple counts of assault, and public outrage over her mistreatment of Mary Ellen helped to galvanize efforts to protect neglected and abused children.[5]

By the dawn of the twentieth century, states had begun to make safeguarding children's welfare a public-policy priority. Expanding police powers to include more stringent regulation of relationships between parents and their offspring, legislatures throughout the country enacted statutes proscribing such crimes against children as abuse, neglect, overwork, and unnecessarily cruel punishment. (Indiana even went so far as to prohibit parents from allowing their children to work as contortionists or acrobats.) States also created juvenile court systems specifically designed to address and rectify the conditions that made youngsters either the perpetrators or victims of crime. These efforts were not uniformly successful: all too often, beleaguered juvenile courts and local "poor law" officials found themselves overwhelmed by the task of shielding large numbers of vulnerable children from so many potential threats. But even their piecemeal efforts represented progress. For all of their failures, reformers in both the public and private spheres successfully "championed the idea that the state had a responsibility to ensure that all children had a childhood," in the words of scholar David Tanenhaus.[6]

The state's emerging role in protecting children was grounded in part in the doctrine of *parens patriae* (a Latin phrase meaning "parent of the country"). Although U.S. Supreme Court Justice Abe Fortas suggested in 1967 that "its meaning is murky and its historic credentials are of dubious relevance," the roots of this principle, under which the state acts as protector of minors and incompetent adults, ran deep: they could be traced at least as far back as medieval and late medieval English chancery courts, which concerned themselves with children primarily within the context of preserving feudal hierarchies. The doctrine became more clearly associated with the state's role in protecting children's welfare in Britain in the eighteenth century through such litigation as *Blisset's Case* (1774). Countenancing state-imposed limits on parental authority, Lord Mansfield's decision in that case highlighted "the public right of the community to superintend the education of its members, and disallow what for its own security and welfare it should see good to disallow," even if that meant encroaching upon "the right and authority of the father."[7]

American courts began to explicitly invoke the doctrine of *parens patriae* around 1840. A case known as *Ex Parte Crouse* involved a father who challenged the commitment of his incorrigible daughter to a state-operated "house of refuge." Ruling against the father, the Supreme Court of Pennsylvania suggested that "the natural parents, when unequal to the task of education, or unworthy of it, [can] be superseded by the parens patriae, or common guardian of the community" (that is, the state). Voicing a refrain commonly heard in cases involving abuse and neglect, the court noted that the rights of parents, though natural, were not inviolable, particularly when the parents apparently had failed to provide adequate care of their children. Subsequent cases in a variety of jurisdictions further recognized the right of public authorities to intervene on behalf of youngsters when their parents failed to provide for "the nurture and education of the child," as one court put it.[8]

Efforts by private charitable organizations and public authorities—the latter armed with the emerging doctrine of *parens patriae*—to shield children's welfare burgeoned in tandem with the rapid advancement of medical science in the latter half of the nineteenth century. Together, these advancements created an expectation that the health of children was a matter of public concern that should and in fact *could* be protected by entities outside a child's family, the state being the most prominent among them. At roughly the same time, thanks to the emergence of Christian Science and various Pentecostal sects that stressed exclusive reliance on prayer as the means of ensuring physical health, spiritual-healing practices gained more widespread popularity throughout the United States.

In the late nineteenth and early twentieth centuries, these simultaneous developments generated a series of sharp legal conflicts pitting parents and clergy against state authorities who, in the name of safeguarding children's welfare, sought to regulate their religious practices. Like the Peculiar People in Great Britain, Americans who relied exclusively on prayer for healing their children fiercely opposed these efforts on a variety of grounds, claiming that they violated the teachings of the scriptures; they encroached on individuals' religious liberty; they undermined long-established legal norms that allowed parents to direct the upbringing of their children; and they placed undue weight on the reliability of medical science, which had yet to be proven conclusively. The battles waged in this era over these thorny issues ushered in more than a century of criminal (and, in a few notable instances, civil) litigation generated by failed efforts to heal children through prayer.

A few clear trends emerged in these early American legal conflicts. One was general confusion over how statutes that governed medical practice, child neglect, and manslaughter could be applied to cases of religion-based medical neglect of children. Common-law doctrines regarding manslaughter, which seemed to permit defenses based on the accused's religious beliefs, only added to this persistent muddle. (As one observer noted in the early 1920s, "under the common law no conviction of manslaughter predicated upon a failure to provide medical attention due to conscientious scruples could be sustained.") Nevertheless, as medical science grew in reliability and stature, there emerged among law enforcement authorities and the general public a growing consensus that the failure to furnish medical treatment to a child, even when caregivers sincerely believed that prayer represented an adequate substitute, might result in criminal sanctions for the child's parents. Yet prosecutions in such cases often foundered because existing criminal laws failed to provide a clear framework for addressing issues raised by spiritual healing, a practice that privileged powerful and long-standing religious traditions over the claims of medical science.[9]

As part of another trend that emerged in these initial American cases, law enforcement authorities and the general public began to distinguish between the conduct of clergy who advocated spiritual healing and the actions of parents who treated their ailing children primarily through prayer. Outside their flocks, ministers like John Alexander Dowie and Frank Sandford commonly were viewed as charlatans who preyed upon the gullible in order to accrue power and wealth. Prosecutors zealously pursued these contentious figures, arguing that they merited severe punishment because they used the mantle of religion to propagate doctrines that endangered children. Grounded in the notion that members of professions or trades must adhere to broadly recognized standards of conduct, "clergy malpractice" is a term of relatively recent vintage that mainly has been used to describe the purported negligence of clergy in connection with instances of sexual abuse and faulty pastoral counseling. Had it been coined a century earlier, prosecutors almost certainly would have applied the term to the conduct of Dowie, Sandford, and other clergymen implicated in cases of religion-based medical neglect of children.[10]

That the criminal justice system took a more sympathetic view of parents was most evident when they were sentenced in cases of religion-based medical neglect of children. Trial or appellate court judges repeatedly justified imposing lower-than-typical sentences on mothers and fathers who were convicted of crimes relating to the death of a child by mentioning that the parents' actions had been rooted in their sincere religious beliefs and in their genuine desire to help their sick children. The frequent imposition of these lenient sentences—which sometimes amounted to no temporal punishment at all—suggested that many judges believed parents convicted of religion-based medical neglect, though legally guilty, did not bear complete moral responsibility for the deaths of their children. (Some courts even went a step further, hinting that parents were themselves victims who had been duped by unscrupulous clergy.) The pervasiveness of this notion further complicated the welter of legal and ethical issues that became the hallmark of cases of religion-based medical neglect of children.

John Alexander Dowie began to devote his ministry to what he called "the gospel of healing through faith in Jesus" in 1876, when an epidemic swept through his congregation in suburban Sydney, Australia, and left dozens of people dead. At one point he was summoned to the bedside of a young woman who appeared to be hovering near death. Desperate to help her, Dowie despaired that he lacked "some sharp sword of heavenly temper keen to slay [the] cruel foe"—namely, the devil—that threatened to extinguish her life. Dowie then experienced an epiphany, realizing that he had come into possession of just such a noble weapon: "the Spirit's sword, the Word of God." Armed with this divine cutlass, he prayed over the woman, and she recovered a short time later. Dowie previously had dabbled in a variety of social reform movements (temperance chief among them), but in time he abandoned those causes and focused his formidable energies on building a ministry devoted to what he termed "divine healing." No one could accuse Dowie of lacking passion for this endeavor: he later confessed that he had been "almost frenzied with Divinely imparted anger and hatred of that foul destroyer, disease, which was doing Satan's will."[11]

A powerful orator and more than a bit of a showman, Dowie gained a reputation as a gifted healer, and the ill and infirm flocked to his services, which he held in an impressive tabernacle in the middle of Melbourne. (He had moved there after breaking with the Congregational Church and establishing an independent ministry.) To carry his ministry abroad, Dowie founded the International Divine Healing Association in 1886 and used the organization to forge links with like-minded religious healers in the United States and Great Britain. These connections proved to be so strong that he left Australia for the United States, stopping first in California before settling in the Chicago area in 1890. There he "reigned as the most important and notorious divine healer in America," according to scholar Jonathan Baer, and became the center of fierce debates over the legitimacy of spiritual healing and the state's use of neglect, abuse, and manslaughter laws to deter religion-based medical neglect of children.[12]

"God's way of healing," as Dowie saw it, was firmly grounded in a few cardinal principles. One was the doctrine of atonement, a touchstone for many spiritual healers of his era. (Dowie was fond of quoting Isaiah 53:5, which promises that "by [Jesus'] wounds we are healed.") He also insisted that there was but one source of disease: the devil. Sickness, Dowie maintained, "is the Devil's work, consequent upon Sin, and it is impossible for the work of the devil ever to be the Will of God." He believed that there were four primary means of combating this malevolent work: direct prayer by the afflicted; intercessory prayer on behalf of the sick; anointment by church elders; and the laying on of hands. Since the apostolic age, these methods—all of them clearly outlined in the scriptures—had proven to be formidable means of healing.[13]

Physicians had no place in Dowie's healing ministry. Waging what he described as a "holy war against doctors, drugs, and devils," he routinely mocked medical science, at one point dismissing it as "medical bosh!" Dowie scorned the lack of consistency among—and sometimes the clear contradictions between—emerging schools of medical science. It seemed absurd to him that men who advocated such a jumble of ideas should wield any kind of influence. "You doctors think you can control the whole population from cradle to grave?" he asked in one sermon. "We cannot be born without you, we cannot live without you, and we cannot die without you?" For Dowie, the foolishness of medical science stood in stark contrast to the scriptures, which afforded the surest path to healing.[14]

Those who heeded Dowie's warnings and avoided doctors could seek spiritual and physical rehabilitation by joining the overflow crowds that packed his Christian Catholic Church for services or by checking into one of the several "divine healing homes" he operated in the Chicago area. These institutions were designed to, as one observer has written, "provide a hospice where the sick could secure board and room at a reasonable rate while they undertook a disciplined regimen of prayer and Bible study." Testimonies from those cured in the healing homes filled the pages of *Leaves of Healing*, a journal devoted to trumpeting Dowie's accomplishments as a healer. Its pages brimmed with accounts of him using prayer to help vanquish ailments ranging from blood poisoning and Bright's disease to epilepsy and cancer. In one typical story, a woman with the Dickensian name Mary Casey-Cough reported that nineteen cancerous tumors, which had been plaguing her for more than seven years, had disappeared after Dowie "prayed with me in the name of Lord Jesus."[15]

Although church publications understandably downplayed Dowie's failures as a healer, Chicago's mainstream periodicals routinely documented them as proof that he was a swindler. Throughout the 1890s and early 1900s, the deaths of women and children who had been placed in his care occasioned dramatic and damning newspaper articles aimed at exposing Dowie as a fraud. When an eight-year-old named Homer Harrison expired at Dowie's home in the spring of 1894, an alliterative front-page headline in the *Chicago Daily Tribune* blared, "DIES IN DOWIE'S DEN." In maudlin prose, the accompanying story explained that Harrison had suffered from several large (and presumably cancerous) tumors and that his desperate parents had been deluded by Dowie "into believing what they were so willing to believe—that their boy was improving all the time—until he died." In this instance, as in countless others, the irascible Dowie compounded the negative publicity generated by the tragedy by berating a reporter who had the temerity to ask about the circumstances of the child's death.[16]

But Dowie had more to contend with than bad press. Almost from the moment he arrived in Chicago, he was targeted by law enforcement and public-health authorities who were disturbed by how he and members of his church treated the illnesses and injuries of children. In 1899, for instance, his church came under fire during an outbreak of scarlet fever and diphtheria that afflicted children in several neighborhoods in the city. Like the Peculiar People in England and members of several other spiritual-healing churches, such as the Faith Tabernacle in Philadelphia (which would be ravaged by a measles outbreak in the early 1990s), the "Dowieites" seemed reluctant to help contain the spread of these highly contagious illnesses. They failed to report new cases to public authorities, and they refused to obtain prompt medical treatment for children who had become sick. To make matters even worse, they also seemed lackadaisical about quarantining victims, thereby potentially exposing hundreds of other children to the illnesses. One city official bemoaned the fact that Chicago was now threatened by a serious outbreak of both scarlet fever and diphtheria because of the "so-called religious enthusiasm" of Dowie and the church members who blindly followed him.[17]

Such episodes—and there were several every year—took their toll. Mounting public outrage over Dowie's apparently dangerous ministry prompted authorities in Chicago to consider enforcing state and municipal laws to limit his activities. After his "healing homes" opened, authorities explored the possibility that he might be violating statutes used to regulate medical care, among them a state law prohibiting the practice of medicine without a license. In 1894, the secretary of the state board of health, J. W. Scott, called for Dowie's arrest, declaring that "there is no doubt in my mind that the fellow is practicing [medicine] in violation of our law" by operating what were essentially unlicensed hospitals. Scott said he was eager to have Dowie and other faith healers prosecuted so that he could "put a stop to their nonsense." But perhaps the most serious threat to Dowie's ministry was a freshly minted city ordinance requiring the presence of a licensed physician in dwellings used for care of the sick. City officials pilloried Dowie under the latter charge: in 1895 alone, he later claimed, it was brought against him nearly one hundred times. "For one whole year they arrested me on an average of twice a week," he groused in one sermon. "I had lots of fun, and lost a good deal of money. It cost me twenty thousand dollars."[18]

Never one to shrink away from a fight, Dowie responded forcefully. The charges were unfounded, he proclaimed time and again, because he performed religious rituals rather than practiced medicine, and thus was protected by both common law and the First Amendment's safeguards for religious liberty. "Divine healing homes are not hospitals," he said once in court. "No 'medicine' is used. No 'treatment' is given. . . . Divine healing has no association with doctors and drugs, or surgeons and their knives." He also frequently reminded his accusers that, by attempting to treat the sick through prayer, he followed in the tradition of the greatest healer of all, Jesus Christ. Dowie wondered aloud what would happen if the Savior appeared in contemporary Chicago and resumed his miraculous healing ministry. Because public authorities absurdly wanted to police religious rituals, he probably would "be indicted and brought before the court and charged" with a whole host of crimes, Dowie speculated.[19]

Several of Dowie's most serious brushes with law-enforcement authorities resulted from his purported role in instances of religion-based medical neglect of children. For example, in the spring of 1901, newspapers throughout the country carried accounts of two sensational cases involving the apparent neglect of young members of his church. A church member named Emma Judd and her newborn child were, as one paper put it, "lulled into eternity by the prayers of John Alexander Dowie and two elders" after they failed to receive medical treatment during a prolonged and difficult childbirth. The deaths created an uproar in Chicago, and both Dowie and H. W. Judd, Emma's husband and the deceased child's father, soon came under intense scrutiny from the press, law enforcement authorities, and child-welfare advocates for their roles in the tragedy. Barraged by criticism, both men were unapologetic, if not downright defiant. At a coroner's inquest, Judd explained that he had not summoned a physician to his wife's bedside "because I have taken God as my healer." Dowie, who also had been on hand throughout Emma Judd's ordeal, stated flatly that he had treated her solely through prayer because he was "absolutely against doctors and drugs. . . . They are a great hindrance."[20]

The press responded to such explanations with incredulity and called for both men to be prosecuted. "Dowieism must answer to the law for the death of Mrs. Emma Judd" and her child, the *Chicago Daily Tribune* thundered.[21] But as would happen in numerous other apparent cases of religion-based medical neglect of children in the United States over the next century, law enforcement authorities struggled to determine which laws, if any, had been violated. Could Dowie be prosecuted for encouraging his followers to forsake medical care for both themselves and their children? Could authorities file criminal charges against church members like H. W. Judd after their decision to rely solely on prayer for healing resulted in the death of a child? At least initially, no one— not even the newspapers that were calling for Dowie's scalp—seemed to have definitive answers to such questions because they never had been put before the state's courts or debated by the legislature. "Some difficulty has arisen," the *Daily Tribune* admitted, "as to just what section of the law will apply to such a case as the death of Mrs. Judd and her newly born child without medical attention."[22] Similarly plaintive refrains would become common when cases of religion-based medical neglect of children aroused public outcries over the practices of spiritual healers.

With public sentiment squarely on their side—at one point, hundreds of angry demonstrators marched outside Dowie's church and burned him in effigy—prosecutors explored their options. The state's attorney instructed two of his deputies to scour Illinois's criminal code for any statute that might be applicable to Dowie, H. W. Judd, or any of the other church members who had witnessed Emma Judd's ordeal without attempting to secure medical help for either her or her newborn. The search proved largely fruitless; although their behavior was morally reprehensible to most people, Dowie and his followers apparently had not broken any laws. "The general opinion . . . among lawyers," the *Daily Tribune* reported, "was that the laws as at present shaped were inadequate to cope with this modern evil."[23]

The apparent lack of an applicable statute did not deter the state's attorney and the coroner from pursuing charges against Dowie and H. W. Judd. They mounted an inquest into the circumstances of the deaths of Emma Judd and her child, and the coroner's jury held that the two men (as well as two other members of their church) should be charged with what was vaguely termed "criminal responsibility" for their roles in the tragedy. Several local physicians played crucial roles in the proceedings by insisting that both mother and child could have survived if they had received prompt medical attention. An indignant Dowie later said that the doctors were eager to see him imprisoned because they rightly feared that he represented a dire threat to their bogus profession. He also scoffed at the suggestion—made in the *Daily Tribune* and elsewhere—that the state legislature should respond to the furor over the Judd deaths by beefing up the state's criminal code, claiming that "all this talk of censure and of a law to compel everyone to be born, to live, to die 'with the aid of a doctor' is so much nonsense."[24]

The case next went to a grand jury, where it stalled. The panel refused to return indictments against any of the Dowieites because the state had failed to demonstrate that they had broken any specific statute. The grand jury panelists were so frustrated by their inability to hand down an indictment that they issued a statement calling for the legislature to enact a law aimed at spiritual healers who denied medical treatment to children. "We believe there should be a law on our statute books providing that in cases of children under the age of 12 years (who of necessity are not capable of judging what is best for themselves), medical attendance should be furnished when such children are attacked by malignant diseases," the statement read. "We strongly recommend that the Legislature enact a law making it a crime for the parents, guardians, or persons charged with the custody and control of such children who fall into neglect to call medical attendance in such cases." Had such a law been on the books, the grand jurors asserted, Dowie and H. W. Judd might have been brought to justice for their roles in the deaths of Emma Judd and her child.[25]

As the Judd case played out in the spring of 1901, Dowie and his followers were targeted by prosecutors, judges, and child-welfare advocates who were determined to prevent other instances of religion-based medical neglect of children. Their ire was raised by the case of a two-year-old named Mabel Christensen, who had been badly burned in the same fire that had killed her mother. After the blaze, the Chicago police—acting in concert with the Illinois Humane Society, a child-welfare organization—refused to relinquish custody of the girl to her father, a follower of Dowie who vowed that she would not receive conventional medical treatment for her burns. When the father angrily demanded that his daughter be returned to his care, a defiant police captain said, "An order of the Court is the only thing that can force us to give the child to her [father] until she is cured."[26]

For Dowie's critics, the Christensen case provided additional proof that he was a fraud who merited prosecution. One Chicago newspaper, in calling for Dowie to be run out of town, responded to reports of the young girl's ordeal by suggesting that "if there is a law under which the confidence operator, the holdup man, and the thug can be reached, then there is a law under which that brawling imposter, John Alexander Dowie, can be brought to justice." Censure for Dowie came from such distant quarters as Lincoln, Nebraska, where William Jennings Bryan was serving as a newspaper editor as he awaited another quadrennial bid for the presidency. Bryan—himself a man of no small religious convictions—reacted to the Christensen case by penning a stern article entitled "Dowieism Run Mad." In it, he concluded that the Dowieites' insistence on treating Mabel Christensen solely through spiritual means "illustrates distressingly the extremes to which religious fervor . . . will drive a devotee." Aghast at the excesses of Dowie and his followers, Bryan went so far as to suggest that "there should be a limit to so-called religious freedom, and the limit should be reached when folly usurps the throne of Christian faith."[27]

A juvenile court judge named Tuthill took up the Christensen matter and heard impassioned pleas from both an attorney representing the humane society and the girl's father. Tuthill eventually ruled in favor of the humane society, giving it custody of the girl until she recovered. A short time later, he rendered a similar decision in a case involving a young Christian Scientist whose parents, citing their religious beliefs, had refused to furnish medical care. Summarizing his approach to such cases, the *Daily Tribune* reported that "when parents refuse to call in a physician, and when the child is subjected to long-continued suffering . . . it is time for the court to step in and demand protection for the young."[28]

Tuthill's actions sent John Alexander Dowie into a fury. Excoriating the judge from his pulpit, he articulated sentiments that would be shared by many spiritual healers when law enforcement authorities implicated them in cases of religion-based medical neglect of children. Members of his church, Dowie intoned, should devote themselves to following the law of God, not the law of man, particularly when the two seemed to be in conflict. In what could have been a rallying cry for all spiritual healers who ran afoul of criminal statutes, he said, "We must obey God. . . . Forget about the law. You are Christians first, citizens afterward."[29]

Dowie could strike such a defiant posture because he managed to weather the legal campaign waged against him. Working in concert with children's welfare and medical regulation organizations, Chicago authorities hauled him into court on dozens of occasions and hurled a variety of charges at him, but few stuck. The *New York Times* reported in dismay that, despite his apparent role in a horrifying array of misdeeds, the "laws do not reach him." This was true in large part because, as the Judd case demonstrated, city officials strug-gled to find and apply statutes that were well suited for regulating Dowie's ac-tivities. There were gaps in the era's embryonic medical practice, manslaughter, and neglect statutes, and Dowie was masterful in slipping between them.[30]

The legal onslaught took perhaps its greatest toll on Dowie in the court of public opinion. The ongoing barrage of charges leveled at him—all of them duly reported, in high dudgeon, in Chicago's newspapers—made Dowie a pariah in the city, and it became increasingly difficult for him to pursue his ministry. Eventually, Dowie realized that his days in Chicago probably were numbered. Weary of combating antagonistic city officials and reporters, he eventually left the city and established his own religious community in Zion City, Illinois, which historian Grant Wacker has called one of "the largest and most grandly conceived utopian communities in modern American history." Dowie's healing ministry thrived as scores of the infirm flocked to Zion City (located about forty miles north of Chicago, near the Wisconsin border) for spiritual and physical rehabilitation. On the walls of his church he proudly displayed the "trophies" he had accumulated in dealing with these afflicted multitudes: the crutches, braces, and wheelchairs they had discarded after being healed.[31]

Like most members of the Christian Catholic Church, J. Luther Pierson ardently backed Dowie during his travails in the courts. Pierson, a clerk for the New York Central Railroad, felt that Dowie was "justified in carrying on his work," even if authorities in Chicago thought otherwise. At any rate, their re-peated efforts to undermine Dowie's healing ministry were destined to fail be-cause he had a powerful guardian. "God will protect him," Pierson explained.[32]

Pierson himself became embroiled in a prolonged court battle in New York because he followed Dowie's edicts on healing when his daughter fell ill with catarrhal pneumonia. Although he realized that she was gravely sick, Pierson did not call a physician to treat the girl. Indeed, he believed that doing so would have been a colossal blunder. Members of his faith, he said, thought that summoning a physician might result "in the destruction of the child, and that instead of the child being saved it would surely die." Instead of relying on medicine to treat his daughter, who he knew "was slipping away," Pierson turned to the Epistle of James for guidance and decided to pray for her healing with other members of his faith. "To avoid [her] death," he explained, "we adopted the mode and prayer of our creed and our belief and exerted ourselves for the child's protection and safety."[33]

Pierson believed that prayer was necessary in part because of the origins of his daughter's illness. The girl was not simply the victim of a physical malady, he thought, but rather suffered from a profound spiritual ailment precipitated by Satan. "All diseases are of the devil," he said, "and it was the devil's work in that child." Given their source, such illnesses only could be combated by prayer, not the work of physicians, for "God will cure [them] without medicine."

Pierson was sure of this because he knew that "the Almighty would arrest disease if I asked him," he said.[34]

Like many spiritual healers, Pierson blamed himself for his child's death. It was not that he regretted having adhered so strictly to his religious beliefs that he had failed to provide the one thing that might have saved her—the services of a physician. If anything, in fact, he lamented that he had not shown enough faith in God's ability to heal through prayer. Had he been more resolute, his daughter might have survived: "I attribute the child's death to a lack of faith on my part," he said, "and to the fact that I am not pure in the sight of God."[35]

New York authorities charged Pierson with criminal neglect. In May 1901, a White Plains, New York, jury found him guilty, and the judge levied a fine of five hundred dollars. "I believe he is honest in his views," the judge said of Pierson, "but they lead him into a violation of the law. The child died of neglect, and the law requires that a man shall care for those depending upon him." That Pierson's actions were sincerely rooted in his religious beliefs was no defense. As was also true in many of the Peculiar People cases in England, the judge expressed his exasperation with Pierson's stubbornness, castigating the defendant for his unwillingness to follow the strictures of temporal laws even after he had been convicted for violating them. "The trouble with him," the judge said from the bench, "is that he will do the same thing over again—he would do it tomorrow.... He violates the laws because he wants to." Pierson bore out the judge's point by stating that he refused to pay the fine. The judge responded by committing Pierson to the county jail and adding one dollar a day to his fine until he paid it. "You can pay it or be a martyr to your faith, if you wish to be," the judge groused.[36]

Pierson's fortunes worsened the day after the judge sentenced him to jail. His two-month-old son, Earl, had been sick with catarrhal bronchitis, and, despite his lack of success in saving his daughter, he had treated the boy's illness through prayer alone until his trial and sentencing. At that point, his wife, wary of exacerbating his already formidable legal troubles, took the boy to a physician. Earl died anyway, leaving Pierson distraught. "It is thought Pierson may lose his reason," a New York newspaper reported. "He seems fearfully downcast by the death of the child, and takes much blame upon himself because faith cure was not closely adhered to." Despite losing two children to illness in quick succession, Pierson remained convinced that prayer would heal.[37]

Pierson appealed his conviction to the appellate division of the New York Supreme Court in Brooklyn. In oral arguments there, his attorney, Robert Farley, pursued several complementary lines of argument. Underscoring the fact that medical science hardly was infallible, he quoted Oliver Wendell Holmes's quip that homeopathy was little more than "a mingled mass of perverse ingenuity, a tinsel of erudition, of imbecile credulity, and of artful misrepresentation." Farley's point was clear: although spiritual healing had failed to save Pierson's daughter, there was certainly no guarantee that a physician would have done much better. Perhaps more persuasively, the defense attorney also contended that no specific state law compelled parents to furnish medical treatment to their children and that any such law would be unconstitutional even if it were on the books. J. Addison Young, the Westchester County district attorney, countered Farley by citing the precedent of the British courts, which had ruled against the Peculiar People in a series of cases that clearly were analogous to Pierson's. "It does not matter what the religious prejudices and superstitions are," Young said. "People must supply medical aid." The district attorney's arguments fell on deaf ears: the appellate panel ruled in favor of Pierson and reversed his conviction.[38]

The case wound up in the Court of Appeals of New York, which ruled in 1905. In its opinion in *People v. Pierson*, that panel acknowledged that "there are people who believe that Divine power may be invoked to heal the sick and that faith is all that is required." It also noted that physicians had been viewed skeptically for many centuries and that belief in spiritual healing and miracles had been widespread. Perceptions had changed, however, starting in the eighteenth century, with discoveries of effective drug treatments and the establishment of credible medical schools. According to the appellate panel, these advances had "gone a long way in establishing medicine as a science, and [as] such it has come to be recognized in the law of our land." Over the previous two centuries, "the practice among the people of engaging physicians has continued to increase until it has come to be regarded as a duty, devolving upon persons having the care of others, to call upon medical assistance in case of serious illness." In short, a practice that had once been viewed with skepticism gradually came to be seen as an integral part of parents' legal duty to children.[39]

Pierson claimed that he was not bound by this duty because the protections of religious liberty included in the First Amendment shielded the practice of spiritual healing. The Court of Appeals tackled this claim by noting that the U.S. Supreme Court, in *Reynolds v. United States* (1879), had made an important distinction between religious beliefs and religious conduct. In *Reynolds*, the high court had upheld the conviction of a Mormon in the Utah Territory for polygamy, a practice that he claimed was an integral part of his religious faith. "Full and free enjoyment of religious profession and worship is guaranteed," the New York panel wrote in its assessment of the holding of *Reynolds* and its applicability to *Pierson*, "but acts which are not worship are not." The implication for Pierson was clear: he was free to believe as he pleased, but his conduct was subject to state regulation.[40]

After tracing the emergence of medical science and the development of First Amendment jurisprudence, the Court of Appeals held that Pierson's religious belief in the power of spiritual healing did not relieve him of the legal obligation to provide medical treatment for his sick child. The court wrote,

He cannot, under the belief or profession that he should be relieved from the care of children, be excused from punishment for slaying those who had been born to him. Children when born into the world are utterly helpless, having neither the power to care for, protect or maintain themselves. They are exposed to all the ills to which the flesh is heir, and require careful nursing, and at times, when danger is present, the help of an experienced physician. But the law of nature, as well as the common law, devolves upon the parents the duty of caring for their young in sickness and in health, and of doing whatever may be necessary for their care, maintenance and preservation, including medical assistance if necessary, and an omission to do this is a public wrong which the state, under its police powers, may prevent.[41]

The court's decision to uphold the trial verdict in *Pierson* pleased the new Westchester County district attorney, J. Addison Young. Young noted that while the Peculiar People cases in Britain had established the state's right to prosecute spiritual healers for failing to provide medical treatment to their sick children, such precedent was rare in the United States. Indeed, the holding in *Pierson* apparently was the first of its kind in New York. Young welcomed it, saying that "it is of the highest importance, and means absolutely that these faith curists and others of the same sort must obey the law, compelling them to call in regular physicians in the event of dangerous illness of minors in their families. The fact that they have called in 'readers' of their churches, layers-on-of-hands, and others will not shield them from the law."[42]

Other observers reached similarly hopeful conclusions about the potentially wide-ranging impact of *Pierson*. A celebratory editorial in the *American Lawyer* hailed the decision as a blow "to all members of the great cult of humbuggery," whether they were followers of John Alexander Dowie or devotees of Mary Baker Eddy, the founder of Christian Science. The journal argued that the Court of Appeals decision was a setback for all such "fanatics" practicing faith healing because it would circumscribe their religious practices. Although people like Pierson remained free to treat themselves through prayer alone, "they will not be permitted to wantonly neglect those whom nature has entrusted to them for care and protection."[43]

Like many spiritual healers of his era, Frank Sandford was profoundly influenced by Reverend Albert B. Simpson. Initially, Sandford—a former Bates College baseball standout who found himself drawn to the ministry in the late 1880s—viewed claims of divine healing with skepticism. When his sister Maria reported that she had been healed of chronic back pain at a revival meeting, Sandford insisted that there was "no such thing as healing by faith." He held fast to this belief until he heard the dynamic Simpson speak at a camp meeting held in Orchard Beach, Maine. At the time, Sandford did not completely fathom Simpson's interpretations of the scriptures and his approach to healing, but he resolved to "preach that part of the Bible" in his own ministry.[44]

In 1893, Sandford founded "The Kingdom," a small Christian movement whose members devoted themselves to readying the world for the millennium. Sandford and his followers established a largely self-contained community in Durham, Maine, known as Shiloh. Their village—located, as the scriptures dictated, on a hilltop—included an impressive church, a hospital dedicated to divine healing, and an immense dormitory, all of which were intended to create "the architectural image of a New Jerusalem," as one observer has put it. The community also featured prayer towers. In one of them, Shiloh's women offered continuous intercessory prayers over a period of two decades.[45]

The women and men who flocked to Shiloh had middle-class backgrounds. Moses and Eliza Leger, for instance, both had built solid careers in Lynn, Massachusetts, before casting their lot with Sandford. A successful printer, Moses Leger shipped his entire press to Maine and churned out issue after issue of a sect publication bearing the somewhat ominous title *Tongues of Fire*. His wife had been a charismatic evangelist; after watching her spellbind crowds, some observers had compared Eliza Leger to Carrie Nation, the eminent prohibitionist. A broad assortment of other working folk—farmers, sailors, teachers—joined the Legers in Maine.[46]

Healing through prayer and anointment, as prescribed by the Epistle of James, was central to Sandford's ministry. Doctors had no role at Shiloh. "The preachers of the land are saying, 'Call for the physicians,'" Sandford explained, "and are giving God's Word the lie." If *Tongues of Fire* is to be believed, few residents of Shiloh suffered from the lack of medical attention: its pages brimmed with accounts of maladies healed through prayer. These ranged from typhoid, pneumonia, and cancer to "utter exhaustion" and "sick headache." One famous instance involved a blind girl whose case been pronounced hopeless by a team of Bowdoin College doctors. She reportedly regained her sight after prayers were offered for her at Shiloh. "Whatever the cause of the girl's blindness in the first place," one of Sandford's biographers has written, "enough community members witnessed the incident to make the account a sobering one."[47]

But no story of healing at Shiloh was more spectacular than the reported resurrection of a diminutive woman named Olive Mills. Late in the summer of 1899, Mills fell victim to a disease believed to be spinal meningitis. Sandford was so concerned about her ailment that he postponed a scheduled trip to England in order to remain at Shiloh and pray for her recovery. His initial efforts failed, and Mills apparently succumbed to the ailment. She was found lifeless in her bed, neither breathing nor showing signs of a pulse. According to the account that circulated among members of the sect, Sandford simply refused to believe that Mills was beyond hope. After fervently praying over her, he clasped her head and exclaimed, "Olive Mills! Come back! In the name of Jesus of Nazareth, come back!" Miraculously, Sandford's entreaties worked: Mills awoke, and a short time later she was able to leave bed and get dressed.[48]

In the early twentieth century, authorities and the local citizenry concerned with the church's spiritual-healing practices engaged in running battles with Sandford and his followers. Several local newspapers waged long-running campaigns against Shiloh: in one typical salvo, an editor denounced it as "a damnable institution, a hell upon earth and the worst blot that ever disgraced the fair pages of Maine's history." These simmering conflicts finally boiled over early in 1903 as a result of the death of a fifteen-year-old named Leander Bartlett. Bartlett's passing—along with Sandford's alleged mistreatment of his own son John—gave local officials a dramatic opportunity to strike at Shiloh's leader.[49]

Bartlett developed a sore throat in the middle of January 1903. At first, the illness did not seem life threatening, and the youngster continued to tackle farming chores around the community. After a few days, however, the boy's mother, Elvira Bartlett, noted that he seemed uncharacteristically lethargic. As his condition deteriorated, Leander was kept under quarantine, as state law required in cases where diphtheria was suspected, but neither his mother nor any other person living at Shiloh summoned a physician for diagnosis and treatment (this despite the fact that one community member was trained as an osteopath). As one history of the community put it, "No determined steps were taken to save his life."[50]

Instead, Elvira Bartlett called in two community ministers, Ralph Gleason and Joseph Sutherland, for a prayer session. Part of this process required Leander to confess to any sinful or disobedient acts that might impede his healing. Leander admitted to some mischief. He and another youngster, he said, had used some lumber scraps to construct a hut in a pine grove. When a community elder ordered the boys to stop, they resolved to run away from Shiloh and strike out on their own. Confessing to this rebellion seemed to briefly lift Leander's spirits: his fever abated, and he was able to eat solid food. But his rally proved brief. In the words of one observer, he became "too weak to walk and [was] hardly able to speak" before falling "quickly into stupor and delirium."[51]

There was some dispute over Frank Sandford's response to Leander Bartlett's illness. According to several witnesses, Sandford addressed Bartlett's sickness during a community meeting and suggested, either directly or indirectly, that the youngster had fallen ill because he had been rebellious. (Sandford apparently ruled Shiloh with an iron hand, and such behavior was anathema to him.) Some spectators later said that Sandford had expressed open indifference to Bartlett's fate. "I don't remember his exact words," one said, "but he said [he] didn't care if he saw [Bartlett's] dead body lying before him." There also were questions about Sandford's willingness to pursue spiritual remedies for the infirm youngster: at least one community member later said that Shiloh's leader had not prayed for Bartlett's recovery.[52]

Sandford's treatment of his own son, John, also was called into question. Although the precise circumstances were not entirely clear, Shiloh's leader apparently punished the youngster by forcing him to endure a lengthy fast in which he was denied both food and water. One woman who lived in the community later said that John Sandford—who, unlike Leander Bartlett, had survived his ordeal—had been in agony in the fast and that he had pleaded for water at least seventy-five times. Her testimony suggested that the elder Sandford had been fully aware of his son's misery but had done nothing to abate it.[53]

Sandford's roles in Bartlett's death and in the apparent mistreatment of two other youngsters—his son John and another Shiloh resident named John Swart—resulted in the county attorney filing six criminal charges against him. As usual, the local newspapers pilloried Sandford, insisting that he had had a legal duty to provide medical treatment. The *Lewiston Evening Journal* approvingly quoted a local official who had claimed, "This man, by virtue of his authority unquestioned by his followers as far as we can see, was the parent of children and as such was obliged to furnish proper support and care for them."[54] Only two of the charges, however, came to trial: one count of cruelty in the case of John Sandford and one count of manslaughter in the case of Bartlett. Public interest in the cases was intense, thanks in part to breathless coverage in the local newspapers. (One headline proclaimed, "The charge is manslaughter!")[55]

Prosecutors convicted Sandford on the cruelty charges, but their manslaughter case foundered because it was anchored by "a vague premise," as one observer put it. As the presiding judge explained in his instructions to the jury, "the particular kind of manslaughter" mentioned in the indictment of Sandford could not have been found in the Maine criminal code. It was instead based on the common-law definition of manslaughter, in which the "negligent omission" of care constituted an offense. Invoking that principle, the indictment had charged that Sandford had committed manslaughter because "he willingly, knowingly, and feloniously did fail, neglect and refuse to furnish" medical treatment and sufficient nourishment to Bartlett. This argument failed to persuade the jury. It hung on the manslaughter charges, forcing authorities to retry Sandford a few months later.[56]

At his retrial, Sandford's attorney tried to refute the notion that he exercised absolute control over everyone at Shiloh. Elvira Bartlett, he said, maintained authority over her son because "a parent is in control of his child unless he gives control to someone else" and she never had ceded control to Sandford. As a result, the responsibility for Leander Bartlett's death lay with her, not Sandford. What is more, the community's leader, through his teachings and example, had been "doing all he could" to help residents of Shiloh "save themselves from sickness and trouble." Because he wanted to heal Bartlett rather than hurt him, Sandford had not said or done anything acrimonious during the youth's fatal illness, the lawyer said; "There was not any anger or passion or ill will displayed" toward the boy. If there had been talk of the implications of Bartlett's adolescent revolt, it was because the religious doctrines of the Shiloh community included a general belief that "rebellious persons would suffer."[57]

The retrial—and the appeal that followed—turned on the judge's instructions to the jury. He informed the panel that, under Maine law, if Sandford "believed in the prayer of faith, he ought to apply that" in circumstances when members of his community fell ill and required healing. Since it was his legal obligation to apply such methods of healing, jurors could find "a basis for manslaughter [and] evidence of negligence" if they believed that "the omission to use the prayer of faith did hasten the death of Leander Bartlett." In other words, if spiritual healing could have saved the youngster and Sandford had knowingly withheld that effective treatment, then he had been negligent. But if jurors believed that the prayer of faith "did not produce any results"— that is, if they lacked faith in faith healing—they should not find Sandford negligent because his lack of prayer had been irrelevant.[58]

Acting under these curious instructions (which apparently made no mention of any duty that Sandford might have had to provide medical treatment), the jury convicted Sandford of manslaughter. He appealed the verdict, and in 1905 Maine's Supreme Judicial Court reversed it. The trial court's error had been in the jury instructions, which had put members of the panel in the legally untenable position of basing their verdict on their religious faith. The appellate court concluded, "We do not think the guilt or innocence of any person accused of crime, whatever his belief may be, . . . or that the result of a criminal trial should depend upon the beliefs of the members of a jury on the question of the efficacy of prayer as a means of cure for the sick, or upon their religious beliefs in any other respect." After the state high court's ruling, the case sputtered on, with authorities mounting yet another prosecution of Sandford for his role in Bartlett's death. This third trial ended in a hung jury, and prosecutors finally decided to let the matter drop in 1906.[59]

The torturous course of *State v. Sandford* typified the struggle of American courts to develop uniform and effective approaches to prosecuting parents and clergy involved in religion-based medical neglect of children. To be sure, judges and juries, following the trend established by *Pierson* and the Peculiar People cases, often acknowledged the sincerity of parents' religious beliefs but nonetheless held them accountable under manslaughter or neglect statutes for their failure to provide medical care. In Oklahoma, for instance, a spiritual healer named Lawrence Owens was convicted for failing for provide medical assistance to his daughter, who fell ill with typhoid fever and died. "A case of more wanton neglect," the Court of Criminal Appeals of Oklahoma noted in 1911, "could hardly be found." The appellate panel upheld Owens's conviction, holding that "the proposition that religious belief constitutes no defense for violation of a penal statute" was applicable in this instance.[60]

Even when unrelated procedural issues forced them to reverse convictions in spiritual healing cases, some courts went out of their way to stress the duty of parents, whatever the strictures of their religious faith, to furnish medical care to their ailing children. In Indiana, for instance, authorities filed involuntary manslaughter charges against a follower of John Alexander Dowie after his infant son died from bronchial pneumonia. Joseph Chenoweth had treated the boy in accordance with the Epistle of James, summoning elders of his church for prayer and having them anoint the child with oil. (He also apparently communicated directly with Dowie and had him pray for the boy.) The prosecution of Chenoweth foundered when the trial judge, J. V. Kent, directed the jury to return a verdict of not guilty as a matter of law. State authorities apparently botched their appeal of Kent's ruling by failing to file a bill of exceptions with his court in a timely manner. In 1904, the Supreme Court of Indiana held that this error so limited the record before it that it could not reverse Kent's ruling favoring Chenoweth.[61]

Technically, the procedural error barred the state high court from ruling on the merits of the state's case against Chenoweth, but it chose to discuss them anyway because they presented a question "of public importance." The court reviewed analogous cases from a variety of jurisdictions, including England and Canada (where another Dowie follower had been convicted of manslaughter). It concluded that these spiritual-healing cases had firmly established that "the religious doctrine or belief of a person can not be recognized or accepted as a justification or excuse for his committing an act which is a criminal offense under the law of the land." Thus, Chenoweth's acts, even though they were grounded in sincere religious belief, "should be condemned and punished by law." The justices felt so strongly about the matter that they urged the state legislature to bolster the ability of Indiana's criminal code to deal with cases of religion-based medical neglect.[62]

Florida's highest court reversed a manslaughter conviction precisely because it found that the state's criminal code lacked an applicable statute. The details of *Bradley v. State* were horrific. When James Bradley's daughter, an epileptic named Bertha, was seriously burned in a fire, he treated her in accordance with the Epistle of James. Elders from his church were summoned to the girl's bedside; they prayed over her several times a day and anointed her with oil. "We were trusting in the Lord," Bradley later said, "and looking to the Lord and believing in divine healing of the body." He chose this course of treatment because, as he told an acquaintance, "the greatest physician is God."

In the end, though, Bradley's efforts at spiritual healing failed, and Bertha died from her injuries.[63]

The suffering that his daughter endured appalled some of Bradley's friends and family members. When F. S. Sanchez, his brother-in-law, arrived at Bertha's bedside, she was "plumb raving crazy. . . . She didn't know anybody and was biting herself and tearing up the bedclothes, and they were rubbing her [with oil] and I had to help hold her on the bed." When it became obvious to Sanchez that the healing ritual was not working, he pulled Bradley aside and offered to pay for medical treatment for the girl. (He said he would sell his best horse to raise the money, if need be.) Bradley demurred, claiming that he was following the scriptures and restoring his daughter's health. Sanchez—who later called his niece's suffering "the horriblest thing I ever saw"—eventually left the scene in disgust.[64]

Florida authorities charged Bradley with manslaughter, and a jury convicted him. In 1920, however, the Supreme Court of Florida reversed his conviction, holding that "there is no statute in this state specifically making the failure or refusal of a father to provide medical attention for his child a felony, and the general definition of 'manslaughter' contained in the statute does not appear to cover a case of this nature." As Justice Thomas West mentioned in a lengthy and bitter dissenting opinion in *Bradley*, this narrow reading of state law put the court at odds with an evolving line of judicial precedent that included the Peculiar People cases in Great Britain and *Pierson* and *Reynolds* in the United States. It was clear from these precedents, West wrote in dismay, "that [the] defendant's belief was not sufficient justification or excuse to exonerate him."[65]

Reviewing a conviction on a charge of failure to provide medical aid, the Court of Criminal Appeals of Oklahoma echoed West's reasoning. J. H. Beck, a member of an unnamed faith-healing sect, first attempted to treat his eleven-year-old son's tetanus "by prayers and appeals for divine aid," as the appeals court later put it. When that failed to restore his health, Beck reluctantly summoned help from two nearby physicians, but it was too late to do Johnnie Beck much good; he died just a few hours after they administered medical treatment. A trial court found the elder Beck guilty of failing to furnish medical aid to his son, and he was fined and sentenced to six months in jail. Invoking its earlier holding in the *Owens* medical neglect case, the appeals court upheld Beck's conviction in 1925. According to the panel, it had been reasonable for the trial court jury to find "that the defendant was grossly remiss in his duty towards his child in not calling a physician earlier."[66]

But even as the appeals court reaffirmed its conclusion that Oklahoma's abuse and neglect laws should be applied to parents regardless of their religious beliefs, the judges took Beck's faith into account when they mitigated the severity his sentence. At the end of their opinion in *Beck v. State*, the panel members held that Beck's punishment was excessive because he "seems to have been a member of a religious sect which believes in faith or divine healing, and . . . he may have been influenced by other members of the sect" as he attempted to choose a course of treatment for his son. The court left Beck's fine in place but eliminated his jail time altogether. The appeals court thus reached a paradoxical conclusion: while holding that the state's criminal code should be applied without regard to defendants' religious beliefs, it ruled that those beliefs effectively could shield defendants from serious punishment for their crimes.[67]

Part of a dynamic and ongoing interplay between the church and state in the late nineteenth and early twentieth centuries, *Beck* demonstrated a growing willingness by states to regulate manifestations of conduct that, while inspired by individuals' sincere religious beliefs, appeared to lack the imprimatur of traditional Protestantism. Such prosecutions for faith healing meant that, for perhaps the first time in the nation's history, courts repeatedly reviewed widespread and sustained efforts by state authorities to regulate conduct that was defended as fundamentally religious behavior, beyond the reach of secular laws. These cases heralded a new era in which such elemental matters of faith as prayer and worship increasingly were drawn into the political process and treated as matters of broad public concern. In that sense, they clearly foreshadowed later legal disputes over the state's role in governing the proselytizing activities of Jehovah's Witnesses, the ceremonial use of peyote by Native Americans, and the ritualistic sacrifice practices of members of the Santeria faith.[68]

Early criminal cases involving Christian Scientists demonstrated the limits of using state power to regulate forms of religious conduct—behaviors based on underlying religious doctrines—that were perceived as threats to public order. In the interests of promoting the welfare of children, authorities throughout the country repeatedly attempted to use manslaughter, neglect, and medical practice statutes to protect children from harms associated with the healing rituals that formed the core of the church's religious practices. These cases, despite the resolve of prosecutors, produced ambiguous results, as courts struggled to reconcile the nation's long-standing tradition of safeguarding religious liberty with emerging cultural and legal norms relating to the rights of children and the efficacy of medical science.

5

"Does the Science Kill a Patient Here and There?"

Christian Science, Healing, and the Law

The list of writers who have ridiculed Mary Baker Eddy and the religious faith she founded, Christian Science, reads like a who's who of American literature. One of the main characters in Henry James's *The Bostonians* is Verena Tarrant, a lecturer (and daughter of a mesmerist) who bears more than a passing resemblance to Eddy. What she offers the public, James scoffs, is little more than "fluent, pretty, third-rate palaver, conscious or unconscious, perfected humbug." The poet and physician William Carlos Williams, the grandson of an ardent Christian Scientist, wrote movingly in his autobiography of the disastrous results of the faith's approach to healing. Williams once had been called upon to save a child whose diphtheria had been treated solely by spiritual means. He had found the youngster hovering near death, he wrote, "strangling on the floor because of an excess of religious fervor on the part of the parents." A character in a John Updike novel, expressing the view of many of those who have questioned Eddy's teachings, sputters, "Christian Science! As if there could be such a thing!" Willa Cather and Mark Twain published entire books on Eddy's church, and both were caustic. Twain's characteristically scathing *Christian Science* so consistently mocked Eddy that the church attempted to suppress its publication.[1]

Eddy long had been a lightning rod for criticism. She had risen to prominence in the late nineteenth century by developing teachings grounded in the notion that there is "no Life, Substance, or Intelligence in matter. That all is mind and there is no matter." In this scheme—which Eddy codified in her often-updated book *Science and Health*—an individual's sickness is merely an illusion that can be

overcome by eliminating erroneous thinking and embracing Eddy's interpretation of Christ's teachings. Summarizing the essentials of this philosophy,
former Christian Scientist Caroline Fraser has written, "The material world,
physical illness, and disease are an illusion, and a complete understanding of
these revelations about man's true spiritual nature is said to heal illness, as well
as sorrow, moral flaws, and all forms of suffering." Not surprisingly, this unconventional approach to healing—which does not emphasize prayer so much
as it stresses close adherence to Eddy's teachings and avoidance of most standard medical practices—attracted legions of critics, as did Eddy herself. In
Boston, where her church was headquartered, physicians railed against Eddy's
methods, calling them "thundering humbug," among other epithets.[2]

As part of his own withering assessment of Eddy, Twain addressed her
faith's apparently dismal track record in healing. It was a difficult topic to ignore: throughout the late nineteenth and early twentieth centuries, the failures
of Christian Science were documented in sensational accounts published in
newspapers throughout the country. "Does the Science kill a patient here and
there and now and then?" he asked. "We must concede it." After acknowledging such losses, Twain sarcastically noted that Christian Science was
"still . . . ahead on the credit side" because it had secured for numerous individuals "life-long immunity from imagination-manufactured disease." His
implication was clear: Eddy's teachings were all but useless in fighting ailments beyond the psychosomatic.[3]

Later editions of Twain's tirade included an intriguing note regarding the
prosecution of Christian Scientists who had chosen to spurn conventional medicine and treat their children's ailments solely by spiritual means. Twain reported that, following the publication of the first edition of his book, he had
received letters objecting to Christian Science parents making life-and-death
decisions regarding the care of their children. Adults should be free to treat
themselves in whatever fashion they deem fit, Twain's correspondents suggested, but "it is a burning shame that the law should allow them to trust their
helpless little children in their deadly hands." Although he obviously was no
fan of Christian Science, Twain was loath to strip parents, even the misguided
ones who adhered to Eddy's spurious teachings, of their right to direct the upbringing of their children. He mockingly paraphrased the arguments of these
critics: "I know that to a parent his child is the core of his heart, the apple of his
eye, a possession so dear, so precious that he will trust its life in no hands but
those which he believes, with all his soul, to be the very best and the very safest,
but it is a burning shame that the law does not require him to come to *me* to ask
what kind of healer I will allow him to call." Having framed the issue as mere
presumptuousness, Twain implicitly criticized the notion that public officials
should hold Christian Science parents legally accountable when their children
perished. "The public," he wrote, "is merely a multiplied 'me,'" and as such it
had no more right to second-guess parents than an individual.[4]

Few faiths have been implicated in more cases of religion-based medical neglect of children than Christian Science. From Twain's time to the present day, dozens of parents have been prosecuted for manslaughter, neglect, and other offenses after they chose to follow the teachings of Mary Baker Eddy. That Twain, a legendary skeptic and certainly the foremost critic of Christian Science of his time, would caution against infringing on the rights of these parents illustrates just how perplexing cases involving the faith's healing practices could be. The overlapping legal and ethical challenges presented by such cases proved all the more complicated in the late nineteenth and early twentieth centuries, when scientific medicine was still establishing its credibility. With conventional medicine making rapid but sometimes uneven progress against illness, courts in that era struggled to determine if Christian Scientists should be held legally accountable when their shunning of physicians—a repudiation grounded in the fundamental tenets of their faith—apparently resulted in a child's injury or death.

Mary Baker Eddy's unlikely rise to prominence as a spiritual healer began in Bow, New Hampshire, where she was born in 1821. The child of devout Congregationalists, she learned the teachings of the scriptures at an early age, largely as a result of her father's insistence that she pray frequently and listen to his long-winded disquisitions on the Bible. If religion represented one cornerstone of Eddy's formative years, sickness served as the other. A succession of vague illnesses debilitated her throughout her childhood and young adulthood. Although the sanitized accounts later published by her church usually glossed it over, there seems to be a consensus among church historians and Eddy's many biographers that her maladies were psychosomatic. The critic Harold Bloom has made this point particularly forcefully, asserting that she was a "monumental hysteric of classic dimensions, indeed a kind of anthology of nineteenth-century nervous ailments."[5]

Whatever their exact nature, the persistence of Eddy's maladies prompted her to seek help from Phineas Parkhurst Quimby, a healer who had long been fascinated by the mind's ability to conquer illness. In the mid-nineteenth century, there were, in the words of scholar Catherine Albanese, "a series of alternative healing movements [that] were subtly and unsubtly marrying nature to mind," and the colorful Quimby seems to have flirted with many of them, including mesmerism. Eventually, he developed an approach to healing suggestive of a crude form of psychotherapy. Quimby sometimes attacked his patients' illnesses by simply talking with them and attempting to convince them to abandon the faulty reasoning that lay at the heart of their ailments. He felt that doing so would bring "physical nature into harmony with its spiritual principle," as Albanese has described it, and thereby restore an individual's health. Eddy flourished under Quimby's unconventional care and passionately defended him in several letters to newspapers in New England.[6]

According to a well-worn story that appears in every church-sanctioned history of Christian Science, Eddy's own healing ministry began in the winter of 1866, after she slipped and fell on a patch of ice in Lynn, Massachusetts. The ill effects of this mishap were serious for someone with such a delicate constitution, but Eddy said she overcame them by reading a Biblical account of one of Jesus' many healings. At the time, Eddy did not quite understand how she had been healed, but she knew that she had stumbled on something profoundly important. "Even to the homeopathic physician who attended me, and rejoiced in my recovery, I could not then explain the modus of my recovery," Eddy later wrote. "I could only assure him that the divine Spirit had wrought the miracle—a miracle which later I found to be in perfect scientific accord with divine law."[7]

Over the next decade, Eddy attempted to formulate a coherent approach to healing by reconciling the teachings of Quimby with her transformative experience in Lynn. The result was her magnum opus, *Science and Health*, which appeared in the first of numerous editions in 1875. The book's central premise is now inscribed on the wall of the Mother Church of Christian Science in Boston: "Disease is mental." Under Eddy's doctrines, sickness and disease are strictly ailments of the human mind and not physical manifestations of God's will. "God has nothing to do with [sickness], because God is perfect," the writer Alfie Kohn has observed in a pithy summary of Christian Science doctrine. "Our problem is that we are alienated from God's perfect will. To return to it, we have to understand how we ourselves are perfect creatures of God, and how spirit rather than matter is the essential nature of being." Individuals seeking to regain physical health thus do not require the services of doctors; they need only to right the mental "errors" causing their illnesses.[8]

In subsequent years, *Science and Health* went through frequent revisions and reprintings, and Eddy began to attract a small but dedicated following. By 1890, according to one count, the Christian Science Church (which Eddy had formally founded in 1879) boasted nearly nine thousand members in thirty-two states. The church's growth was documented in such publications as the *Christian Science Journal*, which contained numerous accounts of healings experienced by those who followed Eddy's teachings. Newspapers outside the church documented its expansion as well, albeit with a healthier degree of skepticism. A typically quizzical headline in a Boston newspaper read, "What is 'Religious Science'?"[9]

As the church rapidly grew in the 1890s and early 1900s, newspapers throughout the country carried sensational stories of criminal prosecutions involving members of Eddy's church. Perhaps the most scandalous of these resulted from the death of Harold Frederic, an American novelist and journalist who succumbed to heart disease and rheumatic fever in 1898 after being treated by a Christian Science practitioner in London. (Practitioners are specially trained Christian Science healers who attempt to heal the sick with prayer and explications of Eddy's teachings.) Arguing that the writer would have survived if he had received prompt medical treatment, British authorities pursued manslaughter charges against two church members who had been involved in his care. When one of the accused was asked by authorities what she had done for Frederic, she said "she did not treat Mr. Frederic with drugs, but with God's power only," as a London newspaper summarized. "She told him when he said that his hand was paralyzed that he must reflect God, and he would be strong and well." Although the charges eventually were dropped, the case stirred outrage on both sides of the Atlantic over Christian Scientists' healing practices.[10]

Before long, American authorities leveled similar charges against Christian Science parents who had failed to provide conventional medical treatment for ailing children. In the spring and summer of 1899, for instance, newspapers in New York provided extensive coverage of the death of a seven-year-old boy named Ralph Saunders. Saunders, the son of Christian Scientists, died of double pneumonia while his family visited friends at Fort Porter, located near Buffalo. Because the death occurred on a military base, federal authorities investigated, and eventually they pursued manslaughter charges against four people: the boy's parents and two Christian Science practitioners, George and Elizabeth Kinter, who had attended him during his illness.[11]

During a preliminary hearing, a fellow Christian Scientist articulated the views of the accused toward healing. "She declared she had no faith whatever in medical treatment," according to one newspaper account. "She would not summon a doctor if her own children or her husband were close to death. She trusted entirely in God." Mary Ramer, who worked as a servant for this Christian Scientist witness and observed Ralph Saunders in the days leading up to his death, testified at the same hearing and provided a chilling account of how the Kinters' Christian Science treatment had failed. Two days before Ralph's death, she said, she recognized the specter of death in his visage. Also testifying was a physician who reported that the boy probably would have survived if he had received timely conventional medical treatment.[12]

The Saunders parents and the Kinters ultimately escaped formal punishment. In September 1899, a federal grand jury in Buffalo could not reach a consensus on the manslaughter charges, and it failed to return indictments against them. Apparently not chastened by this brush with the law, George Kinter continued to work as a practitioner and forcefully defended the right of Christian Scientists to practice their faith without interference. "I myself have treated thousands of cases," Kinter said in 1901 in testimony before the New York State Assembly's Committee on Public Health. "I have not killed anybody, and I am still a respected member of my community." When a skeptical legislator asked if his minimal formal training (which consisted of a single course taken at a school operated by the Christian Scientists in Boston) adequately had prepared him to diagnose illnesses, Kinter archly replied that his numerous successes as a Christian Science practitioner amply demonstrated that he knew "something about diagnosing disease."[13]

Kinter's efforts to legitimize Christian Science healing—and his success in evading prosecution after the death of Ralph Saunders—failed to dissuade authorities in New York from pursuing criminal charges against other members of his faith. Three years after Saunders's death, authorities in White Plains, New York, mounted a manslaughter prosecution of a Christian Science practitioner and two parents after a seven-year-old named Esther Quimby died in that city from diphtheria. (White Plains officials were not shy about pursuing such cases: the *Pierson* case, involving a follower of John Alexander Dowie, originated there as well.) Dragging on over a period of three years, the case illustrated how tenaciously Christian Scientists at the turn of the century battled authorities and fought to establish the legitimacy of their methods of healing.

Esther Quimby's death in October 1902 followed a common pattern in Christian Science cases of the era. Her parents, John and Georgianna Quimby, summoned John C. Lathrop, a prominent practitioner in the area, after both Esther and her sister Bessie fell ill with what appeared to be tonsillitis. Lathrop, believing that the illness was in fact "merely a mortal belief," proceeded to treat the children according to Christian Science doctrine. Asked later to describe what he had done for the girls, the practitioner said he had furnished "a realizing prayer, an enlightened faith, and a spiritual understanding of God." Ideally, this treatment would have "eradicate[ed] the belief in disease, which we consider is purely in the human mind," but in Esther's case it had failed. An investigation conducted by the local coroner revealed that she had succumbed to diphtheria.[14]

The girl's death did little to shake Lathrop's faith in Christian Science. Echoing a refrain voiced by numerous members of his faith, he commented, "I regret exceedingly that the child was not cured, but at the same time I think it is very well to remember that Christian Scientists are not the only people who occasionally lose a patient." Georgianna Quimby announced that Esther's death could not be blamed on Christian Science because "nothing could have been done that would have saved my little girl." The county coroner strongly disagreed. Convinced that the responsibility for Esther's death lay with her parents and Lathrop, he vowed "to make a test case of this child's death." He promised to pursue manslaughter charges against all three after determining that they had failed to provide adequate medical care to the girl.[15]

Christian Scientists in the New York City area rallied to the defense of Lathrop and the Quimbys. According to scholar Rennie Schoepflin's trenchant account of the case, church members "gathered funds for a war chest and launched a public relations blitz" on behalf of the accused. Many pledged financial backing for their defense, while others offered rhetorical support. "The Christian Scientists do not fear that anything will come of this case, for we are sure that we have broken no law," one said. "There is no law that will prevent one man praying at the bedside of his fellow-beings." Another member of the faith offered an incisive critique of how the still-murky state of medical science made it difficult for the state to proscribe particular forms of healing. "The law has never yet established any standard of correct medical treatment," Christian Scientist W. D. McCracken said, "and it would be impossible to accomplish this along the lines of material remedies, because the advocates of the different schools [such as homeopathic and eclectic medicine] cannot agree among themselves as to a common standard." Furthermore, if the state prohibited individuals from receiving new forms of treatment, "there could be no advance in the art of healing" and humankind as a whole would suffer.[16]

It fell to a Westchester County grand jury to sort out these conflicting claims and determine if manslaughter indictments were warranted. Its findings, issued in October 1902, offered a biting condemnation of Christian Science in general and Lathrop and the Quimbys in particular. In returning manslaughter indictments against all three, the grand jury pointed to the fact that Esther Quimby "was allowed to die without any of the remedies known to medical science being used." After hearing testimony from several medical experts, the members of the panel became convinced that "the life of the child could have been saved" if she had received such treatment. Sharing one of the coroner's chief concerns, the grand jury also noted that Esther Quimby had not been quarantined (as state law mandated in all diphtheria cases) and had "mingled with the inhabitants of the county both upon the street and in public conveyances." The failure of Christian Science treatment to cure Esther's illness thus had not endangered her alone; it also had put the general population at risk. Given that their practices had imperiled the lives both of the girl and of her neighbors, the grand jury concluded, Lathrop and the Quimbys merited prosecution under the state's manslaughter law.[17]

Although Christian Scientists in the New York City area seemed to remain steadfast in their support of the White Plains defendants, the controversy generated by Esther Quimby's death and the grand jury's indictment caused the church to reassess its stance on treating contagious diseases. In a startling turnabout, church leader Mary Baker Eddy issued a directive stating that "until public thought becomes better acquainted with Christian Science, the Christian Scientists shall decline to doctor infectious or contagious diseases." (She declined to address the paradox inherent in acknowledging diseases as contagious while insisting that they are illusionary.) Archibald McLellan, editor of the *Christian Science Sentinel*, also weighed in on the matter, specifying that members of the faith no longer would treat diphtheria, smallpox, cholera, and a host of other contagious diseases. Hereafter, members of the faith were to report cases of such ailments to public health authorities (as state law required) and generally be "prompt and unfailing in their obedience" to health regulations.[18]

The church's backtracking on contagious diseases did not deter J. Addison Young, the Westchester County district attorney, from pursuing manslaughter charges against Lathrop and the Quimbys. As the case moved forward in the fall of 1902, their attorney, Austin G. Fox, filed a demurrer to the indictment, arguing that it was defective on several grounds. In court, Fox supported his claims by invoking the U.S. Supreme Court's recent opinion in *American School of Magnetic Healing v. McAnnulty* (1902), a case involving the mail fraud prosecution of a purportedly disreputable healing institution located in Missouri. In his opinion for the high court in *Magnetic Healing*, Justice Rufus Peckham seemed to buttress the Christian Scientists' contention that the turbulent state of medical science made it nearly impossible to judge which cures were effective and which were fraudulent. "Just exactly to what extent the mental condition affects the body, no one can accurately and definitely say," Peckham wrote. "One person may believe it of far greater efficacy than another, but surely it cannot be said that it is a fraud for one person to contend that the mind has an effect upon the body and its physical condition that even a vast majority of intelligent people might be willing to admit or believe." Fox shrewdly cited such language to bolster his claim that prosecutors could not conclusively prove that Christian Science was ineffective. As Peckham put it, since "there is no precise standard by which to measure the claims" made by advocates of various methods of healing, it was nearly impossible to establish that one was fraudulent.[19]

The outcome of the *Pierson* case—in which New York's highest court upheld the manslaughter conviction of a spiritual healer in Westchester County—seemed to bode well for the district attorney, but his efforts to prosecute the Christian Scientists ultimately failed. As Rennie Schoepflin has noted, the outcome of cases like *Pierson* appeared to indicate that "the courts had moved toward the opinion that parents broke the law when they did not provide medical care for their children. However, courts remained ambivalent about whether Christian Science treatment constituted medical treatment; and if it did, courts balked at convicting parents for practicing their religion in what they had believed to be their children's best interests." The disposition of the Lathrop case vividly illustrated this ongoing uncertainty over Christian Scientists' legal culpability in cases of religion-based medical neglect of children: in August 1905, almost three years after Esther Quimby's death, a county judge dismissed the manslaughter charges against Lathrop and the Quimbys. "This is a victory for the followers of the sect," one newspaper reported, "who contend that they had a right under the Constitution of the United States to care for the sick as they thought best."[20]

The Quimby case was merely one battle in an ongoing war between Christian Scientists and state officials in New York. In the late nineteenth and early twentieth centuries, as Christian Science treatment became more common (and controversial), prosecutors were joined by lawmakers and representatives of the state's emerging medical establishment in an effort to regulate the work of practitioners like John Lathrop. They met with mixed success. Prodded by medical doctors who believed that spiritual-healing practices threatened both public health and their own profession, legislators in Albany introduced a succession of bills aimed at Christian Science, but few of them made much headway. In fact, several observers have argued that these proposed measures actually were counterproductive in that they gave Christian Scientists an opportunity to publicly defend their practices and establish their legitimacy. Christian Scientists were so effective in this regard that some laws passed by state legislatures in this era actually included provisions exempting the practices of their church, making it an era of "legal recognition" for the church.[21]

The late nineteenth and early twentieth centuries marked a period of significant maturation for American medical science. The healing profession became, according to one study of the period, "more coherent, more stable, and probably more prestigious," and for good reason. As the nineteenth century progressed, growing numbers of aspiring physicians attended medical schools that provided clinical and demonstrative instruction and met increasingly strict standards for medical education. Once they met beefed-up licensing standards and launched their practices, physicians began to follow an established code of medical ethics that outlined their duties to their patients, their professional colleagues, and the public as a whole. Some of them conducted research to test the safety and efficacy of various treatments, then published their findings in reputable journals.[22]

The American Medical Association (AMA), an umbrella organization founded in 1847, spearheaded many of these developments. From the outset, AMA members battled to keep nonconformist healers—essentially anyone who had the temerity not to practice the prevailing iteration of scientific medicine—from sullying the reputation of their profession. The AMA pilloried these "sectarians" as thinly disguised frauds who threatened public health by "follow[ing] a dogma, tenet, or principle based on the authority of its promulgator to the exclusion of demonstration and practice." For a time in the mid-nineteenth century, homeopathy (in which patients ingest minute quantities of remedies that, if given in larger doses, would produce symptoms analogous to ones being treated) had emerged as the strongest rival to mainstream medicine. Described by one critic as "the dominant medical delusion of the day," its practitioners were in such high demand that, in 1860, almost seven hundred of them were employed in the state of New York alone. The AMA mustered all of its institutional might to counter the influence of these and other sectarians, such as Thomsonians and "eclectics." Its members railed against the sectarians in journals (one typical attack branded homeopathy "the *abominable thing*") and pressured local medical societies to expel them. These efforts, though spirited, met with only mixed results: finding common cause (if not espousing common practices), intersectarian groups sprouted up throughout the nineteenth century and stubbornly resisted the AMA's efforts to impose hegemony on the healing profession.[23]

And then there was Christian Science. The faith was anathema to members of the AMA, and they railed against it at every turn. In the late nineteenth and early twentieth centuries, the *Journal of the American Medical Association* (*JAMA*) frequently featured vituperative editorials decrying Christian Scientists. Linking Christian Science with another faith that had become notorious because of its approach to healing, one of the journal's condemnations analogized it to "the kindred though rival delusion known as Dowieism." (The comparison was not meant to flatter either religion, for "each is alike damnable in every sanitary point of view.") *JAMA* was so concerned about the spread of this "aggressive delusion" that it called for states to enact legislation aimed at circumscribing the healing practices of Christian Scientists. One typical broadside read, "Steps should be taken to restrain the rabid utterances and irrational practices of such ignorant and irresponsible persons. Liberty is one thing, and license another, and the crime of even suggesting such obviously false doctrines and immoral practices should be prevented by severe punishment." Other editorials went even further, hinting (without much credible evidence) that Christian Scientists engaged in aberrant sexual practices. Like many nonchurch publications of the era, *JAMA* painted a consistently unappealing portrait of Eddy's church.[24]

Such attacks were part of the AMA's dogged attempt to help "legislate Christian Science out of existence," as Caroline Fraser has written in her insightful study of the faith's stormy history. In the 1880s and 1890s, the organization took aim at Christian Scientists by urging legislators in several states to pass laws designed to limit the practice of medicine to those who met criteria established by statewide medical boards, bodies comprised of members of the medical establishment—men who by and large viewed Christian Science as quackery. These standards often required prospective physicians to pass an examination and register with the state before they began practicing medicine. In 1889, the U.S. Supreme Court effectively gave its imprimatur to such regulatory schemes by rejecting a challenge to West Virginia's medical licensure system. In *Dent v. West Virginia*, the high court held that establishing appropriate occupational standards fell within the parameters of "the power of the state to provide for the general welfare of its people."[25]

Not surprisingly, Christian Scientists thought otherwise, and they attacked efforts to apply medical licensing laws to their healing practices. That they viewed these measures as a serious threat to their church was evident in the frequency and vigor of their criticisms. Writing in the *Christian Science Journal* in 1905, Clifford Smith asserted that church members resisted the application of such measures because "the spirit which gave our system of government birth and form forbids any group of citizens, though temporarily clothed with the power of making laws, to define or regulate the relations between God and men, set limits to His salvation, or prescribe what method all citizens shall employ in the case of sickness." Church publications repeatedly leveled similar blasts at individual state medical-licensing measures. Claiming that it plainly infringed on church members' religious liberty, the *Christian Science Journal* condemned an Iowa licensing statute as being "so rankly unconstitutional and so evidently a blow at man's 'inalienable rights'" that it deserved to be immediately repealed.[26]

Legal experts of the time puzzled over when and if such measures should be applied to the healing practices of Christian Scientists. "Christian Science, embodying as it does both the treatment of disease and religious belief, presents . . . a difficult subject to deal with by the law," Irving Campbell wrote in the *Virginia Law Register* in 1904. "And the questions involved being of recent development, it is not surprising that courts differ in their views of the law, and legislatures in their policy." After reviewing church teachings, the halting development of medical science, and judicial opinions in a variety of cases involving spiritual-healing practices, Campbell came to favor a middle course that would allow Christian Scientists "to practice their system, but under reasonable and proper regulation" that would not infringe on their religious liberty. Others in the legal community favored taking a harder line against Christian Scientists. New York attorney William Purrington contended in 1898 that "there seems no good reason, as [a] matter of law, why they should not be punished for the evil they actually do." Insisting that Christian Scientists should be prosecuted under medical-practice and manslaughter laws, he questioned "why unqualified persons should be allowed to pretend to cure disease, by their pretenses deprive the sick of the benefits of science, and yet escape the just consequences of their imposture."[27]

Even Purrington, who penned several anti–Christian Science articles in the late nineteenth and early twentieth centuries, had to acknowledge the pitfalls of legislative efforts to circumscribe the healing activities of Christian Scientists. Although he did not object to the enactment of laws aimed at curbing the practices of "religious fanatics" such as Eddy and her followers, Purrington suggested that there was a quicker and less cumbersome way to protect the public from their charlatanry. "Publicity," he counseled, "will destroy the cult [of Christian Science] far more quickly than legislation." Although few had kind words for the doctrines or practices of Christian Scientists, other observers also criticized anti–Christian Science measures, some of which seemed absurdly broad. The *Chicago Daily Tribune*, troubled by the potential scope of an Illinois medical-practice law, joked that a mother who administered castor oil to her constipated child without first obtaining a prescription from a physician now could be imprisoned for providing such routine care.[28]

In Massachusetts, where the church was headquartered, anti–Christian Science legislation that was introduced in 1898 ignited a political firestorm. The proposed law, which would have required the licensing of anyone who pre-scribed "treatment for a person for the purpose of curing any real or supposed disease," met with what the *Christian Science Journal* prosaically called "lively and formidable opposition." This included several of the city's newspapers, among them the *Boston Herald*, which remonstrated that "this is a matter in which more harm than good may be done by the interference of the law." Several members of the faith testified against the bill, and they were joined by such luminaries as William Lloyd Garrison, Jr. (the son of the famed ab-olitionist), and Harvard University philosopher and psychologist William James.[29]

James's testimony, coming as it did from a prominent scientist, proved especially damning for the bill. Testifying before a legislative committee, James made several telling observations about the bill's origins, its potential impact on medical science, and the state's role in regulating both medicine and reli-gion. He bluntly questioned the motives of the state medical society, the mea-sure's main champion, suggesting that it was not inaccurate to term that body "a trade union trying to legislate against scabs." James also pointed out that since medicine hardly was a "finished science, with all practitioners in agree-ment about methods of treatment," it was difficult for anyone to determine which healing practices were valid and which were spurious. And, he con-tinued, the state was particularly ill equipped to make such a judgment. "The Commonwealth of Massachusetts is not a medical body, has no right to a medical opinion, and should not dare to take sides in a medical controversy," James concluded. Thanks in part to such opposition, the bill foundered and ultimately died.[30]

It was in New York, where cases of faith-based medical neglect frequently made headlines, that Christian Scientists embarked on perhaps their longest-running battle against the medical establishment. In 1898, a bill limiting the practice of medicine to licensed physicians drew trainloads of protesting Christian Scientists to Albany. The measure's opponents, according to one news account, "saw in the bill a direct attempt on the part of the regularly constituted medical fraternity to prevent their sect from treating the sick." As often happened when lawmakers targeted Christian Science practice, mem-bers of other faiths rallied to their defense. Among those testifying against the medical practice law was a Brooklyn judge who, like William James in Mas-sachusetts, questioned the motives of "the real movers of this measure," the medical profession. He expressed dismay that physicians sought "a monopoly, giving to them the sole and only right to heal, making it penal for anyone else to minister to the sick and save from death the thousands in our midst who are stricken with disease." (For good measure, the judge also knocked the bill as "a blow at religious liberty.") The tumult over the bill effectively ended when its sponsor, Senator Henry Coggeshall, surrendered to the protests by asking that the measure be amended to exempt Christian Scientists who were attempting healings.[31]

This defeat did not deter opponents of Christian Science in the Empire State, and they continued to lobby for legislation to circumscribe the faith's healing activities. In the years after Coggeshall's bill stalled, members of the New York County Medical Society repeatedly called for state lawmakers to pass a statute that would regulate Christian Science practice. In 1901, the intro-duction of one such measure drew scores of protesting Christian Scientists back to Albany. Henry Call insisted that the bill had been introduced simply because "the medical fraternity, which finds itself being invaded, claims that Christian Science is a sham," while another member of the faith called it "an attempt to make null and void the final command of the Savior before his ascension: 'Go ye into the world and heal the sick.'" The bill did have its champions, however. The *New York Times*—in addition to railing against "mis-chievous and, in many cases, criminal folly of so-called Christian Science, [which is] neither Christian nor scientific"—maintained that failure to enact such a measure would be "a public calamity."[32]

But even as the editorial page of the *Times* lauded the measure, its news columns were reporting that the bill stood little chance of passing, chiefly because Christian Scientists played political hardball with members of the state legislature. One unnamed lawmaker explained how the bill's opponents op-erated. "They went into the district of every member of the assembly," he said, "and when they had developed to its fullest extent the Christian Science senti-ment in each district, the member representing the district was cold-bloodedly informed that unless he voted against the . . . bill he could not be returned to the Assembly." Another observer was more stark in his assessment of the bill's failure, claiming that lawmakers had been "terrorized" into killing it.[33]

As Caroline Fraser has observed, the AMA's campaign against Christian Science ran out of steam by 1910. Events in New York typified the organiza-tion's repeated failures to regulate Christian Science practice. In many states, proscriptive measures failed to garner much support among state legislators, and the few laws that did earn passage usually were vetoed by skittish gover-nors. Like many of his colleagues who killed similar measures, Governor John Mickey voiced two serious objections when he vetoed the anti–Christian Sci-ence law passed by the Nebraska legislature in 1905. Mickey questioned the motives of the bill's sponsors, suggesting that it had been "conceived in a spirit of professional intolerance" by physicians eager to guard their turf. He further argued that it represented "an infringement on the constitutional guaranty of religious freedom."[34]

Although broad efforts to "legislate Christian Science out of existence" generally failed, authorities throughout the country responded to religion-based medical neglect of children in a more piecemeal fashion by mounting

criminal prosecutions of individual Christian Science parents and practitioners. They typically based these charges on existing neglect, manslaughter, and
medical practice laws, not new statutes crafted specifically to target Christian
Scientists. This ad hoc approach to regulating Eddy and her followers resulted
in a case involving Abby Corner, a Christian Science practitioner from suburban Boston who was indicted for manslaughter in 1888. Authorities charged
Corner after she supervised a childbirth in which both the mother and the
child died. (The victims, as it happened, were Corner's own daughter and
granddaughter.) The case generated so much negative publicity for Christian
Science that Mary Baker Eddy, eager to keep her faith's reputation from becoming further tarnished, attempted to distance the church from Corner by
publishing a letter claiming that the accused could not properly call herself a
Christian Science midwife because she never had completed the obstetrics
course offered by the church's Massachusetts Metaphysical College. Eddy also
resisted efforts to use church funds to assist in Corner's defense. Although a
jury acquitted Corner—the evidence at trial was unclear as to whether a licensed
physician would have managed the complicated delivery more effectively—
Eddy's handling of her case caused a serious rift among Christian Scientists in
Boston.[35]

Other turn-of-the-century cases of religion-based medical neglect of children resulted in authorities charging Christian Science practitioners under
state medical practice acts. In Beatrice, Nebraska, Ezra Buswell faced charges
in 1893 of practicing medicine without a license after a child left in his care
died of cholera. The indictment offered a harsh assessment of his purported
misdeeds, claiming that he "falsely, unlawfully, craftily, and wickedly" attempted to "deceive and defraud the people." At his trial, Buswell attempted to
explain to an incredulous prosecutor how members of his faith attempted to
deal with people who were afflicted by the illusion of illness. "We treat them as
a mother treats her child that is frightened at some object it fears, by showing
them that God is love, and, [in] understanding the all-presence of love, there is
no fear," he said. "We treat it as a question of fear—that is, we seek to dispel
the fear by showing them the presence of love." Such airy answers failed to
satisfy Buswell's questioner. Bewildered by the Christian Scientist's responses,
he wondered aloud, "There is no real, actual sickness? It is all in the mind?
There is no sickness?"[36]

Buswell's attorneys did not delve too deeply into the arcana of Christian
Science doctrine. Instead, they criticized the application of Nebraska's medical-
practice act to Christian Scientists, calling it an obvious violation of the guar-
antees for religious freedom codified in the state constitution. According to
that provision, one of the lawyers reminded jurors, "All men have a natural and
indefeasible right to worship Almighty God according to the dictates of their
own conscience." Regulating Christian Scientists' spiritual-healing practices
clearly violated that stricture. The state's attempt to categorize these traditions

as medical practice was, he averred, not only unconstitutional but also patently absurd. "That is their belief—that God through prayer heals the sick, and learned gentlemen who represent the prosecution say, that in believing that, and praying for their afflicted brothers and sisters, they are violating the law of the state of Nebraska and by prayer are practicing medicine," the attorney said. "It seems to me that this is ridiculous; this is a form of religion; it is their religion."[37]

Christian Scientists' healing practices had ancient roots, Buswell's attorneys claimed. One of them referred to the Epistle of James, a touchstone for many spiritual healers, to underscore the fact that Buswell treated the sick in the manner mandated by the scriptures. "There is his authority," the attorney told jurors, "drawn from the Scriptures, from the inspired word of God." After touching on the scriptures, the lawyer also shrewdly invoked Jesus' prowess as a healer to highlight the ridiculousness of attempting to regulate religious rituals through medical-practice legislation. "What would you think today if Christ were on earth?" he asked. "Do you think if he were, people would compel him to go to Lincoln [the state capital] and say: 'Gentlemen, I want a diploma to pray'?"[38]

As they attempted to undercut the prosecution's case against Buswell, his attorneys also trotted out the familiar claim that his healing practices probably were no more unreliable than those employed by accredited doctors. "There is nothing more proverbial than the uncertainty of medicine," one of the defendants' lawyers stated. "Medicine is not a science." This fact was underscored, he said, by the fact that "regularly licensed physicians are continually losing their patients under seemingly trifling ailments" by repeatedly making errors in both diagnosis and treatment. The attorney noted that one prominent victim of bungling doctors had been President Garfield. (After an assassin's bullet felled him, a battalion of doctors had repeatedly probed Garfield with unclean instruments, causing the blood poisoning that eventually killed him.)[39]

After the jury acquitted Buswell on all counts, the county attorney and George Hastings, the state's attorney general, brought an appeal before the Supreme Court of Nebraska. The high court ruled in favor of the state, holding that Buswell had been "within none of the exceptions provided by the statute" because he had in fact been "treating physical ailments of others for compensation." The case involved "no question of . . . religious practice or duty," the justices concluded.[40]

The *JAMA* hailed the high court's ruling as a "too long deferred blow" against "irreverent charlatans," and the *Lincoln Evening News* proclaimed that the justices had "delivered a body blow to the Christian Science healers that have grown so numerous in Nebraska of late." And, indeed, the decision could have given prosecutors throughout Nebraska a green light to prosecute Christian Scientists under the state's medical-practice act. However, authorities apparently had little enthusiasm for pursuing such cases. According to one account published in 1918, the *Buswell* decision "has been a dead letter for many years, as the liberal views of the Nebraska people are opposed to prosecution for prayer." Although there was widespread dismay over the deaths of children treated by spiritual means, the public seemed ambivalent about attaching criminal liability to actions grounded in individuals' sincere religious beliefs.[41]

The prosecution of Emma Nichols and Crecentia Arries—Christian Science healers implicated in a case of religion-based medical neglect in Milwaukee, Wisconsin—produced a similarly ambiguous result. In 1900, authorities charged Nichols and Arries under Wisconsin's medical-practice act after they unsuccessfully treated an eleven-year-old named Irma Grossenbach for diphtheria. That measure, like analogous measures in other states, mandated licensing for anyone "who shall, for a fee, prescribe drugs or medical or surgical treatment for the cure or relief of any wound, facture, bodily injury, infirmity or disease." Prosecutors claimed that both women fell under those provisions; the defendants asserted that they were merely practicing their faith.[42]

Speaking at length at their trial, both healers described the evolution of their religious beliefs and healing practices. Nichols said that she had been drawn to Christian Science after being debilitated by a spinal ailment at the age of twenty-one. That time, the prognosis had been bleak—the family doctor gave her six months to live—but she eventually recovered after she read some of Mary Baker Eddy's writings and submitted to Christian Science treatment. Inspired by her recovery, Nichols became a Christian Science practitioner herself and treated nearly seven hundred people over a four-year period. (This despite her family's commitment to conventional medicine: Nichols reported that six members of her immediate family were physicians.)[43]

On the stand, Nichols stubbornly defended Christian Science and its approach to illness. Asked to describe her religious faith, she claimed it was "Christianity revived" and represented "the teachings of Jesus understood and administered." Nichols applied these teachings in her own treatment of sicknesses. In order to counter the profound misapprehensions that lay at the heart of all individuals' illnesses, she endeavored to "remove that wrong thinking by giving them the right idea" through prayer and the study of Mary Baker Eddy's writings. This was a far cry from medical treatment, she insisted, for "the material physician gropes among phenomena which fluctuate every instant, under influences not embraced by his diagnosis, and so he stumbles and falls into darkness." Physicians erred so gravely, she believed, because they, unlike Christian Scientists, refused to accept the fact that God heals.[44]

Assistant district attorney A. C. Umbreit subjected both Nichols and Arries to vigorous cross-examinations, and in doing so he highlighted several apparent weaknesses in their defense. As he questioned Arries about her healing methods, Umbreit established that Christian Science practitioners did not "lay hands" on their patients. To the prosecutor, this seemed to contradict their claim that their methods were "patterned after Christ's system of healing." Umbreit sputtered at one point that "in every recorded instance we find in Scriptures where a report is given of any act of healing, Christ either lay hands on the patient" or had some other form of physical contact with the patient. If Christian Scientists really followed the scriptures, he suggested, they would act as Christ did and touch their patients.[45]

Umbreit maintained in his closing argument that Christian Science healing practices, whatever their religious trappings, should fall under the provisions of the state's medical-practice act. As he called for the judge to convict Arries and Nichols, the prosecutor mixed ridicule for Christian Science doctrines with an appeal to mainstream Christian beliefs regarding healing. Umbreit mocked the defendants' stubborn—and lethal—resistance to employing the tools of conventional medicine to combat disease. Christian Scientists insist "that God is good, that God created everything, that God not only created everything, but everything he created was good," he said. "If that is so, then God created the drugs and created them for a good purpose"—namely, healing sick children like Irma Grossenbach.[46]

The prosecutor paired such jibes with a careful examination of relevant state and federal law. Wisconsin's medical-practice act, Umbreit contended, covered "every kind or method of healing . . . not merely the practice of medicine by means of certain drugs, but any healing treatment which is applied for the purpose of curing or healing a disease or ailment." Moreover, the defendants' claims that their activities were religious in nature and thus beyond the scope of state regulation had to be viewed in light of a succession of U.S. Supreme Court rulings in cases involving Mormons and the practice of polygamy. In these cases (the most prominent of which was *Reynolds v. United States*, decided in 1879), the high court had drawn a distinction between religious beliefs and conduct. Summarizing the court's holdings in those cases, Umbreit said that although all citizens were "entitled to the freest exercise of [their] religious beliefs," they still were required to remain "amenable to the law of the land" in terms of the conduct that resulted from those beliefs. When such behavior violated a law, he added, an "appeal to the constitutional guaranty of freedom of religious worship or religious belief is no defense." This was perhaps doubly true, the prosecutor stressed, in cases such as the one at hand, where the defendants' botched handling of an infectious disease could have resulted in multiple deaths.[47]

Judge N. B. Neelen, who heard the case in the Milwaukee police court, agreed with Umbreit that the standards established by the U.S. Supreme Court in the Mormon polygamy cases applied to the prosecution of Arries and Nichols. "No interference can be permitted" with individuals' religious beliefs, Neelen said, "provided always the laws of society, designed to secure its health, peace and prosperity are not interfered with." Arries and Nichols, by providing medical treatment to the sick without having first obtained the requisite license, had done just that by practicing medicine without licenses, and they had to be held accountable. "However free the exercise of religion may be," he said, "it must be subordinate to the laws of the land." Neelen was convinced that his guilty verdict (which carried with it a penalty of fifty dollars or thirty days in jail) had not infringed on the defendants' First Amendment freedoms: "This in no way interferes with the religious belief of anybody," he concluded.[48]

As so often happened in cases of religion-based medical neglect involving Christian Scientists, an appellate court overturned the trial court's guilty verdict. Judge Eugene Elliott of the Milwaukee County Circuit Court held that Arries and Nichols had not been practicing medicine when they treated Irma Grossenbach. "They have not claimed to be doctors or to be qualified as such," Elliott wrote. "Not only have they not prescribed drugs or other medicaments, but they disclaim, denounce and oppose the use of such agencies. . . . The treatment given by them may have been theological. It certainly was not medical; and so believing, I must find the defendants not guilty and order their discharge." The reversal was not especially well received among the medical community in Milwaukee: one local physician said that Elliott's ruling was itself a crime and railed against "a learned judge, listening to the ravings emanating from the sepulchral voice of an ephemeral fifteenth century delusion—for Eddyism is but a recrudescence of this mediaeval mania."[49]

In prosecutions of Christian Science practitioners under medical-practice acts and other related measures, such outcomes tended to be the rule rather than the exception. Just as lawmakers largely failed to enact legal provisions specifically tailored to limit Christian Science healing rituals, prosecutors—acting in concert with the emerging medical establishment—generally were unable to regulate them as practitioners of an alternative form of medicine. In Kansas City, Missouri, for instance, prosecutors secured the conviction of a Christian Science practitioner named Amanda Baird after she failed to report a fatal case of diphtheria to the local board of health. At Baird's trial, the dead girl's mother asserted, "There is no disease. The child was under the illusion of disease and the object [of treatment] is to remove the illusion." The Kansas City Court of Appeals reversed the conviction in 1902, holding that the ordinance in question clearly was meant to apply to physicians, and "there is no doubt whatever that [Baird] was not a physician."[50]

For all their broad legal implications, prominent religious liberty cases often arise from relatively localized and narrow state efforts to regulate religious practice. Nineteenth-century federal prosecutions for polygamy, for instance, involved members of a single church (Mormons) who lived in one region (primarily Utah and neighboring Idaho). Over a hundred years later, the notable First Amendment case *Church of the Lukumi Babalu Aye v. City of Hialeah* (1993) centered on the efforts of a modest-sized Florida city to regulate the ritual sacrifice practices of a particular Santeria church. Although their suppression had potentially far-reaching consequences for members of all religious faiths, neither polygamy nor the ritual sacrifice of animals were particularly widespread practices that concerned authorities in a variety of jurisdictions.

From the start, prosecutions in cases of religion-based medical neglect of children—which highlight equally profound cultural and legal issues—have been far less limited by denomination or geography. These manslaughter, neglect, and medical-practice prosecutions of parents and clergy have involved a number of different Protestant churches, and they have occurred in every region of the country. In the late nineteenth and early twentieth centuries, Christian Scientists alone faced criminal charges from Boston to the Dakota Territory because of their religious healing practices. The geographical pervasiveness of these prosecutions for inherently religious behavior probably has been matched only one other time in American history—in the late 1930s and early 1940s, when Jehovah's Witnesses across the country faced charges because of their aggressive proselytizing activities and refusal, on religious grounds, to salute the American flag.

Although the churches and historical eras are different, there are striking parallels between these efforts by states to regulate religious conduct. Both Christian Scientists and Jehovah's Witnesses were members of what scholars would later describe as "new" or "alternative" religions. As also was true of the Mormons, their faiths emerged from a period of intense religious ferment in the nineteenth century. These embryonic denominations espoused doctrines and practiced rituals that placed them outside the mainstream of conventional Protestantism. (Indeed, these faiths were regarded as so unconventional at the time that some questioned whether they even could be termed bona fide religions.) Their existence on the periphery of the country's religious culture left these churches stigmatized and politically vulnerable, and, like many fringe groups throughout the course of American history, they were easy targets for state control.

Also analogous are the justifications that authorities offered for this regulation. Public officials asserted that they had significant—and somewhat high-minded—secular reasons for attempting to govern the conduct of members of these marginal churches. Christian Scientists in the late nineteenth and early twentieth centuries allegedly endangered the welfare of children by substituting prayer for medicine; Jehovah's Witnesses during World War II were said to both disrupt public order with their obstreperous proselytizing activities and to threaten national unity with their resistance to saluting the American flag. As would be the case in every significant legal dispute over state regulation of religious practices, officials claimed that they acted merely to safeguard the broad public interest.

Christian Scientists and Jehovah's Witnesses responded to state meddling in remarkably similar ways. Both made the rhetorically savvy move of tracing the origins of their controversial conduct to the Christian scriptures. (Given that the New Testament is in many ways a chronicle of Jesus and the apostles healing and proselytizing, this was not especially difficult.) Bibles in hand, members of these alternative churches attempted to fortify the authority of their claims by repeatedly linking their activities to the formative era of Christianity. If the country truly valued religious liberty, their argument went, what could merit more legal protection than the religious practices of truly authentic Christians who modeled their conduct on the work of the apostles?

Both groups further bolstered their legitimacy by contesting state regulation within the accepted framework of American political and legal culture. Neither Jehovah's Witnesses nor Christian Scientists shied away from vigorously defending their rights in court, and members of the latter church even went a step further, effectively lobbying lawmakers to change laws that were applied to their religious practices. This engagement in the political process served a dual purpose. In the immediate sense, it helped members of these marginal faiths contest specific criminal charges. But more broadly, it also demonstrated that they were dutiful citizens rather than peculiar cultists lingering on the fringes of society. As scholar Eric Michael Mazur has argued, the process of "confronting the constitutional order" helped these groups become perceived as more fully Americanized.[51]

Religious healers clearly benefited from this posture. Whether or not they prevailed in individual legal cases, Christian Scientists and members of other faiths targeted for their healing practices were destigmatized by their willingness to voice a kind of principled defiance to state authority within the accepted political framework of the judicial system. But the specter of regulation never entirely disappeared, and, after weathering an initial storm of state oversight in the late nineteenth and early twentieth centuries, parents and clergy who relied solely on spiritual means to heal children's illnesses received renewed scrutiny by public authorities in the later half of the twentieth century. Once again, Christian Scientists throughout the country faced criminal charges for their religious practices. It was not so much that the church lost standing in this period but rather that the stature of medical science—which Christian Scientists stubbornly dismissed as irrelevant or even counterproductive to the process of physical healing—grew enormously. Whatever its shortcomings, the cultural ascendance of scientific medicine made it increasingly difficult for church members to mount compelling legal defenses of their healing practices.

6

"The Pain Has No Right to Exist"

Contemporary Christian Scientists in the Courts

On January 29, 1959, a fifty-eight-year-old man named Edward Whitney strode into an office on the eighth floor of Chicago's Orchestra Hall, a neo-Georgian building located on Michigan Avenue. Once inside, Whitney pulled a .32 caliber pistol from his overcoat and brandished it at William Rubert, a Christian Science practitioner who had unsuccessfully treated his daughter more than two decades earlier. "How would you like to die?" the enraged Whitney said as he leveled the gun at Rubert. "You murdered my little girl." With that, Whitney began firing. He hit Rubert three times—doctors later removed bullets from his chest and right hand and arm—as the victim sprang from his desk and ran down a hallway toward an elevator. ("That wasn't so bad," Whitney later said of his aim, "for a man who doesn't know anything about guns.")[1]

Whitney and Rubert had a tangled relationship that dated back to 1937. In December of that year, Whitney's daughter, Audrey Kay, fell sick with diabetes while her father was away on a business trip. The relative in whose care Whitney had left his daughter was a Christian Scientist, and she took the girl to Rubert for treatment. Although a regimen of insulin shots likely would have saved Audrey Kay's life, Rubert relied solely on Christian Science practices in an effort to remove the purported "illusion" of the girl's illness. This treatment failed, and Audrey Kay died. Whitney, livid over his daughter's death, pressed authorities to bring manslaughter charges against Rubert, but a jury acquitted the practitioner in 1938. Despite Whitney's repeated calls for the case to be reopened, authorities chose not to revisit it. Whitney, now desperate to bring Rubert to justice, accosted Dwight Green, the governor of Illinois, at a public appearance in 1941 and urged him to investigate the circumstances of his daughter's death. (Green ignored him, but the police did not: they arrested Whitney after the confrontation.)[2]

Audrey Kay's death haunted Whitney, and he brooded over the fact that Rubert had, in his view, gotten away with murder. With all official channels apparently closed, he eventually decided to take matters into his own hands. Whitney made no secret of his intentions: in the mid-1940s, he mailed the practitioner a letter that read in part, "I will return to Chicago and when I do, I will hunt you like the beast you are and kill you with as little mercy as was shown to [my daughter]." This grim promise so distressed Rubert that he contacted local authorities, and eventually Whitney was charged in federal court with using the mails to threaten the practitioner's life. Perhaps sympathetic to Whitney's plight as a distraught father, a jury acquitted him.[3]

Early in 1959, Whitney resolved to make good on his threat. He spent $27.50 on a .32 caliber pistol and traveled from his home in Birmingham, Alabama, to Chicago. After waiting twenty-one years to exact his revenge on Rubert, Whitney proved to be a determined assailant. When he confronted Rubert at the latter's office, the Christian Scientist bolted down a hallway toward an elevator operated by a man named Francis Houston. Already wounded, he exclaimed to Houston, "My god, he's shooting at me!" Rubert might have assumed that he had at last reached safety when the elevator's glass doors closed, but Whitney literally shattered that illusion by firing one last shot through them.[4]

As the elevator reached the building's lobby, Houston told Rubert, "I'll call a doctor." This notion was, of course, anathema for a practitioner of Christian Science, and Rubert responded, "No, no doctor!" Perhaps fortunately for Rubert, the police officers who soon converged on the scene ignored his demand and parceled him off to a nearby hospital. There, doctors removed all three bullets that had lodged in Rubert's body and stabilized his condition. (When asked to comment on this apparent breach of Christian Science practice, a church spokesman later said that emergency operations did not violate its proscription of medical treatment.)[5]

Whitney fled the scene after the shooting, but he quickly surrendered himself and his gun to a traffic policeman stationed at a nearby street corner. When police questioned him, Whitney made no attempt to conceal his role in the shooting or his motive. "I shot him and intended to kill him," he said. "I did it because he killed my daughter." This admission apparently did not hurt Whitney when he was tried later that year for attempted murder. "The temper of public sentiment," according to one account of the case, "was reflected in this heartbroken man's prompt acquittal by a Chicago jury."[6]

Following a period of intense activity around the turn of the century, there was in the mid-twentieth century a relative lull in prominent manslaughter and neglect cases involving Christian Scientists. (This reflected the overall downturn in outside scrutiny of the church that followed the death of the ever-controversial Mary Baker Eddy in 1910.) The post–World War II era, however, witnessed a notable upsurge in such litigation. The saga of Edward Whitney's vendetta against William Rubert (replete with sordid details seemingly borrowed from one of the era's pulp novels) helped to inaugurate an era in which church members faced intensifying scrutiny from the general public and the courts because of their healing practices. Over the final third of the twentieth century, a succession of deaths of children who had been treated in accordance with Christian Science principles resulted in high-profile manslaughter and neglect prosecutions of parents, as well as civil actions filed against both individual church members and the Mother Church of Christian Science in Boston.

It is intriguing to note that this trend paralleled an exceptional growth throughout the United States in medical-malpractice litigation. The legal historian Lawrence Friedman has suggested that the increase in medical-liability claims filed in the latter part of the twentieth century was rooted in part in a growing expectation among the general public that the courts should provide redress to individuals who have been denied the presumably certain benefits of modern medicine by incompetent or negligent physicians. A similar expectation seems to have driven the late-century rise in prosecutions of (and, to a lesser extent, civil suits filed by individuals against) Christian Scientists implicated in cases of religion-based medical neglect of children. With dramatic advances demonstrating almost daily the remarkable benefits of medical science, those who denied medical treatment to the sick or injured—whether out of professional incompetence or religious fervor—increasingly were perceived as legally culpable.[7]

Other broad trends influenced and complicated these later Christian Science cases. Starting with the Jehovah's Witness cases of the World War II era, judicial protections for religious practice grew steadily throughout the middle part of the twentieth century, with the U.S. Supreme Court handing down a series of opinions that made it increasingly difficult for states to regulate religious conduct. This development culminated in *Wisconsin v. Yoder* (1972), in which the high court ruled in favor of Old Order Amish parents who had resisted, on religious grounds, the application to their children of a state law mandating school attendance. There followed, however, a prolonged period of retrenchment in which the Supreme Court chipped away at legal protections for religious conduct. In *Employment Division v. Smith* (1990), for instance, the high court gutted one of the central holdings in *Yoder* by ruling that states did not have to demonstrate that they possessed a "compelling interest" in regulating religious behavior. The Supreme Court did not rule in a case directly related to spiritual-healing rites in this tumultuous period, but its evolving First Amendment jurisprudence suggested that statutes could pass constitutional muster if they exhibited surface neutrality toward religion. Under this relatively permissive standard, there was no significant constitutional barrier to the application of manslaughter and neglect laws to Christian Scientists who had engaged in religious-healing practices.[8]

But even in the later part of the twentieth century, prosecutions of some Christian Scientists for religion-based medical neglect often produced ambiguous results that left both the church and its critics unsatisfied. Although broader legal trends regarding medical liability and state regulation of religious conduct seemed to cast a long shadow over their legal claims, church members could fall back on one particularly effective defense: specific provisions in state manslaughter and neglect statutes that appeared to exempt conduct grounded in sincerely held religious beliefs. The impediments posed by these little-known stipulations—many of which were added in the mid-1970s to state criminal codes at the behest of the federal government—infuriated prosecutors, confounded appellate courts, and precipitated calls from children's welfare advocates for their repeal.

Christian Scientists, still holding fast to their religious beliefs, continued to view state regulation of their healing practices as a dire threat to their faith, and they battled it fervently. Often with the assistance of lawyers dispatched by the Mother Church in Boston, individual Christian Scientists zealously defended themselves in court against criminal charges and civil suits. Church leaders further bolstered these piecemeal defenses of the faith by extolling the virtues of Christian Science in a public relations campaign that included newspaper columns, television appearances, and public testimony. As time passed, however, and young Christian Scientists continued to die as a direct result of their church's approach to healing, the defenses marshaled by church members—that the Constitution defended their religious practices, that Christian Science was every bit as effective as medical science in treating illness, that the state had no business meddling in the relationship between parents and their children—rang more and more hollow.

Like Audrey Kay Whitney, seven-year-old David Cornelius suffered from diabetes. The diagnosis came late in 1955, after the boy's weight dropped and he found it increasingly difficult to breathe. Although they were Christian Scientists, David's parents, Edward and Ann Cornelius, were so concerned by his symptoms that they took him to a physician. The doctor quickly determined the cause of David's illness and admitted him to a hospital in Ridley Park, Pennsylvania. As part of his recovery there, David adhered to a regular schedule of insulin injections, the standard treatment for juvenile-onset diabetes. The youngster quickly recovered, and doctors released him from the hospital early in 1956. They informed David's parents that his health depended on ongoing insulin treatments. Without them, the physicians warned, David most likely would die.[9]

Edward and Ann Cornelius refused to heed this advice, choosing instead to treat their son's diabetes by employing the techniques prescribed their religious faith. Christian Science failed to sustain David's health, however, and his condition deteriorated rapidly. Although they had seen the obvious benefits offered by insulin, his parents admitted him to a Christian Science nursing home, which offered no medical treatment of any kind. Just as doctors had predicted a few weeks earlier, David could not survive without insulin. He fell into a coma and died shortly after arriving at the Christian Science facility.[10]

Citing their "persistent and willful" failure to provide adequate medical treatment for David, the Philadelphia district attorney filed involuntary manslaughter charges against the boy's parents. They did not have to fight the charges alone. Always vigilant about shielding the faith from state regulation, the Mother Church of Christian Science became so concerned with the potential implications of the case that it hired a white-shoe law firm in Philadelphia to defend the couple. C. Brewster Rhoads, a distinguished attorney who served as one of the firm's partners, worked closely with one of the Mother Church's lawyers to craft a legal brief arguing that the charges should be dropped. At first glance, this seemed to be an uphill battle: in two earlier cases that seemed analogous to the Cornelius prosecution, spiritual-healing parents had been convicted of manslaughter in Pennsylvania courts. But Rhoads and his colleagues nonetheless mounted such a persuasive case that they were able to convince the district attorney to enter a declaration of *nolle prosequi*, meaning that he now wished to drop the charges altogether. With both parties now satisfied that the charges were without merit, the presiding judge granted the prosecutor's motion. As he effectively ended the case before it reached the trial stage, the judge seemed to endorse the long-held Christian Science position on state regulation of their religious practices. He said that if "the failure to provide medical care is the result of religious tenet or in a sincere belief in the inefficacy of medical treatment there may be no criminal responsibility under the law."[11]

Prosecutors on Cape Cod in Massachusetts took a harder line against Dorothy Sheridan, a Christian Scientist whose daughter Lisa fell sick in February 1967 with what proved to be pneumonia. At least initially, the child's illness appeared to be nothing too out of the ordinary: Lisa complained of feeling listless and developed both a deep cough and a high fever. Following Christian Science practice, Sheridan gave her daughter no medication but instead relied on the services of two practitioners licensed by her faith. The efforts of the second of these practitioners appeared to be effective, and Lisa briefly seemed to rally. Her condition soon worsened, however, and she died. Sheridan later said that Lisa's death had come as something of a shock. "Lisa never complained," she said, "of having pain.... I expected her to recover."[12]

The circumstances of Lisa Sheridan's death troubled many Cape Cod residents, including her grandmother. She was incredulous at her own daughter's apparent neglect. "How could a mother let a sweet, dear child die of gross neglect," she asked, "when the laws of our land make us pick up a dog hurt in an accident and take it to the nearest veterinarian?" Local authorities were similarly perplexed: after examining Lisa's corpse and determining her cause of death, the medical examiner said she had suffered "an unnecessary death" and termed her mother's behavior "nothing short of criminal." Another incensed physician said that Dorothy Sheridan had been "inexcusably negligent" in failing to provide adequate medical care for her daughter.[13]

District attorney Edmund Dinis shared these sentiments and decided to prosecute Sheridan for manslaughter. He based his charge on a provision in the state criminal code that made it illegal for any parent to "willfully [fail] to provide necessary and proper physical, educational or moral care and guidance" to a child under the age of sixteen. Even though this statute failed to mandate medical treatment, Dinis believed that its reference to a parent's duty to provide "proper physical . . . care" clearly exposed Sheridan to criminal liability for involuntary manslaughter. Manslaughter was a more appropriate charge than murder, the district attorney concluded, because she had not acted with malice aforethought or intent to kill.[14]

The charges leveled against Sheridan created a minor sensation in Massachusetts, the home of the Mother Church of Christian Science. Many members of the faith were livid, believing that Dinis essentially had charged their entire church with a crime. Even some observers outside the church expressed concern over the prosecutor's actions. In an editorial on the case, the *Boston Globe* highlighted the apparent pointlessness of the state's belated decision to concern itself with Lisa Sheridan's welfare. The paper noted that "the child is beyond healing now, and perhaps the mother, too. Can any good purpose be served by pursuing the case to a still more bitter conclusion?"[15]

At Dorothy Sheridan's trial, her attorney, Walter Jay Skinner, took a different tack. Skinner zeroed in on the fact that Massachusetts law did not specifically mandate that parents furnish medical treatment for their sick children. Instead, they were required to provide "proper physical care," a vague standard that Skinner called "a very general commandment for taking care of children." Sheridan, by following the doctrines of Christian Science, clearly had met her burden under this imprecise standard, Skinner maintained. Far from ignoring Lisa's illness, she had responded to it aggressively, calling upon two different Christian Science practitioners and offering fervent prayers herself. In Skinner's reckoning, these were not the actions of a reckless or negligent parent.[16]

Skinner, like many champions of Christian Science, paired his defense of the faith's practices with a sharp attack on medical science. Despite the claims of the prosecution (which offered testimony from several doctors who believed that Lisa Sheridan's pneumonia could have been treated and cured), medicine was an "inexact science," Skinner said, and patients under the care of physicians died every day in the nation's finest hospitals. Given medicine's imperfect record in treating illness, Skinner professed shock that Sheridan could be prosecuted for attempting to heal her daughter according to the tenets of Christian Science, which was "not a fringe religion, but one widely accepted by reasonable people" (such as the phalanx of church members who attended and testified at Sheridan's trial). It was a testament to Christian Science's stature, Skinner said, that it stood "just as well in the eyes of the law" in Massachusetts as medical science.[17]

Dinis grasped this final point as well as anyone in the courtroom. He knew that in the Christian Science stronghold of Massachusetts, his decision to prosecute a parent in the church for religion-based medical neglect of a child was unprecedented. (About the only case that came close to paralleling it was the prosecution of Abby Corner in Boston in 1888, but she had been a midwife, not a parent.) Still, Dinis felt that he was on solid legal ground in pursuing manslaughter charges against Sheridan. At her trial, the prosecutor acknowledged that Americans were a diverse people who practiced a wide array of religious faiths. All of these religious beliefs merited respect, he told jurors, but when they "collid[ed] with the law of the land, the law of the land must prevail. And the law must be applied equally to all. That is the issue you've got to decide!"[18]

In the end, the panel decided that Dinis was right: it convicted Sheridan of involuntary manslaughter. Although it permeated the trial, the jurors did their best to avoid the religious dimension of the case. One member of the panel later said that all of the jurors "decided not to have religion play any part in our verdict." The facts of the case made it clear that Lisa Sheridan had been denied the proper care mandated by state law "no matter which way you look at it, whether her mother believes in God or not. It's as simple as that." Journalist Leo Damore, who wrote an account of the case that was decidedly sympathetic to Dorothy Sheridan, refused to believe that the jurors had been able to arrive at their verdict while discounting the role played in the case by religion. He thought, in fact, that little else ultimately mattered in the case. "In effect," he wrote, "Christian Science had been found guilty of killing Lisa Sheridan."[19]

Like most parents implicated in cases of religion-based medical neglect of children, Dorothy Sheridan escaped with a relatively lenient sentence: five years' probation (along with a stipulation that she would rely on the care of a physician if her remaining child fell sick). While the prospect of an appeal might have held some promise for Sheridan, its potentially wide-ranging negative implications frightened the leaders of Christian Science, who had played an integral role in mounting her defense. An unfavorable decision from a state appellate court, after all, might have restricted the practice of Christian Science throughout Massachusetts. Unwilling to take that risk, church officials directed Sheridan to forego an appeal.[20]

The Sheridan case, happening as it did in the backyard of the Mother Church, served as a kind of wake-up call for the leaders of Christian Science. Her conviction raised the specter of further manslaughter and neglect prosecutions of church members who chose to treat their children according to the church's teachings. Christian Scientists, recoiling at the prospect of continuously defending themselves in court, resolved to carve out exemptions in state criminal codes for their religious practices. As one church attorney put it, "We don't look for litigation over individual cases. . . . Christian Scientists have too much sense to make a case, and we seek instead a recognition by the state of the validity of the doctrine through the form of exemptions."[21]

According to Rita Swan, head of the advocacy group CHILD, Christian Science leaders scored an enormous victory in this realm by successfully lobbying the federal government to change its guidelines for child protection programs. Several Christian Scientists—among them White House staffers H. R. Haldeman and John Ehrlichman—held prominent positions during the Nixon administration, and Swan has surmised that they might have exercised their influence to persuade the Department of Health, Education and Welfare (HEW) to promulgate new regulations that states were obliged to follow if they hoped to receive federal funding for child protection programs. The federal mandate (which individual states had to codify) read,

> A parent or guardian legitimately practicing his religious beliefs who thereby does not provide specified medical treatment for a child, for that reason alone shall not be considered a negligent parent or guardian; However such an exception shall not preclude a court from ordering that medical services be provided to the child, where his health requires it.

Prior to implementation of HEW's new policy, fewer than a dozen states allowed religious exemptions to civil or criminal charges. Afterward, however, most states followed Washington's lead and enacted such provisions. Even after HEW—responding largely to the Herculean efforts of Swan and her husband—rescinded its requirement in 1983, most of these exemptions remained on the books.[22]

California was among the many states that changed its child-neglect laws in the mid-1970s to reflect the new HEW mandate. The state criminal code had first addressed child neglect in 1872, after legislators enacted a statute requiring parents "to furnish necessary food, clothing, shelter, or medical attendance" to their children. Lawmakers had made a significant change to the law in 1925: parents were now obliged to provide "medical attendance or other remedial care." Whether "other remedial care" applied to spiritual-healing practices remained somewhat uncertain until 1976, when legislators more thoroughly defined the term to conform with HEW regulations. "If a parent provides a minor with treatment by spiritual means," the statute read, "through prayer alone in accordance with the tenets and practices of a recognized church or religious denomination, by a duly accredited practitioner thereof, such treatment shall constitute 'other remedial care.'" Recognizing its potential impact on the faith, the Christian Science Church organized a sophisticated and intense lobbying campaign to help ensure the law's success in the legislature.[23]

The parameters of this new law were tested in the mid-1980s by a series of Christian Science cases involving parents accused of religion-based medical neglect of children. In 1984, three children in the church in California died from bacterial meningitis. Four-year-old Shauntay Walker's death followed a disturbingly familiar pattern. Over a period of two weeks, she fell sick, weakened, failed to respond to Christian Science treatment, and died in agony—all without the benefit of medical treatment. Shortly thereafter, the district attorney in Sacramento filed felony child-endangerment and manslaughter charges against the girl's mother, Laurie Walker. As had been the case with the prosecution of Dorothy Sheridan in Massachusetts, this was an almost unprecedented step; no Christian Science parent had faced such charges in California since 1902.[24]

The decision to prosecute Laurie Walker set in motion a lengthy battle that ultimately reached the Supreme Court of California. The central issue throughout Walker's case was the precise meaning of the amendment to California's child-neglect law passed by the state legislature in 1976. Attorneys representing Walker and the Christian Science Church—a powerhouse team that included Warren Christopher, who later would serve as secretary of state under President Clinton—moved to dismiss the charges against her by arguing that the addition of language referring to "treatment by spiritual means" meant that Christian Science treatment fell into the category of "other remedial care" permitted by the statute. During oral arguments before the state's highest court, Christopher buttressed this claim by maintaining that "society has recognized the practice of Christian Science as a reasonable and acceptable alternative to conventional care." He also made a more visceral appeal to the judges, urging them not to put Laurie Walker "through the additional trauma, the additional tragedy, of [the] trial" that would follow if they failed to dismiss the charges against her. The deputy attorney general representing the state responded with a familiar argument himself, invoking the U.S. Supreme Court's opinion in *Prince v. Massachusetts*, which held that parents were not free "to make martyrs of their children."[25]

The Supreme Court of California's opinion in *Walker v. Superior Court* tackled the central issue of the case head-on, with the justices tracing the evolution of the 1976 amendment and the legislature's intent in passing it. A review of documentary materials relating to the bill's passage (including a legislative-committee staff report finding that "no exception is made under the manslaughter statutes for parental liability should the child die") made it clear that legislators had not intended to shield parents from serious criminal charges when they permitted spiritual-healing practices to be grouped under "other remedial care." The justices also analyzed the earliest cases involving religion-based medical neglect of children—those involving the Peculiar People in England in the nineteenth century—and subsequent prosecutions involving diverse faiths. A survey of these cases revealed that standards of neglect had evolved over time to include denial of medical treatment to children, regardless of the parents' religious faiths. In general, such beliefs were not compromised, the court held, if parents who treated their children's illnesses by spiritual means were charged criminally under neglect statutes. In the case at hand, Laurie Walker's right to due process of law had not been violated by what her attorneys characterized as the lack of a clear demarcation in the California criminal code between lawful and criminal prayer treatment.[26]

The high court denied Walker's motion, and the case against her was allowed to proceed. She subsequently reached a deal with prosecutors in which she pled guilty and received a characteristically lenient sentence: a term of probation, a small fine (three hundred dollars), and some community service. The agreement also compelled her to allow her surviving daughter to choose medical treatment, if that was the teenager's wish. The severity of the deal did not impress Marci Hamilton, an expert on church-state relations at the Cardozo School of Law. "Considering she permitted a child to die, the failure to sentence this mother to any jail time is troubling," Hamilton wrote, "but at least criminal liability attached to a parent's actions that culminated in the death of her child."[27]

The *Walker* ruling also cleared the way for the two other Christian Science cases that had arisen in California in 1984: the prosecutions resulting from the deaths of children named Seth Glaser and Natalie Middleton-Rippberger. Initially, Seth Glaser seemed to be suffering from a simple cold or the flu—the first symptoms of his illness were coughing, a runny nose, and sneezing—but his condition deteriorated rapidly over a period of a few days. Despite the attention of a Christian Science practitioner and periodic moments of recovery, his condition worsened dramatically over a relatively short time, and he began suffering from convulsions, vomiting, and fever. On the morning of March 28, "he didn't want to sit up, he just wanted to lie down," his mother later said. "After he ate something and when I picked him up, he would clutch at me like he had lost his balance." Seth died later that day after his parents, responding to his worsening condition, rushed him to the home of a Christian Science practitioner named Virginia Scott. Although he never saw a doctor (who might have diagnosed and treated his meningitis), his mother was convinced she and her husband, Eliot, had done all they could to save his life. "We never knowingly do anything wrong," she later said of Christian Scientists, "or withhold what a child needed."[28]

Local Christian Scientists reacted angrily when authorities in Los Angeles County charged the Glasers with child endangerment and involuntary manslaughter. An article in a newsletter published by the local church maintained that the prosecutor was guilty of "arbitrarily singling out parents because of their religious beliefs." The same piece also trotted out the familiar argument that the many failures of medical treatment rarely attracted such intense scrutiny from authorities. "The parents of hundreds of children suffering from meningitis who receive the most up-to-the-minute medical care—and yet pass on—are not similarly objects of criminal proceedings," the article stated. For local Christian Scientists, this was an infuriating double standard.[29]

At the Glasers' trial, their attorney, Douglas Dalton, did not focus his energy on portraying his clients as victims of religious persecution. Instead, falling back on an argument used by numerous spiritual healers, he claimed that there was no guarantee that medical treatment could have saved Seth. Because he first exhibited flu-like symptoms, the Glasers had been fooled by the apparently unthreatening onset of Seth's meningitis. By the time they had grasped the seriousness of their son's illness, he already was so gravely sick that it was unlikely any treatment would have preserved his life, Dalton argued. The meningitis overwhelmed the boy so rapidly that "the child could have been in the Mayo Clinic and it would not have made a bit of difference," the attorney added. Even if the Glasers had been negligent, Dalton averred, it had not contributed to their son's demise.[30]

In 1990, almost six years after their son's death (the prosecution proceeded only after the courts resolved the *Walker* case), Los Angeles County Superior Court Judge Robert Thomas acquitted the Glasers on all counts. Thomas found that there was insufficient evidence to sustain the child-endangerment and involuntary manslaughter charges against the couple. For the judge, the case turned on the brief rallies Seth had made during his illness. These promising moments, the judge believed, might have convinced the Glasers that their spiritual-healing treatments were indeed working. And if they failed to obtain medical treatment for Seth because they genuinely believed that he was recovering, there was reasonable doubt as to whether they could be held legally accountable for gross negligence in their care for him.[31]

The third Christian Science meningitis death in California came near the end of 1984. When eight-year-old Natalie Middleton-Rippberger fell sick in December of that year, her parents relied on the services of a Christian Science nurse named Therese Miller. As Miller visited the Middleton-Rippberger home over the course of several days, she saw Natalie's condition plummet despite her efforts in "voicing the truth to the baby." Apparently failing to respond to Christian Science treatment, Natalie was wracked by "what appeared to be heavy convulsions," Miller later said, and she "was very rigid, [her] eyes were really rolling back, and she appeared not responsive." The nurse urged Natalie's parents to look past these signs of distress and focus instead on "the reality of the child being healed and well through the prayers." But Natalie never healed. She died on the morning of December 9, 1984.[32]

The first doctor to inspect Natalie's body was the physician who performed her autopsy, a forensic pathologist named Dr. A. Jay Chapman. He found that Natalie had suffered from acute purulent meningitis of the brain and spinal cord. The disease had ravaged the girl's body over the period of approximately two weeks, leaving her brain swollen and softened. Chapman later said that inflammation probably had left Natalie in excruciating pain. He and another doctor who reviewed Natalie's case later reported that readily available antibiotics could have alleviated her pain and vanquished the meningitis that caused it. Dr. Michael Witwer, an expert on infectious diseases, called her case "eminently treatable" and estimated that, had she received antibiotics, she had better than a 90 percent chance of surviving her illness. Without such treatment, however, she had essentially no hope of pulling through, Witwer said.[33]

After Natalie's death, authorities in Sonoma County charged her parents, Mark Lynn Rippberger and Susan Edna Middleton, with involuntary manslaughter and felony child endangerment. With Chapman and Witwer serving as their key witnesses, prosecutors put on a relatively straightforward case at the couple's trial. The two doctors testified that Natalie probably had endured intense physical pain as the meningitis had swollen and softened her spinal cord and brain. They also stated that treatments with penicillin almost certainly would have restored the girl's health. The couple had committed neglect and manslaughter, prosecutors told jurors, by failing to take their obviously sick daughter to a physician who could have provided this treatment. The defendants countered with their own medical experts, who downplayed Natalie's suffering and disputed the idea that treatment with antibiotics would have guaranteed her recovery. Mark Rippberger took the stand as well and explained his rationale for treating his daughter's illness solely through spiritual means. He explained that, as a lifelong Christian Scientist, he never had considered providing medical treatment for his daughter.[34]

The Rippberger's attorney, David Mackenroth, complained that the charges were tantamount to "put[ting] Jesus Christ on trial for quackery." His defense, mirroring the claims of myriad other Christian Scientists who have faced criminal charges in cases of religion-based medical neglect of children, insisted that the parents' actions were safeguarded by the First Amendment and its protections for religious liberty. To buttress this argument, Mackenroth elicited testimony from Samuel Hill, a professor of religion at the University of Florida. Hill provided some context for the couple's approach to treating their daughter's illness, explaining that spiritual healing was "the hallmark" of Christian Science, and that the kind of medical treatment advocated by the prosecution's expert witnesses was "incompatible" with the church's main teachings. For Christian Scientists to pursue such treatment, Hill said, they would have to "betray [the] faith, to cut the heart out of Christian Science." The defense used Hill's testimony to support its claim that the couple's decision to treat Natalie solely through spiritual means was fundamentally a religious choice and that, as such, the First Amendment protected it.[35] Although the jury acquitted Rippberger and Middleton of manslaughter, it convicted them of neglect. The Christian Science couple then challenged their convictions in the Court of Appeal of California. The most compelling portion of the panel's ruling in *People v. Rippberger*, handed down in July of 1991, dealt with the defendants' assertion that their right to the free exercise of religion had been violated by the state. Lawyers for the couple argued that state efforts to compel medical treatment for children represented a grave threat to Christian Scientists because they would in effect force members of the church to make "an admission that illness is 'real' " and thereby forsake "the most central belief" of their faith. The appellate court disagreed, citing several relevant cases, including *Walker* and the ever-present *Prince v. Massachusetts*, to back up its holding that the child endangerment convictions should stand. "Free exercise of religion is not an absolute right and must be balanced against the rights of others, including one's children," Justice Robert Merrill wrote in his opinion for the court's majority. "It would be denigrating to the First Amendment if parents could use it as a shield to justify conduct which is life-threatening to an offspring."[36]

The California meningitis cases were among a string of prominent religion-based medical neglect prosecutions involving Christian Scientists in the late 1980s and early 1990s. In cases in Florida, Massachusetts, and Minnesota, other Christian Science parents also stood accused of manslaughter and neglect for failing to provide medical care for their sick children. These prosecutions featured familiar arguments from both sides: while prosecutors asserted that even parents who believed in the efficacy of spiritual healing were legally obligated to furnish medical care for their gravely ill children, Christian Science defendants maintained that the religious exemptions found in most state criminal codes shielded their right to treat their children in accordance with the doctrines of their religious faith. Although this line of argument rarely worked at the trial level for Christian Scientists, it proved enormously effective when appellate courts reviewed their cases, and defendants in several prominent religion-based medical neglect prosecutions had their convictions reversed. These were somewhat Pyrrhic victories for the church, however, because they called attention to religious exemptions to manslaughter and child-neglect laws and intensified the efforts of those who believed that such provisions should be eliminated.

No one disputed the basic facts of Amy Hermanson's death: the seven-year-old died in Sarasota, Florida, in 1986 after her parents chose to provide spiritual rather than medical treatment for her juvenile diabetes. (As was true in many such cases, a regimen of insulin shots probably would have saved the girl's life.) Her parents, Christian Scientists named William and Christine Hermanson, were charged with child abuse and third-degree murder for their roles in her death. "If the Hermansons wanted to make martyrs of themselves, that's fine," said the prosecutor in the case. "But they had no right to make a religious martyr of their child." The Hermansons were convicted, and they appealed to the Supreme Court of Florida. Its decision in *Hermanson v. State* focused on the apparent conflict between Florida's child-abuse and third-degree-murder statutes. Although the latter measure stated that a parent who furnished spiritual healing in lieu of medical care for a child could not be considered neglectful, the child-abuse statute contained no such exception. Parents like the Hermansons thus were left in a quandary, for adhering to their religious faith's approach to healing absolved them of criminal liability under one statute but failed to provide a defense under another. Seizing on that paradox, the state high court found that the ambiguous statutes failed to "establish a line of demarcation at which a person of common intelligence would know his or her conduct is or is not criminal." It reversed the Hermansons' convictions because "the legislature has failed to clearly indicate the point at which a parent's reliance on his or her religious beliefs in the treatment of his or her child becomes criminal conduct."[37]

The manslaughter prosecution of Christian Scientists David and Ginger Twitchell followed a similar course. The case began when the couple's two-and-a-half-year-old son, Robyn, fell victim to sickness in the spring of 1986. The Twitchells called in an experienced Christian Science practitioner named Nancy Calkins, and she treated the boy over a period of five days. Although there were some potentially ominous signs—Ginger, for instance, reported that Robyn had vomited a foul-smelling brown substance—Calkins believed that she was facilitating "a good healing." Apparently rebounding as a result of her treatments, the boy showed increased signs of vigor; his parents claimed that he rolled over on his bed and crawled after the family's cat. But Robyn's condition deteriorated on the fifth day of his illness, and he expired in his father's arms. Calkins, who watched the boy's death, did not try to revive the boy through mouth-to-mouth resuscitation or cardiopulmonary resuscitation. Instead, she prayed for a few minutes for his resurrection (a relatively common response among spiritual healers in such circumstances). The Twitchells eventually summoned paramedics to their home, but they arrived far too late to do anything for Robyn. One paramedic later testified that, by the time he arrived, the boy had been dead for at least an hour. Just by touching Robyn, he could "tell right away" that the boy was dead, the paramedic said. "Cold is cold."[38]

An autopsy revealed that Robyn Twitchell, like many victims of religion-based medical neglect, died of what one physician called "a medically correctable condition": a bowel obstruction. Dr. William Hardy Hendren, chief of pediatric surgery at Children's Hospital in Boston, later said that Robyn's bowel had twisted and then perforated over the course of several painful days. Given that Robyn had suffered from telltale symptoms of a bowel obstruction—cramps, fecal vomiting, and dehydration—Hendren surmised that a knowledgeable physician might have been able to diagnose his malady simply by speaking to his parents via telephone. Such a consultation, followed by corrective surgery, probably would have saved the boy's life. (The success rate for such procedures, Hendren said, was "nearly 100 percent.")[39]

Because he was familiar with the excruciating pain that typically accompanies bowel obstructions, Hendren scoffed at the notion that Robyn's death had come so suddenly that he had been happy and active just a few hours earlier, chasing the family cat. "In my experience, that would be totally impossible," he said. "I think that is pure fantasy." Two neighbors of the Twitchells also suggested that Robyn's battle had been prolonged and painful. The boy cried so loudly and persistently that it became "absolutely unbearable," as one put it, and they had to shut their windows to block out the chilling sound.[40]

The Twitchells were tried for manslaughter in the spring of 1990, four years after Robyn's death. Countering defense efforts to portray them as loving, caring parents, prosecutor John Kiernan told jurors that the couple had been "indifferent" to the "natural consequences of their child being desperately ill." Throughout the trial, Kiernan highlighted the sometimes gruesome details of Robyn's death to demonstrate the obvious seriousness of his illness. The boy had shown the "signs and symptoms of a dying baby," and his parents must have known that the Christian Science treatments were having no effect. By failing to act on that knowledge by pursuing the medical treatments that probably would have saved Robyn's life, Kiernan argued, the Twitchells had neglected their son and caused his death.[41]

Not surprisingly, the Twitchell's attorney portrayed them in a dramatically different light. Rikki Klieman disputed the notion that Robyn's parents had neglected him during his illness. Far from ignoring his sickness, they had done everything in their power to heal the boy, relying on the proven treatments prescribed by their religious faith. "These parents did everything that they thought was humanly possible in a method of healing that they thought was right, that they believed was proven correct and that they had seen work for three generations in their families," Klieman said. She also advanced a pair of claims frequently made by defendants in numerous spiritual-healing prosecutions. The Twitchells, she said, had been unaware of the seriousness of Robyn's illness until it was too late. And even if they had sought medical treatment for the boy, Klieman asserted, there was no guarantee that it would have preserved his life. Prosecutors could present no evidence that "the medical care would have saved this child," she said.[42]

The Twitchells' manslaughter trial was long and contentious. Both sides elicited testimony from doctors who commented on the duration and severity of Robyn's illness, and they came to radically different conclusions about whether his bowel obstruction could have been easily diagnosed and treated by medical science. The defense, for instance, produced a pediatric radiologist who testified that Robyn's bowel obstruction had resulted from a rare birth defect that doctors often have trouble detecting. (There was no small irony, of course, in Christian Scientists—diehard foes of medical treatment—using testimony from a doctor to *support* their legal claims.) Perhaps the most controversial aspect of the trial involved the prosecutor questioning David Twitchell at length about his religious beliefs. Over the protests of the Twitchells' attorney, Judge Sandra Hamlin permitted this testimony as a means of determining the reasonableness of the couple's treatment of their son. She did not intend to "litigate anyone's religion," the judge cautioned, but rather meant to probe the couple's motives in relying on spiritual treatments.[43]

In his testimony, David Twitchell did his best to explain how his adherence to Christian Science doctrines influenced his response to his son's illness. Pain, he told jurors, was not created by God; it was an illusion that could be eradicated by prayer. "[P]ain has no right to exist because God did not authorize it," he said. "Consequently, when I feel pain, I deny its right to be there. If I believe God's power is greater than it, it will be healed." He also addressed the relationship between sin and sickness. Because infants and children are typically thought of as being free from sin, this has long been an enormously difficult issue for parents who have attempted to heal their children through spiritual means and failed. As they search for answers, many parents come to believe that their own transgressions somehow triggered the illnesses that killed their children. Twitchell might have fallen into this category himself, hinting to jurors that Robyn's death perhaps resulted from his own lack of fidelity to God's word. "From a spiritual sense," he said, "I felt if I was closer to God and closer to Christ Jesus' footsteps as we always try to be, Christ Jesus wouldn't have lost this child, and I don't think I would have."[44]

The Twitchells' jury deliberated for fourteen hours before finding them guilty of manslaughter. The verdict outraged their attorney, who felt that the panel should have taken no longer than a few minutes to find them not guilty. An attorney representing the Christian Science Church was similarly dismayed by the verdict, claiming that it validated a prosecution that was an "unmitigated attempt to undermine the Christian Science way of life." David Twitchell agreed: after the verdict, he bemoaned the trial as "a prosecution against our faith." Prosecutors had no such reservations about the verdict. A triumphant John Kiernan asserted that the verdict sent an unmistakable message: "Every parent of whatever religious belief or persuasion is obligated to include medical care in taking care of his or her child."[45]

When the Twitchells appealed their convictions to the Supreme Judicial Court of Massachusetts, the central issue of their case proved to be neither religion nor parental rights. Instead, the case turned on a booklet entitled "Legal Rights and Obligations of Christian Scientists in Massachusetts," to which David Twitchell had referred during the course of Robyn's illness. That publication contained language borrowed from an opinion on Massachusetts' child-neglect law (and its apparent exemption for religious healing) issued in 1975 by the state's attorney general. Relying on that opinion (but not explicitly referring to it), the booklet stated that the criminal statute "expressly precludes imposition of criminal liability as a negligent parent for failure to provide medical care because of religious beliefs." At their trial, the Twitchells had attempted to use their reliance on the pamphlet as part of their defense, but the judge had refused to allow them to present such evidence to the jury. In a tortured opinion, the members of the Supreme Judicial Court found that while the attorney general's opinion had been misleading (it failed, for instance, to address spiritual healers' potential criminal liability for manslaughter when they failed to provide medical care to their children), the Twitchells should have been able to tell the jury about their indirect reliance on it.[46]

Although it reversed the couple's guilty verdicts, the high court's opinion in *Twitchell* hardly was an unequivocal victory for Christian Scientists. The ruling found that, despite the child-neglect statute's provisions relating to spiritual healing, state law provided "no complete protection to a parent against a charge of involuntary manslaughter that is based on the parent's wanton or reckless failure to provide medical services to a child." The *Boston Globe* recognized this silver lining. In its editorial on the *Twitchell* ruling, the paper pointed out that, whatever their religious beliefs, "parents have a legal duty to provide medical care for their children." (To eradicate any lingering confusion on this matter, legislators in Massachusetts later repealed the child-neglect law's spiritual-healing exemption.)[47]

Complications arising from spiritual-healing exemptions also thwarted the prosecution of Christian Scientists in Minnesota. After eleven-year-old Ian Lundman died from diabetes in the spring of 1989, authorities in Hennepin County, Minnesota, filed second-degree manslaughter charges against his mother and stepfather, Kathleen and William McKown, as well as the Christian Science practitioner who had unsuccessfully treated the boy during his illness, Mariano Victor Tosto. Three different courts—the last being the Supreme Court of Minnesota—ruled that the charges should be dismissed because of apparent conflicts between the state's child-neglect statute (which contained an exemption for spiritual-healing practices) and its manslaughter law (which contained no such caveat). Echoing a refrain heard in many states, all of the courts found that indicting the Christian Scientists under one law for conduct that was explicitly protected under another statute violated their right to due process of law. "The spiritual treatment and prayer exception to the child-neglect statute expressly provided [the defendants] the right to 'depend upon' Christian Science healing methods so long as they did so in good faith," the state's highest court held. "Therefore the state may not now attempt to prosecute them for exercising that right."[48]

As the criminal case against the Christian Scientists misfired, Ian Lundman's father, Douglass Lundman, hit upon a different strategy: he filed a civil suit against a host of people who allegedly had been responsible for his son's death—its targets included his former wife, her husband, practitioner Tosto, and Christian Science nurse Quinna Lamb—as well as the church itself. Because the suit would be heard in a civil court, the apparent conflict between the state's child-neglect and manslaughter statutes no longer was an issue.

Lundman's strategy was not entirely new. A few other cases of religion-based medical neglect of children also had resulted in civil actions against individual Christian Scientists and their church, but none of them had gone very far. In 1958, for instance, a California couple had filed a $350,000 civil suit against a variety of parties, including public health authorities and a Christian Scientist named Robert Czapkay, after their son contracted tubercular meningitis. Alfred Jones and his wife claimed that Czapkay, their neighbor, had contracted the disease but then had failed to observe the requisite quarantine. Because of his recklessness and the negligence of the public health authorities who were responsible for enforcing the quarantine, they argued, the disease had been communicated to their son, and he had been crippled by it. The Jones's suit sputtered to an end in 1960, when the Court of Appeal of California ruled in favor of the few remaining defendants. Decades later, Rita Swan, the founder of the advocacy group CHILD, had been involved in a more ambitious civil suit against individual practitioners of Christian Science and their church. (The case arose from the death of her son Matthew, when Swan herself had been a Christian Scientist.) But this civil action also had been unsuccessful: a trial judge had issued a summary judgment against Swan, and her appeal foundered.[49]

Undaunted by those precedents, Lundman's attorneys pressed forward with the claim that their client deserved to collect a damage award because all of the defendants had contributed to Ian's death. The defendants filed a pretrial motion to have the suit dismissed on the claim that it abridged their freedom of religion under the state constitution, but Hennepin County district court judge Sean Rice denied it. In a careful ruling, Rice acknowledged that the state constitution safeguarded the defendants' right to the free exercise of religion. Those rights, however, were not absolute, and they could be curbed in the interests of safeguarding the welfare of children. "The competing interests between [the] defendants' right to freely exercise their religion and the paramount interest of the plaintiff and the state to protect the lives of children, like Ian, appears to justify an imposition on [the] defendants' religious liberties," Rice held. The lawsuit could go forward.[50]

The defendants had been negligent, lawyer James Kaster told jurors at the civil trial, because they had ignored a series of obvious signs indicating that Ian was seriously ill and had failed to provide him with the relatively simple medical care (insulin shots) that almost certainly would have saved his life. The church itself also had been partially responsible for Ian's death because it had essentially certified Tosto and Lamb as being qualified to provide competent care. In an emotional appeal, Kaster reminded jurors who had suffered as a result of this combination of negligence and religious zeal. "This is a case of the death of an eleven-year-old boy who died for the religious beliefs of others. He had no choice," the attorney said.[51]

A small battalion of lawyers rebutted these claims at the civil trial. Kathleen McKown's attorney, Terence Fleming, asserted that she had relied on spiritual healing to treat Ian because it had proven so successful in her own life: it had cured the deafness she had experienced as a child, just as it had restored her father's sight after he had been temporarily blinded. Such experiences had left her so convinced that Christian Science worked that it would have been unimaginable for her to try another method of healing, such as medical science. Asking a doctor to care for Ian, Fleming said, "would have been unthinkable for her just as it would be for a person used to medical care to switch to prayer." He also underscored the purity of Kathleen McKown's motives, informing jurors that her "every step was motivated by love of her son."[52]

Douglass Lundman's testimony marked the emotional peak of the trial. From the witness stand, he recounted the telephone conversations he had had with his former wife during the course of his son's illness. The former Christian Scientist said he had volunteered to drive to Minneapolis from his home in Kansas in order to help monitor Ian's condition, but Kathleen McKown had assured him that the boy was recovering. Lundman told jurors that he deeply regretted having stayed home; if he had been on hand, he might have recognized the seriousness of Ian's condition and taken him to a doctor. In a poignant moment, he confessed that he probably bore some of the responsibility for the boy's death. "I was Ian's father," Lundman said. "I should have found a way to learn the circumstances. I should have prevented it."[53]

On August 18, 1993, a jury awarded Lundman $5.2 million in compensatory damages. The panel assigned degrees of responsibility to the defendants that ranged from 25 percent (Kathleen McKown) to 5 percent (Quinna Lamb). A court-imposed gag order prevented all parties from immediately commenting on the verdict, but the state's largest newspaper quickly weighed in with an editorial applauding it as a means of warning parents that, whatever their religious beliefs, they were responsible for safeguarding the welfare of their children. "[M]oney has been known to talk, and the message in this verdict is hard to miss," the *Minneapolis Star Tribune* posited. "It tells parents that religious freedom doesn't entitle them to deny medicine to an ailing youngster.

It warns that, when a child's life is at stake, no one is free to shrug off science in favor of faith."[54]

For the punitive damages phase of the case, Lundman chose to proceed only against the Christian Science Church (which already had been ordered to pay 10 percent of the compensatory damage award). Kaster told jurors that Lundman had one goal in mind when he filed his civil suit: he hoped to prevent other innocent children from suffering as Ian had. "If you want to establish change," he said, "it's by [assessing] punitive damages against the church," the institution "that sets the policies, that gets involved in the serious illness of a child." The church's attorney argued that it was being targeted for a far less noble reason: among the defendants, it obviously had the deepest pockets. In addition to impugning Lundman's motives, William Christopher claimed that it was unfair to pin the blame for Ian's death on devout people who simply had been following the teachings of their religious faith—a faith that had healed thousands of afflicted souls over the previous century. "The defendants honestly believed what they were doing for Ian was the best they [could do]," Christopher said. "They believed what they were doing was effective."[55]

In the punitive damages phase of the case, jurors struggled to decide upon an award that would appropriately punish the church for its role in Ian's death and also send a message to society about the duty of institutions to protect the welfare of children. After deliberating more than seven hours, the panel settled on a $9.15 million award—reportedly the largest such judgment ever granted in a civil case involving religion-based medical neglect of children. Jurors later told reporters that throughout the civil case, they tried to downplay its religious dimension and focus instead on matters like children's welfare and parental responsibility. "This wasn't a case based on religion. It was about health care, the protection of children and the rights of children," one juror said. "The rights of children need to be protected."[56]

But Douglass Lundman ultimately could hope to collect only a fraction of the more than $14 million in compensatory and punitive damages awarded to him by the jury. First, a district court judge whittled the compensatory damage award down to $1.5 million. (The original amount, he ruled, was not in line with awards in other wrongful-death cases in Minnesota.) Then, in the spring of 1995, the Court of Appeals of Minnesota struck down the entire punitive damage award and the church's share of the compensatory damage award (which together totaled over $9 million). The court found that the imposition of such awards against a church violated its right—protected by both the state and federal constitutions—to promote religious faith and doctrine. In refuting the argument that the church bore responsibility for the actions of those who followed its teachings, Judge Jack Davies asserted,

A church is not a lawn-mower manufacturer that can be found negligent in a products liability case for failing to affix a warning sticker near the blades.... [T]he constitutional right to religious freedom includes the authority of churches—not courts—to independently decide matters of faith and doctrine, and for a church as an institution to believe and speak what it will. When it comes to restraining religious conduct, it is the obligation of the state, not a church and its agents, to impose and communicate the necessary limitations—the warning sticker. A church always remains free to espouse whatever religious belief it chooses; it is the practices of its adherents that may be subject to state sanctions.

But while the court essentially absolved the church of liability, it let stand what remained of the compensatory damage award. Because "religious freedom ends when one's conduct offends the law by, for example, endangering a child's life," the four Christian Scientists who had most closely directed Ian's care still owed Douglas Lundman $1.5 million.[57]

The remaining defendants mounted an appeal to the U.S. Supreme Court, claiming that the importance of the case to Christian Scientists "can scarcely be overstated." Members of other faiths apparently cared about it as well: religious bodies ranging from the Roman Catholic Archdiocese of St. Paul and Minneapolis to the National Association of Evangelicals filed amicus curiae briefs recommending the high court hear the case. These entreaties failed to persuade the Supreme Court, however, and it refused to take the appeal.[58]

Although the outcome of the *Lundman* civil case could have been worse for Christian Scientists from a monetary standpoint, some observers argued that their church nonetheless had suffered serious harm. Church spokesmen lamented the fact that members of their faith might now face a barrage of civil suits simply because they chose to adhere to a central tenet of their church's doctrines and treat their children's illnesses through spiritual means. Protests came from outside the faith as well: Yale Law School's Stephen Carter expressed dismay that Americans who exercised their religious liberty were being forced to pay "ruinous damages." As he lamented the Supreme Court's refusal to hear the Christian Scientists' appeal, Carter—echoing arguments made by the Freethinkers who had defended the Peculiar People more than a century earlier—highlighted a paradox in societal views toward prayer. He accused the justices of "reinfor[cing] a societal message that has grown increasingly common: It is perfectly O.K. to believe in the power of prayer, so long as one does not believe in it so sincerely that one actually expects it to work—a peculiar fate indeed for our 'most inalienable right,' " religious liberty.[59]

Carter's complaint underscored a profound challenge confronting Christian Scientists at the turn of the twenty-first century. From the outset, Christian Science—perhaps more than any other Protestant church—had staked its legitimacy on its promise to effect healing (or, as church members themselves would put it, its promise to help individuals return to full health by eliminating the illusion of their illnesses). Save for such routine mechanical matters as setting bones and caring for teeth, doctors were to play no part in this process of physical restoration for church members. But, in the last third of the twentieth century, these core claims increasingly were cast into doubt by the accusations leveled at church members implicated in cases of religion-based medical neglect of children. In the church's formative era, the impact of such charges had been mitigated somewhat by lingering doubts regarding the reliability of the still-emerging therapies being offered by physicians. A century later, with such questions about the value of medical science essentially mooted in public consciousness, Christian Scientists struggled to refute legal charges that challenged the very foundations of their faith.

Their defenses increasingly were narrow and legalistic claims grounded in the alleged vagueness of criminal laws rather than bold arguments based on the purported sacredness and practical value of their religious practices. For all its expediency as a legal strategy, this approach had significant drawbacks for a church already battling a steady decline, both in terms of membership and public stature. Legal disputes such as the *Lundman* case challenged the legitimacy of Christian Science in a very public forum, the court system. In the late nineteenth and early twentieth centuries, church members had used this stage to their advantage, making forceful claims in court (and behind the scenes, in the halls of state legislatures) that gave a patina of credibility to their church's doctrines. Later manslaughter and neglect cases involving Christian Scientists had precisely the opposite effect: by juxtaposing the uncertainty of prayer as a means of healing with the growing reliability of medical science, they seemed to fundamentally—and very visibly—undercut the church's main ideological underpinnings.

7

"Nightmare Would Not
Be Too Strong a Term"

Life and Death in the Faith Tabernacle

The measles virus incubates within its victims for approximately a dozen days before its symptoms begin to manifest themselves. The first sign of the malady usually is a fever that rises incrementally and peaks as high as 103 to 105 degrees Fahrenheit. Victims then suffer a cough, runny nose, and sometimes conjunctivitis (pink eye) before the virus's trademark symptom, a rash, develops. Lesions first take form along the hairline, then creep down the body and outward until finally reaching the hands and feet. After roughly a week, the rash begins to disappear just as it has spread, with the extremities clearing up last.[1]

Although they are uncomfortable, the fever and rash that accompany measles generally are not life threatening. Approximately a third of measles victims, however, develop complications from the virus that can imperil their lives. These range from the comparatively innocuous (diarrhea, for instance) to the deadly. About six percent of those afflicted with measles develop pneumonia, which causes about two out of every three deaths associated with the virus. Among adults, acute encephalitis (the inflammation of brain tissues) is another potentially lethal complication.[2]

Accounts of the fatal consequences of the measles date back at least as far as the seventh century. Rhazes, the famed Persian physician and philosopher, highlighted the virulence of the virus by writing that it was "more dreaded than smallpox." For centuries thereafter, the virus afflicted adults and children living in every corner of the globe. Before 1963, between three and four million cases of the measles—several thousand of them resulting in deaths—were reported every year in the United States alone. Up to that point, about half of all American children suffered from the measles before they reached age six, and more than 90 percent experienced it before age fifteen.[3]

The introduction of a measles vaccine in 1963 caused the number of measles cases in the United States to plummet dramatically. Over the course of the next few years, as researchers tinkered with strains and doses, the number of reported cases dropped by a staggering 98 percent. After the virus made a brief comeback in the late 1970s, a national effort called the Measles Elimination Program endeavored to completely eliminate transmission of it by 1982. This goal was not reached, but by the late 1990s there were fewer than one hundred cases reported annually in the United States (and about half of these typically were acquired by children when they traveled outside the country). What three experts have described as "the remarkable impact of immunization on measles transmission in the United States" raised hopes for the worldwide eradication of the disease.[4]

In the United States, however, one group of children has remained at risk of contracting the measles virus: youngsters who never receive vaccinations. State laws mandating vaccinations have a long history, and the U.S. Supreme Court upheld their constitutionality more than a century ago, in *Jacobson v. Massachusetts* (1905). Yet all state immunization statutes contain exemptions for medical reasons (such as the likelihood that a child will have a severe allergic reaction to the components of a vaccine), and more than a dozen permit exemptions based on parents' philosophical or personal beliefs. Moreover, all but two states (Mississippi and West Virginia) allow parents to forego vaccinations for their children on the grounds that receiving such preventive medical treatment would violate the tenets of their religious faith. (Members of some churches believe that immunizations render the blood "unclean" in a manner prohibited by the Bible.) Some states require parents seeking the religious exemption to submit a personal affidavit explaining their opposition to vaccinations; others require a bit more documentation, such as a letter from a church leader.[5]

Not surprisingly, children exempted from vaccination laws for religious reasons are particularly vulnerable to the measles. Recent studies have shown that they are exponentially more likely to contract the potentially deadly virus than those who have received the vaccine. A study of religious exemptors in Colorado found that they were twenty-two times more likely to acquire the measles, and a similar study found the risk to be thirty-five times greater. Such vulnerability poses a threat not only to the unvaccinated children themselves but also to their vaccinated friends and classmates, who are not rendered totally immune to the disease by the vaccine. As one study flatly put it, religious exemptors "put vaccinated children at risk of acquiring measles."[6]

A measles outbreak in Philadelphia in 1991 demonstrated the lethal consequences of religious exemptions to immunization laws. Over a period of several harrowing weeks, the virus swept through the Faith Tabernacle, a small church with a long history of withholding medical care from children on the basis of religious conviction. More than 120 children in the church fell sick in the outbreak, and five of them died. City public health authorities had not contended with such a deadly outbreak in decades, and it left them aghast. "This is very bad. I think nightmare would not be too strong a term," one official said, acknowledging the difficulty of containing the virus among a group of people who spurned medical treatment.[7]

The toll from the measles outbreak in Philadelphia might have been worse if public health and law enforcement authorities had not taken extraordinary steps to curb the spread of the virus. Acting under the aegis of the city health commissioner, a team of doctors drawn from area hospitals made dozens of visits to Faith Tabernacle homes and identified children requiring immediate medical attention. If parents refused to permit their sick children to be admitted to a hospital, the city sought court orders compelling treatment. In order to stop the spread of the outbreak, city officials also asked judges to mandate measles immunizations for several Faith Tabernacle children. Although church members and some local civil-liberties groups protested that the city's actions violated the First Amendment's protections of religious liberty, Mayor W. Wilson Goode felt that he had little choice but to take dramatic action to halt the spread of the virus and save lives. "We recognize that this a First Amendment issue which must be balanced with public health concerns," Goode said. "We are prepared, however, to ask the court to intervene in the lives of at-risk children."[8]

It was neither the first nor the last time that members of the Faith Tabernacle would be involved in a clash with state officials over their healing practices. Although their losses have not been as widely documented as those of Christian Scientists, dozens of children in the church have died in the absence of medical care since its founding late in the nineteenth century. Many of these deaths have gone unnoticed by the world outside the church's insular community, but a few of them—such as the demise of Michael Heilman, the hemophilic toddler who bled to death after cutting his foot in his family's backyard—have resulted in the prosecution of parents for neglect or manslaughter. These cases, like the measles outbreak, have shown not only the tragic consequences of faith-based refusals of medical treatment but also the remarkable intransigence of parents who choose prayer over medicine. One Faith Tabernacle family, for instance, lost six small children to illness, and none of them received medical treatment before dying. The abysmal record of spiritual healing in his own family did not seem to faze the father: after the last child died, he told a reporter, "When you believe in something, you have to believe in it all the way."[9]

From the era of the Peculiar People to the present day, one tragic irony of religion-based medical neglect cases has been that the prosecution of parents under criminal statutes often can do nothing to help their alleged victims. (In the worst instances, many of them die long before their parents actually make it to court.) Although this occurred in many Faith Tabernacle cases, in other instances officials managed to intervene in time to prevent children in the church from suffering serious physical harm or even death. In the 1930s and again during the 1991 measles outbreak, authorities did not simply wait to prosecute church parents after their children died from illness. Instead, they were proactive, initiating legal actions designed to preserve the lives of ailing children by mandating medical treatment. As also would be the case roughly a decade later with a separate faith-healing sect in New England known as The Body, these preventive measures proved to be a legally controversial but effective means of combating religion-based medical neglect.

The Faith Tabernacle has eight branches in the United States and several outposts in such far-off lands as Sri Lanka and India. Church members are most heavily concentrated in Pennsylvania, where there are seven branches, including the main church, a modest building that stands on the corner of Fifth and Erie streets in Philadelphia. The families that file into the "home station," as it is called, have been called "urban Amish" by one wry observer because the church community is extraordinarily close-knit. Faith Tabernacle members tend to marry within their faith, and their children often attend church-run schools that are permeated with the teachings of the scriptures. ("What else is there to go by?" one church member pointed out. "Anything else is a false foundation. It's gonna crumble.") Children in the church are taught to adhere to traditional gender roles: husbands work and exercise unquestioned authority over their families, while wives stay home and submit.[10]

Nineteen articles of belief guide the church, which was founded in the 1890s. Most of these, including the article on healing, are based in narrowly literal interpretations of the scriptures. Faith Tabernacle members believe that Christ will "heal our bodies from sickness and disease" after they submit to the rite of prayer and anointment with oil described in the Epistle of James. This method, they believe, renders physicians unnecessary. Moreover, the scriptures prohibit such treatment: "[W]e believe the Bible is opposed to all means of healing apart from God's way . . . and all medical and surgical practice whatever." A church pamphlet entitled "How to Receive Perfect Healing" points out that adhering to the lessons of the Bible when illness strikes can be a challenge, because Satan "usually makes our symptoms worse and tries to persuade us to turn back from the Lord. But if we are steadfast . . . victory is sure."[11]

The church's approach to illness, particularly as it relates to the welfare of children, periodically has attracted the interest and concern of public authorities. In the early 1930s, for instance, cases involving two ailing Faith Tabernacle children garnered widespread attention when their parents resisted state efforts to compel their medical treatment. In the first case, authorities in New York intervened to protect a child named Helen Vasko, who suffered from a malignant growth in one of her eyes. Eager to "let God have His way," as one of them put it, the girl's parents held fast to the tenets of their faith, refusing to authorize the surgery that was necessary to prevent the growth from spreading to Helen's brain and killing her. In one of the first cases of its kind in New York, state authorities sought to override the parents' religious objections and compel medical treatment for the child. A state appeals court sided with the state, and doctors performed the necessary surgery. Underscoring the extraordinary circumstances of the case, a later court pointed to *Vasko* as an illustration of "the extreme to which a court will go in the interests of a child."[12]

On the heels of the Vasko imbroglio came the 1934 case of John Hoffman, Jr., a sixteen-year-old from Philadelphia whose parents also belonged to the Faith Tabernacle. A tubercular infection developed in one of Hoffman's legs after he broke it, but his parents refused to treat it with anything other than prayer over a period of a year. John Hoffman, Sr., adamantly expressed his opposition to surgery, at one point insisting, "It isn't right to take matters like this out of God's hands." A Philadelphia children's welfare organization disagreed and sought a court order mandating surgery for the youngster's leg. When the case came before a local judge named Theodore Rosen, the elder Hoffman sparred with him over the efficacy of medical science and the constitutionality of state efforts to regulate his religious practices.[13]

"My chance with the living God is as good as your chance with the physicians," he fumed at Rosen. "The responsibility is not on me. The boy and myself have a legal right under the law of this land to act according to our conscience."

"But your boy has a right to health and a straight body, too," Rosen responded.

"There's only one thing involved here—that's God," Hoffman insisted.[14]

This colloquy failed to persuade the judge, and he ordered the surgery for the teenager. A distraught John Hoffman, Sr., accompanied his child to the hospital and bemoaned Rosen's decision, claiming that the operation was simply "against God's will." (He also had a warning for those who were to perform the surgery: "Any man who lays hand or knife on my boy does so at his own peril. It is a defiance of God.") Other observers of the case had a more favorable view of Rosen's decision. A Philadelphia newspaper praised the judge for both his legal reasoning and his fairness in dealing with the somewhat temperamental Hoffman. The paper, reflecting a general public consensus on the need to balance religious liberty against children's welfare, editorialized, "It is not a strained interpretation of the principle of law to assume that the State may intervene in the child's welfare as against a purpose of the parent which is sincere and in concern for the child, but which the Court may determine on the evidence and advice of science to be a fallacy." Such assessments seemed all the more valid after the successful surgery on the younger Hoffman's leg, in which doctors removed several inches of bone that had decayed as a result of the infection.[15]

Not all cases of religion-based medical neglect of children in the Faith Tabernacle concluded so happily. All too often, authorities learned that young-sters in the church had been denied medical treatment only after it was too late to save their lives. Justin Barnhart's death—and his parents' subsequent prosecution—typified these grim cases. In the summer of 1981, the two-year-old's mother and father detected a small lump in his abdomen. The mass grew over the summer, leaving the boy's midsection "quite large and distended," according to one account. Neither of Justin's parents, William and Linda Barnhart, ever had been treated by a doctor, and they determined that there was only one way to shrink the growth—through prayer and anointment, as pre-scribed by the Epistle of James. In keeping with that mandate from the scriptures, Justin was anointed several times, both at church and at home, and church members prayed fervently for him throughout his illness.[16]

The Barnharts' decision to rely on spiritual healing for Justin had nothing to do with money. William Barnhart was a state employee and thus was eligible for health insurance. "I could take Justin to the finest hospital in the country," he explained, "and it wouldn't cost me nothing." But, through the experiences of members of his own family, Barnhart had seen how powerful a force prayer could be. His father had been an alcoholic who had seemed destined to drink himself to death until he found the Faith Tabernacle. With the church's help, he sobered up and lived a happy, productive life. His father's physical and spiritual rehabilitation had convinced Barnhart to "never doubt" the healing power of prayer. His commitment to prayer was only reinforced when his son Bill (Justin's brother) fell ill. During the course of his sickness, Bill turned pallid, and all of his hair fell out. By following the teachings of the Epistle of James, the elder Barnhart helped to restore Bill's health. He expected that pro-viding the same treatment for Justin would produce similarly positive results.[17]

Justin's summer-long illness left him emaciated. "His arms and legs were so thin as to outline the shape and markings of his bones," according to one account. "His skin was just hanging loose." The boy died on September 10, 1981. An autopsy revealed that the growth in the boy's abdomen was a Wilms' tumor, a cancerous growth that had originated in his left kidney and metas-tasized to his lungs and lymph nodes. The pathologist who performed the autopsy found that Justin essentially had starved to death because of the enormous tumor, which measured a little more than twenty-one inches in diameter (about the size of a volleyball) and weighed more than five pounds. The tumor—which the pathologist described as "the largest single structure in

Justin's body"—had absorbed the bulk of the nourishment the boy had received each day. To make matters worse, the growth had so compressed and obstructed Justin's intestines that they could not deliver the little remaining nourishment to his organs. In short, as the tumor had ballooned inside Justin, it had more or less starved his increasingly frail body.[18]

Prompt medical treatment probably could have saved Justin's life. According to the National Cancer Institute, "Wilms' tumor is curable in the majority of affected children." When doctors detect it early enough, the malady can be treated with a combination of surgery, chemotherapy, and radiation therapy, provided that a patient has a favorable histology. (More than 90 percent of patients fall into this category.) A physician who reviewed Justin's case asserted that if the boy had received appropriate medical treatment when the tumor first had been discovered, he would have had a 90 percent chance of surviving. Dr. Giulio D'Angio said that Justin even might have survived if he had been taken to a hospital and received treatment on the day of his death.[19]

Because Justin apparently could have been saved by medical treatment, the coroner of Cambria County, Pennsylvania, conducted an inquest into the circumstances of his death. In his testimony, William Barnhart acknowledged that the couple had "realized [Justin] was going downhill" because his deteriorating condition had reminded them of a young neighbor's unsuccessful battle against leukemia. Yet Barnhart made no apologies for his decision to treat his son's illness solely through prayer and anointment. When he was asked if he still believed in the efficacy of spiritual healing, Barnhart replied, "I do, a hundred percent. And if the good Lord don't change my mind or I don't change it or something else, I intend to leave this earth that way." After hearing from Barnhart and other witnesses, the coroner's jury unanimously recommended that further legal proceedings be conducted against Justin's parents. The combined efforts of the coroner, the state police, and the district attorney eventually resulted in the filing of involuntary manslaughter and child-endangerment charges against both Barnhart and his wife. The state claimed that the couple had caused Justin's death by their "failure and omission to provide ordinary expert medical treatment for [his] apparent ailments."[20]

At their trial, the Barnharts attempted to explain how their conduct had been shaped by their religious beliefs—beliefs that were protected by both the federal and state constitutions. Testifying about his adherence to the teachings of the Epistle of James, William Barnhart stated, "In my belief, I know no other way . . . and if I would go to a doctor, I would be turning my back on my faith." A leader of their local church made much the same point. In his testimony for the defense, Charles Nixon pointed out that members of the Faith Tabernacle would not forsake their spiritual well-being for the blind pursuit of physical relief. "We would consider going to a doctor and trusting in medicine doing greater harm," Nixon said, "because . . . it would be harming the spiritual and eternal interest of the child and parents as well in doing so."[21]

Many parents accused of religion-based medical neglect are forced to explain why their purported abhorrence of medical treatment has not prevented them from seeking treatments from a dentist. A great deal of testimony in the manslaughter trial of Massachusetts Christian Scientists David and Ginger Twitchell, for instance, was devoted to the former's seemingly incongruous decision to receive dental treatment. (Twitchell, like many spiritual healers, explained that dentists were acceptable because they do not purport to "heal" teeth; they merely perform mechanical functions such as filling cavities.) This issue cropped up at the Barnharts' trial and seemed to undercut their claim that they relied solely on prayer and anointment for healing. "Although they profess not to believe in professional medical help," assistant district attorney Patrick Kiniry noted, "both Mr. and Mrs. Barnhart have gone to a licensed dentist on many occasions, and Mr. Barnhart admitted to receiving novocaine for some dental procedures." As has often happened in faith-based neglect trials, the prosecutor's strategy of highlighting their reliance on dentists was intended to undermine the Barnharts' credibility by making them seem inconsistent, if not hypocritical.[22]

When it came time for the jurors to deliberate, they received a lengthy charge from the trial judge, H. Clifton McWilliams, Jr. As he attempted to focus the panel's attention on the legal questions at issue, the judge did his best to downplay the religious dimension of the case. "Now, this case is really not a question of Christian faith or the efficacy of prayer," Judge McWilliams said. "It is whether the parents of Justin failed to seek medical attention for a seriously ill child and that that failure caused his death." After outlining this broad framework, the judge described the elements of the charges that the state had leveled at the Barnharts. The key to the manslaughter charge, as McWilliams described it, was its third element. For the jury to find the couple guilty, it would have to find that their failure to furnish medical treatment to Justin "was done in a reckless or grossly negligent manner," the judge said. "This means that the defendants were aware and conscientiously disregarded a substantial and unjustifiable risk that death would result from their conduct, or that they should have been aware of such a risk." Judge McWilliams instructed the jurors to "use your good common sense" when considering such questions in their deliberations.[23]

After the jury found the Barnharts guilty of both manslaughter and child endangerment, their attorneys, Fremont McKendrick and Bruce McKendrick, filed motions asking the judge for a new trial. They objected to his charge to the jury, saying that it had essentially strait-jacketed the panel into returning guilty verdicts, and to the prosecution's use of a red rubber ball to demonstrate the size of the tumor that had killed Justin. The Barnharts' attorneys also claimed that the verdict, by punishing the couple for following the tenets of their faith, represented an infringement on their religious liberty. McWilliams brushed aside these objections and let the verdicts stand. "All rights," he said, "have limitations."[24]

Like most parents who have been convicted of crimes associated with religion-based medical neglect of children, the Barnharts were sentenced to probation (fifty-nine months for William, twenty-three for Linda). Despite the relative leniency of their sentences, they appealed their convictions to the Superior Court of Pennsylvania. On appeal, the couple's attorneys sought review of the trial judge's rulings on their earlier motion for a new trial, criticizing the judge's charge to the jury as well as claiming that the charges were vague and violated their religious liberty. They also attacked the cornerstone of the prosecution's case: its claim that Justin had died as a result of his parents' inaction. In making this argument, the Barnharts' attorneys pointed out that the prosecution's own expert had testified that as many as 10 percent of Wilms' tumor patients die even after they receive state-of-the-art medical treatment. If Justin had been part of this hopeless 10 percent, the attorneys insisted, his parents' behavior could not have contributed to his death; he would have died regardless of what they did or failed to do. The state countered these claims by citing myriad appellate court decisions in similar cases, including *People v. Pierson* and the oft-quoted *Prince v. Massachusetts* (with its admonition that parents are not free "to make martyrs of their children").[25]

The Superior Court followed the state's lead and upheld the Barnharts' convictions. A workmanlike analysis of the case's primary legal issues, the court's opinion in *Commonwealth v. Barnhart* lacked much in the way of soaring rhetoric. It did include, however, a poignant aside on the difficulties posed by cases of religion-based medical neglect. "Our decision today directly penalizes [the Barnharts'] exercise of their religious beliefs," the judges held. "They ask how we can hold them criminally liable for putting their faith in God. No easy answer attends."[26]

Although Justin Barnhart's death and his parents' later prosecution for their roles in it attracted relatively little public attention, print and broadcast media extensively covered subsequent incidents involving the church's healing practices. The church made national headlines in 1991, for instance, when public officials in Philadelphia intervened after a measles outbreak focused public attention on how spiritual healers' resistance to preventive and therapeutic medical treatments could endanger not only their own children but also youngsters outside their church community.

Children in the Faith Tabernacle in Philadelphia apparently started falling victim to the measles in November 1990, when the city experienced an overall spike in cases of the virus. Because none of them had been immunized (Pennsylvania is one of the many states that permits religious exemptions to such preventive health measures), the virus quickly spread through the roughly 150 pupils enrolled at the church's Philadelphia school. According to a study later published in the *Pediatric Infectious Disease Journal*, the lack of immunizations left those students and their fellow young church members particularly vulnerable: compared to children from groups that were immunized, youngsters in the Faith Tabernacle were roughly one thousand times more likely to contract the measles during the Philadelphia outbreak. They also were, according to the study, roughly four times more likely to die from the virus once they had caught it.[27]

By early the following February, two girls in the church had fallen seriously ill. Nine-year-old Karyn Still became so sick with the measles that she vomited repeatedly over the course of several days, but her parents, following the Faith Tabernacle's interpretation of the scriptures, did not attempt to provide medical care for her. Monica Johnson exhibited similarly dire symptoms, gasping for air and going limp, but the nine-year-old's parents also refused to take her to a doctor. The girls died within a few days of each other in the second week of February. Karyn Still's death hit her parents hard, according to a neighbor who watched as the girl's lifeless body was wheeled from her family's home. "I saw their faces when the rescue service got here for Karyn," the neighbor said, "and they were so distraught, they were just out of their minds."[28]

Eager to stop the spread of the virus, which already had infected a majority of the school's pupils, city public health officials urged the church to temporarily close its school. "Right now," said Robert Ross, the city's deputy health commissioner, "we have to get this thing controlled." The church agreed to suspend classes at the school, but its leaders balked at the city's suggestion that all youngsters in the church receive measles immunizations. According to one public health official, a member of the church said "immunization was against their religious beliefs."[29]

Although they encountered resistance from the church, public health officials in Philadelphia organized an unprecedented effort to canvass Faith Tabernacle families and determine if any of their children were seriously ill from the measles. Teams of doctors from St. Christopher's Hospital for Children and Children's Hospital of Philadelphia telephoned and then visited the homes of dozens of families with children enrolled in the school. The house calls were unlike anything the physicians previously had experienced. Most of the parents, citing their religious opposition to medical care, initially would not permit the doctors to touch their children, making it impossible for them to conduct thorough physical examinations. As they tried to determine if any of the children were seriously ill and in need of immediate medical care, the doctors were limited at first to simply looking at the sick youngsters.

The physicians met with varying degrees of cooperation as they visited the Faith Tabernacle homes. One later said that he had found the parents to be, on the whole, "extremely courteous and caring and honest." But Deputy Health Commissioner Robert Ross had an entirely different experience when he entered the home of a grandmother who was caring for a half dozen children, two of whom had fallen sick with the measles. The condition of one of the ailing youngsters stunned Ross: she was pallid, and she struggled to breathe. "She was propped up on some pillows in front of the TV, but she was not watching TV," Ross recalled. "She was dying." Convinced that the girl's life was in jeopardy, Ross searched for a telephone so that he could summon emergency medical technicians and have her transported to a hospital. The diminutive grandmother—"who couldn't have been more than five feet tall and 90 pounds," Ross later said—so opposed this course of action that she tried to physically restrain the strapping health official from using the phone. This effort failed to prevent Ross from dialing 911, and the girl was transported to a nearby hospital, where she received treatment for bilateral pneumonia and dehydration. Ross believed that this basic treatment—the girl received antibiotics and intravenous fluids—saved the youngster's life, but members of her family treated him coldly when he monitored her progress at the hospital. He later said that they "clearly [were] resentful of my interference," even though his meddling almost surely had saved the girl's life.[30]

Despite such efforts, public health authorities struggled to determine the extent of the measles outbreak and the severity of victims' illnesses. Part of the problem was that some Faith Tabernacle parents were, as one Philadelphia newspaper put, "less than candid in describing their children's health" to Ross and his colleagues. This lack of candor apparently prevented authorities from intervening on behalf of fourteen-year-old Linnette Milnes, whose sister attended the Faith Tabernacle school. When Ross called the Milnes home, a family member informed him that there was no cause for alarm: two children had contracted the virus, but they were in good condition. This was not true: Linnette died from the virus shortly thereafter. (When authorities asked her father about how his religious beliefs influenced his treatment of the girl, "We told them we don't believe in taking anything," he later said.) The girl's death nettled Ross, who publicly expressed his concern "that the information we're getting by phone may not be completely accurate." Fearing that parents were not being completely forthcoming, public health authorities stepped up their efforts, endeavoring to visit every home associated with the Faith Tabernacle and its school.[31]

By the middle of February, the measles outbreak in Philadelphia had become so serious that the Centers for Disease Control (CDC) dispatched two epidemiologists to assist the city with its investigation. The death toll reached five when two girls succumbed to the virus on February 15. One of the two new victims was thirteen-year-old Tina Louise Johnson, whose sister Monica had died just days earlier. Wayne Johnson was distraught after losing two of his children to the virus, but he refused to repudiate his religious beliefs. "We strongly believe in our faith," he said of his family, "and we love our children dearly." A few weeks later, *Philadelphia Inquirer* columnist Steve Lopez visited

Johnson and asked him if his girls' deaths had shaken his faith. Despite the enormity of his loss, Johnson reiterated his belief "that only God heals," Lopez recounted, "that his daughters are safe in God's care, and God took them to strengthen their family's own faith."[32]

The city's district attorney, Ronald D. Castille, doubted that much good would come from prosecuting Wayne Johnson or any of the other Faith Tabernacle parents who had lost children in the measles outbreak. "Unfortunately," he said, "when a parent is willing to risk the death of their children because of their religious beliefs, it is unlikely that the threat of prosecution would in any way act as a deterrent to these families." But as the outbreak worsened, Castille and Mayor W. Wilson Goode signaled that they would seek court orders compelling medical treatment for seriously ill Faith Tabernacle children. Goode announced that while the city intended to respect the religious beliefs of church members, authorities had a duty to both protect the welfare of sick children and prevent other youngsters from becoming ill.[33]

The city made good on these threats on February 17. Over the preceding few days, public health officials had stepped up their efforts to visit the homes of families belonging to the Faith Tabernacle and the First Century Gospel Church (whose members also were affected by the measles outbreak). During this extensive canvass, doctors identified ten measles cases that they deemed serious enough to warrant daily follow-up visits. A youngster named Daniel Kirn was in such dire condition that the physician who examined him determined that he needed immediate hospitalization. When his parents balked, citing their religious faith, the physician contacted the city solicitor, and she in turn obtained a court order mandating the child's removal and hospitalization. That same day, city officials obtained a similar court order for a nineteen-month-old girl who had fallen victim to the virus. (She recovered relatively quickly and was released from the hospital within a few days.)[34]

After city officials obtained court orders to compel medical treatment for two more Faith Tabernacle children, Charles Reinert, one of the church's leaders, made his first extensive public comments on the measles outbreak. Critics might have seen the tally of the epidemic—up to that point, it stood at four deaths and four court-ordered hospitalizations—as reflecting poorly on the church's reliance on spiritual healing. But Reinert stressed the overall success of the church's efforts at restoring health, pointing out that hundreds of children had weathered the epidemic, with many having "recovered and been raised up" thanks to prayer. As a result, he said, "We believe God has proved his faithfulness." Reinert regretted the deaths of the four children, but he pointed out that the tragedy had drawn members of the church more closely together. (They reached out to one another by helping to cover funeral expenses, for instance.)[35]

City officials had a considerably less sanguine view of the outbreak, and they continued to pursue legal actions designed to stem its spread. To protect the handful of Faith Tabernacle children who had not been exposed to the virus, authorities debated a plan to obtain court orders mandating immunizations for the youngsters. Reflecting public health and law enforcement officials' sensitivity to church members' potential objections, discussion of this unprecedented scheme involved medical ethicists as well as city, state, and federal representatives. "Obviously the children are the priority," Robert Ross said, "but we want to make sure if we do something it is the right thing." In the end, the city asked family court judge Edward R. Summers to order vaccinations for six Faith Tabernacle children.[36]

Experts in the fields of public health, constitutional law, and bioethics were divided over whether the city's request should be granted. Underscoring the unusual nature of the city's efforts to compel inoculations among children in the Faith Tabernacle, a medical epidemiologist at the CDC remarked that he was unaware of any recent cases of forced immunizations involving members of any religious faith. Although the city's actions were unprecedented, Dr. Arthur Caplan, a biomedical ethicist at the University of Minnesota, favored them as a means of protecting the health of children in the church community and throughout Philadelphia. But Caplan predicted that the courts would balk at compelling inoculations because judges "have generally been reluctant to intervene when the stakes do not clearly involve death." Kathleen Sullivan, then a professor at Harvard Law School (and later dean of Stanford Law School), disagreed, arguing that the state generally had a right to step in whenever there was a danger of imminent physical harm.[37]

To the horror of local civil libertarians, Judge Summers issued a much broader order than the city had requested. In addition to mandating the inoculations, the judge ordered that all preschool children in the Faith Tabernacle congregation receive monthly medical examinations and that the school operated by the church report student absences lasting longer than three days to the city's human services department. According to a lawyer involved in the case, Summers also instructed the city "to locate any church that believes only in faith healing." A representative of the Philadelphia chapter of the American Civil Liberties Union (ACLU) called the judge's broad order—which seemingly would have put the city in the business of monitoring the beliefs and practices of religious denominations—"appalling" and "astonishing." Representatives of the city's five Christian Science churches worried that Summers's order would infringe on their religious liberty. Referring to the church's practice of reporting communicable diseases to the city's health department, one official said, "Christian Scientists obey the law. But at the same time we are anxious to see that the law recognizes our religious rights."[38]

Two observers from outside the city offered more positive assessments of Summers's controversial actions. Writing in the *National Law Journal*, New York attorneys Jennifer Trahan and Susan Wolf put the court orders in historical context, favorably comparing the judge's rulings to others involving parents who had resisted, on religious grounds, compulsory medical treatment for their children:

> When constitutionally protected parental rights endanger the lives of children, courts consistently intervene. The rationale is most clearly stated in *Prince* [*v. Massachusetts*]: Parents are not free to deprive their children of the chance to reach majority and to decide then whether to embrace the parents' religion. The family court acted well within that tradition in ordering the hospitalization of ill children. The immunization orders were an extension of that doctrine, arguably mandated by the nature of the disease, the imminence of the threat of infection and the lack of adequate alternatives.

According to the analysis of Trahan and Wolf, Summers had acted appropriately in compelling the young church members to receive medical treatment.[39]

However, because of its concerns over the scope of Summers's ruling, the ACLU worked to broker a compromise between the city and the Faith Tabernacle. Under a proposal negotiated with the help of ACLU attorney Stefan Presser, the city would have dropped its demand for inoculations in exchange for a promise from church members that they would report all measles cases and permit medical treatment for children who had been stricken by the virus. The proposed agreement fell apart, however, when it was revealed that a toddler named James Jones was hovering near death at St. Christopher's Hospital. The severity of Jones's illness vexed city officials because his parents previously had assured public health authorities that there were no serious measles cases among their children. Now convinced that it simply could not rely on Faith Tabernacle parents to be completely forthcoming about the condition of their children, the city walked away from the compromise and asked Judge Summers to order the inoculations. City solicitor Charisse Little, summing up authorities' feelings about the fate of children in the church, said, "We are very nervous."[40]

After Judge Summers acceded to the city's request for immunizations (and agreed to reconsider the remainder of his far-reaching order), the church appealed to the Superior Court of Pennsylvania. Arguments before Judge Vincent Cirillo involved lawyers representing the city and church parents, as well as an attorney appointed by the court to represent the children who were to be immunized. Their debate over Judge Summers's order was interrupted by news that the death toll among children in the Faith Tabernacle had risen to five with the passing of James Jones. The boy's death only served to underscore the seriousness of the city's efforts to preserve the health of youngsters in the church. Although he applauded Faith Tabernacle parents for "adhering to the Good Book," Cirillo refused to block Summers's immunization order. In doing so, he maintained that the refusal of church members to seek medical

treatment for their children posed a serious risk not only to their faith's adherents but also to the public as a whole. "These parents have a right to choose
the religion they want for their children and to practice it," Cirillo said, "so long
as it does not unduly risk the health of other children." After the state supreme
court refused to hear the parents' appeal of Cirillo's ruling, public health officials administered the measles inoculations to the children as family members
and church elders looked on. Less than a week later, three more Faith Tabernacle children received court-ordered immunizations.[41]

The city's aggressive actions during the measles outbreak raised a host of
compelling legal and ethical issues that civil libertarians, church members, and
children's welfare advocates debated long after the epidemic had passed. What
remained indisputable was the practical impact of the moves made by local
authorities: their unprecedented efforts clearly prevented the fatal measles
outbreak from turning even more deadly. In a break from the usual pattern of
state activity in faith-based medical-neglect cases, they were proactive, intervening to save children before they were harmed by a lack of medical treatment. This assertiveness arguably might have compromised parents' religious
liberty, but its concrete benefits were undeniable—lives were saved.

Nonetheless, families in the Faith Tabernacle were not pleased with the
courts' seeming interference with the practice of their religious faith. "They're
not too happy," their attorney said. "They have belief in faith and they are really
convinced that what happens is due to a higher force."[42]

Northwest of Philadelphia, in the central Pennsylvania city of Altoona, another
Faith Tabernacle congregation lost two youngsters in the same family. Dennis
and Lorie Nixon were fiercely dedicated to the church and its tenets, including those relating to healing. Whenever one of their children fell sick, they
turned to prayer rather than medicine. "They will usually come to us [and say]
'Mommy or Daddy, would you pray for me? I don't feel good, and my belly
hurts,' or something like this," Dennis Nixon explained. "We'll say, 'Sure,' and
we'll get out and we'll kneel down along the bed, and we'll say a little prayer.
And time after time, they go back to bed, and you don't see them or hear from
them until morning." The Nixons believed so strongly in this method that
none of their thirteen children ever visited a doctor or took even the most
common pain medications.[43]

In the early 1990s, this approach to healing was put to the test when the
Nixons' son Clayton fell victim to a common childhood malady, an ear infection. The family chose to treat the infection with prayer instead of antibiotics,
and Clayton never recovered. The infection worsened and spread, and he developed a high fever and lost his appetite. Stricken by an illness that is easily
treated millions of times every year by pediatricians, Clayton eventually died
from extreme dehydration and malnutrition. Blair County District Attorney
William Haberstroh charged the couple with involuntary manslaughter and

child endangerment, and they pleaded no contest to both counts. (Not surprisingly, the Nixons were sentenced to probation.) Haberstroh said his intention in charging the couple was to ensure that their religious practices no
longer would imperil their remaining children. "What I want to do is not
change their belief," he said, "but change their conduct."[44]

Haberstroh would be profoundly disappointed on this score. Like many
spiritual healers who have been charged with serious crimes, the Nixons
stubbornly refused to abandon the tenets of the faith when another one of their
children, sixteen-year-old Shannon, subsequently fell sick. The teenager's ordeal started midway through 1995, when she began losing weight and con-
stantly feeling thirsty. When Shannon subsequently complained to her parents
of feeling fatigued and dizzy ("She said that she didn't feel her body was right,"
he mother later explained), the family decided that, in accordance with the
teachings of the scriptures, she should be prayed for and anointed with oil.
This rite was performed at the home of her grandfather, Charles Nixon, the
pastor of the local Faith Tabernacle congregation. The family's hope was that
God "would have mercy on her," Dennis Nixon later said, "give her the healing
touch that she need[ed] in her body." Although Shannon did not feel well
enough to attend worship services with her family the following day, she
promised to listen to a tape of the sermon when they came home. Dennis and
Lorie returned from church to find Shannon in an exultant mood. The prayers
and anointment had worked; she was feeling better. "I feel I have my victory!"
she said.[45]

But Shannon Nixon's exultation proved to be short-lived. She began vomiting the following morning, and she was unable to keep down much food.
With her illness worsening, Charles Nixon presided over another session of
prayer and anointment, and it seemed to benefit Shannon; she was able to eat
without throwing up. But Shannon clearly had the sense that she was faring
poorly: at one point she told her brother, "The devil is fighting me hard." More
fervent prayers followed, but they had little effect on the teenager's condition.
After repeatedly losing consciousness, she fell into a coma and died on June 21,
1995, three days before what would have been her seventeenth birthday. When
her family buried her, they gave Shannon a headstone that testified to her
unswerving commitment to her religious beliefs. It read:

> I have fought a good fight.
> I have finished my course.
> I have kept the faith.[46]

Even though prayer had proven fatally ineffective during their son Clayton's illness, at no time throughout Shannon's hardship did her family even
consider taking her to a doctor. After Shannon's death, Dennis and Lorie Nixon
insisted that they would have taken their daughter to a doctor if she had
requested such help. "All her actions proved what she wanted," her mother

later said, "and she was trusting God for her healing." Because Shannon had been so mature at the time of her illness, the Nixons had decided to leave such choices up to their daughter; they had not directed the course of her treatment, even though she technically had been a minor at the time of her illness. "That was Shannon's decision, whether she wanted medical [treatment] or not," Dennis Nixon said. "That wasn't our decision."[47]

Regardless of how it had been made, the decision not to seek medical treatment for Shannon had proven to be disastrous. An autopsy revealed that the teenager had suffered from diabetic ketoacidosis (DKA). Although the condition—which caused Shannon's blood to become more acidic than her body tissues—is incurable, it is readily treated with regular insulin injections that typically cost less than a dollar each. There is little hope for victims of DKA who do not receive this relatively cheap treatment: diabetes experts say that their survival rate is zero. The decision not to seek medical treatment for Shannon thus sealed her fate.[48]

After Shannon's autopsy was performed, the Altoona Police Department filed criminal complaints against her parents and arrested them. District Attorney William Haberstroh, who had earlier prosecuted the Nixons after their son Clayton's death, again filed involuntary manslaughter and child-endangerment charges against the couple. After seeing two children die as a result of the family's adherence to its faith, he had little sympathy for the Nixons. "They sacrificed this little girl," he said, "for their religious beliefs." For their part, the Nixons apparently believed that they had become the victims of religious persecution inspired by the most malevolent force known to man: family members reportedly told a police investigator that they believed the prosecution was "an instrument of the devil testing their faith."[49]

At their trial and in the appeal that followed, the Nixons maintained that Shannon herself bore responsibility for the fact that she had not received medical treatment for her DKA. Although she had been a little more than a year shy of her eighteenth birthday at the time of her death, the teenager had been a "mature minor"—a kind of pseudoadult—capable of choosing whatever treatment she deemed appropriate for her illness. "Shannon Nixon was a mature minor," the Nixons' attorney argued, "who had the ability to consent [to] or refuse medical treatment." To back up this claim, the Nixons offered testimony meant to establish that their daughter had been an independent young adult. She had held down a part-time job, and she had traveled frequently on her own—all signs, they insisted, that she had not been a mere child whose decisions were completely controlled by her parents. Effectively an adult, Shannon had the legal right to control the course of her treatment, and "when she became ill, it was her wish to refuse medical care and be treated pursuant to the [tenets] of her faith." Because she had made this decision on her own, her parents "could not be culpable for failure to provide medical treatment to which Shannon properly refused."[50]

Such arguments—which have been made, in one form or another, in numerous cases of religion-based medical neglect of children—proved ineffective during the Nixons' trial, and they were found guilty of manslaughter and child neglect. When they were sentenced, the couple and their attorney apparently believed that they would once again receive a lenient sentence. The couple's attorney made an emotional plea to the judge, pointing out the large family—soon to expand even further with the birth of yet another child—would be "torn apart" if either of the parents received jail time. But Blair County Common Pleas Court Judge Norman Callan stunned the family by imposing the maximum allowable sentence, a minimum of two and one-half years of imprisonment for both parents. Callan scoffed at the argument that consideration of the couple's obligation to their children should lead him to impose a light sentence. "The irony of using their family as justification for probation is not lost on this court," he said. "If they wanted to keep their family intact, there are two more people in that family [Clayton and Shannon] who should be alive today."[51]

When the Nixons appealed their sentence to the Supreme Court of Pennsylvania, their effort to rely on the "mature minor" doctrine met with stiff opposition from a coalition of groups dedicated to children's welfare. The advocacy group CHILD and three like-minded organizations filed an amicus curiae brief urging the court not to accept the Nixons' claims and thereby adopt such an "unprecedented and disastrous" rule of law. The forceful brief—written by James Dwyer, an authority on children's rights and professor at William and Mary School of Law—pilloried the Faith Tabernacle couple for attempting to shirk their legal responsibility to provide medical care for their child. "Mr. and Mrs. Nixon," Dwyer wrote, "should be ashamed for attempting to shift to their deceased daughter responsibility for the choices they made about how to govern her life." Courts in numerous jurisdictions had recognized this obligation in such cases as *Commonwealth v. Barnhart*, which also had involved members of the Nixons' church.[52]

Pennsylvania's highest court held that the "mature minor" doctrine was not applicable to the Nixons' case, and it upheld their convictions. Summing up the court's analysis, one justice wrote in a concurring opinion that Shannon Nixon clearly "did not have the maturity to make an informed decision regarding medical treatment." Vindicated by the court's ruling, District Attorney William Haberstroh reflected on the case and the stubborn refusal of the two defendants to subordinate their religious practice to the rule of law. "I know Dennis Nixon [and he's] not a Charlie Manson," Haberstroh said. "But Shannon Nixon is dead, and Shannon Nixon should not be dead. These two people have to learn, somebody has to convince them that [their church] isn't the last word. The last word is the law."[53]

As the Nixons' case made its way through the courts, authorities in Philadelphia were battling another Faith Tabernacle couple, Daniel and Anne

Foster. The Fosters' case began late in the winter of 1997, when they detected a lump in the abdomen of their two-year-old son, Patrick. Other symptoms of a serious illness soon developed: the boy became fatigued and lost weight, and his nose ran almost continuously. Like William and Linda Barnhart—the Faith Tabernacle members who also had felt a lump in the abdomen of their child—the Fosters did not rush their son to a doctor. Instead, they followed the teachings of the Epistle of James, fervently praying for the boy and anointing him with oil. "We prayed morning and night," Daniel Foster said. "We asked the Lord to change it." Patrick failed to improve, however, and a concerned neighbor eventually reported his deteriorating condition to the Pennsylvania Department of Human Services. When investigators arrived at the Fosters' home, they found Patrick lying near death. "The boy did not look well; he was moaning and wincing," according to one account. "When [a social worker] picked him up, mucous was coming out of his mouth, Patrick had a visible rash along his left cheek, his eye was swollen shut, his left hand was swollen and his hair was matted to the side of his head."[54]

After the human services agency obtained a court order mandating Patrick's removal from his parents' custody, he was taken to a local hospital for treatment. There, doctors discovered that the growth in Patrick Foster's stomach was a massive Wilms' tumor, the same kind of cancerous growth that had killed Justin Barnhart in 1981. According to one person who observed the child, the tumor was "the size of a watermelon." (The veteran oncologist who treated Patrick later said that he never had seen a larger Wilms' tumor.) Surgeons removed the potentially fatal growth, and Patrick subsequently received radiation therapy to ensure that the cancer did not return. As the boy recuperated, his parents faced charges of child endangerment and criminal conspiracy. They also battled an effort by state human-services officials to permanently remove Patrick from their custody.[55]

At their trial, Daniel Foster stressed that he had chosen to treat his son with prayer because he had witnessed on numerous occasions the healing power of prayer. When his attorney, Jonathan James, asked if he believed in divine healing, Foster replied, "Absolutely. I've seen it happen. I've seen walking miracles in my church, in my own family." Even as Patrick's condition had worsened, Foster had expected that the boy would "receive the divine touch" and be healed. The fact that medicine had succeeded where prayer had failed, curing Patrick's illness and sending him down the road toward a complete recovery, in no way diminished Foster's commitment to spiritual healing. Probing his capacity to learn from his apparent mistakes—and the apparent failures of his fellow members of the Faith Tabernacle—Assistant District Attorney Mimi Rose asked Foster how he we would treat Patrick if the boy fell sick again after being returned to his custody. Foster refused to budge. "I would continue to pray," he said. "I do not agree with medical procedures."[56]

After deliberating less than two hours, the jury convicted both Daniel and Anne Foster on both the child-endangerment and criminal-conspiracy counts. Panel members later told reporters that the couple's right to freedom of religion did not trump their responsibility to protect the welfare of their child. Troubled by the church's long history of religion-based medical-neglect cases, they hoped that their verdict would send a clear message to members of the Faith Tabernacle: "They have to make some sort of adjustment to their faith so as not to continue to endanger children," suggested one member of the panel. But Anne Foster's attorney derided the notion that the verdict would have much of an impact on the church. The convictions, Rose Marie DeFino said, "don't settle anything. It's not going to change the practices of the church. It's not going to deter future behavior [of church members]."[57]

DeFino's prediction was borne out late in 2002 with the death of nine-year-old Benjamin Reinert. After receiving an anonymous call indicating that his health was being neglected, a state human-services worker visited his family's home during the last week in December. Benjamin told the worker that his foot had been bothering him—he had trouble walking on it, he said—but the injury did not seem serious enough at the time to merit his removal from the home. Another worker made a follow-up visit a few days later, and once again the boy was permitted to stay with his father, who explained that he was being treated solely with prayer. Human-services officials remained concerned about Benjamin's health, and they decided that if his condition did not improve over the following few days, they would attempt to obtain a court order mandating medical treatment for him. But Benjamin Reinert died on New Year's Eve, before the courts could intervene. It turned out that he had been suffering from acute lymphocytic leukemia. After reviewing the circumstances of the boy's death, local authorities chose not to file criminal charges against his parents.[58]

The circumstances of Reinert's death showed how difficult it was, as a practical matter, for public officials to successfully intervene between parents and children in order to mitigate or even prevent religion-based medical neglect. Until they learned of the boy's illness and appreciated its severity, authorities lacked any kind of motivation for mandating medical treatment for him. (That is, they had absolutely no reason to force him to see a doctor until they knew he was sick.) But by the time they fathomed the danger confronting Reinert and resolved to take legal action on his behalf, it was too late; the illness already was well on its way to killing him. In retrospect, it seems that his only hope would have been if the state—sensing that his parents' reliance on religious practices for healing posed a serious danger to his well-being—had stepped in and taken over supervision of his health *before* he had fallen sick. Had that somehow happened, his leukemia might have been diagnosed early and speedily treated by means more effective than prayer.

This scenario might seem far-fetched and—depending on how one feels about the limits of state power—alarming. But it is essentially what Massachusetts authorities had in mind when they initiated an extraordinary preemptive action against members of The Body, a religious denomination with a grisly record of faith-based abuse. Convinced that it was only a matter of time before another child in the faith suffered because of her parents' religious healing practices, officials there resolved to intervene and protect one child from the earliest possible moment—her birth.

8

"This Ain't Religion"

Spiritual Healing and Reproductive Rights

Rebecca Corneau gave birth to her fifth child, a daughter, at 2:40 PM on October 16, 2000. Aided by a midwife (two doctors were present, but they did not assist with the birth), Corneau experienced less than two hours of labor before delivering a healthy, seven-pound-fifteen-ounce girl at the Neil J. Houston House in West Roxbury, Massachusetts. Four of Corneau's relatives were present in the facility for the baby's arrival.[1]

Although the birth of her daughter itself proved to be relatively routine, the circumstances surrounding Rebecca Corneau's delivery were nothing short of extraordinary. In the preceding few weeks, Corneau, a member of an obscure religious denomination known as The Body, had been the subject of an unprecedented legal proceeding initiated by Paul Walsh, the district attorney of Bristol County, Massachusetts. Fearing for the safety of Corneau's fetus, Walsh had obtained a court order mandating that she be held in state custody and deliver her child under the close supervision of medical experts at a birthing center for prison inmates. Although he repeatedly maintained that she had not been formally incarcerated, Walsh essentially had jailed Corneau so that her child would be born safely.

Walsh took such a controversial step because members of the The Body—who eschewed medical care and relied on prayer to treat everything from potentially fatal illnesses to backed-up septic systems—had been implicated in several macabre and much-publicized cases of religion-based medical neglect of children. As Corneau prepared to give birth in the fall of 2000, Walsh's office was probing the starvation death of Samuel Robidoux, the infant son of church members

Jacques and Karen Robidoux. (That investigation eventually led Walsh to file first-degree murder charges against the boy's father and second-degree murder charges against his mother.) Walsh's office also was investigating the circumstances of a stillbirth of one of Rebecca Corneau's own children, a boy named Jeremiah. Given that abysmal track record, Walsh felt compelled to take preventive measures. "That baby died," Walsh said of Jeremiah Corneau, "and I don't think, as district attorney, I can sit by and let that happen again."[2]

Walsh's actions drew national attention, and not all of it was positive. Numerous civil libertarians criticized his efforts to control the circumstances of Corneau's delivery, calling them a clear threat to the reproductive freedoms of women of all faiths. New England School of Law professor Wendy Murphy, an outspoken critic of Walsh, voiced a typical concern by arguing that the prosecutor's actions threatened to open a Pandora's box of legal issues by interfering with Corneau's right to choose the manner in which she would give birth. "What's to stop a prosecutor tomorrow from locking up all Christian Scientists?" Murphy asked at one point. "They don't believe in medical care either. What's to stop the next prosecutor from saying about a woman who can't afford medical care, 'Well, I better lock you up because you can't afford to get the prenatal help that you need'? . . . So it really is very dangerous."[3]

The Corneau and Robidoux cases—which in some ways paralleled cases involving pregnant Jehovah's Witnesses who refused, on religious grounds, to receive blood transfusions—generated such intense interest throughout the United States because their peculiar circumstances further complicated the already tangled issue of religion-based medical neglect of children. The preventive action taken by Massachusetts authorities against Rebecca Corneau raised questions regarding not only reproductive rights but also criminal procedure. (As her defenders frequently noted, Corneau was ordered into state custody because of the possibility that she might commit a crime in the future.) And when authorities prosecuted Karen Robidoux for second-degree murder after her son died, the case turned on whether she had been a psychologically battered woman who was incapable of freely deciding if medical care had been necessary for her child. Because they bring into collision so many compelling legal and ethical claims, conflicts involving religion-based medical neglect typically are, as law professors like to put it, "hard cases." In Massachusetts, the implication of profound issues relating to due process of law, reproductive freedoms, and women's self-determination rendered them all the more bedeviling.

By most accounts, Roland Robidoux, Jacques's father and founder of The Body, had a fairly typical upbringing in the Catholic Church. Robidoux graduated from an all-boys Catholic high school and became a devout churchgoer as an adult, rarely skipping Sunday services. But his humdrum religious life took a radical turn one Sunday morning in the early 1970s as he drove to mass in

North Attleboro, Massachusetts. While navigating his way to church, Robidoux tuned his AM radio to a program by Herbert W. Armstrong, leader of a small denomination known as the Worldwide Church of God (WCG), entitled *The World Tomorrow*. Robidoux was so taken by the fervor of Armstrong's broadcast, in which he touted the magnificence of his "one true church," that the lifelong Catholic never made it to mass again.[4]

A dynamic preacher and tireless proselytizer, Armstrong had begun his ministry decades earlier by founding what he called the Radio Church of God. Its cornerstone was regular broadcasts in which Armstrong analyzed current events through the prism of various prophetic Biblical texts. The faith that emerged in these programs and Armstrong's other media venture, a magazine called the *Plain Truth*, was an amalgam of doctrines that he apparently borrowed from several faiths, among them the Seventh-day Adventists. By 1968, Armstrong had somewhat grandly renamed his movement the Worldwide Church of God, and he found himself presiding over what one observer has termed "a vast media empire." Armstrong ruled this realm with an iron hand. In both fiscal and doctrinal matters, no one questioned his authority.[5]

Roland Robidoux bridled at Armstrong's absolute control over the WCG, and he resolved to strike out on his own by helping to form a Bible-study group in Attleboro, Massachusetts. Teaming with a man named Roger Daneau, Robidoux led a small group comprised mainly of family members and friends; its membership probably never exceeded more than twenty people. Most of them were drawn by the simplicity of the church—one member later said that a typical meeting involved a handful of people "sitting at a table with their Bibles open"—and Robidoux's charisma. Although the group had formally ceded from the WCG, many of its doctrines mirrored those of Armstrong's church. Among them were a skepticism of medical treatment and a reliance on prayer for healing. As one former member put it, "The Worldwide Church of God really frowned on medical practices. They certainly taught that a person should pray and ask God to heal." Whatever their misgivings about Armstrong's leadership, Robidoux, Daneau, and their followers adopted this philosophy as their own.[6]

The teachings of Carol Balizet, the founder of a Florida sect known as Home in Zion Ministries, profoundly influenced the nascent church's approach toward healing. Balizet advocated a withdrawal from several "worldly" systems—including government, education, and medicine—that were, in her estimation, inherently Satanic. In her books *Born in Zion* and *Egypt or Zion*, Balizet touted what she called "a valid, workable, God-given alternative to submission to the medical system." As she urged individuals to "refuse medical care completely," Balizet advocated a "spiritual" approach to birth that involved neither doctors nor hospitals. Instead, women were to give birth at home and rely solely on prayer for support, even in the most complicated deliveries.

Adhering to such a method, Balizet insisted, would allow women to free themselves from "the stronghold of deceptions about medical care" and enter into the realm of "kingdom healing."[7]

Balizet's teachings took hold among members of the Attleboro church, and they began to closely follow her directives regarding medical care. Dennis Mingo, who married Roland Robidoux's daughter Michelle, fell ill with a mysterious illness that proved to be leukemia. Worried that he had been given a death sentence, he went to his father-in-law for guidance. "He said you need to, basically, put this in God's hands," Mingo recalled. "Just have the faith and he's going to take care of it." Mingo chose to forego conventional medical treatment for his illness, and "it just went away. And of course, I attribute this to God."[8]

But while such experiences solidified Mingo's faith in Robidoux's teachings, other moments made him question the church's direction. One day, Mingo joked with his bespectacled wife that wearing eyeglasses seemed to run counter to the faith's proscriptions on medical care. "And sure enough, like, in about a week's time, she went before the group and said God had shown her that she's not to wear glasses, and everybody else isn't to wear glasses," Mingo recalled. "They were basically against God." This was the first time that a member of the church claimed to have received a "first leading from God." At these moments, Mingo explained, individuals "felt God had told them to do something or change something." Over time, it would become increasingly difficult for sect members to question such powerful revelations.[9]

At no time was this more evident than when Karen Robidoux gave birth to her son Samuel. During the boy's infancy, Michelle Mingo, Karen's sister-in-law, experienced another "leading," this time learning from God that Karen had become thin and vain. This problem would be solved, Michelle said, if Karen drank large amounts of fattening almond milk and nourished Samuel through continuous breastfeeding. Only then would God "relent in his judgment," Michelle said.[10]

The results of this "leading" were nothing short of disastrous for Samuel. Breastfeeding failed to provide him with adequate nourishment, and his weight plummeted. As he withered away, his increasingly frail body showed clear signs of distress. "He began losing weight," his father later said. "His cry wasn't a normal baby's cry. . . . Sometimes his eyes would roll to the back of his head." Although Karen Robidoux wanted to supplement her breastfeeding with other sources of nourishment, she abided by the strictures of Michelle Mingo's leading, even as her son's health unmistakably deteriorated. According to a journal used by various group members, over a two-week period "Samuel was obviously losing much weight and becoming sicker."[11]

While Samuel wasted away, church members showed remarkably little concern for his well-being. During the boy's downward spiral, Rebecca Corneau asserted that "our prayers should not be for Samuel to be healed but for

God's purposes to be fulfilled. This is all we can do for Samuel." Michelle Mingo took a similar position, insisting that the boy's condition was beyond her control (this despite the fact that he obviously was starving to death). The matter was "in God's hands," she claimed. "What can we do for Samuel? Nothing. God is the master. We are his servants."[12]

Samuel died on April 26, 1999, just three days before his first birthday. The medical examiner who officially determined the boy's cause of death ruled that he had died from "severe malnutrition due to starvation." Even in death, Samuel was subjected to callous treatment. According to court documents and press reports, the Robidoux couple did not immediately bury their son's corpse. Instead, they placed the body in a basket, wrapped the container in a plastic garbage bag, and then placed it in a "bulkhead" (a New England term for a horizontal or sloping structure providing access to a cellar stairway) near the playroom in their home. A child who played in the room later reported that the area around the bulkhead was "stinky" and swarmed with "tons" of insects.[13] Members of the church apparently came to view Maine's vast Baxter State Park as a kind of promised land, and they eventually buried Samuel Robidoux there. He was joined in an unmarked grave by Jeremiah Corneau, Rebecca Corneau's son who died at birth.

The church's journal told the bleak story of Jeremiah's birth. After a relatively uneventful pregnancy, Rebecca Corneau went into labor without the assistance of a physician or even a trained midwife. (Thanks in part to the influence of Carol Balizet's book *Born in Zion*, she was attended only by another church member.) The child was breech: its feet emerged first, with the umbilical cord wrapped around them. In time, the baby's head emerged, but not before the child had aspirated the contents of the birth canal and essentially choked to death. "He was pink even before fully birthed," the journal reported. "But he never breathed." Medical authorities who reviewed the case later said that a rudimentary medical procedure—mucus suction—probably would have saved Jeremiah's life.[14]

In the fall of 1999, authorities in Bristol County obtained copies of the church's journal and, working with state child-welfare officials, initiated a flurry of legal proceedings against its members. Following an investigation by the state Department of Social Services (DSS) and the police departments in the towns of Attleboro and Seekonk, Attleboro Juvenile Court Judge Kenneth Nasif awarded DSS temporary custody of the Corneaus' three children, who were identified in court proceedings using the pseudonyms Fran, Sally, and Jane. (All told, about a dozen children were removed from the custody of parents who belonged to The Body.) The girls lived in foster homes for the next ten months as their parents awaited the trial that would determine if the youngsters could be formally adopted without their parents' consent. The Corneaus neither visited nor communicated with their daughters over that time. At one point, the girls (acting through their court-appointed attorney) requested that their father, David Corneau, contact them, but he refused, "telling the judge, in effect, that he would not engage in visitation because he knew what was best for the children," according to the Appeals Court of Massachusetts, which later reviewed the case.[15]

This "benevolent abandonment," as the appellate court termed it, was not the most serious charge leveled at the Corneaus. There was evidence that the couple had repeatedly physically abused their children, spanking them "with a wooden paddle to the extent that the skin on their buttocks was thickened and calloused," the appellate court found. (Spanking was so routine in the household that Rebecca Corneau reportedly attached a paddle to a rope and wore it around her waist.) Both the trial and appellate courts also expressed concerns about the Corneaus' spiritual-healing practices and how they might affect their children. The girls never had seen a physician, nor had they been vaccinated. David Corneau told a DSS investigator that he and wife "would not procure medical attention for their children even if the children were faced with a life-threatening illness."[16]

As they determined if the Corneaus were unfit parents, the trial and appellate courts also focused on the couple's behavior during Jeremiah's birth. The trial court judge, Kenneth Nasif, found that the boy "had been born alive and that he would likely have survived if the father and mother had provided him adequate medical care," according to the appellate court. (Because Nasif presided over an adoption proceeding that was technically unrelated to that case, his finding had no impact on the couple's potential criminal liability for the boy's death.) Although the appellate court disagreed with this conclusion— it found that Jeremiah "never drew a breath after delivery"—it was disturbed by the circumstances of the boy's stillbirth and the Corneaus' disposal of his corpse. (They apparently stored Jeremiah's body in the same bulkhead that held Samuel Robidoux.) After reviewing all of this grim evidence, the trial and appellate courts agreed that the Corneaus were unfit parents, and they approved adoption decrees for all three children.[17]

As the adoption proceedings moved forward, law enforcement officials continued to investigate the circumstances of the deaths of Samuel Robidoux and Jeremiah Corneau. Samuel's death seemed so brutal that District Attorney Paul Walsh filed first-degree murder charges against Jacques Robidoux and second-degree murder charges against Karen Robidoux. When he announced the charges, Walsh downplayed the religious dimension of the case. "I don't see this as being religious prophecy or anything like that," Walsh later said. "There are two adults with their baby in a house full of food. No religious group in the world allows that to happen. This is a clear case of murder. This ain't religion." He also charged Michelle Mingo, whose "leading" arguably had set the entire process of Samuel's death in motion, with being an accessory to assault and battery and thereby contributing to what Walsh called "one of the most chilling homicides that I've ever had to deal with in my life."[18]

Jacques Robidoux was tried first. (His wife's case proceeded more slowly because she initially was ruled mentally incompetent to stand trial.) Although there seemed to be a general consensus among observers that the father bore some legal responsibility for his son's death, some wondered if prosecutors might have had an easier time proving a lesser charge, such as manslaughter. One former prosecutor said, "I think [first-degree murder] is a very tough case. Most juries are going to be looking for some evidence that the parent had hostility toward the child." Others wondered about the credibility of the sect's journal, which contained graphic descriptions of Samuel's demise and his parents' behavior. The journal was a gold mine of information, but prosecutors could not attribute its authorship to any particular member of The Body—a weakness that Robidoux's attorney was sure to exploit at trial.[19]

Another part of Robidoux's defense rested on the notion that he essentially had been brainwashed by the other members of The Body into adopting the religious practices that caused his son's death. "Unfortunately, the religious beliefs that had been drilled into him since he was a youngster clouded his ability to make the right decision," said his attorney, Francis O'Boy. His opposite number, Assistant District Attorney Walter Shea, countered by arguing that "it wasn't a case about religion" but rather a matter of simple, brutal murder. The jury agreed: after deliberating for a little over six hours, it found Jacques Robidoux guilty of first-degree murder. At her own trial for second-degree murder, Karen Robidoux raised a similar defense, with her attorney arguing that she was a psychologically battered woman who had been victimized by "a bizarre, misbegotten group." ("This is not the Partridge Family," he said at one point, "or the Brady Bunch.") The jury found this argument persuasive—one member later told reporters that the panel felt Robidoux's "intent was not to kill her baby"—and acquitted her. She wound up in a group home for former cult members.[20]

The uncertain circumstances of Rebecca Corneau's delivery made it more difficult for Walsh to settle on charges against either her or her husband. Like juvenile court judge Kenneth Nasif, the district attorney believed that Jeremiah had been born and then died as a result of his parents' religion-based medical neglect. "Jeremiah was born alive, aspirated the contents of the birth canal and basically suffocated and died while mother and dad were looking on, accepting no medical intervention because they thought the hand of God would save this child," he said. "It did not." The Corneaus, however, insisted that Jeremiah had been stillborn: David Corneau reportedly told police that the child "never had a breath of life.... The Lord never gave it to him." The distinction between a stillbirth and a live birth had enormous implications for the Corneaus, because they could not face criminal charges if Jeremiah never technically had been alive outside the womb.[21]

Their case was further complicated by the fact that authorities could not find the final resting places of either Samuel or Jeremiah. Initially, church members kept mum about the location of their graves. ("Between myself and God, that's my business and none of the state's," Jacques Robidoux replied when a judge asked him to name the site of his son's grave.) Without finding the boys' bodies and subjecting them to autopsies, prosecutors could not officially determine the causes of their deaths—an essential piece of information in any murder or manslaughter case. David Corneau eventually broke the impasse, agreeing to lead investigators to the boys' gravesite in exchange for immunity from prosecution. In what Walsh termed "a major breakthrough in the case," Corneau took a phalanx of Massachusetts authorities to a remote spot in Baxter State Park. There they found the boys' graves and exhumed the bodies.[22]

By the time authorities located the bodies, Walsh had decided to forego filing charges against the Corneaus for their role in Jeremiah's death. (Although he firmly believed that Jeremiah in fact had been born and then died as a result of his parents' neglect, the district attorney sensed that it would be difficult to make his case before a jury.) Walsh instead focused his attention on the child that the visibly pregnant Rebecca Corneau was going to deliver sometime in October 2000. In a highly unusual move, he sought a court order from Attleboro Juvenile Court Judge Kenneth Nasif mandating that Corneau be confined to a state-operated medical facility so that her fetus would survive its birth. "Someone has to be there when that baby is born," Walsh insisted. "Rebecca Corneau cannot be trusted to keep that little baby alive. Someone must be there."[23]

According to a study of perinatal and maternal mortality among members of another faith-healing church, Walsh had good reason to be concerned about the health of Rebecca Corneau and her fetus. The study, published in the *American Journal of Obstetrics and Gynecology*, examined more than three hundred live births in two Indiana counties between 1975 and 1982 among members of the Faith Assembly, who typically did not receive prenatal medical care and gave birth in their homes with the assistance of midwives rather than physicians. This survey found that the perinatal mortality rate of children of church members was almost three times higher than for the state of Indiana as a whole and that the maternal mortality rate was a staggering ninety-two times higher. The study's findings suggested that "when women . . . avoid obstetric care, they greatly increase the risks of perinatal and maternal death."[24]

In his more candid moments, Walsh conceded that his maneuver probably was not backed by a wealth of legal precedent. After all, he in effect was asking that Corneau be taken into state custody because he believed she would commit a crime (medical neglect) sometime in the future—an approach that in many ways seemed antithetical to some of the fundamental premises of the Anglo-American legal tradition. But Walsh insisted that preserving the life of Rebecca Corneau's fetus should take precedence over legal hairsplitting. "There are some varying legal rights here," he said, "but I'd prefer to save the baby first, and then enter the debate" over the legality of his scheme.[25]

A chorus of critics attacked Walsh for his effort to compel Rebecca Corneau to give birth while in state custody. Few of these detractors endorsed the Corneaus' apparently peculiar religious beliefs or their past behavior; many, in fact, went to great lengths to dissociate themselves from The Body and its opposition to medical science. Swallowing their misgivings about Rebecca Corneau's religious beliefs and practices, her defenders argued that Walsh's efforts represented a clear threat to the reproductive rights of women of all faiths. If the courts permitted the district attorney to effectively control Corneau's pregnancy because she might harm her fetus, they insisted, it would send a signal to law enforcement authorities throughout the country that they too could detain women and similarly take command over their pregnancies.

This prospect chilled two of Walsh's most forceful and persistent critics, Wendy Murphy, a professor at the New England School of Law, and Lynn Paltrow, the founder and director of National Advocates for Pregnant Women. As the Corneau case progressed, both women appeared on numerous television programs and gave dozens of interviews to print and broadcast journalists. In all of these exchanges, Murphy and Paltrow expressed their concern that Corneau was "being deprived of her right to make decisions about her pregnancy," as Paltrow put it. There was only one person who had a legal right to make such choices, they claimed, and that was the pregnant woman herself, not a district attorney.[26]

A few basic arguments undergirded most of the criticisms leveled at Walsh by Murphy and Paltrow. Both attorneys, for instance, were appalled that the district attorney wanted to detain Rebecca Corneau because she might be guilty of neglecting her child sometime in the future. "In our country," Paltrow said, "we do not take anybody into custody, wherever it happens to be, because they might in the future commit a crime." Murphy echoed this critique, asserting that "locking [Corneau] up based on the speculative notion that she might hurt the child in the future after it's born violates every constitutional principle of fairness, and it smacks of paternalism in a very deep way." Whatever transgressions she might have committed in the past, it was unconstitutional to preemptively incarcerate Rebecca Corneau. Doing so, Murphy and Paltrow argued, clearly violated her right to due process of law.[27]

Murphy forcefully argued that Rebecca Corneau's rights, not those of her fetus, were paramount. "The only person with rights in this proceeding is Ms. Corneau," she said. "She's the only real person under the law. Until a child is born, it is not a person with rights." Paltrow made much the same point, insisting in a television appearance that, "under the United States Constitution, a fetus is not a legal person" possessing the rights accorded to all citizens by the Constitution. In the Corneau case, the district attorney wanted not only to give the fetus such rights but also to have its newfound rights trump those of the mother. Although neither Murphy nor Paltrow explicitly stressed it, this inversion of rights had potentially broad implications for reproductive freedoms. After all, if the courts held that a fetus was a person with preeminent rights in this context, the precedent could be used to undermine a woman's right to terminate her pregnancy—a frightening prospect for champions of abortion rights.[28]

Murphy, Paltrow, and other critics of the district attorney repeatedly invoked the notion that the courts might establish a perilous "slippery slope" for all pregnant women if they permitted Walsh to "lock up" Rebecca Corneau. If a prosecutor was able to incarcerate a pregnant woman because her religious practices might harm her fetus, this argument went, what would stop authorities from taking similarly repressive actions based on other potentially risky behaviors? "Where is this going?" asked Andrea Mullin, the president of the Massachusetts chapter of the National Organization for Women. "Are we going to incarcerate women who drink during pregnancy or smoke during pregnancy? Because, I mean, that puts us on a slope that's slippery." For her part, Wendy Murphy illustrated the dangers of the slippery slope by noting that she had climbed a ladder and changed shutters on her home while she was pregnant with her fourth child. Had he seen her, Murphy said half-jokingly, the district attorney "would have sent the police" because he somehow felt empowered to incarcerate pregnant women who engaged in behavior that he deemed unsafe to their fetuses.[29]

For Murphy, the central question posed by the Corneau case was relatively straightforward: "Can you lock up a pregnant woman to protect the unborn fetus?" Although she and other critics of Walsh answered it with a resounding "no," the district attorney did have some defenders. Perhaps not surprisingly, pro-life advocates applauded him for taking actions designed to protect Rebecca Corneau's fetus. Contesting the notion that only Rebecca Corneau's rights were at stake, Father Joseph Howard of the American Life League declared that the case involved "two human lives, two human persons, both of equal value"—morally and legally. He praised Walsh for upholding the state's duty "to protect its citizens [who] are innocent." Maryclare Flynn of Massachusetts Citizens for Life offered praise for Walsh and castigated his critics for exaggerating the dangers posed by forcing Rebecca Corneau to give birth under state supervision. "To try to say the sky is falling and this is somehow going to put all pregnant women in jail is ridiculous," Flynn said. But not all of those who saw the logic in Walsh's actions were formally affiliated with the pro-life cause. Calling the case "beyond gut-wrenching," *Boston Globe* columnist Adrian Walker conceded that he shared "the widespread unease over Corneau's incarceration" because it seemed to be such a draconian measure. "But the concern over the baby is simply too well-founded to ignore," Walker wrote. "In what could easily be a decision of life or death, I think trying to preserve life is the right place to be."[30]

The Corneau case and the other legal proceedings involving members of The Body were so widely publicized that they attracted the scrutiny of such prominent legal scholars as Harvard Law School's Laurence Tribe and Yale Law School's Stephen Carter. Tribe, perhaps the greatest liberal constitutional scholar of his generation, questioned the constitutionality of Walsh's actions. Like many of the district attorney's critics, he wondered if Rebecca Corneau basically could be punished because authorities anticipated that she might commit a crime. But Tribe did not believe that the state's claim for preemptive action was completely without merit. "The closer you get to birth, the closer we come to the point where the state can say, 'We may not be protecting whatever is inside her now, but we are protecting what is going to come out from the time bomb that she, in effect, carries around with her,' " Tribe said. "That is, the state can often act to protect people in imminent danger by taking steps in advance of the explosion that endangers."[31]

Carter spoke more generally about the limits of parental rights and religious liberty. "Although I am a strong advocate of respecting parental authority in creating even a very insular religious and moral world for their child, I also believe that a civilized society must place some limits," Carter said. "The law generally places the limit at the well-being of the child." For Carter, the cases involving Rebecca Corneau and the Robidoux couple also raised broader questions about how spiritual healers could reconcile their practices with the strictures of temporal law. Parents who treated their children's illnesses through prayer, he said, were "not crazy or stupid. They are doing what they believe the Lord requires. But they are, in their innocence, pressing the bounds of religious freedom beyond what a civilized society can allow, and that is why they must not be permitted to do it."[32]

Ultimately, of course, neither law professors nor newspaper columnists determined the outcome of the Corneau case. The task fell to Kenneth Nasif, the Attleboro Juvenile Court judge who also had presided over the adoption proceedings involving the Corneaus' three daughters. Like Walsh, Nasif had a visceral feeling that Rebecca Corneau should be confined until she gave birth, but he struggled to formulate a legal rationale to justify taking her into custody. The case was, he told a reporter, "difficult from a technical, legal, right-or-wrong point of view." In the end, he became convinced of the "morality" of forcing Corneau to give birth under state supervision by figuratively listening to the fetus she carried. "I sense the child is saying to me, 'I want to live. I don't want to die like my brother Jeremiah did,' " Nasif said in court. "There is a real possibility [that this fetus] could die as well. This cannot be allowed to happen again." He ordered that Corneau be taken into custody and transferred to the Neil J. Houston House, a state-run birthing facility for prison inmates that had staff capable of addressing the medical "needs of the mother and the unborn child at this time."[33]

When Corneau chose not to appeal Nasif's order, attorney Wendy Murphy challenged it through an admittedly "novel" maneuver. Murphy represented a Norfolk County woman—court documents identified her only as

"Barbara F."—who appealed the order in the Supreme Judicial Court of Massachusetts. Her appeal maintained that Corneau "was deprived of her liberty" by Nasif's ruling and that other pregnant women, including herself, lacked adequate protection from its potential "chilling effect." Echoing the oft-repeated "slippery slope" claim, the woman asserted that she feared she would be detained if she traveled to Bristol County and authorities there determined that she had failed to obtain appropriate prenatal care or engaged in conduct that purportedly threatened her fetus. Much to Murphy's dismay, the Supreme Judicial Court issued a short ruling against Barbara F., holding that she lacked appropriate legal standing to challenge Nasif's ruling against Rebecca Corneau. Any appeal of that order, the court held, would have to come from Corneau herself.[34]

The Supreme Judicial Court's ruling against Barbara F. removed the last legal obstacle to Rebecca Corneau's confinement at the Neil J. Houston House. She gave birth to a daughter there on October 16, 2000, and DSS immediately took legal custody of the infant. "What we will do now," an agency spokesman said, "is make sure she gets medical attention, that her needs are met and that she's well-cared for." DSS immediately sought to have the Corneaus declared unfit, and, about a year after the girl's birth, a juvenile court judge terminated their parental rights. "Darla," as she was called in court proceedings, thus became the fourth of the couple's surviving children to be permanently removed from their custody.[35]

Even after "Darla" was taken from their custody, gruesome accusations of religion-based medical neglect of children continued to dog the Corneaus. Because of various legal proceedings involving other members of The Body (including Jacques and Karen Robidoux), both David and Rebecca Corneau appeared in court at various times late in 2001. At that time, several observers noted that Rebecca Corneau looked as though she was bearing the couple's sixth child. "I personally observed her at the last trial," attorney John Rego said, "and she was pregnant." However, at subsequent court proceedings, Rebecca no longer appeared to be pregnant. With memories of Jeremiah's demise still fresh in their minds, local authorities began to wonder about the whereabouts of the child: Had there been another stillbirth? Had the child been born and victimized by religion-based medical neglect? Authorities feared the worst. "Let's just hope," one anonymous source told the Boston Herald, "they're not in a van heading up the Maine Turnpike" toward Baxter State Park, where one Corneau child already had been buried.[36]

What followed was another extraordinary legal battle pitting the Corneaus against the Bristol County district attorney's office and DSS. Early in January 2002, investigators from the Attleboro police department and the district attorney's office conducted a search of the Corneaus' home to find evidence that Rebecca had delivered a child sometime in the previous month. Although this search proved inconclusive, investigators eventually pieced together information suggesting that Rebecca Corneau had in fact given birth. (Investigators spoke to a neighbor who believed she had seen Rebecca in labor as she was being carried into a van. According to the neighbor, Rebecca no longer had been pregnant when she returned home several days later.) Acting on the basis of this fragmentary evidence, DSS subsequently filed a "care and protection" petition asserting that there was in fact a sixth Corneau child and that its welfare was imperiled. Judge Kenneth Nasif awarded DSS temporary custody of the infant—even though there was no concrete proof that the child existed—and issued summonses to the Corneaus. He ordered them to appear with their child at evidentiary hearings.[37]

The Corneaus turned up at two hearings in January 2002, but they failed to bring the child along with them. To the chagrin of both the judge and the DSS officials on hand, they also refused to testify and provide an explanation for the child's whereabouts. Their attorney claimed that both the state and federal constitutions protected their right not to incriminate themselves. "The department is alleging that this child is in immediate danger of suffering serious physical harm at the hands of the parents," attorney J. W. Carney told Nasif. "If such harm ever did befall this child, [the parents] cannot be compelled to provide evidence that would support a criminal prosecution in that regard." Outside of court, Carney expressed outrage that the Corneaus once again had been hauled into court even though there was "absolutely no evidence that [they] have ever abused any of their children." He groused that their mistreatment "borders on a witch hunt."[38]

Carney's arguments on behalf of the Corneaus troubled DSS officials. One explained that if all parents involved in care and protection proceedings were allowed to invoke their Fifth Amendment right against self-incrimination, it "would essentially block our work." The attorney's claims also failed to persuade Nasif, who had grown weary of the Corneaus' intransigence. Because the couple would neither produce their sixth child nor explain its whereabouts, the judge initiated civil contempt proceedings against them. Carney protested once more, insisting that "there is absolutely no evidence that [the Corneaus] have done anything wrong," but Nasif remained unconvinced. He found the Corneaus in contempt.[39]

The Massachusetts Court of Appeals denied Carney's appeal of the contempt citation, as did Justice Roderick Ireland of the state's Supreme Judicial Court. In his ruling, Ireland concluded that the Corneau's principal claim—that their right against self-incrimination shielded them from having to provide any information about their child—"defies common sense." Echoing the arguments made by DSS officials, he pointed out that it would be next to impossible for state authorities to conduct care and protection proceedings if all parents effectively could hide behind the shield of the Fifth Amendment. Ireland also spoke more broadly about the limits of the rights of parents, referencing the famous passage from *Prince v. Massachusetts*: "Parents may be free to become martyrs themselves. But it does not follow they are free, in identical circumstances, to make martyrs of their children before they can make that choice for themselves." (The full court later upheld Ireland's ruling.)[40]

Now facing a jail term for the contempt charges, the Corneaus dropped a bombshell. Appearing before Nasif on February 5, 2002, Rebecca Corneau reported that she had suffered another stillbirth. According to the Supreme Judicial Court's ruling in the contempt case (which it would hand down a few months later), Corneau maintained that the fetus "died in her uterus, was decomposed, and had a strong odor" when it was discharged. "There is no live Baby Corneau II," attorney Carney explained. "There never has been a live Baby Corneau II." Neither Rebecca nor her husband, however, could offer many details beyond the simple fact that she had had a miscarriage. They told Nasif that they could not remember the date of the miscarriage or whether the fetus possessed appendages. And the couple once again balked at revealing a burial site. As Carney explained, they did not want the government to "go dig [the fetus] up."[41]

Nasif was incredulous at the couple's eleventh-hour revelation, calling it "stunning information" that, if credible, should have been revealed weeks earlier, when the care and protection order had been issued. Exasperated by several years of battling with the couple, the judge said he was unconvinced by Rebecca Corneau's miscarriage story and denied Carney's request that the contempt case now be dismissed because there was no live child for the couple to turn over. He ordered them jailed. Carney, insisting that his clients were being completely forthcoming, responded by claiming that Nasif was engaged in "religious persecution" and should remove himself from the case because of his bias against the Corneaus. The judge declined, and the district attorney's investigation into the child's whereabouts continued.[42]

Some observers of the ongoing saga in Attleboro agreed with Carney that Rebecca Corneau was being repeatedly victimized because of her religious beliefs. Referring to concerns raised about the treatment of suspected terrorists being held by American authorities in Guantánamo Bay, a *Boston Herald* columnist complained that "we've heard more bleating ... about the constitutional rights of Middle Eastern terrorists in Cuba than those of Rebecca Corneau, who's already lost four children to the state." Lawyer and social critic Wendy Kaminer called the Corneaus victims of "sectual discrimination" and lamented that they were "being deprived of all rights to raise a family" simply because of their "association with a suspect religious group." Kaminer did not minimize the dangers posed by religion-based medical neglect of children, and she called for the prosecution of all parents who engaged in it. "But no parents should be presumed to be abusive, neglectful, or otherwise unfit and denied the right to raise their children," she wrote, "because of their religious beliefs."[43]

The Corneaus spent more than five months in jail before Nasif freed them in June 2002. With the couple continuing to refuse to fully cooperate, the investigation into the fate of the sixth Corneau child had reached a dead end. "It remains unclear," Nasif conceded, "as to whether the child was born alive." Because authorities lacked conclusive evidence about the circumstances of the birth, it seemed that the most serious case that could be mounted against them would be for improper disposal of human remains, a misdemeanor punishable by a maximum of six months in jail. Even if the Corneaus were found guilty under that charge, they probably would be credited with the time they already had served.[44]

It was fitting that a justice sitting on Massachusetts' highest court cited a famous holding in a Jehovah's Witness case when he ruled on the Corneaus' contempt proceedings. *Prince v. Massachusetts* was one of several Witness cases from the World War II era in which courts were asked to determine the limitations placed by the Constitution on religious liberty and the rights of parents. In fact, although they were not mentioned in Justice Ireland's opinion, a succession of later Witness cases dealt more directly with the reproductive rights of women in the context of religion-based medical neglect. Those cases, like so many legal disputes embroiling deeply religious parents who refuse to fully rely on medical science for healing, also featured a welter of sociolegal issues that defied neat resolution by the courts.

Although Jehovah's Witnesses do not typically choose to substitute prayer for medical treatment, members of their faith long have opposed the use of blood transfusions in medical procedures. This resistance—which appears to have softened in recent years—is grounded in their religious beliefs regarding "the sanctity of blood," as it is called in many Witness publications. For members of the faith, blood is a quintessential symbol of life that has special meaning for God. As such, it cannot be disrespected through improper use. For Jehovah's Witnesses, receiving transfusions amounts to "eating" blood, a practice prohibited in such scriptural passages as Leviticus 7:26–27, which cautions that "if anyone eats blood, that person must be cut off from his people."[45]

The widespread use of blood transfusions during World War II led to an official denunciation of the practice in 1945 by Witness authorities. In subsequent decades, Witness publications routinely featured articles condemning the practice—it was termed "cannibalism" on at least one occasion—and questioning its usefulness. One widely distributed tract informed readers that "even from a medical viewpoint, the religious belief of Jehovah's Witnesses on the matter of blood is not unreasonable." Jehovah's Witnesses who failed to heed such injunctions faced potentially serious consequences: an investigation by their congregation and forced excommunication from the church (called "disfellowshipping").[46]

Because American courts have generally recognized the right of competent adults to direct their own medical care, Jehovah's Witnesses have faced few significant legal barriers when they have chosen not to receive blood transfusions, even in the direst circumstances. Witness transfusion cases involving children and pregnant women, however, often have been contentious. In numerous instances, hospitals and child-welfare authorities, citing the state's obligation to safeguard the best interests of children, have sought court orders mandating transfusions that would preserve the lives of minors and fetuses. As has been typical for cases concerning potentially dangerous religion-based healing practices, these dramatic clashes have forced courts to determine the circumstances in which the state legitimately can compromise individual rights in order to protect children's welfare.

When such procedures have been deemed necessary to preserve the lives of minors, American courts generally have countenanced forced blood transfusions for them, ruling that the state's interest in protecting the health of children outweighs the religious objections of Witness parents. In 1952, for instance, a judge in Cook County, Illinois, heard a case involving a Witness infant named Cheryl Linn Labrenz. Three doctors testified that the youngster desperately needed a transfusion so that she could overcome a condition that was destroying her red blood cells. The girl's mother, Rhoda Labrenz, vehemently opposed the procedure, saying that members of her faith "believe it would be breaking God's commandment" to have a transfusion. The judge ordered a guardian appointed for the girl and authorized him to consent to a blood transfusion, and the state's highest court upheld his ruling. In denying Labrenz's appeal, that panel quoted the *Prince* opinion's admonition that "the right to practice religion freely does not include liberty to expose the community or child to communicable disease or the latter to ill health or death."[47]

In 1961, a three-year-old Jehovah's Witness named Joseph Perricone battled for his life in a hospital in Jersey City, New Jersey. At the time he was admitted to the hospital, a physician described the boy as "a blue child." His lips and nail beds had turned that color, the doctor concluded, because a heart defect had caused a chronic deficiency of oxygen in his blood. As his condition deteriorated, doctors believed transfused blood, containing the oxygen that his own blood lacked, was necessary to save Perricone's life and safeguard him from long-term neurological harm. Because of their religious beliefs, however, his parents refused to authorize the procedure. His father later explained,

> I have dedicated my life to do God's work in accordance with the
> scriptures of the Bible. One of the particular scriptures makes
> mention of taking of blood or transferring it from one person to
> another. The one part I have in mind is taken from the book Levit-
> icus, 17th chapter, verse 11–12. It states the life of the flesh is in
> the blood. No soul of you shall eat blood; neither shall any stranger

that so joineth meeting you eat blood. From the view of this scripture and others that point to this, I can assume, then, from my
position, as a dedicated minister of Jehovah's Witnesses, to hold fast
to the belief or to the teachings which were set down in the Bible.

Convinced that the Perricones' adherence to such beliefs amounted to a death
sentence for the boy, the hospital went to court to seek an order mandating the
appointment of a guardian who could authorize the transfusion.[48]

Citing both *People v. Labrenz* and *Prince*, a juvenile court judge granted the
order, and the young Jehovah's Witness received a blood transfusion fifteen
minutes later. Sadly, Perricone's condition already had deteriorated so mark-
edly that the procedure did him little good; he died within hours of receiving it.
New Jersey authorities subsequently charged the boy's parents with neglect for
their failure to provide him with adequate medical treatment, and a jury
convicted them. In an appeal to the Supreme Court of New Jersey, the Perricones challenged both their convictions for neglect and the court-ordered
transfusion (even though the latter issue had been mooted by the boy's death).
The couple asserted that their religious liberty, as well as their right as parents
to direct the upbringing of their child, had been violated by the court order and
their subsequent prosecution for neglect. To help bolster their claims, the
Perricones pointed to language in the state's criminal code that seemed applicable to their decision to adhere to their faith's teachings regarding blood
transfusions. The relevant provision stated that parents could not be prohibited
from treating the illnesses of their children "in accordance with the religious
tenets of any church."[49]

In rejecting the Perricones' claims, the state's highest court cited holdings
in child-neglect and religious-liberty cases dating back to *Queen v. Wagstaffe*,
the Peculiar People case resolved in 1868, and the ever-pertinent *Prince v.
Massachusetts*. This comprehensive review noted that courts in a variety of
jurisdictions had subordinated individual liberties, such as the freedoms
shielded by the First Amendment, to the legitimate interests of the state.
According to the court's unanimous opinion, cases like *Prince* illustrated that
"where the interests of society as a whole necessitate a certain course of action,
they have been held paramount to certain personal freedoms," including religious liberty. Given that the facts of *State v. Perricone* "clearly evidence[d] a
more compelling necessity for the protection of a child's welfare than those in
Prince," the high court had little difficulty adhering to those precedents and
rejecting the parents' claims.[50]

A case resolved by the Supreme Court of Nevada in 2004 demonstrated
the durability of such reasoning in cases involving young Jehovah's Witnesses
and blood transfusions. *In re L. S. and H. S.* centered on the treatment of the
twin sons of Jehovah's Witnesses Jason and Rebecca Soto. The boys (who were
referred to by their initials during court proceedings) struggled throughout

Rebecca's pregnancy with "twin-to-twin transfusion syndrome," a condition in which their circulatory systems were joined at the placenta. The malady resulted in H. S. becoming anemic, and his health was precarious after Rebecca Soto gave birth. Concerned by his abnormally low blood platelet count, doctors concluded that the child needed a blood transfusion, but his parents, citing their religious beliefs, objected to the procedure. To get around the parents' objections, the hospital, in what it called an effort to "provide for the medical care of the two children," sought a court order for temporary guardianship of both boys. The hospital based its request on "the substantial and immediate risk of physical harm, potential death, and the emergency circumstances surrounding the health and well being" of the Sotos' children. A lower court granted the hospital's order, and the state's highest court, following the general trend in such cases, upheld that ruling. "While Jason and Rebecca have a parental interest in the care of their son, the State has an interest in preserving the child's life," the court held. "As H.S. is unable to make decisions for himself, the State's interest is heightened. Jason and Rebecca's liberty interest in practicing their religion must also give way to the child's welfare."[51]

Several other cases have pitted pregnant Jehovah's Witnesses against hospitals that sought to compel blood transfusions that would benefit the health of the fetuses. Shaped in part by the courts' evolving approach to reproductive freedoms, these cases have proven to be especially complex because they pit the rights (or lack thereof) of the unborn against the individual liberties of pregnant women. In 1964, for instance, administrators at the Raleigh Fitkin-Paul Morgan Memorial Hospital in Neptune, New Jersey, sought a court order to administer a transfusion to a pregnant Jehovah's Witness named Willimina Anderson. Anderson suffered from placenta previa, which caused serious bleeding and threatened both her own life and viability of her fetus, but she refused to consent to a transfusion because it would violate the tenets of her faith. New Jersey's highest court granted the order, asserting that that it was "satisfied that the unborn child is entitled to the law's protection," irrespective of the mother's religious beliefs. This holding did not sit well with Anderson's husband, Alex. "Our religion calls for man to do God's will," he said, "yet six men on the Supreme Court of New Jersey have overruled God's will."[52]

An analogous case heard in New York in 1985 reached a similar conclusion. A lower court judge viewed *In re Jamaica Hospital*—a case involving a Jehovah's Witness who required a blood transfusion during her eighteenth week of pregnancy—through the prism of the U.S. Supreme Court's landmark abortion decision, *Roe v. Wade*. Judge Arthur Lonschein of the Supreme Court of New York wrote that the holding in *Roe* had recognized "that the State has a significant interest in protecting the potential of human life represented by an unborn fetus, which increases throughout the course of pregnancy, becoming 'compelling' when the fetus reaches viability." Although the Witness mother's fetus was not yet viable, Lonschein believed that the state nonetheless had "a highly significant interest in protecting the life of a mid-term fetus." Indeed, this interest was so significant that it "outweigh[ed] the patient's right to refuse a blood transfusion on religious grounds." Lonschein appointed a physician to serve as the guardian of the fetus. Under the judge's order, the doctor possessed the authority to safeguard the health of the fetus by compelling its mother to receive a blood transfusion.[53]

In an insightful study of pregnant Jehovah's Witnesses and blood transfusions, Joelyn Knopf Levy has pointed out that, despite the judicial precedents established in cases like *Raleigh Fitkin* and *Jamaica Hospital*, "the right of a pregnant woman to refuse treatment required for her fetus's survival continues to be much debated. Those supporting the right argue that a woman does not surrender her autonomy when she becomes pregnant. Those arguing against point to the U.S. Supreme Court's finding that the state has an interest in protecting a viable fetus." Levy's point regarding the lack of a clear consensus on this issue was illustrated by the case of Darlene Brown, a Jehovah's Witness who opposed, on religious grounds, a blood transfusion during her thirty-fourth week of pregnancy. Although Brown's fetus was viable and the lack of a transfusion left it endangered, the Illinois Supreme Court held in 1997 that she had the right to refuse the procedure. Rejecting the reasoning behind decisions like *Jamaica Hospital*, the court's majority held that "the State may not override a pregnant woman's competent treatment decision, including refusal of recommended invasive medical procedures, to potentially save the life of the viable fetus."[54]

In two controversial Witness cases, courts have weighed the state's interest in preserving a mother's health so that she could care for a healthy child. The *Application of the President and Directors of Georgetown College* case involved a young Witness mother, Jesse E. Jones, who had been rushed to a Washington, DC, hospital after suffering from a ruptured ulcer. The woman's life clearly was in jeopardy—by the time she arrived at the hospital, she had lost about two-thirds of her blood—but her husband, citing the tenets of their religious faith, refused to authorize a blood transfusion. (Jones herself weakly voiced opposition to the procedure, but there was some question as to whether she was competent enough to make such a decision.) After the hospital sought a court order mandating the treatment, Judge J. Skelley Wright of the U.S. Court of Appeals for the District of Columbia conducted an extraordinary firsthand investigation at the hospital. With Jones's life apparently hanging in the balance, Wright convened a meeting attended by doctors and hospital administrators as well as the dying woman's husband. "Mr. Jones [insisted] that the Scriptures say that we should not drink blood, and consequently this religion prohibited transfusions," Wright later wrote. "The doctors explained to Mr. Jones that a blood transfusion is totally different from drinking blood in that the blood physically goes into a different part and through a different process in the body. Mr. Jones was unmoved."[55]

Wright granted the hospital's order, and Jones received the blood transfusion. In his written opinion, the judge stressed the fact that although the Jehovah's Witness was not pregnant, she was the mother of a seven-month-old child, and its welfare might have been endangered if she had died. "The state, as parens patriae, will not allow a parent to abandon a child, and so it should not allow this most ultimate of abandonments," Wright held. "The patient had a responsibility to the community to care for her infant. Thus the people had an interest in preserving the life of this mother." Whatever her religious beliefs, the state could act to preserve the mother's life in order to safeguard the interests of her child.[56]

However, thirty years after *Georgetown College*, a Connecticut case with comparable facts was resolved differently by a state court. Jehovah's Witness Nelly Vega delivered a healthy baby at Stamford Hospital in the summer of 1994, but afterward a retained piece of her placenta caused her to hemorrhage. When Vega refused a blood transfusion, the hospital sought a court order to compel her to receive the treatment. In an emergency hearing—it took place at the hospital at 3:25 AM—a trial court judge granted the order, and in doing so he noted the state's interest in not only preserving Vega's life but also in protecting the interests of her child, who seemed likely to suffer harm if she died. Although Vega received the transfusion and survived her ordeal, she appealed the trial court's judgment to the Supreme Court of Connecticut. As Justice David Borden wrote for the state high court in *Stamford Hospital v. Vega*, the hospital's position was that the Jehovah's Witness essentially would have abandoned her baby, "and, therefore, the hospital had a legitimate interest in protecting the welfare of an innocent third party who was also its patient—the baby—that outweighed Vega's interest in bodily self-determination." The court rejected this argument, saying that the hospital's interest in the baby's welfare was "not sufficient to take priority over Vega's common law right to bodily integrity."[57]

It is tempting to dismiss women like Nelly Vega or Rebecca Corneau as aimless people who have drifted toward "fringe" religions or, even worse, cults. Observers often affix these pejorative terms to emerging religious faiths espousing doctrines that seem so far outside the perceived mainstream of American Protestantism as to be beyond the bounds of religious legitimacy. Corneau's denomination, for example, routinely was disparaged in the news media as the "Attleboro cult." The appellation clearly was meant to distinguish The Body, with its unusual doctrines and insular structure, from churches that purportedly were more legitimate. The irony, of course, is that Christianity itself was similarly marginalized when it was first preached—in part because of the startling religious healing practices of its leader and his followers.

What such dismissive labels gloss over is the undeniable vitality of what an increasing number of scholars—dropping pejorative terminology that implicitly marginalizes such groups—have characterized as "new," "emerging," or "alternative" religious movements. Exhibiting a kind of zealous spiritual entrepreneurialism, these American originals (to borrow an apt term from historian Paul Conkin) continually sprout up and flourish by tapping into devout individuals' dissatisfaction with the doctrines and practices of mainstream churches. The allure of many such churches lies in their promise to provide a more authentic religious experience, one closely modeled on the traditions established by the earliest Christians. Quite often, the foundation of this more genuine experience is a narrowly literal interpretation of the Bible or some other sacred scripture of more recent vintage.[58]

The modest stature of these small denominations, some of which lack formal clergy or even church buildings, often seems inversely proportional to their members' fervor. To outsiders, the intensity of their religious devotion often becomes apparent only when church members clash with public authorities over their religious practices. This was famously the case with the Branch Davidians, whose long-simmering conflict with the FBI in Waco, Texas, boiled over into a full-fledged conflagration in 1993. It also happened—albeit in a somewhat less dramatic way—in Oregon in the late 1990s, when members of two obscure churches, the Church of the First Born and the Followers of Christ Church, gained widespread notice because of their dismal track records as spiritual healers. Until word spread that children in the denominations had been dying after their parents denied them medical treatment, many Oregonians had not even known that the churches existed.

9

"God Can't Cure Everyone"

Spiritual Healing on Trial in Oregon

The first signs of Tony Hays's illness—the illness that eventually would ravage his young body and leave him dying in his father's arms—hardly seemed ominous. In the fall of 1994, the Hays family left its home in Brownsville, Oregon, for an extended trip to visit friends and relatives in Oklahoma and Colorado. Tony became carsick during the first leg of their journey, but his parents, Loyd and Christina Hays, initially did not think his illness was a serious problem. The boy had experienced similar discomfort on other long trips, and he had recovered relatively quickly each time.[1]

By the time the family reached Oklahoma, Tony seemed to be back on his feet. He was able to romp with his cousins and four siblings, playing football and roughhousing like a healthy eight-year-old. But Tony's condition deteriorated when the family traveled through the Rocky Mountains on its way back to Oregon. Usually a robust kid, he now seemed lethargic. He developed bruises and showed signs of a high fever. His neck swelled; he complained of pains in his stomach and back. He also vomited and experienced a series of nosebleeds that became progressively longer and more intense. (One, in fact, lasted for several hours.) Eventually, Tony's health faltered so much that his father decided to cut the vacation short and return the entire family to Oregon.[2]

But Loyd Hays did not rush his son to an emergency room when the family made it back to Brownsville. In fact, even though Tony's health clearly was failing, Hays would not consult with a physician—or any other medical professional, for that matter—for the duration of the boy's sickness. Although he had battled more than his share of physical ailments over the years, Loyd Hays never had taken a pill or received an injection in his life, and he had no intention of having his son treated with such tools of modern medicine. What would heal Tony, he believed, was prayer—and prayer alone.

Religious faith permeated the lives of Loyd Hays and his family. They belonged to the General Assemblies and Church of the First Born, a relatively small Pentecostal church with roots stretching back to the early twentieth century. The church's ten thousand or so members were spread out in about thirty congregations in a handful of states in the Midwest and West, primarily Oklahoma, Indiana, Colorado, and Oregon. Like Loyd Hays (who roofed houses for a living), most church members were hardscrabble, working-class folk, and they did not stand much on ceremony: the church lacked a formal headquarters, and it did not employ paid clergy. Elders guided individual congregations, and Hays proudly served in that capacity in his local church.[3]

Although there is not complete uniformity in doctrine and practice among individual Pentecostal churches, they are united by a belief that spirit baptism is marked by such ecstatic experiences as glossolalia. Commonly known as speaking in tongues, glossolalia is viewed by Pentecostals as a sacred gift that signifies not only God's immense power but also his direct presence. This immediacy—taken as a sign that God is present—minimizes an individual believer's need for formal liturgies or the mediation of clergy.

Describing the particular doctrines of the Church of the First Born, one member of the faith explained that followers believed in "salvation by faith and God, the authority of the Bible, the necessity of repentance and baptism, [and] obedience to the orders of the church, [with] the orders being faith, baptism and penitence." For Loyd Hays and his religious brethren, heeding "the authority of the Bible" meant adhering to a narrowly literal interpretation of the scriptures. They routinely followed the guidance set forth in both Romans 16:16 ("greet one another with a holy kiss") and John 13:14 ("you also should wash one another's feet").[4]

Perhaps not surprisingly, when a member of their flock fell ill, church members turned to James 5:13–15, the much-cited passage that prescribes prayer and anointment as a means of physical healing. Another verse they relied on was Mark 6:13, which describes the apostles' method of healing the sick as they went forth among the people and preached: "They drove out many demons, and they anointed with oil many who were sick and cured them." The teachings of these passages in the scriptures seemed perfectly clear to Loyd Hays. If prayer and anointment with oil had been good enough for Christ and the apostles, they were surely good enough for him. Prayer would heal Tony's illness. Medical treatment, as the elder Hays later put it, simply was "not an option."[5]

Loyd Hays's decision came as no surprise to members of his local Church of the First Born congregation. Their worship services—held in a local elementary school because the church could not afford to erect its own structure—often were punctuated by wondrous accounts of the healing power of prayer. People talked of bent backs straightening and of sores healing. Arnold Jensen, Hays's father-in-law and the acknowledged leader of the congregation, sometimes regaled listeners with stories from his boyhood that illustrated just how miraculous a healing tool prayer could be. When he was four, Jensen said, he tumbled out of a wagon and broke his arm. His folks did not summon a doctor; they brought in church elders for a prayer session, and the break healed.[6]

At one worship service, Jensen told a group of a dozen or so rapt youngsters another tale from his childhood. He recounted how he had stumbled into a beehive as a toddler and received more than six dozen bee stings. Red welts had covered his young body, Jensen said, and he had been in agony—until, that is, his mother summoned church elders to pray over him and anoint his body with oil, as stipulated in the Epistle of James. "My mama did what she read in the Bible," he recalled. "Those who came [and prayed] did what they read in the Bible. God had mercy and spared my life."[7]

Loyd Hays could tell similar stories. Tony's father claimed that one of his other children once had fallen into a pool of water and drowned. The girl had been revived on the family's kitchen table—not through cardiopulmonary or mouth-to-mouth resuscitation, he said, but through prayer. Witnessing such miracles confirmed Loyd Hays's belief that the plain-spoken spiritual healers in his congregation were far more effective at curing the sick than the high-toned physicians at the local hospital. "I feel if they put us on a percentage rate against what the doctors do," he asserted, "our percentage would be a lot better."[8]

Others were not so sure. Skeptical observers from outside the Church of the First Born claimed that its ineffective healing practices had resulted in the deaths of at least two dozen children nationally since 1964. "They've lost children in several states," said Rita Swan of the advocacy group CHILD. Church of the First Born congregations in California, for instance, experienced a series of highly publicized child deaths in the 1980s and early 1990s. Because faith-based neglect deaths typically are underreported (authorities often chalk them up to natural causes or simply fail to investigate them very thoroughly), such cases probably were only the tip of the iceberg. "I'm sure that we don't have a quarter of what there really is," said Swan of the cases of neglect involving Church of the First Born that were tracked by CHILD.[9]

One of the Church of the First Born neglect cases documented in Swan's files dated back to the mid-1960s. Sandra Kay Arnold, a thirteen-year-old girl from California, became ill early in May 1964. After complaining to her mother, Florence Arnold, of stomach pains, she vomited several times. Other unmistakable signs of illness soon followed. Sandra began to lose weight; she could neither retain liquids nor defecate, nor could she walk without help. At one point, a convulsion lasting nearly half an hour wracked Sandra's body.

Florence Arnold, a Church of the First Born member, knew that her daughter was grievously ill, but she chose to treat her worsening ailment with prayer rather than conventional medical treatment. On May 15, members of her church came to Sandra's bedside and prayed over her, and five days later they transported her to a nearby river, where she was immersed and baptized. (Church doctrines proscribed infant baptism.) She died three hours after that service.[10]

The doctor who performed Sandra's autopsy quickly found the cause of her illness. He was amazed to discover that a ball of human hair measuring over two inches in length (it apparently had accumulated over a period of several months) had lodged in her small intestine, obstructing her bowels and causing the aspiration of fecal material into her lungs. Had surgery been performed up to twelve hours before Sandra's death, the doctor later testified, her life probably would have been spared. The dreadful circumstances of the death prompted authorities in Sacramento County, California, to charge Florence Arnold with manslaughter, and a jury later convicted her on that charge. (The Supreme Court of California threw out Arnold's conviction in 1967, but its ruling focused almost solely on how police had obtained her confession and not on her culpability in Sandra's death.)[11]

The healing practices of Church of the First Born members also came under intense scrutiny in another California case from the 1980s. Church members Geneva Northrup and Julia Young faced criminal charges for practicing midwifery without proper certification after they were implicated in two botched baby deliveries. In accordance with church doctrine, Pat Bell, Northrup's daughter, did not consult an obstetrician after she went into labor late in 1984. Instead, she received help only from two unlicensed "helpers"—her mother and Julia Young—who attempted to expedite the delivery. (Among other things, they helped to enlarge Bell's vaginal opening and cut the umbilical cord.) Their efforts failed to preserve the health of Bell's daughter, who was stillborn. Northrup and Young were similarly unsuccessful when they attended at the labor of Northrup's daughter-in-law early in 1985; her child was stillborn as well. Soon thereafter, the pair faced charges of practicing midwifery without the certification mandated by California law.[12]

The defense mounted by Northrup and Young demonstrated how religious exemptions to state criminal laws—provisions that effectively excuse criminal conduct if it is grounded in sincere religious belief—could complicate efforts to prosecute members of the Church of the First Born. The accused pair argued that they had not been performing midwifery but rather simply "fulfilling their calling" by attending to the women in labor in a way that conformed with their religious faith. They could not obtain the state-mandated certification, Northrup and Young claimed, because doing so would have required them to violate the tenets of their religious faith. California law required certified midwives to refer to a physician any patient who exhibited a specified set of symptoms or conditions, and Church of the First Born doctrine pro-hibited such connections with mainstream medicine. In their defense, the pair pointed to the state's medical-practice act. The law stated that none of Cali-fornia's myriad laws regulating the practice of medicine could be construed to "regulate, prohibit, or apply to any kind of treatment by prayer, nor interfere in any way with the practice of religion." In an opinion handed down in 1987, the California Court of Appeal held that the religious exemption applied to Northrup and Young and that they could not be prosecuted for failing to obtain midwifery licenses.[13]

In Oregon, one particularly notable Church of the First Born neglect case involved one of church leader Arnold Jensen's own children—Tony Hays's aunt, Sara Jensen. As an infant, Sara suffered from hydrocephalus. The con-dition caused fluid to build in her skull, and her head became abnormally enlarged. Although the disease did not immediately threaten to kill her, the hydrocephalus so debilitated Sara that she could not sit up without assistance, and in the long term she faced the prospect of severe developmental problems, including retardation. There was a widely accepted treatment for Sara's con-dition. Through a low-risk procedure known as surgical shunting, a tube could be inserted into her brain in order to drain off the excess fluid. But Arnold Jensen refused to authorize the surgery, claiming that his child's malady was best treated with prayer.[14]

Sara's case gained a degree of notoriety in Oregon because local authorities intervened to protect her. Officials in Linn County obtained an order from a juvenile court judge ordering Sara to be placed in the custody of the state's Children's Services Division. The court then directed that agency to "obtain and provide medical care and other special treatments to [the child] for the condition of hydrocephalus, such treatment to include but not be limited to a surgical operation." Arnold Jensen and his wife appealed the court's order, claiming that it violated their "constitutionally protected right to family in-tegrity, privacy and freedom to practice religion," as their attorney put it. The Jensens asserted that the state had no grounds to infringe on these freedoms because Sara's condition, though clearly debilitating, was not yet life threat-ening. The Oregon Court of Appeals denied their appeal in 1981. Its opinion in *State v. Jensen* held that "the most basic quality of the child's life is endangered by the course the parents wish to follow. Their rights must yield." Sara had the surgery, and the hydrocephalus abated.[15]

Then there was Loyd Hays himself. He sported thick, tinted eyeglasses and a hearing aid, and spots from a nagging fungal infection dotted his fingernails. Hays also suffered from a chronic kidney ailment that sometimes left him in such excruciating pain that he was unable to work as a roofer. His condition was serious: when the state's Vocational Rehabilitation Department referred him to a physician for an examination (church doctrine permitted such man-dated interaction with doctors), Hays learned that stones had rendered one of his kidneys useless. The doctor warned Hays that he was risking total kidney failure—and perhaps death—if he failed to receive proper medical treatment for the stones, but he stubbornly insisted on continuing to treat his ailment with prayer alone.[16]

His faith in the healing power of prayer unmitigated by his own checkered medical history, Loyd Hays did not take Tony to a hospital when the family returned to Oregon from its abbreviated vacation—this despite the fact that he read some medical literature and surmised that his son might be suffering from leukemia. Instead, he summoned a group of Church of the First Born elders to his home for a prayer session. Tony seemed to rally briefly, but then his condition steadily declined. According to one observer's account, his "energy level decreased, he began to vomit again, his stomach protruded and he complained a couple of times a day that his stomach bothered him." At one point in his downward slide, a worried neighbor telephoned the local sheriff's office and urged authorities to check on Tony's worsening condition. A sheriff's deputy came to the Hays home on the night of November 3, 1994, to inquire about the boy. Christina Hays answered the door but quickly deferred to her husband, who refused to permit the deputy to see Tony.[17]

Tony's condition turned grave that night, and Loyd Hays slept for several hours on the floor near his son's bed. Early on the morning of November 4, the elder Hays carried Tony to a couch in the family's living room. After complaining of pain in his back and stomach, the boy asked his father to beckon church elders for a prayer session. They arrived soon thereafter and kneeled around the couch in prayer. As they prayed for Tony's recovery, he reached up several times and clutched his father around the neck, indicating that he wanted to be held. Loyd Hays obliged, lifting Tony from the couch and taking him to a recliner located near the wood stove that heated the living room. The youngster died a few minutes later as his father cradled him.[18]

An autopsy confirmed Loyd Hays's suspicions about his son's illness: Tony died from acute lymphocytic leukemia (ALL). In victims of ALL (there are about four thousand new cases diagnosed in the United States every year), bone marrow fails to generate blood stem cells that turn into a healthy balance of white blood cells, red blood cells, and platelets. Instead, too many immature white blood cells (called "blast cells") are generated. The resulting deficiency in red blood cells and platelets can cause recurring infections, frequent bruises, slow-healing cuts, and anemia. The acute nature of the disease means that the health of victims—most of whom are children under the age of ten—worsens quickly.[19]

Dr. Steven Fletcher, the pathologist who performed Tony Hays's autopsy, said of ALL, "It's very treatable." In the overwhelming majority of ALL cases, chemotherapy restores proper blood-cell production within a relatively short period of time and drives the disease into remission within a few months, if not weeks. Although there is no guarantee that chemotherapy (or more dramatic treatments, such as blood stem cell transplants) will eradicate a patient's ALL, most of those treated can look forward to surviving for a significant number of years. Dramatic advances in the treatment of ALL prompted Dr. Grover Bagby, director of the Oregon Cancer Center at Oregon Health Sciences University, to comment, "It's viewed as one of the biggest success stories in clinical cancer research."[20]

Because of his family's religious faith, Tony Hays never benefited from the readily available treatments that would have mitigated his pain and prolonged his life. The autopsy performed by Fletcher revealed just how clearly spiritual healing had failed to match the effectiveness of those standard medical treatments. When Fletcher examined Tony's corpse, he discovered that ALL had caused his spleen to balloon to more than six times its normal weight. Tony's liver had likewise swelled, doubling in size as the disease laid waste to his body.[21]

In the wake of Tony's death, these findings did not seem to faze Loyd Hays or the other members of the Church of the First Born in Brownsville. They were devastated by the boy's death, but they apparently had no regrets about how they had attempted to heal him. "None of this changes anything," said Vernon Flandermeyer, one of the congregation's elders. "People die. God can't cure everyone. But he cures more than they do in hospitals." Stan Fitzjarrell seconded Flandermeyer's defiant comments, telling a newspaper reporter that the brutal circumstances of Tony Hays's death would not change the way he treated the illness of his own children, boys aged three and six. "If my child were hurt, I'd pray for him first, then bring in the elders to pray for him," Fitzjarrell said. "We'd leave it in God's hands." Fitzjarrell's wife agreed with him wholeheartedly. She claimed that the next time one of her boys fell ill, she would call in the congregation's elders for a prayer session, "just like they did with Tony. We'd trust in the Lord."[22]

Arnold Jensen remained firm in his faith as well. Despite his daughter's battle with hydrocephalus and the death of his grandson Tony, Jensen held fast to the belief that the teachings of the scriptures mandated prayer for the treatment of illness. "We have no instruction in the Old Testament or the New to go to a medical practitioner for healings," he said shortly after Tony Hays's death. "Jesus healed. He didn't refer them to this doctor or that doctor." As for Tony's passing, it was simply a part of the cycle of life. "Death is a natural thing," Jensen commented. He even managed to speculate that there might be a silver lining to Tony's death. One of the happy consequences of the legal battle that raged over the treatment of his daughter Sara's hydrocephalus, he recalled, was that the publicity generated by the case had caught the attention of an errant member of the faith and brought him back into the Lord's fold. Jensen wondered if Tony's death—which attracted widespread media coverage in the Pacific Northwest—might serve a similar purpose.[23]

Loyd Hays was not about to abandon his faith, either. "I was raised in this church," he said after Tony's death, "and I'll always be a member." His son's passing had been a tragedy, to be sure, but it had been part of the Lord's plan. "Obviously, the Lord didn't spare my son. But he knows what is best. I believe there is a heaven and a hell. If the Lord had spared him, maybe he wouldn't have walked with God [in heaven]." For her part, Christina Hays remained as steadfast as her husband. "I believe prayer works," she said.[24]

When local authorities mounted an investigation into the circumstances of Tony Hays's death, the residents of Brownsville, a town of about fourteen hundred residents nestled into the Willamette Valley, seemed somewhat ambivalent about the prospect of Loyd and Christina Hays facing criminal charges for their failure to seek medical treatment for their son. They were known around town as solid citizens and devoted parents. "I think they're good people," one neighbor commented; another described Loyd Hays as being "just a hard-working, honest guy." To some in Brownsville, it seemed inappropriate to mount a criminal case against such seemingly harmless people when they merely had been following the dictates of their conscience. Summing up this sentiment, a local newspaper editorialized that "these parents appear to be as far removed from criminality as anyone." There was a sense, too, that the parents might have been punished enough already by the loss of their beloved son.[25]

But not everyone sided with the parents. Some critics of the couple conceded that Loyd Hays should be left free to treat his own kidney stones with prayer alone; he was an adult, after all, and it was his own body. But Tony Hays had been a child, these observers said, and he had been left at the mercy of his parents' seemingly peculiar religious beliefs. "A line needs to be drawn," one Brownsville resident said. "I don't care what religion you are—kids should be able to count on getting proper care from their parents." It somehow seemed wrong that Tony had paid such an enormous price for his parents' adherence to religious doctrine.[26]

Early in 1995, authorities in Linn County, Oregon, determined that Loyd and Christina Hays had been responsible for Tony's death. Prosecutors alleged that the boy's parents had been negligent in relying on spiritual healing and not seeking proper medical treatment for the illness that proved to be ALL. Both parents were charged with one count each of first-degree manslaughter, second-degree manslaughter, and criminally negligent homicide. If convicted, they faced jail sentences of up to twenty years.[27]

Over the years, authorities in Oklahoma—one of the Church of the First Born's strongholds—had charged several of the Hays's coreligionists with similar offenses. These prosecutions had met with varying degrees of success. In 1982, for instance, an Enid, Oklahoma, couple, Palmer and Patsy Lockhart, faced manslaughter charges after their nine-year-old died of complications resulting from a ruptured appendix. At their trial, Palmer Lockhart detailed the tenets of the Church of the First Born as they related to healing and explained how his ailing son had been treated with prayer. After the defendants described their religious practices, their attorney asserted that the state's child-neglect statute contained a provision specifically exempting their conduct from criminal sanction. As was true in many states, Oklahoma mandated medical care for children unless the parent combated the sickness or injury by relying on "spiritual means alone through prayer, in accordance with the tenets and practice of a recognized church or religious denomination." The Lockharts' jury acquitted them, apparently finding that the faith-healing exemption excused their conduct.[28]

The Lockharts' acquittal prompted Oklahoma legislator George Vaughn to take action. Vaughn, the Democrat who had authored the child-neglect statute, introduced legislation aimed at narrowing the loophole that the Lockharts had slipped through. Vaughn's measure permitted parents to treat children with prayer unless the youngsters were seriously endangered and faced "permanent physical damage" if they failed to receive standard medical treatment. Realizing that the measure was aimed largely at them, Church of the First Born members rallied against Vaughn's bill. Several church members testified before lawmakers and argued that narrowing the faith-healing exemption would violate constitutional safeguards for their religious liberty. Their lobbying efforts failed, and the law passed.[29]

In 1983, prosecutors in McCain County, Oklahoma, filed second-degree manslaughter charges against Church of the First Born members Kevin and Jamie Funkhouser after their three-month-old baby died from complications from pneumonia. The faith-healing exemption to Oklahoma's child-neglect statute was still in effect at the time of their alleged offense, but the couple was not as successful as the Lockharts in convincing a jury that state law shielded their decision to treat their son through prayer alone. Prosecutors persuaded jurors that the couple was guilty of the "culpable negligence" provision outlined in the Oklahoma statute covering second-degree manslaughter. The Funkhousers received two-year sentences, which the Court of Criminal Appeals of Oklahoma subsequently upheld. "Good faith reliance on spiritual means alone," the court held in 1988, "is not a defense to Manslaughter."[30]

Prosecutors in Oregon hoped to have similar results in their effort to convict Loyd and Christina Hays. Like their counterparts in Oklahoma, Linn County authorities had to navigate the shoals of state laws covering criminal mistreatment of children. Oregon statutes in that area exempted parents who withheld medical treatment from dependent children if they provided "spiritual treatment through prayer from a duly accredited practitioner of spiritual treatment . . . in accordance with the tenets of a recognized church or religious denomination." This provision seemed to bar prosecution of the Hays parents for criminal mistreatment, but, as prosecutors argued in court, the loophole appeared not to provide a defense under either the manslaughter or criminally negligent homicide statutes. The latter law provided that individuals were guilty of a crime if they caused the death of another person "with criminal negligence" (a term defined elsewhere in the Oregon criminal code as meaning that "a person fails to be aware of a substantial and unjustifiable risk that the result will occur or that the circumstances exist"). By failing to take Tony to a doctor and furnish readily available treatments for his ALL, prosecutors asserted, his parents had been criminally negligent and had caused his death.[31]

At their trial, Tony's parents mounted a two-pronged defense. They maintained that since their religious conduct was afforded a complete defense under the state's criminal mistreatment statute, they should be similarly protected under the manslaughter and criminally negligent homicide laws. In addition to these somewhat dry matters of statutory interpretation, Loyd and Christina Hays stressed that they had been following Tony's explicit request when they had treated him solely with prayer. Had he asked to see a doctor, the couple maintained, they would have taken him (although Loyd Hays conceded that he "would have been pretty persistent in asking him not to" seek medical treatment, had the boy asked for it).[32]

The jury in the Hays's trial deliberated for about ten hours over two days. Trial testimony established that Loyd Hays, acting with Tony's assent, had directed the boy's care, but members of the panel struggled to determine what Christina Hays's role had been because, as one of them later put, she "was only on the stand for about two minutes" during the trial. Left to work with scant evidence, some jurors focused on her behavior when the sheriff's deputy appeared at the Hays home the night before Tony's death. The fact that the boy's mother "didn't refuse to let the deputy in" but rather deferred to her husband (who barred the deputy's entry) convinced some jurors that Christina Hays simply had not exercised any control over Tony's care. "You had to take into account," one panel member later said, "that the Hayses practice a kind of archaic religion where the man is supposed to be the dominant figure." The jury acquitted Christina Hays on all counts.[33]

Jurors deliberated more intensely over the charges leveled at Loyd Hays. Mindful that his treatment of Tony had been grounded in his sincere and long-held religious beliefs, panel members eventually turned their attention to the less serious charge facing the deceased boy's father, criminally negligent homicide. At one point in its deliberations, the panel seemed to have reached an impasse on that count, with the vote to convict sticking at nine to three. In time, however, another juror became convinced of Hays's guilt, and the panel convicted him. (In Oregon, a 10–2 jury vote is sufficient for conviction in many criminal cases.) After the verdict was handed down, several jurors conceded that their deliberations had been "very difficult," as one put it. Deciding the case, they said, had required them to sort out the clash between Hays's religious beliefs and his responsibilities as a parent. "The freedom of religion is what our country was based on, and they have their right to believe that," one juror said. "But we believed that a human life is more precious than religious beliefs." She added, "There's no doubt that they did love their child. But we believed that [Loyd Hays] seemed to think that putting his own soul in jeopardy was more important than his son."[34]

Prosecutors expected Loyd Hays to receive a sentence of between sixteen and eighteen months' incarceration, as was called for in the state's sentencing guidelines. Judge Daniel R. Murphy surprised them by sentencing Hays to five months of probation. Hays also was instructed to report to his probation officer if one of his children faced a serious illness. If such a situation arose, Hays was required to permit a medical examination of the child and assent to appropriate medical treatment.[35]

In justifying the relatively light sentence, Murphy cited Hays's cooperation with authorities after Tony's death and his previously clean criminal record. He also made several revealing comments regarding the potential impact of sentencing Hays to prison. Like many close observers of legal cases involving spiritual healing, Murphy doubted that imposing severe punishment would alter Loyd Hays's behavior or serve as an effective deterrent to others who held similar beliefs about the healing power of prayer. "Incarceration will not likely deter [Hays] nor others in society from engaging in the negligent conduct that led to the death of the victim in this case," Murphy wrote. "Incarceration is not likely to reform [him] in any sense that would reduce the likelihood of re-offending; that is, should similar circumstances arise there is no reason for the court to conclude that [his] conduct would be any different following a period of incarceration."[36]

Even though he had avoided jail time, Hays appealed his conviction to the Oregon Court of Appeals, which heard the case in 1998. Hays's attorney, deputy public defender Peter Gartlan, argued that the Oregon statutes governing criminal mistreatment and criminally negligent homicide were unconstitutionally vague. Gartlan highlighted the apparent inconsistency between the two laws: the former provided an exemption for spiritual treatment, but the latter did not. As a result, the attorney claimed, parents like Loyd Hays never could be sure if their reliance on religious treatment was permissible or subject to criminal sanction. Indeed, it seemed that spiritual treatment was legal until a child receiving it died—by which point it obviously was too late for a parent to change course and call a doctor. Highlighting this conundrum, Gartlan asked the court to determine exactly when Hays had started breaking the law by withholding medical treatment from Tony: Had it been "when the family traveled to Oklahoma? In Oklahoma? On the return from Oklahoma? While the victim was still alive in Oregon? Ten minutes before the victim's death? Or only at the time the victim died?" Such vagueness made it virtually impossible, Gartlan asserted, for "a person of average intelligence [to] possibly know when the exact conduct, which appears ostensibly privileged by statute, becomes criminal." Indeed, making this kind of subtle judgment probably was beyond the ken of most laypeople. "Asking people to comprehend that the spiritual-treatment defense applies to criminal mistreatment but not to homicide," Gartlan argued, "requires a near-expert appreciation of the law."[37]

Gartlan also made two broader claims, maintaining that the prosecution had jeopardized Loyd Hays's right to freely practice his religion and to direct the upbringing of his children. The facts of the case forced the public defender to frame the religious liberty claim in an audacious way. Gartlan conceded that a long line of judicial precedent had established the state's right to regulate religious conduct. (The line of such decisions stretched back to at least the 1870s, when the U.S. Supreme Court held that the Mormon practice of polygamy was not entitled to protection under the First Amendment.) But the courts had permitted such intrusions, Gartlan insisted, only when government could demonstrate that it was safeguarding a "compelling interest." Protecting the life of a child surely would be such an interest, but it clearly was not in jeopardy in the case of Loyd Hays because his son already was dead when the charges against him were filed. Once Tony Hays passed away, Gartlan argued, the state's interest was so diminished that it could not justify infringing on the father's religious practice.[38]

Although their final form was somewhat daring, Gartlan's arguments were based on a relatively straightforward claim: the state of Oregon could not impose criminal sanctions on Loyd Hays for having practiced his religious faith. The First Amendment protected him.

As Loyd Hays's appeal wound its way through the courts, a succession of spiritual healing–related deaths involving members of another religious faith, the Followers of Christ Church, made headlines in Oregon. After authorities learned of two deaths of children in the church in early 1998, investigations by journalists and state officials revealed that dozens of child deaths over the preceding three decades had been linked to the healing practices of this obscure church. The probes also revealed that few, if any, members of the faith ever had faced charges of neglect, manslaughter, or criminally negligent homicide.

Healing practices aside, there were more than passing similarities between the Church of the First Born and the Followers of Christ Church. Both, for instance, had roots in the Pentecostal and Holiness movements that swept through the Great Plains in late nineteenth and early twentieth centuries. Although its early history remains murky, the first Followers of Christ Church is reported to have been founded in Chanute, a small town in Kansas. A dynamic preacher named Marion Reece helped to foster the church's growth there before his calling took him to Oklahoma. The Followers apparently gained a foothold in the West during the 1920s, when Reece's brother-in-law Charlie Smith began preaching in Idaho and California. Smith eventually teamed up with George White, and White in turn ordained several of his nephews to preach. Among them was Walter White. After quarreling over church doctrine with another minister in the early 1940s, White settled down in Oregon City,

Oregon. There he dominated the affairs of a Followers of Christ congregation for the next thirty years.

Like many of his Pentecostal brethren, White could be a spellbinding orator. He gripped listeners in part by telling them that the stern messages he delivered came to him directly from the Almighty. But White relied on more than showmanship to keep the church in line. By most accounts, he ruled the Oregon City congregation with an iron hand, stifling dissent and harshly suppressing even the smallest challenges to his authority. Followers who were impudent enough to challenge his interpretation of the scriptures or commit transgressions of doctrine found themselves being called to account in front of the entire congregation or banished from it altogether. "Walter became a Christlike figure," according to one member of the faith who later left. "People believed the only way to get to God was through Walter White."[39]

White's death in 1969 left an enormous void in the Oregon City congregation. He had been in such complete control of the local church for so long that no clear successor emerged. By the 1990s, after the last member of White's inner circle had passed away, the Followers in Oregon City had neither a minister nor elders to turn to for guidance. With no one stepping forward to lead them, services at their church—a modest but well-kept building located next to the town's fire station—consisted mainly of hymns and silent prayers. These listless sessions were a far cry from the dynamic services that marked White's heyday. (One man who ultimately left the church grumbled, "I got tired of going out there and doing nothing but singing songs.") Visiting ministers from nearby Followers congregations in Oregon and Idaho sometimes presided over worship, but their offers to help establish more permanent leadership for the local church usually were rebuffed.[40]

Perhaps because of this vacuum in leadership, the Followers of Christ congregation in Oregon City became even more tightly knit. More than one observer went so far as to say that it became "cultlike" in its closeness and intolerance of dissent. Outsiders were not welcomed into the faith; only those born into the church could worship among them. To keep the church pure, nearly all youngsters were married off to other church members before they reached the age of twenty (and many were wed as early as age fifteen). Viewing themselves as the "chosen people" described in the scriptures, they kept largely to themselves and ostracized members deemed too eager to experience the allegedly corrupt world outside the confines of the church. Those who were cast out of the church for transgressions faced complete shunning: even immediate family members would greet them on the streets of Oregon City with nothing more effusive than a nod.[41]

Also shunned from the Oregon City congregation were those who too openly deviated from the faith's interpretation of the scriptures, which included a narrowly literal reading of passages dealing with prayer and healing. Like the members of the Church of the First Born, they took their cue from the

Epistle of James whenever illness or injury struck, avoiding physicians and instead relying on prayer. Many Followers were unwavering in their commitment to this practice. "Faith healing works. There is no question in my mind," said Russell Conger, a church member from Idaho. Members of the church were so resolute in believing in the healing power of prayer, he said, that their faith was "strong to the point of death." Followers did not need temporal doctors because they could rely on a spiritual healer who was far more potent. "Our physician is always there," Conger boasted. "He's always there through prayer."[42]

There seemed to be some differences of opinion among Followers regarding the appropriateness of seeking medical care when prayer failed. One deacon in Idaho said that members of his congregation were not sanctioned if they sought treatment from a doctor. (Indeed, he said that he had gone into hospitals and prayed at the bedsides of members of his church.) Even though they ran the risk of being expelled from their congregation for doing so, some members of the Oregon City congregation apparently traveled to cities like Portland and Salem to furtively seek medical treatment. For instance, when skin cancer appeared on his forehead, church member Tommy Nichols visited a doctor and had it removed. Although not everyone had the courage to admit it, "we're all not against doctors," he said. A critic of the church's drift in the years since Walter White's death, Nichols was among the few Oregon City Followers who openly questioned the wisdom of church members steadfastly refusing to seek medical treatment in cases where lives were stake. "I think they're selling out their religion," he said of those who spurned doctors altogether. "They have no religion if they allow their children or their women to die."[43]

When he criticized members of his faith for failing to protect the welfare of women and children, Nichols could point to a series of untimely deaths involving members of the Followers of Christ Church. Authorities in Idaho and Oklahoma, two other states with significant populations of Followers, documented numerous deaths among members of the faith that might have been prevented by timely medical treatment. Many of these deaths involved children. For instance, a newspaper investigation of the Followers' healing practices uncovered a dozen child deaths in two counties in Idaho. Physicians who reviewed reports of these deaths determined that several of the children—among them a youngster who suffered a ruptured appendix and another who died from a strangulated hernia—probably would have faced decent chances of survival if they had received timely medical treatment. The same newspaper investigation also discovered an alarming number of stillbirths among the Followers in those two counties.[44]

Among the Followers in Oregon City, childbirth proved to be especially perilous for both mothers and newborns. Four women in the church—none of whom was attended by a physician—died while giving birth between 1986 and 1998. Over that same period, only two women died in childbirth at a large

Portland hospital that recorded a total of twenty-five thousand births. As one specialist on high-risk pregnancies put it, "Their population base is way too small to justify four maternal deaths. These were probably healthy mothers who didn't have underlying disease who should have had healthy babies." In the summer of 1996, for instance, Janae McDowell fell victim to a massive infection after delivering a breech baby, who died as well. A physician who later reviewed a report on McDowell's death concluded that both mother and child probably would have survived if the birth had occurred in a hospital.[45]

Russ Briggs left the Followers in 1981 after watching two of his own children die in childbirth. In neither case was a doctor or nurse present; the boys died without receiving medical treatment. Almost twenty years after the deaths, Briggs was still haunted by how he had failed to secure medical help for his dying children. "I could have saved them," he said in 1998, "but I let them die." Wracked by guilt, Briggs often visited the boys' graves and reflected on how tightly he had been bound by his faith in divine healing. "It's only when you no longer have that belief," he mused, "that all of the sudden it comes to you: How could I ever have done that?"[46]

Briggs could take cold comfort in the fact that his newborn sons had not suffered as long as Alex Morris, a four-year-old boy from Oregon City who fell ill in the winter of 1989. When the youngster developed a fever and chest pains, his parents treated him in accordance with Followers doctrine, anointing his body with oil and organizing prayer sessions with other members of their church. Alex's illness continued for well over a month, and his condition progressively worsened. At one point a local police officer—acting on an anonymous tip that the boy's life was endangered—visited his home but left after the ailing boy reported that he was "all right." This self-diagnosis was far too optimistic, and Alex died of a massive chest infection two days later. Dr. Larry Lewman, Oregon's medical examiner, surmised that the child had suffered through an especially painful ordeal. "It was a horrible thing," he lamented. "The kid was getting sicker for days and days. At times, the child would have been overwhelmed with fever and pain." Lewman later said that basic medical treatment—nothing more complicated than a regimen of antibiotics—probably would have saved Alex.[47]

Two deaths of Followers children early in 1998 focused statewide attention on the faith's reliance on divine healing. On New Year's Day, an infant named Valarie Shaw died in Oregon City from an infection caused by a congenital kidney defect. Two months later, police detective Jeff Green investigated the death of Bo Philips, the eleven-year-old son of two Followers. When he arrived at the Philips home a few hours after the boy's passing, Green found a large group of Followers praying and consoling the parents. The officer found the dead child in his parents' bed; he was significantly underweight and clad in a single sock, an adult diaper, and a T-shirt. An autopsy revealed that Philips had died from juvenile onset diabetes, an illness that is usually controlled with regular insulin shots. To Larry Lewman, the state medical examiner, it was another senseless death. The diabetes "was easily treatable," he said. "It's a simple, everyday thing."

The deaths of Shaw and Philips prompted an extensive investigation of the Followers by Mark Larabee, a talented reporter for the state's largest newspaper, the *Oregonian*. Working with medical experts (including medical examiner Lewman), Larabee examined the circumstances of the sixty-three children who had been buried in the Followers' cemetery since 1955. His investigation determined that at least twenty-one of the deceased youngsters had died from causes that probably could have been successfully treated by physicians. Not all of the ailments would have required sophisticated medical treatment, the reporter found; in many cases, doctors could have relied on remedies as simple as antibiotics. Larabee learned that more than half of the child victims—thirty-eight of them—had perished before reaching age one. He also uncovered more than a dozen stillbirths over the three-decade span. Larabee's investigation of these fatalities concluded that the Followers in Oregon City had "amassed one of the largest clusters of child deaths recorded among the nation's spiritual-healing churches."[48]

What made the investigation in the *Oregonian* even more remarkable was the fact that none of the numerous deaths examined by the paper had resulted in charges of any kind being filed against parents of the deceased children. Although they seemed vulnerable at the very least to the kind of criminally negligent homicide charges that were leveled at Church of the First Born member Loyd Hays in 1996, no Followers parents had been charged with any kind of felony or even misdemeanor in connection with the dozens of child and maternal deaths associated with the Oregon City church. Nor had authorities acted preemptively to remove Followers children from their parents' custody when serious harm resulting from lack of adequate medical treatment seemed imminent. Ironically, the Oregon legislature had passed a statute authorizing the child-welfare authorities to act in such cases in 1965 after two young Followers died from meningitis in a single month. Appalled by reports of Followers children suffering from want of medical care, state representative Richard Groener had crafted a measure that allowed state officials to trump the religious objections of parents and mandate appropriate medical treatment for sick children. But authorities became so wary of infringing on the religious liberty of Followers parents that they failed to use this potential weapon for safeguarding the welfare of children in the church.

After the death of Bo Philips in 1998, Clackamas County District Attorney Terry Gustafson announced that she would not attempt to prosecute the dead boy's parents. The district attorney claimed that she did not lack the will to file charges in the latest death of a Followers child. "I want desperately to prosecute this case," she insisted. "I think that what happened to Bo Philips is a horrible, horrible thing." The problem with prosecuting the boy's parents, she said, was the apparent conflict between Oregon's criminal neglect and manslaughter statutes (which included exemptions for religious treatment) and its criminally negligent homicide law (which contained no such waiver for spiritual healing). Given the seeming inconsistency between the various laws—behavior that was sanctioned under one was illegal under another—it would violate the parents' right to due process of law to prosecute them under the more restrictive measure. To support her position, Gustafson pointed to recent court decisions in spiritual-healing cases in Minnesota (relating to the death of Ian Lundman) and Massachusetts (*Twitchell*) where appellate courts had ruled that similar conflicts between statutes did in fact represent a violation of parents' due process rights. The district attorney said that even though she was not obliged to honor rulings in those other jurisdictions, it would be "presumptuous" for her to interpret the law differently than the highest courts in two different states had.[49]

Gustafson's decision not to prosecute Bo Philips's parents was greeted with a chorus of criticism in Oregon. Among those who questioned the district attorney's judgment was Attorney General Hardy Myers. Gustafson had consulted with attorneys in Myers's office before she reached her decision, and she later said that they had advised her that a prosecution of the Philips parents was not in order because of the apparently conflicting statutes. But a spokesman for Myers disputed the district attorney's interpretation of the guidance provided by the attorney general's office, claiming that its attorneys had not in fact told her that a prosecution was inappropriate. Myers himself apparently believed that Oregon's criminally negligent homicide law contained no exemption for spiritual healing and that it was possible for the Philips parents to be prosecuted under it, just as Loyd Hays had been. Although the attorney general's spokesman suggested that Gustafson had misconstrued his office's guidance, he acknowledged that the ultimate authority to determine if particular cases merited prosecution lay with the district attorney.[50]

Several of Gustafson's fellow district attorneys also suggested that she had erred in deciding not to prosecute the Followers parents. Deriding Gustafson's claim that the confusing nature of Oregon's statutes made it impossible for her to act, one district attorney remonstrated, "I'm not confused. I think the law is sufficient to deal with this." His sentiments were echoed by John Bradley, an assistant district attorney who had helped the state legislature revise the state's child homicide laws. Bradley asserted that if a serious crime had been committed in Oregon City, as appeared to be the case, it could be prosecuted under existing state law. "If this conduct came up in Multnomah County," he said, referring to his own jurisdiction, "and the facts were present, we'd prosecute."[51]

Adding to the uproar over Gustafson's decision was the decision rendered by the Oregon Court of Appeals in the case of Loyd Hays. Just as the controversy over the Followers of Christ was reaching a crescendo in the summer of 1998, the state appellate court denied Hays's appeal. In effect, the panel gave its imprimatur to prosecutions under Oregon's criminally negligent homicide statute. The law in question, the court held, "is not legally ambiguous when applied to a parent's duty to provide medical treatment to a child." The three-judge panel held that a parent could treat a sick child by spiritual means until the illness threatened the youngster's life. At the point where there was "a substantial risk that the child will die without medical care, the parent must provide care, or allow it to be provided."[52]

Although the appellate court's decision effectively ended the Loyd Hays case, it failed to quell the rancorous public dispute over how Oregon's manslaughter and neglect laws should be applied, both in letter and in spirit, by prosecutors in cases involving spiritual healing. That debate headed to the state's legislature in the fall of 1998, and its intensity did not wane.

10

"We Need to Change the Statute"

The Promise (and Limits) of Statutory Reform

No voice was louder than Rita Swan's in calling for Oregon to bolster legal protections for children against religion-based medical neglect. A leading public campaigner against religious exemptions to manslaughter and neglect laws, Swan—the founder and leader of the advocacy group CHILD—knew that the Bo Philips case was no isolated incident. Throughout the country, in cases involving a variety of religious denominations, measures meant to safeguard spiritual-healing practices had derailed prosecutions of parents who had failed to provide adequate medical treatment for their children. Swan believed that, by allowing their parents to rely exclusively on prayer and spurn medical treatment altogether, these provisions in state criminal codes imperiled the lives of hundreds of youngsters in faith-healing churches.

Swan had painful firsthand knowledge of the dangers of religion-based medical neglect of children. Her own parents converted to Christian Science when she was a girl, and throughout her childhood she never questioned the church's teachings regarding healing. "My parents raised six kids and never took any of us to doctors," Swan later said. "We all survived and, in fact, we were pretty superior about it. We felt that we were better off than people who went to doctors and had to take drugs." When Swan married and started a family of her own, the church remained a central part of her life. She and her husband, Doug, taught Sunday school, and the couple spent part of every day praying and reviewing the works of church founder Mary Baker Eddy. In order to adhere to Eddy's teachings, Swan later said, "You deny the reality of sin, disease and death; they are all tied to matter and the false belief that we are mortal."[1]

Swan's faith in Eddy's approach to disease was tested in the early and mid-1970s. Over the period of a few years, she suffered from periodic vaginal bleeding and intense pain in her abdomen. Christian Science treatment failed to completely eliminate the problem, and Swan grew increasingly concerned about her health when she became pregnant with her second child, Matthew, in 1975. Because church doctrine permitted Christian Scientists to work with doctors for standard prenatal care, she consulted with an obstetrician during her pregnancy, and the physician diagnosed the cause of her discomfort, reporting that there was a cyst growing on one of her ovaries. Swan once again turned to her faith for healing. She worked with a Christian Science practitioner, and the results appeared to be dramatic: no cyst was visible in a subsequent ultrasound examination. Swan was "absolutely convinced" that she had benefited from "a Christian Science miracle."[2]

But Swan's religious "miracle" proved to be short-lived. Follow-up visits to her obstetrician revealed that her cyst had not disappeared; it merely had been obscured by the growth of her fetus. Swan's obstetrician, now convinced that the growth threatened her life, counseled her to have the cyst removed immediately via surgery. Swan resisted medical treatment until the pain from the cyst became unbearable. "An hour and a half of surgery [took] care of a desperate situation that Christian Science hadn't been able to heal in six years of treatment," she later explained. But Swan paid a heavy price for her decision to ignore one of the central teachings of Christian Science: she and her husband were placed on probation by their church for six months, and Swan was relieved of her post as a Sunday school teacher.[3]

Swan was such a firm believer in the Christian Science approach to healing that this potentially transformative experience—in which she had seen firsthand the undeniable merit of medical treatment—failed to shake her faith. As she later confessed, she "went crawling back to Christian Science" after her surgery. At least initially, it seemed that she had made the right decision. Her son Matthew battled a few high fevers in his infancy, and Christian Science treatments appeared to restore his health each time. His grateful parents, believing the work of church practitioners had been instrumental in the boy's recoveries, told fellow church members that his experience offered further proof of the wisdom of Eddy's teachings—and of the fallibility of medical science. As Swan later put it, Matthew's apparent ability to recover without the help of a physician seemed to confirm the Christian Science doctrine that "doctors don't heal diseases."[4]

It took Matthew's death to shatter Swan's faith in Christian Science. The boy's downward spiral in 1977 was sadly typical of many cases of religion-based medical neglect of children. When Matthew came down with another fever in the spring of that year, his parents once again summoned a Christian Science practitioner to guide his recovery. This time, however, the boy failed to re-bound, and his condition worsened; his fever spiked, and convulsions wracked his body. Matthew was "delirious and totally incoherent . . . thrashing around wildly," his mother later said. At one point in Matthew's Christian Science treatment, a church member who had been involved in his care suggested that he might be suffering from a broken bone—a condition which, under church doctrine, could be treated by a doctor. Swan carried Matthew into an emer-gency room, and physicians quickly surmised that he was suffering from an ad-vanced case of bacterial meningitis (the same virulent infection that has killed many other victims of religion-based medical neglect). Despite the entreaties of fellow church members, who urged them to remove the boy from the hospital, the Swans authorized doctors to perform emergency neurosurgery on Mat-thew. Unfortunately, the couple had waited too long to seek appropriate med-ical treatment for their son; he died less than a week after the procedure.[5]

Although the Swans blamed themselves for the loss of Matthew ("It was terribly, morally wrong for us to let this happen," Rita Swan later said), they also held responsible Christian Science and the church members who repeat-edly had counseled them to spurn medical treatment for the boy's illness. The Swans not only broke with the church; they also filed a wrongful death suit against it and two individual church members who had supervised Matthew's failed Christian Science treatments. The Swans' efforts in the courts made little headway: citing First Amendment concerns, a trial court judge dismissed the case, and an appellate court upheld the ruling. Undaunted by this failure, Swan chose to battle the dangers posed to children by spiritual-healing practices by founding CHILD, an organization devoted to safeguarding youngsters "from abusive religious and cultural practices, especially religion-based medical neglect."[6]

Religious exemptions to neglect and manslaughter laws—the provisions that stirred so much controversy in Oregon—quickly emerged as one of Swan's primary targets. Like nearly all opponents of religion-based medical neglect, Swan was not eager to suppress the religious liberty of parents or to unfairly cir-cumscribe their right to make important child-rearing decisions. Nonetheless, she adamantly believed that holding all parents, whatever their religious beliefs and practices, legally responsible for the health and welfare of their children was essential to ensuring that the rights of these vulnerable youngsters were adequately protected. "Should states prosecute parents who, acting out their sincere religious beliefs, have denied a child life saving medical care and the child has died?" she asked in one of her many articles on the subject. "I have to say yes."[7]

Public opinion seemed to support Swan's position. In 1992, two scholars at the University of Nevada-Reno, James Richardson and John Dewitt, sur-veyed four hundred adults in a community where a spiritual-healing parent recently had been tried in a case relating to religion-based medical neglect of a child. Richardson and Dewitt found overwhelming support for the general idea that the Constitution protected religious beliefs and practices. Nearly two-thirds of their respondents also agreed with the notion that "there is strong evidence that spiritual healing is an effective way of treating illness." Yet Richardson and Dewitt found that there was little public backing for religious exemptions to manslaughter and neglect laws. More than 90 percent of their respondents agreed with the assertion that "spiritual healing may have its place, but medical care should be required by law if it will prevent [manslaughter and abuse of children] from occurring again."[8]

Public support of efforts to repeal religious exemptions was tested in Massachusetts in the wake of the case of David and Ginger Twitchell, Christian Scientists who had been prosecuted for manslaughter after their son died of a bowel obstruction in 1986. As that controversial case made its way through the courts in the early 1990s, lawmakers in Boston began to consider a major overhaul of the state's child-abuse laws. Citing the Twitchells' prosecution, which had highlighted language in the laws that seemed to shield spiritual-healing practices, a broad coalition of law enforcement, children's welfare, and public health organizations urged legislators to repeal the religious-healing exemption. Among those pushing for the repeal were Joyce Strom of the Massachusetts Society for the Prevention of Cruelty to Children and John Kiernan, who had prosecuted the Twitchells. Kiernan called the repeal effort an important children's rights issue; Strom warned that failure to promptly remove the religious exemption "may result in inexcusable harm to our most vulnerable population."[9]

Repeal advocates faced a formidable opponent: the Christian Science Church, which was headquartered in Boston and wielded considerable political clout in the state capitol. In an effort that would be repeated in several other states where religious exemptions came under fire, church representatives and their allies protested that any effort to remove statutory protections for spiritual-healing practices essentially would "make criminals of good families," as one prominent Christian Scientist put it. Christian Scientists, they asserted, were not child abusers but rather caring parents, and they had adopted an approach to healing that was not only effective but also protected by both the federal and commonwealth constitutions. These claims were backed by Rev. Dean Kelley of the National Council of Churches, who objected to the criminal prosecution of compassionate parents who engaged in neither child abuse nor neglect when they attempted to heal their children's ailments through religious methods.[10]

Energetic lobbying by Christian Scientists helped to stall attempts to repeal the religious exemption to Massachusetts's child-abuse-and-neglect laws. In the fall of 1993, lawmakers took up the issue once more, and the church voiced its opposition with customary vigor. Warren Silvernail, legislative liaison for the church, asserted that "spiritual treatment is a right, a right we've proven we've been using responsibly" for over a century. Efforts to remove the religious exemption, he warned, left the church "in special jeopardy" because spiritual healing was so central to Christian Science. Church spokesman Victor Westberg made much the same point when he warned that lawmakers were on the verge of "legislating spiritual healing out of existence" by removing the religious exemption. Like Silvernail, Westberg cautioned that such a move represented a dire threat to the religious practices of tens of thousands of upstanding Christian Scientists.[11]

At least initially, it seemed that Governor William Weld backed legislators' efforts to repeal the religious exemption. At one point in the debate over the revised child-abuse bill, the governor favorably referred to the U.S. Supreme Court's oft-quoted opinion in *Prince v. Massachusetts*—a sign, it seemed, that he favored removing exceptions for spiritual-healing practices from child-abuse-and-neglect laws. But then Weld backtracked. After the state legislature formally repealed the religious exception in December of 1993, Weld said that he would reject the "minor amendment" because it was unnecessary. Under existing case law, he asserted, it was apparent that spiritual-healing practices were not in fact exempted from child-abuse laws. (This in fact had been the conclusion of the Supreme Judicial Court of Massachusetts in the *Twitchell* case.) The governor's about-face drew sharp criticism from a variety of quarters. Among those suggesting that he had succumbed to political pressure was *Boston Globe* columnist Bella English, who hinted that Weld might have "caved in to some heavy-duty lobbying by high-level Republican officials in the Christian Science Church." However, in the waning days of 1993, Weld's office announced that he would sign the bill, which repealed the ambiguous religious exemption and stiffened penalties for serious abuse. Despite the protests of the Mother Church, the governor apparently chose to scuttle the generally unpopular spiritual-healing provision in order to preserve one of his "top crime initiatives," as one Boston newspaper termed it.[12]

Although Maryland, Hawaii, and South Dakota also repealed apparent religious exemptions to their child-abuse-and-neglect laws, aggressive lobbying by Christian Scientists slowed or stalled the pace of reform in other states. Indiana, for instance, seemed primed for change in the early 1980s after a newspaper investigation revealed that dozens of children in the Faith Assembly church had died as a result of religion-based medical neglect. Responding to those reports, lawmakers made several attempts to clarify and strengthen state child-abuse laws by removing any apparent exemption for spiritual-healing practices. But, thanks largely to the opposition of Christian Scientists, such efforts repeatedly failed. "It was impossible to get it by the Christian Science Church," one lawmaker later complained.[13]

In Oregon, Christian Scientists actually succeeded in *bolstering* legal protections for their spiritual-healing practices. In 1995, shortly after the widely reported death of Tony Hays, lawmakers in Salem crafted a revision to the state's criminal code that included more severe penalties for parents found guilty of murdering their children by abuse. Christian Scientists met on several occasions with the legislators and district attorneys who were drafting the revision, and they were able to add a provision that would allow parents charged with murder by abuse to claim as a defense that they had substituted spiritual-healing practices for medical treatment. The *Oregonian* later reported that church representatives had "played a behind-the-scenes role in getting the religious defense into the 1995 Oregon law," an assertion confirmed by a district attorney who had helped draft the measure. "Our negotiation with them," he said of the Christian Science lobbyists, "was to come up with language that left [church members] alone."[14]

The *Oregonian*'s revelations about dozens of suspicious deaths of children in the Followers of Christ Church—none of which had resulted in criminal prosecutions for manslaughter or neglect—prompted lawmakers to revisit the state's criminal code. Early in 1999, two legislators introduced measures requiring parents to obtain medical treatment for their sick or injured children. Representative Bruce Starr, who introduced one of the bills, stressed that the state possessed the authority to act on behalf of children like Bo Philips when their parents, citing the tenets of their religious faiths, failed to protect them. "When, because of religious beliefs, parents refuse to intercede in life-threatening situations for their children, it is the right of the state to intervene in order to prevent the death of that child," Starr said.[15]

Several legislators spoke out against Starr's bill, claiming that it was too harsh and threatened to infringe on individuals' religious liberty. The measure's critics pointed out that, because of mandatory sentencing guidelines, parents convicted under the revised law faced sentences of up to twenty-five years in prison. This seemed to be excessive punishment for people who were "not malicious murderers," as one lawmaker put it, but rather caring parents who simply had relied on prayer to heal their children. Another cautioned that the bill, while safeguarding the rights of children, threatened to trample on the First Amendment's protections for individual rights. "I'm worried about protecting a child," said Representative Juley Gianella, "and destroying religious freedom at the same time."[16]

Christian Scientists in Oregon worked diligently to exploit such doubts and derail the revision. Although they were unable to duplicate the backstage maneuvering that had proven so effective in 1995, church members did a masterful job of lobbying lawmakers and offering public testimony designed to undermine support for Starr's bill. At one meeting of the state senate's judiciary committee, no fewer than eight church members spoke, and all of them delivered the same message: in the interests of protecting religious liberty and acknowledging a proven form of treatment, legislators should retain the religious-healing exemption. One observer compared the intensity of the church's grassroots efforts to the lobbying done by members of the National Rifle Association on behalf of gun owners.[17]

For a time, it appeared that the church would once again stymie statutory reform aimed at stiffening penalties for parents who engaged in religion-based medical neglect of children. After Starr's bill won passage in the state House of Representatives, members of the Senate Judiciary Committee restored most of the spiritual-healing defenses that the original version of the measure had eliminated. The move infuriated many of the bill's supporters: one groused that restoring the defenses for religious healing "kind of guts the whole goal of the bill." The *Oregonian*, which had played no small role in bringing the issue of religion-based medical neglect of children to the legislature's attention, also weighed in, urging lawmakers to reject the "watered down" bill and instead enact a measure that would serve as "a deterrent to the reckless practice of faith that endangers children."[18]

A main sticking point for the bill's opponents continued to be the fact that it brought faith-healing parents convicted of second-degree manslaughter under the purview of the state's mandatory sentencing law. Some legislators balked at the prospect of parents receiving a minimum sentence of seventy-five months (more than six years) for their roles in faith-healing deaths. Following several months of wrangling, both houses of the legislature finally passed Starr's bill after lawmakers agreed to remove the mandatory minimum sentence in such cases and permit a judge to determine punishment. One of the legislators who helped to forge the compromise bill—which Governor John Kitzhaber signed into law in August 1999—echoed the words of *Prince v. Massachusetts*. "We have a constitutional right to die for our religious convictions," Senator Peter Courtney said. "We don't have a constitutional right to make our children do so."[19]

Would the toughening of penalties for religion-based medical neglect actually influence deeply religious parents to seek adequate medical treatment for their sick or injured children? Expressing the hopes of many observers, one lawmaker asserted that members of the Followers of Christ Church and other churches that practiced spiritual healing were "law-abiding people" who would adhere to the newly clarified manslaughter and abuse statutes. The initial signs were encouraging. A few months after the statutory changes went into effect, Representative Bruce Starr reported that the district attorney for Oregon City, where the Followers were based, had been "flooded with phone calls from members of the church asking what they need to do to stay within the bounds of this law." And in the years since the bill's passage, there have been few (if any) reports of deaths involving children either among the Followers or in the Church of the First Born.[20]

Two years later, in 2001, lawmakers and children's welfare advocates in Colorado hoped to achieve similar success in their own long-running battle against religion-based medical neglect. Events in that state followed a familiar and dispiriting pattern in which a series of highly publicized deaths of children in faith-healing churches highlighted the need for reform in statutes covering manslaughter and neglect. As had been its habit for a century, the Christian Science Church launched a well-orchestrated lobbying effort to head off any such changes, insisting to state lawmakers (and their constituents) that removing exemptions for religious healing would compromise the individual liberties of parents who relied on spiritual means to treat the illnesses of their children.

Colorado had been struggling with religious exemptions since at least 1989, when legislators attempted to strengthen state laws governing child abuse and neglect. At the behest of Christian Scientists, lawmakers inserted into the revised statutes a provision stating that religious-healing treatments determined to be valid by insurance companies and the Internal Revenue Service were to be considered among the legitimate forms of medical treatment mandated for sick or injured children. Although this stipulation was narrowly tailored to benefit Christian Scientists, it "had a chilling effect on prosecution" across a range of religious faiths, according to the head of the state's district attorneys council. Indeed, as neglect-related deaths mounted in Colorado in the 1980s and 1990s among members of sects such as the Church of the First Born (which had been implicated in fatalities in Oregon as well), relatively few parents were held legally accountable. According to one tally, religion-based medical neglect claimed the lives of more than a dozen children in the state between 1974 and 2001, but in only three instances were parents convicted of any crime.[21]

In 1993, state representative Doug Friednash resolved to close the statutory loophole and remove the state's religious-healing exemption for child neglect. A former prosecutor who had taken a special interest in children's welfare issues, Friednash had been prompted to act by the tragic neglect death of a young girl whose parents belonged to the Church of the First Born. Friednash's bill sailed through a legislative committee, "but then the Christian Science onslaught began," he later said, "and the bill was killed." Friednash, outraged over the church's maneuvering, offered a dire prediction about the impact of the bill's failure. "At the time," he said, "I warned that more children would die because of religious exemptions."[22]

Friednash was prescient. In subsequent years, several cases of religion-based medical neglect of children were reported in Colorado. Early in 1999, for instance, an infant in Mesa County named Warren Trevette Glory died from pneumonia and bacterial meningitis—ailments that his parents, devout members of the Church of the First Born, had treated solely with prayer and anointment, as prescribed in the Epistle of James. (Asked to explain the boy's death, his grandfather said, "It's the will of God. God knows what's best.") Despite the apparent ambiguity of the state's abuse and neglect laws, the child's parents soon faced a host of serious criminal charges, including manslaughter and reckless child abuse. They eventually pled guilty to criminally negligent child abuse and received sentences of sixteen years of probation (as well as an order to provide medical care for their surviving child). "I recognize the right of parents to practice their religion," the sentencing judge offered, "as long as it does not endanger the life of someone too young to make a decision for themselves."[23]

It soon became clear that the prosecution of Glory's parents would do little to change the healing practices of members of the Church of the First Born. After the couple pled guilty, an elder insisted that church members would continue to treat their children through prayer and anointment. "The laws of God supersede the laws of this court," Marvin Peterson said shortly after the sentencing. "This is not going to change our belief any." The church's intransigence was demonstrated a year later, when another Mesa County child died from apparent religion-based medical neglect. In July 2000, a newborn named Billy Ray Reed turned pallid and struggled to breathe. His parents, adhering to the teachings of their religious faith, summoned church members and elders to pray for the boy, but their efforts failed; he eventually turned blue, stopped breathing completely, and died. An autopsy later revealed that Reed had died from respiratory problems triggered by a common heart defect. Doctors who later reviewed the case concluded that the ailment could have been diagnosed and treated relatively easily—had his parents sought medical treatment. Frank Daniels, the Mesa County district attorney, ultimately decided not to press criminal charges against the victim's parents under the state's "convoluted" and "very murky" abuse and neglect laws because it was unclear whether they had fathomed the seriousness of Billy Ray's condition. Daniels nonetheless had strong words for members of the Church of the First Born and other faiths who refused to furnish medical treatment for ailing children: "I strongly favor the right of individuals to pray for the sick and infirm. But the use of prayer to the absolute exclusion of medical care is a remnant of the Dark Ages. This practice endangers children."[24]

The Glory and Reed deaths prompted renewed calls for reform in the laws governing child abuse and neglect in Colorado. Daniels, who had pursued criminal charges in the former case but not in the latter, grumbled that "the current statutory scheme is seriously flawed and should be changed." Daniels asserted that prosecutors would be able to file charges in more cases of religion-based medical neglect—and thereby deter parents from engaging in it—if legislators clarified the statutes and removed the exemption for religious healing. Russell George, the speaker of the state's House of Representatives, echoed his point, stating plainly, "We need to change the statute."[25]

State lawmakers responded to such calls early in 2001 by taking up a bill designed to remove the religious-healing exemption that they had approved in 1989 at the behest of Christian Scientists. The proposal elicited impassioned oratory from both spiritual healers and their critics. Rita Swan, in characteristically stern testimony before a House subcommittee, criticized the exemption and scoffed at the notion that spiritual healing provided an adequate substitute for medical care. Bluntly questioning the core of spiritual healers' beliefs, she said that their practices did not merit statutory protection because there was scant proof that prayer actually worked. "Colorado's present law gives parents and church officials the impression that exclusive reliance on prayer is not only legal but safe," Swan stated. "We do not think either the [Christian Science Church] or the Church of the First Born has credible evidence that they can heal serious diseases of children."[26]

As Swan and other child-welfare advocates made their push for reform in Colorado, the death of yet another child in the Church of the First Born seemed to give their arguments added weight. In February 2001, as lawmakers began to debate the merits of removing the spiritual-healing exemption, a thirteen-year-old Mesa County resident named Amanda Bates died from complications—among them gangrene that had spread to her genitals and buttocks—caused by diabetes. The county coroner, Dr. Rob Kurtzman, later said that if the girl's parents had sought medical treatment, the massive infection that had killed her easily could have been diagnosed and treated. Although it saddened Kurtzman to chronicle another death caused by religion-based medical neglect, he thought it "may have come at a good time" because it dramatized the need for clarifying the state's abuse and neglect laws. (As it happened, Bates's death seemed to be such a clear-cut case of religion-based medical neglect that Daniels felt confident in filing criminal charges against her parents under existing statutes, and they eventually pled guilty to felony child abuse.)[27]

In the wake of Amanda Bates's death, the repeal measure, sponsored by Representative Kay Alexander, gained narrow approval in the House of Representatives and then moved to the state Senate, where it was shepherded by Bob Hagedorn. "I don't think freedom of religion should allow a child to die for not getting proper medical care," Hagedorn explained as he promoted the bill. Although Denver's two daily newspapers disagreed over the merits of the bill—the Rocky Mountain News said the measure was unnecessary, while the Post called it "long overdue"—the Senate passed it, and Governor Bill Owens signed it into law. As had been the case in Oregon, those who supported the religious exemption's repeal expressed the hope that it would "act as a deterrent," as one put it, "and save some kids' lives."[28]

Following the hard-won success of statutory reform efforts in Oregon and Colorado, children's welfare advocates like Rita Swan had reason to feel optimistic. After a series of high-profile cases had exposed possible weaknesses in abuse and neglect laws in those states, lawmakers had at last rebuffed the entreaties of the Christian Science Church and eliminated exemptions for religious healing. These statutory clarifications seemed to have had their desired effect among members of spiritual-healing denominations like the Church of the First Born, apparently deterring parents from relying solely on prayer in treating their children's illnesses. Here, the political process appeared to work (albeit creakily) as a means of preventing religion-based medical neglect. Without there being a significant infringement on individual liberties, the state nudged parents into changing their behavior and thereby safeguarding their children's health *before* the youngsters suffered grievous harm from want of medical care.

But it would be a mistake to conclude that these two prominent victories marked a conclusive end to the long-running conflict between spiritual healers and state authorities who hoped to ensure that their religious practices did not endanger or kill children. Dozens of states still retained religious exemptions to their manslaughter and neglect statutes, and many devout individuals continued to pursue spiritual treatments for their children's illnesses, often with disastrous results. In August 2003, for instance, a two-year-old in Milwaukee, Wisconsin, named Terrance Cottrell, Jr., died during a religious ritual that was meant to rid him of autism. Cottrell's death demonstrated that spiritual-healing practices remained widespread in the United States at the dawn of the twenty-first century and that they still posed a threat to ailing children whose parents substituted prayer for conventional medical treatment. Moreover, it showed that a century of litigation, statutory reform, and dramatic technological advances in the field of medical science had failed to resolve the fundamental clash between spiritual healers and public authorities. After decades of sharp conflict, both groups remained convinced—for diametrically opposite and seemingly irreconcilable reasons—that they were acting in the best interests of children.

As she waited in the lobby of a Milwaukee office building, Pat Cooper struggled to keep under control her four-year-old son, Terrance Cottrell, Jr. (who was known to friends and family simply as "Junior"). Two years earlier, doctors had discovered that Junior suffered from autism, a complex developmental disability that generally appears during the first three years of life. The boy's disability—it resulted from a neurological disorder that affected the functioning of his brain—had left him with limited social interaction and communication skills. Like many autistic children, Junior had difficulty expressing himself verbally, and he sometimes flailed his arms wildly. In an effort to mitigate Junior's disruptive behavior, a physician had prescribed him the antipsychotic drug ziprasidone, but controlling his outbursts still posed a formidable challenge for his mother. She often felt overmatched.[29]

A woman named Tamara Tolefree approached Cooper and struck up a conversation as she tried to control Junior. The two discussed the boy's disability and his apparent lack of response to medication and therapy. Tolefree, sensing Cooper's despair, suggested that both she and her son might benefit from attending services at the Faith Temple Church of Apostolic Faith, a storefront church located in a strip mall on Fond du Lac Avenue in Milwaukee. The idea appealed to Cooper because, as a police report later put it, she "felt that going to church and appealing to a higher authority might help her with her son," whom she loved dearly. Tolefree provided her telephone number, and Cooper contacted her a few weeks later in order to determine when the church held its services.[30]

Like most storefront churches, the Faith Temple Church was physically nondescript, even "dingy," as one newspaper reporter jibed. (The strip mall's other tenants—they included a modest pizzeria and a dry-cleaning store—certainly were no more glamorous.) Its main room contained a small stage and ten pews; a half dozen ceiling fans kept the air circulating on warm days. But the church's aesthetic shortcomings belied its importance to the neighborhood. One observer has described storefront churches as "a lifeblood in urban communities," furnishing a desperately needed source of spiritual and temporal renewal for the disenfranchised. Since its founding in 1977, a handful of Milwaukee residents had spurned mainstream churches and regularly come to the Faith Temple Church for worship services led by its "bishop," a man named David Hemphill.[31]

Hemphill, as was typical for many leaders of storefront churches, never had received formal training in the ministry, but he hardly viewed his lack of schooling as a shortcoming. All that was necessary to preach the word of God, he felt, was a genuine understanding of the teachings of the scriptures and a profound commitment to spreading them. "If a person believes that the King James Version of the Bible is the word of God, you just read it and believe it," he once said. "It's nothing that you have to go to school for." Hemphill felt so confident in his qualifications for the ministry that he ordained his brother Ray as an evangelist.[32]

Something more than fraternal loyalty prompted the bishop to bring his brother into the ministry. From his close study of the scriptures, David Hemphill knew that God, acting through talented ministers, responded to the prayers of the sick and healed them. Over time, the bishop came to believe that his brother—who worked as a school custodian when he was not preaching the gospel—could help the afflicted embrace God's word and thereby conquer illness. And he thought he knew how Ray Hemphill accomplished this task: "He has the gift to cast out devils," the bishop explained.[33]

From the outset, Pat Cooper seemed enthralled by the Hemphill brothers and their church. The church usually held two services on Sundays—one at noon and the other at 7 PM. On the first day she visited Faith Temple Church with Junior and her daughter Zarria, Cooper arrived in time for the earlier service but stayed the entire day and participated in the later session as well. Before long, she became immersed in the church and the apparent promise it held for her son. A neighbor later claimed that as Cooper's interest in the church grew, she became "secluded and isolated," closing herself off from friends and acquaintances and venturing from her apartment only to attend church services with Junior—something she did as many as three times a day.[34]

It was clear to Monica Tarver, a youth leader in the church, that Cooper desperately wanted to help her son. She told Tarver that Junior was being so disruptive at his school (and on the bus that transported him there) that the social worker assigned to her family had threatened to remove him from her custody. As she learned more about Cooper and her troubled son, Tarver, who fashioned herself as a prophet within the church, thought she understood the root causes of Junior's woes. At one point, she explained to the boy's mother that she had received a prophecy revealing "that Terrance was not only suffering from autism but also has demons in his soul," according to a later police report. Cooper would not have to look far for help in ridding her son of those demons, Tarver and other church members explained, because God had given minister Ray Hemphill a talent for vanquishing them.[35]

Church members' efforts to heal Junior in both body and spirit began modestly enough, with specific prayers for his physical recovery being offered during worship services on Sundays. Ray Hemphill then intensified matters by formulating a special "deliverance prayer" aimed at facilitating the boy's recovery. This measure was followed by a more dramatic attempt to cast out the demons that were contributing to Junior's flagging physical and emotional health. In the middle of a worship service, Hemphill placed Junior on the church's floor and seemingly tried to squeeze the evil out of the boy. Because Junior, like many autistic children, often recoiled when other people touched him, the minister used one hand to hold down the child's upper body and the other to restrain his legs. For good measure, he also placed a knee across Junior's chest. The boy's mother helped by pinning his legs to the floor. With the child thus restrained, Hemphill leaned toward Junior's ear and muttered a series of imprecations into it, including, "In the name of Jesus, devil get out." Cooper and the minister held the prostrate child to the floor for approximately an hour and a half.[36]

It was a testament to Cooper's desperation over her son's autism that she turned to this unconventional method of treating Junior's disability. Convinced that Hemphill's efforts represented the child's best hope for recovery, she decided to subject him to a regimen of daily exorcism sessions that involved not only the minister but also such church members as Monica Tarver and Tamara Tolefree. (Like Cooper, they helped to restrain the boy.) A police report later summarized Cooper's account of how these profoundly religious people attempted to heal Junior:

> She stated that these sessions would last two hours, during which time Terrance would be forced to the floor and pinned down while minister Ray Hemphill would be holding Terrance's head to the floor with his knee across his chest prohibiting him from moving. She stated that he, Ray Hemphill, would always be saying words to the effect of "In the name of Jesus, devil get out." She also stated that they . . . wrapped a sheet around one of Terrance's hands to stop him from scratching the people that were holding him down. Pat Cooper

stated that it was always the minister, Ray Hemphill, who was holding the victim's head down and with his knee on the victim's chest.

As one of the participants later put it, church members went to such extraordinary lengths because they "wanted God to work a miracle" and heal Junior.[37]

As the exorcism sessions continued and her commitment to the church intensified, several of Cooper's acquaintances noticed "a change in her personality," as a police report later summarized. Alisa Dawkins, whose sister lived in an apartment located above Cooper's, later reported that both Junior and his mother seemed to have isolated themselves in their apartment, only rarely venturing outside. What apparently transpired inside their apartment left Dawkins aghast. Although she never saw Cooper striking her son, Dawkins later claimed that when she and her sister sat on some steps near Cooper's apartment, she could "hear Junior being struck by [a] belt near the front door and hear Junior fighting to get out of the door as he was being beaten." The apparent beatings occurred so frequently that Dawkins approached Cooper and questioned her about the propriety of physically abusing an autistic child. According to Dawkins, Cooper justified her actions by citing the scriptures, asserting that "the Bible says to chastise your children." Dawkins's concerns about Junior's well-being only grew when she came to suspect that other church members were joining Cooper in abusing her child inside her apartment.[38]

The church's efforts to, in Ray Hemphill's words, "release the demons" that were plaguing Junior ended tragically on the night of August 22, 2003. As was customary, that evening's service began with a song, some readings from the scriptures, and various prayers. Then Junior came to the front of the church for another attempted exorcism, in which the minister would "ask God to heal this child [from] his violent problems with autism," as a police report later summarized. Hemphill lay atop the boy as various church members, including Junior's mother, helped to restrain him. They took turns clutching his limbs and keeping them from thrashing. The minister whispered imprecations in the child's ear throughout the session, imploring Jesus to "deliver Terrance from his demons and this state" of disability. The church lacked air conditioning, and on that warm evening its ceiling fans did little to keep the worshippers and their minister cool. The session was physically strenuous for Hemphill, and it left him drenched with sweat.[39]

After about two hours, Hemphill lifted himself from Junior and walked toward a restroom, and the session broke up. When the child—still lying on his back on the church floor—failed to stir, a church member said to him, "Junior, let's go." He remained motionless, and several women rushed over to check his condition. They were stunned to discover that the child had stopped breathing. Church member Tamara Tolefree responded by calling 911 from her cellular phone. As they awaited the arrival of emergency medical technicians, the 911 operator provided Hemphill with instructions for performing cardiopulmonary resuscitation, which he attempted with the help of a church member. Paramedics from the Milwaukee Fire Department arrived a short time later and took over the attempt to revive the boy.[40]

Paramedic Cansell Mitchell made a desperate effort to save Junior's life. Attempting to gauge the possible extent of the child's injuries, Mitchell asked the boy's mother what had transpired in the church. Cooper apparently was reluctant to be completely forthcoming about the circumstances of Junior's injuries. She did not mention that Hemphill had been laying atop her son for a prolonged period or that his limbs had been restrained. "He was praying," she said, "and just stopped breathing." When Mitchell attempted to insert an IV into Junior's right arm, he observed what appeared to be fresh "pressure bruising," typically caused by broken capillaries beneath the skin's surface. Mitchell asked Cooper how the boy might have received such bruises, and she again dissembled. Instead of mentioning that Junior's arms had been restrained throughout the exorcism, she told the paramedic that she could offer no explanation for the marks.[41]

As soon as he inserted the IV into Junior's arm, Mitchell realized that he probably was fighting a losing battle. The color of the boy's blood was dark red, which indicated that it had been deprived of oxygen for an extended period. And when the EMT hooked up Junior to a monitor and checked his vital signs, he saw that the boy "had already flatlined, with no pulse," in the words of a later police report. Even before they reached a nearby hospital, a doctor had pronounced Junior dead. An autopsy later revealed that he had died of mechanical asphyxiation. A criminal complaint later prepared by police concluded that it had been caused by "pressure placed on Terrance Cottrell's chest to the point . . . where he could not breathe and was denied oxygen."[42]

After the Milwaukee Police Department received word that Junior had died in unusual circumstances, several detectives arrived at the storefront church and began questioning people who had witnessed or participated in the exorcism, including the boy's mother and Ray Hemphill. Although some of the details of their accounts differed, most told essentially the same story: believing that the boy was possessed by demons, Hemphill had performed the last in a series of exorcism rituals, rites that had involved church members restraining Junior and the minister himself lying across the child's body for a period of approximately two hours. According to a police department summary of her interview, Junior's mother, like all of the participants and witnesses, "did not realize that there was anything wrong" during the exorcism. "She stated that she did not feel that they were hurting her child because his actions during the incident were consistent with his actions in the previous prayer ceremonies that had been conducted in the past three weeks." It was not until Junior actually had stopped breathing, she said, that she had realized that something had gone horribly wrong, and by then it had been too late to save him.[43]

Ultimately, prosecutors decided not to file criminal charges against Cooper or any other lay participant in the exorcism because their roles in the ritual had been secondary. Ray Hemphill, however, soon faced charges of felony child abuse. For his failed effort to heal Junior, the minister faced penalties that included up to ten years in prison and as much as twenty-five thousand dollars in fines. A judge—who termed Junior's death "one of the most troubling cases ever to come before this court"—released the minister on bail but ordered him not to "engage in or even attempt any sort of exorcism or spiritual healing" as he awaited trial.[44]

E. Michael McCann, the Milwaukee County district attorney, felt that, given the circumstances of Junior's death, his office might have had difficulty convincing a jury to convict Hemphill of a more serious crime, such as homicide, because the minister clearly had lacked the intent to harm the victim. To substantiate a murder charge, prosecutors would have had to prove that Hemphill had been "consciously . . . aware that what he was doing had a great likelihood of causing death," McCann explained. "We did not feel we could prove it." After all, the intention of all the participants in the exorcism had been to restore Junior's health; hurting him had been the furthest thing from their minds. As an assistant district attorney put it, Hemphill had been "trying to help this child," and that mitigated against filing a more serious charge.[45]

Even in pursuing lesser criminal charges against Hemphill, McCann appeared to face a potential hurdle. Within the state laws governing child abuse lurked a caveat addressing "treatment through prayer." The provision, like ones that had confounded prosecutors in other states, stated that a person could not be found guilty of child abuse "solely because he or she provides a child with treatment by spiritual means through prayer alone for healing in accordance with [a bona fide] religious method of healing . . . in lieu of medical or surgical treatment." Another section of the statute stated that a determination of abuse or neglect "may not be based solely on the fact that the child's parent, guardian or legal custodian in good faith selects and relies on prayer or other religious means for treatment of disease or for remedial care of the child."[46]

McCann was an experienced prosecutor—he had served as district attorney since 1968—and he was wary of how the statutory language protecting "spiritual" and "religious" means of healing might complicate, if not simply derail, his case against Hemphill. "I've been aware of that provision and concerned about it for a number of years," McCann said. "I think it has the potential for mischief." He insisted that the minister's behavior during the exorcism had been so egregious that it could not be covered by the religious-healing exemption to the child-abuse statute. Hemphill had not simply prayed for Junior; the minister essentially had squeezed the breath out of the helpless child's body. In McCann's estimation, the statute never had been intended to shield such conduct.[47]

As McCann attempted to navigate the shoals of Wisconsin's child-abuse laws, a variety of critics blasted his handling of the Hemphill case. Mary Luckett, the victim's grandmother, voiced a common sentiment when she expressed bewilderment over the district attorney's reluctance to pursue more serious charges against the minister. "How can a child be dead," Luckett asked, "and these people get charged with child abuse?" It mattered little to her that her grandson had died during a religious-healing ritual. "I don't care if it was a church. I don't care what they were trying to do." The victim's father (who was estranged from Junior's mother and apparently played a secondary role in his upbringing) also ridiculed the notion that Hemphill should be treated more leniently because he had been trying to help the child in a religious rite. According to the elder Cottrell, the exorcism "was just a way to kill somebody." Even more casual observers of the case seemed disturbed by McCann's charging decision: a typical letter to the *Milwaukee Journal Sentinel* asserted, "That our district attorney is only charging this so-called preacher with felony child abuse . . . is unthinkable. That this monster is now out on bond is just insane."[48]

Criticism of McCann soon came from outside Milwaukee as well. Marci Hamilton, a church-state expert from the Cardozo School of Law in New York, called the charges leveled against Hemphill weak and suggested that the religious dimension of the case had given McCann cold feet. "He should have been charged with reckless homicide at least," she asserted, "but the prosecutor did not have whatever it takes to do what is right: this man's deeds killed this boy, and their religious quality does not alter that fact one iota." Annie Laurie Gaylor, head of the Madison-based Freedom From Religion Foundation, also condemned McCann for his apparent reluctance to "throw the full force of Wisconsin law" at Hemphill. A frequent and vocal critic of entanglements between church and state, Gaylor insisted that the district attorney had reached a "gutless and . . . immoral decision" in determining that the minister only should be charged with felony child abuse for his role in Junior's death. Like Hamilton, she lamented McCann's hesitancy in pursuing more severe criminal charges against those responsible for Cottrell's death, saying that it sent "a message that Milwaukee County does not value the life of [the victim], and that cruelty and criminal conduct in the name of religion will be rewarded with token charges."[49]

Unshaken by such condemnation, McCann refused to alter the charges filed against Hemphill, and the minister went to trial on the felony child-abuse count in July 2004. Annie Laurie Gaylor had cautioned the district attorney that "the world is watching" the case unfold, and she hardly was exaggerating: Court TV broadcast the trial live into millions of households in the United States and abroad. Viewers who tuned in witnessed a clash that echoed the dozens of cases of religion-based medical neglect of children that had been heard in American and British courts during the previous century and a half.

Sparring with prosecutor Mark Williams, the minister's brother, David Hemphill, attempted to explain how religious faith could vanquish sickness, testifying that "there's nothing too hard for God, and nothing too hard for his believers." When the skeptical Williams pressed him by suggesting that the minister had perhaps taken the church's dedication to religious healing to a dangerous extreme during the exorcism ritual, Hemphill snapped that "my church is going to do exactly what the word of God tells us to do."[50]

Williams responded, "So, you're saying God is giving you the power to take away . . ."

"I say, he has the power," Hemphill thundered. "If I lay down on someone and he passes away—God took him, I didn't!"

"He did it to Terrance, didn't he? Your brother did it!"

"No, he didn't!"

This explanation apparently was too much for Pat Cooper to bear. Upon hearing David Hemphill claim that his brother had not in fact taken Junior's life, the victim's mother began sobbing and left the courtroom in tears.[51]

Although his brother apparently hoped to pin the ultimate responsibility for Junior Cottrell's death on the Almighty, Ray Hemphill's attorney had a more temporal and prosaic explanation for the youngster's demise. Cottrell's autopsy revealed that elevated levels of ziprasidone (also known by the brand name Geodon) had been present in the boy's bloodstream at the time of his death. The medical examiner acknowledged that the drug levels had been relatively high, but he insisted that they had not played a factor in Cottrell's death. Defense attorney Thomas Harris, however, argued that the boy appeared to have been "heavily medicated" at the time of the exorcism and that the elevated levels of Geodon—not Hemphill's "good works," as the attorney called them—had been primarily responsible for the child's death. "I'm saying it's the drugs," Harris explained.[52]

Hemphill's attorney faced an uphill battle, but he gamely offered several other claims in his defense. Harris argued that the minister should not be found guilty of child abuse because he had not been irresponsible in performing the exorcism that evening. Hemphill, after all, had performed similar rituals on several prior occasions, and the child's mother had consented and participated each time. "Minister Ray did no act in a reckless fashion that day," Harris said in court. "There was nothing reckless about this admittedly nontraditional prayer service. It had been performed numerous previous times, and [Junior's] own mother was there supervising and assisting." The defense attorney also zeroed in on the religious dimension of Hemphill's activities, arguing that Junior had died in a church during a religious service and the district attorney had no business attempting to regulate such matters. "The government is attempting to equate a voluntary church-prayer service, participated in by the victim's mother, as somehow criminal conduct," he added.[53]

As he built his case against Hemphill, prosecutor Mark Williams expressed a dim view of the "makeshift exorcism," as he called it, and the minister who had presided over it. Williams told jurors that the ceremony had been nothing short of "bizarre" and that Hemphill should have known better than to think it was safe for a grown man to lie atop a small disabled child for several hours. "Any normal—and any abnormal—adult is going to say, 'Yeah, you can hurt that child very seriously,'" the prosecutor jibed. Williams also attempted to shift the jury's focus from the alleged perpetrator of the crime to his victim. He underscored the fact that Junior—tiny, autistic, and essentially defenseless—apparently had tried to writhe his way free of those restraining him during the exorcism. "All the child could do was struggle," the prosecutor said, "and literally fight for his life."[54]

Throughout the case against Hemphill, prosecutors seemed confident that there was sufficient evidence to sustain a charge of physical abuse of a child/recklessly causing great bodily harm. But before jurors began their deliberations, Williams gave them the option of considering a lesser charge of physical abuse of a child/recklessly causing bodily harm—a sign that prosecutors perhaps harbored doubts about the strength of their case against the minister. Nonetheless, after four hours of deliberations, jurors returned a guilty verdict on the more serious charge. The victim's father found cold comfort in the verdict, and he once again blasted McCann for his decision to charge Hemphill merely with felony child abuse. "I don't feel we got justice," he said. "The state wasn't too zealous to up the charge. They could've gotten a conviction on a higher charge."[55]

At Hemphill's sentencing, Milwaukee County Circuit Court Judge Jean DiMotto told him, "It was your unreasonable and reckless conduct that caused this child to die." She sentenced the minister to thirty months in prison and seven-and-a-half years of probation thereafter. DiMotto also barred him from performing exorcisms during the period of state supervision unless he first received formal training in how to conduct them. The judge believed that such a stiff sentence was needed in part to warn others against risking the lives of children in religious ceremonies. "The community cannot risk another child being hurt, much less being killed, in a religious ritual," DiMotto warned.[56]

At the time, it seemed that the widespread publicity generated by the death of Junior Cottrell and Ray Hemphill's subsequent trial would prompt Wisconsin lawmakers to reexamine—and eliminate—the spiritual-healing exemption to the state's child-abuse statute, as their counterparts in Massachusetts, Colorado, and Oregon had done. Hemphill had not been able to wriggle through that loophole; he simply had gone too far in his conduct during the botched exorcism. Yet the provision and the values it reflected nonetheless seemed to constrain prosecutors, and many observers speculated that it would only be a matter of time before the exemption resulted in real "mischief," as E. Michael McCann put it. The district attorney was among those who called for lawmakers to repeal the exemption as a means of discouraging parents from engaging in religion-based medical neglect of children. One of McCann's sharpest critics, Annie Laurie Gaylor, challenged him to "take the lead in advocating the repeal of this statute, if you sincerely find it to be a potential barrier to justice," as she most certainly did.[57]

In the following two years, legislators in Madison took up a number of issues of varying degrees of importance. They wrangled over the state's budget, debated the merits of a bill allowing state residents to carry concealed weapons, and argued over such matters as minimum wage laws, smoking bans, and a proposal to pick an official state tartan design. But no legislator introduced a measure to repeal or modify the religious-healing exemption.

The death of Junior Cottrell—involving as it did an exorcism, a religious rite with its own set of distinct and ancient roots—was uniquely tragic. However, with its agonizing facts and unsatisfactory outcome, the legal case arising from the boy's passing in many ways typified more than a century of litigation in American courts over religion-based neglect and abuse of children. In the Cottrell case, as in so many others of its kind, a child died as the direct result of a religious ritual that was meant to heal rather than harm him. Authorities pursued legal action against the minister they deemed responsible for the victim's death (and took a softer line against his mother), but they found their task complicated by provisions in state law that appeared to afford legal protections for religious-healing practices. Although the jury found the accused guilty, his conviction provided no guarantee that other children might not fall victim to the same kind of religious conduct. And, after the case had demonstrated the need for statutory reform, politicians failed to muster the will to take decisive action in the realm of public policy. This bleak course of events, which seemed to leave no one involved fully contented, fit into a pattern that had been established over a century earlier and then repeated dozens of times in communities across the United States.

If this pattern has shown anything, it is that secular political forces, whatever the noble intentions of the individuals who marshal them, still face an awkward task when they endeavor to police religious conduct. Despite the best efforts of the Founders, who hoped that the nation would avoid such strife, state and church have maintained a contested relationship throughout the course of American history. Some of their discord has been generated by efforts of state authorities to limit religious behavior that, for a variety of reasons, has been deemed a threat to public order. It is a testament to Americans' longstanding and fierce attachment to the principle of religious liberty that public officials have wielded this police power so infrequently and so reluctantly. Even when it apparently has cost children their lives, prosecutors have been skittish—sometimes to a fault—about zealously and consistently applying manslaughter and abuse laws to parents who have spurned medicine for prayer in the treatment of their children.

Not that representatives of the other two branches of government have been especially bold in dealing with religion-based medical neglect of children. Legislators—sometimes responding to political pressure exerted by religious denominations—have crafted and then defended loopholes in various criminal laws for religious healing practices. Judges throughout the country have been diffident as well, imposing remarkably lenient sentences on religious parents convicted for their roles in the neglect-related deaths of their children. Their tentativeness, grounded in a sincere desire not to infringe on individuals' First Amendment freedoms, has typified the overcautiousness evidenced by all three branches of government in dealing with crimes related to prayer-based healing rituals.

Despite this hesitancy, some distinct trends have emerged with regard to regulation by secular authorities of parents' spiritual-healing rituals. Starting in the late nineteenth century, these rites increasingly have been drawn into the orbit of state control, thanks in large part to the evolution of an interrelated set of legal norms that have afforded the state a more expansive role in safe-guarding the rights of children, curbing potentially disruptive or dangerous religious practices, and protecting public health. Over time, there have emerged legal standards—though not always precise ones—mandating medical treat-ment for sick and injured children, even when their parents voice objections on religious grounds. These standards have developed in piecemeal fashion through a halting and imperfect political process. Its features have included criminal prosecutions of parents and clergy, as well as the evolution of judicial precedent and the institution of statutory reforms by elected officials.

The smooth functioning of this process has been impeded by the princi-pled defiance of the Christians around whom it revolves. Healing rituals are such a long-standing and essential part of their religious experience that they have fiercely resisted state attempts to regulate their efforts to treat their chil-dren's illnesses solely by prayer, anointment, and other spiritual means. Chris-tian Scientists have provided perhaps the most prominent example of this in-transigence. Refusing to be deterred by the specter of temporal punishment for their actions, they have endured more than a century of intermittent scrutiny by public officials without abandoning the healing practices that comprise the core of their faith. Other spiritual healers—all of them convinced that they are loyally following the teachings of the scriptures—generally have been just as obdurate in refusing to accept state regulation of their religious conduct.

It is tempting to use broad strokes in characterizing the many legal clashes in which these stubborn individuals have been implicated. Their ongoing con-flicts could be depicted as emblematic religious persecutions pitting devoted and deeply religious parents against characteristically overzealous political of-ficials who fail to respect basic principles of tolerance. Or, conversely, they could be portrayed as efforts by well-meaning public authorities to exercise their power wisely and thereby prevent innocent children from becoming martyrs to their parents' reckless religious practices. Depending on one's point of view, the central actors on either side of these disputes easily might be represented as heroes, villains, or just plain fools.

These extreme depictions gloss over, however, what fundamentally links spiritual healers to the public officials who attempt to restrict their religious conduct. As the preceding pages have shown, the realms of law and religion often come into conflict even in the most broad-minded and tolerant societies, but they are by no means inherently oppositional. Indeed, as legal historian Harold Berman has argued, they can be viewed as being in many ways complementary and interdependent. To borrow Berman's framework, both parents who spurn medicine for prayer and public officials value belief systems grounded in ritual, tradition, authority, and universality. Furthermore, both groups genuinely treasure children and hope to protect their health. Their methods of shielding youngsters are, of course, dissimilar, if not simply antithetical, yet their intentions are very much the same. Neither group wants to see children get hurt.[58]

Nonetheless, what divides spiritual healers and legal authorities—and what has generated the heated conflicts that comprise the heart of this book—is striking. They possess dramatically different perspectives on such potentially life-and-death matters as the efficacy of medical science and the legal duty of parents to furnish it to their children. More broadly, their views of the obligations of citizenship are fundamentally at odds. At least in theory, prosecutors and politicians devote themselves to defining the rule of law and making sure that all citizens uphold it, irrespective of their personal beliefs. Spiritual healers often struggle to match this fidelity to what some scholars have described as "the idea of the good liberal citizen." While they generally are law abiding, many of those who spurn medicine for prayer would agree with John Alexander Dowie's assessment that they should "forget about the law" as it relates to furnishing medical treatment to their children because they "are Christians first, citizens afterward."[59]

Dowie's comment cuts to the heart of the dilemma that still confronts devoutly religious parents who choose to treat their sick or injured children with prayer rather than medicine. Not only must they endeavor to safeguard the flagging health of their sons and daughters; they also must try to reconcile their devotion to God with their duties as citizens in a society that, while ostensibly honoring the principles of tolerance articulated in the First Amendment, boasts a long and sometimes checkered history of regulating the religious conduct of adherents to uncommon faiths. For spiritual healers, balancing those sacred and secular responsibilities—weighty obligations that often dramatically conflict with one another—remains no less vexing a task today than it was in Dowie's time.

Notes

CHAPTER 1

1. *Commonwealth v. Dean Heilman* and *Commonwealth v. Susan Heilman,* "Statement of Facts for Guilty Plea," 1–4 (hereafter *Heilman* Guilty Plea); *Commonwealth v. Dean Heilman,* "Criminal Complaint" (hereafter *Heilman* Criminal Complaint); Macarena Hernandez and Denise Leobet, "More Tests Planned in Toddler's Death," *Philadelphia Inquirer,* 10 July 1997, B3. All primary documents relating to these prosecutions are in the case files for *Commonwealth v. Dean Heilman* (No. 1757) and *Commonwealth v. Susan Heilman* (No. 1758), Court of Common Pleas of Philadelphia County, Criminal Section, Trial Division, August Term, 1997. I am grateful to court personnel for making these materials available to me.

2. *Heilman* Criminal Complaint; *Heilman* Guilty Plea, 1–4.

3. Ibid., 1–4.

4. Michael E. Ruane, "Church Believes in Healing through Faith," *Philadelphia Inquirer,* 12 February 1991, B1. Except when indicated otherwise, Bible quotations throughout this volume are from *The Holy Bible: New Revised Standard Version with Apocrypha* (New York: Oxford University Press, 2001).

5. *Heilman* Guilty Plea, 1–4; Linda Loyd, "Court Told How Tot Bled to Death," *Philadelphia Inquirer,* 15 October 1997, B1.

6. *Heilman* Guilty Plea, 1–4.

7. *Heilman* Criminal Complaint; *Heilman* Guilty Plea, 1–4.

8. *Heilman* Guilty Plea, 1–4; Loyd, "Court Told How Tot Bled to Death," B1. For a standard reference work on hemophilia, see Christine Lee, Erik Berntorp, and W. Keith Hoots, eds., *Textbook of Hemophilia* (Malden, MA: Blackwell, 2004). A helpful resource for information on hemophilia is the Web site of the National Hemophilia Foundation: http://www.hemophilia.org.

9. Barbara Laker, "Faith Tabernacle Parents Face Trial," *Philadelphia Daily News*, 15 October 1997, 16.

10. Barbara Laker, "Tiny Victims of Blind Faith," *Philadelphia Daily News*, 10 July 1997, 10; Barbara Laker, "Docs: Dead Tot Was Hemophiliac," *Philadelphia Daily News*, 29 July 1997, 14.

11. *Heilman* Criminal Complaint.

12. Laker, "Faith Tabernacle Parents Face Trial,"16.

13. Ibid.

14. Loyd, "Court Told How Tot Bled to Death," B1.

15. *Commonwealth v. Dean Heilman* and *Commonwealth v. Susan Heilman*, "Written *Nolo Contendre* Plea Colloquy," 7 October 1998; Dave Racher, "No Jail for Parents in Tot's Death," *Philadelphia Daily News*, 19 February 1999, 14.

16. Julie Stoiber, "Parents Get Probation in Son's Death," *Philadelphia Inquirer*, 19 February 1999, B1.

17. Racher, "No Jail for Parents in Tot's Death," 14.

18. Ibid.

19. These cases, and the Peculiar People in general, are discussed more extensively in chapter 3.

20. *People v. Pierson*, 68 N.E. 243 (N.Y. 1903), 244–247.

21. "Child Died Without Medical Attendance; 'Diphtheria and Christian Science Neglect' the Causes," *New York Times*, 22 October 1902, 16.

22. Daniel Rubin, "Measles Epidemic Spurs a Rush of Doctor Visits," *Philadelphia Inquirer*, 17 February 1991, 1; Idris M. Diaz and Denise-Marie Santiago, "Phila. Compels Hospitalization in Measles Case," *Philadelphia Inquirer*, 18 February 1991, 1B.

23. Bill Gifford, "A Matter of Faith," *Philadelphia*, September 1997, 100.

24. Bette Bottoms et al., "In the Name of God: A Profile of Religion-Related Child Abuse," *Journal of Social Issues* 51 (1995), 85–111.

25. Don Finley, "Child Health Group Targets Faith Healing Exemptions," *San Antonio Express-News*, 25 May 1988, 1A; Mark Sauer, "Suffer the Little Children," *San Diego Union-Tribune*, 22 June 1999, E1; Seth Asser and Rita Swan, "Child Fatalities from Religion-Motivated Medical Neglect," *Pediatrics* 101 (1998), 625–629.

26. Finley, "Child Health Group Targets Faith Healing Exemptions," 1A; Sauer, "Suffer the Little Children," E1; Asser and Swan, "Child Fatalities," 625–629.

27. Asser and Swan, "Child Fatalities," 625–629.

28. Ibid.

29. Jim Quinn and Bill Zlatos, "More Than Half the Faith Assembly's Fatalities . . . Were Babies Too Young to Choose for Themselves," *Fort Wayne (IN) News-Sentinel*, 2 May 1983, 7A.

30. Asser and Swan, "Child Fatalities," 625–629; Caroline Fraser, *God's Perfect Child: Living and Dying in the Christian Science Church* (New York: Holt, 1999), 305–309, 333, 334.

31. David Van Biema, "Faith or Healing?" *Time*, 31 August 1998, 68–69.

32. Mark Larabee, "An Oregon Case Shines a Light on the Issue," *Portland Oregonian*, 29 November 1998, A1.

33. Wis. Stat. Ch. 948 (2005); Rita Swan, "On Statutes Depriving a Class of Children of Rights to Medical Care: Can This Discrimination Be Litigated?" *Quinnipiac Health Law Journal* 2 (1998/1999), 73–95. Swan also discusses these statutes in some detail in the "Policy and Legal" section of the Web site operated by CHILD, http://www.childrenshealthcare.org.

34. American Academy of Pediatrics Committee on Bioethics, "Religious Exemptions from Child Abuse Statutes," *Pediatrics* 81 (1988), 169–171; Massachusetts Citizens for Children, "Death by Religious Exemption," http://www.masskids.org/dbre_1.html, accessed on 11 July 2005.

35. Rita Swan, "When Faith Fails Children—Religion-Based Neglect: Pervasive, Deadly . . . and Legal?" *Humanist*, November/December 2000, 11–16.

36. Jennifer Rosato, "Putting Square Pegs in a Round Hole: Procedural Due Process and the Effect of Faith Healing Exemptions on the Prosecution of Faith Healing Parents," *University of South Florida Law Review* 29 (1994), 43–119; James G. Dwyer, "The Children We Abandon: Religious Exemptions to Child Welfare and Education Laws as Denials of Equal Protection to Children of Religious Objectors," *North Carolina Law Review* 74 (1996), 1321–1478; James G. Dwyer, "Symposium: Spiritual Treatment Exemptions to Child Medical Neglect Laws: What We Outsiders Should Think," *Notre Dame Law Review* 76 (2000), 147–178; and Henry J. Abraham, "Abraham, Isaac and the State: Faith-Healing and Legal Intervention," *University of Richmond Law Review* 27 (1992–1993), 951–988.

37. Jim Quinn and Bill Zlatos, "52 Deaths Tied to Sect," *Fort Wayne (IN) News-Sentinel*, 2 May 1983, 1A; Jordan Cohn, "When God Is the Doctor," *Student Lawyer*, February 1987, 31–36.

38. Quinn and Zlatos, "52 Deaths Tied to Sect," 1A; Mark Larabee, "The Battle Over Faith Healing," *Portland Oregonian*, 28 November 1998, 1A.

39. Jim Quinn and Bill Zlatos, "Law Sought to Protect Sect Children," *Fort Wayne (IN) News-Sentinel*, 6 May 1983, 1A; "Indiana Parents Not Charged after Children's Deaths," *Fort Wayne (IN) News-Sentinel*, 5 May 1983, 8A.

40. Randy Frame, "Indiana Grand Jury Indicts a Faith-Healing Preacher," *Christianity Today*, 23 November 1984, 38–39; Chris Lutes, "Former Staff Pastor Says Faith Assembly Is a Cult," *Christianity Today*, 7 November 1986, 61–62; *People v. Lybarger*, 700 P. 2d 910 (Colo. 1985), 911–917.

41. *People v. Lybarger*, 700 P. 2d 911–917; *People v. Lybarger*, 790 P. 2d 855 (Colo. App. 1989), 857–862; *Lybarger v. People*, 807 P. 2d 570 (Colo. 1991), 571–583.

42. Rebecca Gardyn, ed., "Quackery No More," *American Demographics*, January 2001, 10; Patricia Barnes et al., "Complementary and Alternative Medicine Use among Adults: United States, 2002," *Advance Data from Vital and Health Statistics* 343 (2004): 1–19.

43. Barnes et al., "Complementary and Alternative Medicine," 1–19.

44. Ibid., 10; Meredith B. McGuire, *Ritual Healing in Suburban America* (New Brunswick, NJ: Rutgers University Press, 1988), 10–13.

45. Daniel M. Johnson et al., "Religion, Health and Healing: Findings from a Southern City," *Sociological Analysis* 47 (1986), 66–73; Margaret M. Poloma, "A Comparison of Christian Science and Mainline Christian Healing Ideologies and Practices," *Review of Religious Research* 32 (1991), 337–350.

46. Larry Dossey, *Prayer Is Good Medicine: How to Reap the Healing Benefits of Prayer* (New York: HarperCollins, 1996).

47. Stephen Gottschalk, "Spiritual Healing on Trial: A Christian Scientist Reports," *Christian Century*, 22–29 June 1988, 602–605; Tom Black, "Real Power," *Christian Science Sentinel*, 14 June 2004, 8; *Today*, NBC, 23 October 1998.

48. Bruce Nickerson, ed., "Faith Healing in Indiana and Illinois," *Indiana Folklore* 6 (1973), 33–99.

49. Stephen Gottschalk, "Spiritual Healing and the Law: A Dispute," *Christian Century*, 19 October 1988, 928–929.

50. Grant Wacker, "Marching to Zion: Religion in a Modern Utopian Community," *Church History* 54 (1985), 496–511; Ellis E. Conklin, "Trial Tested Town's Faith: Oregon Case Pitted Prayer vs. Medicine," *Seattle Post-Intelligencer*, 27 April 1996, A1; Mark O'Keefe, "Boy's Death Reinforces Faithful, Splits Town," *Portland Oregonian*, 26 March 1995, A1; Cheryl Martinis, "Man Argues Conviction in Death of His Son," *Portland Oregonian*, 30 May 1998, A1.

51. Asser and Swan, "Child Fatalities," 625–629; G. E. Wilson, "Christian Science and Longevity," *Journal of Forensic Science* 1 (1965), 43–60; William Franklin Simpson, "Comparative Longevity in a College Cohort of Christian Scientists," *Journal of the American Medical Association* 262 (22–29 September 1989), 1657–1658.

52. James McClendon, "Spiritual Healing and Folklore Research: Evaluating the Hypnosis/Placebo Theory," *Alternative Therapies* 3 (January 1997), 61–66.

53. Amanda Porterfield, *Healing in the History of Christianity* (New York: Oxford University Press, 2005), 16–18.

54. Bill Gifford, "A Matter of Faith," *Philadelphia Magazine*, September 1997, 96–101, 154–156.

55. Suzanne Shepard, "Suffer the Little Children," *Redbook*, October 1994, 66, 68, 70, 72.

56. Larry Parker, *We Let Our Son Die: A Parent's Search for Truth* (Irvine, CA: Harvest House, 1980), 27, 55–56.

57. Ibid., 82–83, 95, 98.

58. Ibid., 159–174; "Probation in Faith-Healing," *New York Times*, 29 September 1974, 55; Larry Parker, *Assumptions About Faith and Tradition* (Frederick, MD: PublishAmerica, 2002).

59. Shawn Francis Peters, *The Yoder Case: Religious Liberty, Education, and Parental Rights* (Lawrence: University Press of Kansas, 2003); Shawn Francis Peters, *Judging Jehovah's Witnesses: Religious Persecution and the Dawn of the Rights Revolution* (Lawrence: University Press of Kansas, 2000); Ronald B. Flowers, *That Godless Court? Supreme Court Decisions on Church-State Relationships*, 2d ed. (Louisville, KY: Westminster John Knox, 2005), 21–50.

60. *Meyer v. Nebraska*, 262 U.S. 390 (1923); *Pierce v. Society of Sisters*, 268 U.S. 510 (1925); *Prince v. Massachusetts*, 321 U.S. 158 (1944), 159–176.

61. The Corneau case and The Body in general are discussed more thoroughly in chapter 8.

62. Lawrence Friedman, *Total Justice: What Americans Want From the Legal System and Why* (Boston: Beacon, 1985), 3–5, 147–152.

CHAPTER 2

1. Lawrence Sullivan, "Healing," in Mircea Eliade, ed., *The Encyclopedia of Religion*, vol. 6 (New York: Macmillan, 1987), 226–233.

2. John Wilkinson, *The Bible and Healing: A Medical and Theological Commentary* (Grand Rapids, MI: Eerdmans, 1998), 64–77; Morton Kelsey, *Healing and Christianity: In Ancient Thought and Modern Times* (New York: Harper and Row, 1973), 54–57; John T. Carroll, "Sickness and Healing in the New Testament Gospels," *Interpretation* 49 (1995): 130–142.

3. Carroll, "Sickness and Healing," 130–142.

4. Wilkinson, *Bible and Healing*, 179.

5. Daniel R. Hayden, "Calling the Elders to Pray," *Bibliotheca Sacra* 138 (1981): 258–266; Martin Albl, " 'Are Any Among You Sick?' The Health Care System in the Letter of James," *Journal of Biblical Literature* 121 (2002): 123–143; Roderick Graciano, "The Prayer of Faith and Healing in James 5," 1–19, accessed through the Timothy Ministries Web site at www.tmin.org on 12 October 2005.

6. Amanda Porterfield, "Healing in the History of Christianity: Presidential Address, January 2002, American Society of Church History," *Church History* 72 (2002): 227–242.

7. Porterfield, *Healing in the History of Christianity*, 53; Darrel Amundsen and Gary Ferngren, "The Early Christian Tradition," in Numbers and Amundsen, eds., *Caring and Curing*, 52; Darrel Amundsen, "Medicine and Faith in Early Christianity," *Bulletin of the History of Medicine* 56 (1982): 326–350.

8. Amundsen and Ferngren, "Early Christian Tradition," 40–60.

9. John Calvin quoted in Porterfield, "Presidential Address," 233.

10. Martin Luther, *Luther's Works*, vol. 35 (Philadelphia, PA: Muhlenberg, 1960), 362, 395–397; John Calvin, *Calvin's Commentary on the Epistle of James* (Aberdeen, Scot.: J. Chalmers, 1797), 1–109.

11. Richard W. Fox, *Jesus in America: Personal Savior, Cultural Hero, National Obsession* (New York: HarperCollins, 2005), 29–67.

12. George Fox, *The Journal of George Fox*, vol. 2 (Cambridge: Cambridge University Press, 1911), 227; George Fox, *The Journal of George Fox*, vol. 1 (Cambridge: Cambridge University Press, 1911), 234; George Fox, *Book of Miracles* (Cambridge: Cambridge University Press, 1948).

13. George Fox, *Book of Miracles*; George Fox, *Journal of George Fox*, vol. 2, 227; George Fox, *Journal of George Fox*, vol. 1, 234; *The Brethren Encyclopedia*, vol. 1 (Philadelphia: Brethren Encyclopedia, 1983), 39–40; Jonathan Baer, "Redeemed Bodies: The Functions of Divine Healing in Incipient Pentecostalism," *Church History* 70 (2001), 735–771; Jonathan Baer, "Perfectly Empowered Bodies: Divine Healing in Modernizing American" (PhD diss., Yale University, 2002); Robert Bruce Mullin, *Miracles and the Modern Religious Imagination* (New Haven, CT: Yale University Press, 1996), 107.

14. Grant Wacker, "The Pentecostal Tradition," in Numbers and Amundsen, eds., *Caring and Curing*, 524–525.

15. Baer, "Redeemed Bodies," 735–771.

16. Maria Woodworth-Etter, *Maria Woodworth-Etter: The Complete Collection of Her Life Teachings*, comp. Roberts Liardon (Tulsa, OK: Albury, 2000), 763–774.

17. Mullin, *Miracles and the Modern Religious Imagination*, 91–93; Charles Cullis, *Faith Cures; or, Answers to Prayer in the Healing of the Sick* (Boston: Willard Tract Repository, 1879), 5.

18. Cullis, *Faith Cures*, 5, 15–17.

19. Raymond J. Cunningham, "From Holiness to Healing: The Faith Cure in America, 1872–1892," *Church History* 43 (1974): 499–513.

20. A. B. Simpson, *The Gospel of Healing*, in Jonathan Graf, ed., *Healing: The Three Great Classics on Divine Healing* (Camp Hill, PA: Christian, 1992), 370.

21. Ibid., 359–369.

22. Donald Dayton, "The Rise of the Evangelical Healing Movement in Nineteenth Century America," *Pneuma: The Journal of the Society for Pentecostal Studies* 4 (1982): 1–18.

23. A. J. Gordon, *The Ministry of Healing*, in Jonathan Graf, ed., *Healing: The Three Great Classics on Divine Healing* (Camp Hill, PA: Christian, 1992), 130, 232–244.

24. Cunningham, "From Holiness to Healing," 504–506.

25. "Driven Crazy by Religion," *New York Times*, 12 April 1891, 1.

26. Mark Noll, *The Work We Have to Do: A History of Protestants in America* (New York: Oxford University Press, 2002), 83; Benjamin Warfield, *Counterfeit Miracles* (New York: Scribner's, 1918), 157–196.

27. Mullin, *Miracles and the Modern Religious Imagination*, 102–103.

28. Carrie Judd Montgomery, *The Life and Teaching of Carrie Judd Montgomery* (New York: Garland, 1985), 79–92; Wacker, "The Pentecostal Tradition," 522.

29. Grant Wacker, *Heaven Below: Early Pentecostals and American Culture* (Cambridge, MA: Harvard University Press, 2001), 66–67.

30. Grant Wacker, "Marching to Zion," 500, 510–511; Baer, "Redeemed Bodies," 765.

31. Wacker, "The Pentecostal Tradition," 522.

32. F. F. Bosworth, *Christ the Healer* (Grand Rapids, MI: Revell, 1973), 163–189.

33. Ibid., 232–234.

34. David Edwin Harrell, Jr., *All Things Are Possible: The Healing and Charismatic Revivals in Modern America* (Bloomington: Indiana University Press, 1975), 27–52.

35. Ibid.; C. Douglas Weaver, *The Healer-Prophet, William Marrion Branham: A Study in the Prophetic in American Pentecostalism* (Macon, GA: Mercer University Press, 1987).

36. Harrell, *All Things Are Possible*, 100–101.

37. Kathryn Kuhlman, *I Believe in Miracles* (Englewood Cliffs, NJ: Prentice-Hall, 1962); Kathryn Kuhlman, *God Can Do It Again* (Englewood Cliffs, NJ: Prentice-Hall, 1969); Wayne Warner, "At the Grass-Roots: Kathryn Kuhlman's Pentecostal-Charismatic Influence on Historic Mainstream Churches," *Pneuma: The Journal of the Society for Pentecostal Studies* 17 (1995), 51–65.

38. William Nolen, *Healing: A Doctor in Search of a Miracle* (New York: Random House, 1974).

39. James Randi, *The Faith Healers* (Buffalo, NY: Prometheus Books, 1987), 1–11, 89–98, 257.

40. Ibid., 183–195.

41. Nickerson, "Faith Healing in Indiana," 47–50. Nickerson's lengthy article is comprised of transcripts of interviews with faith healers.

42. Ibid.

43. Ibid., 51–53.

44. Ibid., 78–79, 85–87.

45. Larry Dossey, *Prayer Is Good Medicine: How to Reap the Healing Benefits of Prayer* (New York: HarperCollins, 1996), 5.

46. Francis Galton, "Statistical Inquiries into the Efficacy of Prayer," *Fortnightly Review* 12 (1872): 125–135. I have benefited from a discussion of Galton's work in Larry Dossey, *Healing Words: The Power of Prayer and the Practice of Medicine* (San Francisco: HarperSanFrancisco, 1993), 234–238.

47. Dossey, *Healing Words*, 238–239; William R. Parker and Elaine St. Johns, *Prayer Can Change Your Life: Experiments and Techniques in Prayer Therapy* (Carmel, NY: Guideposts, 1957), ix.

48. Randolph C. Byrd, "Positive Therapeutic Effects of Intercessory Prayer in a Coronary Care Unit Population," *Southern Medical Journal* 81 (1988), 826–829; Dossey, *Healing Words*, 248–250.

49. Harold Koenig, *The Healing Power of Faith: Science Explores Medicine's Last Great Frontier* (New York: Simon and Schuster, 1999), 22–25. For a mammoth compendium of studies in this field, see Harold Koenig, Michael McCullough, and David Larson, eds., *Handbook of Religion and Health* (New York: Oxford University Press, 2001).

50. "The Act of Prayer and Its Benefits," *Talkback Live*, CNN, 27 November 1997.

51. Dale Matthews, *The Faith Factor: Proof of the Healing Power of Prayer*, with Connie Clark (New York: Viking, 1998), 53; Hampton Sides, "The Calibration of Belief," *New York Times Magazine*, 7 December 1997, 92.

52. *The Edge with Paula Zahn*, Fox News Network, 12 July 2000; R. P. Sloan, E. Bagiella, and T. Powell, "Religion, Spirituality, and Medicine," *Lancet* 353 (1999), 664–667. A thorough review of controversies involving the credibility of scientific studies of prayer is, unfortunately, beyond the scope of this work. For an illuminating example of these impassioned debates, see Bruce Flamm, "Faith Healing Confronts Modern Medicine," *Scientific Review of Alternative Medicine* 8 (2003/2004), 9–14.

53. Stephen Barrett, "Some Thoughts about Faith Healing," http://www.quackwatch.org/01QuackeryRelatedTopics/faith.html, accessed on 14 December 2005.

54. Hector Avalos, "Can Science Prove That Prayer Works?" *Free Inquiry* 17 (1997), 27–31.

55. Ibid.

56. Benedict Carey, "Can Prayers Heal? Critics Say Studies Go Past Science's Reach," *New York Times*, 10 October 2004, 1.

57. Herbert Benson et al., "Study of the Therapeutic Effects of Intercessory Prayer (STEP) in Cardiac Bypass Patients: A Multicenter Randomized Trial of Uncertainty and Certainty of Receiving Intercessory Prayer," *American Heart Journal* 151 (2006): 934–942; Raymond Lawrence, "Faith-Based Medicine," *New York Times*, 11 April 2006, A21.

CHAPTER 3

1. "'Schlatter' at Work," *New York Times*, 9 March 1899, 8.

2. Ferenc Szasz, "Francis Schlatter: The Healer of the Southwest," *New Mexico Historical Review* 54 (1979): 89–104.

3. "Prof. Koch and Malaria," *New York Times*, 24 March 1899, 7.

4. John Waller, *The Discovery of the Germ: Twenty Years that Transformed the Way We Think about Disease* (New York: Columbia University Press, 2002), 1–24.

5. Ronald Numbers and Darrel Amundsen, "Introduction," in Numbers and Amundsen, eds., *Caring and Curing*, 3; Paul Starr, *The Social Transformation of American Medicine* (New York: Basic Books, 1982), ix.

6. Mark Sorrell, *The Peculiar People* (Exeter, U.K.: Paternoster, 1979), 21; Richard Cavendish, ed., *Man, Myth and Magic: An Illustrated Encyclopedia of the Supernatural*, vol. 16 (New York: Cavendish, 1970), 2157; J. S. Cockburn, H. P. F. King, and K. G. T. McDonnell, eds., *A History of the County of Middlesex: Volume 1: Physique, Archaeology, Domesday, Ecclesiastical Organization, The Jews, Religious Houses, Education of Working Classes to 1870, Private Education from Sixteenth Century* (London: Victoria County History, 1969), 139–48; William Osler quoted in C. C. Cawley, *The Right to Live* (South Brunswick, NJ: Barnes, 1969), 34. The New Revised Standard Version of the Bible renders the "peculiar people" passage somewhat differently: "But you are a chosen race, a royal priesthood, a holy nation, God's own people, in order that you may proclaim the mighty acts of him who called you out of darkness into his marvelous light."

7. Sorrell, *Peculiar People*, 21.

8. Fred J. Jiggens, *"Glory Be"* (Elms Court, U.K.: Stockwell, 1978), 44.

9. Ibid., 45.

10. Sorrell, *Peculiar People*, 22–23.

11. "Central Criminal Court, Jan. 27," *Times* (London), 28 January 1868, 9; "Central Criminal Court, Jan. 29," *Times* (London), 30 January 1868, 9; *Queen v. Wagstaffe*, 10 Cox. Crim. Cas. 530 (1868), 530–534.

12. "Central Criminal Court, Jan. 27," 9; "Central Criminal Court, Jan. 29," 9; *Queen v. Wagstaffe*, 530–534.

13. "Central Criminal Court, Jan. 27," 9; "Central Criminal Court, Jan. 29," 9; *Queen v. Wagstaffe*, 530–534.

14. "Central Criminal Court, Jan. 27," 9; "Central Criminal Court, Jan. 29," 9; *Queen v. Wagstaffe*, 530–534.

15. "Central Criminal Court, Jan. 27," 9; "Central Criminal Court, Jan. 29," 9; *Queen v. Wagstaffe*, 530–534.

16. J. H. Merrill, ed., *The American and English Encyclopedia of Law*, vol. 21 (Northport, NY: Thompson, 1889), 199.

17. "Central Criminal Court, Jan. 29," 9; *Queen v. Downes*, 1 Q.B.D. 25 (1875).

18. "Central Criminal Court," *Times* (London), 4 May 1872, 11; "Central Criminal Court, May 6," *Times* (London), 7 May 1872, 11; "Central Criminal Court," *Times* (London), 9 May 1872, 11.

19. "Central Criminal Court," 4 May 1872, 11; "Central Criminal Court, May 6," 11.

20. "Central Criminal Court," 9 May 1872, 11.

21. Ibid.

22. Ibid.

23. "Central Criminal Court, Aug. 19," *Times* (London), 20 August 1874, 9.

24. Ibid.

25. "Central Criminal Court, June 9," *Times* (London), 10 June 1875, 11.

26. *Queen v. Downes*, 1 Q.B.D. 25 (1875).

27. "The Case of John Robert Downes," *Times* (London), 11 June 1875, 9.

28. "Central Criminal Court, Sept. 21," *Times* (London), 22 September 1876, 11.

29. "The Peculiar People," *Times* (London), 13 January 1882, 6; "Central Criminal Court, March 1," *Times* (London), 2 March 1882, 7.

30. "The Peculiar People," *Times* (London), 13 January 1882, 6; "Central Criminal Court, March 1," 7.

31. *Queen v. Morby*, 8 Q.B.D. 571 (1882).

32. "Central Criminal Court, Oct. 28," *Times* (London), 29 October 1897, 11.

33. *Queen v. Senior*, 1. Q.B. 283 (1898).

34. "Central Criminal Court, Dec. 15," *Times* (London), 16 December 1898, 12.

35. The *Freethinker* is still published, and biographical information regarding its founder can be found at the periodical's Web site: http://www.freethinker.co.uk/.

36. G. W. Foote, *Peculiar People: An Open Letter to Mr. Justice Wills on His Sentencing Thomas George Senior to Four Months' Imprisonment with Hard Labor for Obeying the Bible* (London: Secular Society, 1899), 3–14.

37. Ibid.

38. George Bernard Shaw is quoted in Sorrell, *Peculiar People*, 91–92.

39. George Bernard Shaw, *The Complete Prefaces: Vol. 2, 1914–1929* (London: Penguin, 1995), 523.

40. The *London Law Journal* quoted in "Conscientious Scruples," *Green Bag* 10 (1898): 496.

41. Luke Owen Pike quoted in review of *A History of Crime in England*, vol. 2, by Luke Owen Pike, *Law Magazine and Review* 241 (1876–1877), 261–163.

42. "The Peculiar People at Home," *Times* (London), 20 January 1888, 13.

43. Ibid.

44. "Inquests," *Times* (London), 24 August 1898, 5.

45. "Central Criminal Court, Sept. 16," *Times* (London), 17 September 1898, 12; "Central Criminal Court, Oct. 26," *Times* (London), 27 October 1898, 11.

46. "Central Criminal Court, Oct. 26," 11; "Central Criminal Court," *Times* (London), 27 July 1906, 8.

47. Sorrell, *Peculiar People*, 90–91; " 'Peculiar People' and Doctors," *Times* (London), 24 November 1923, 17.

48. " 'Peculiar People' Prosecution," *Times* (London), 15 December 1923, 9.

49. Ibid.

50. Ibid.

51. Ibid.; "Central Criminal Court, July 27," *Times* (London), 28 July 1899, 10.

52. "Central Criminal Court, July 27," 10.

53. Ibid.

54. "Boy's Death from Tonsillitis," *Times* (London), 7 February 1935, 9.

55. Ibid.

CHAPTER 4

1. George Henry Payne, *The Child in Human Progress* (New York: Putnam's, 1916), 184–198, 209–222.

2. Mason P. Thomas, "Child Abuse and Neglect, Part I: Historical Overview, Legal Matrix, and Social Perspectives," *North Carolina Law Review* 50 (1972), 293, 304–305.

3. Ibid., 302; James Kent quoted in Robert Bremmer, ed., *Children and Youth in America: A Documentary History*, vol. 1 (Cambridge, MA: Harvard University Press, 1970), 364.

4. *Johnson v. State*, 21 Tenn. 282 (1840), 283.

5. Lawrence Friedman, *American Law in the 20th Century* (New Haven, CT: Yale University Press, 2002), 19, 178; "Mr. Bergh Enlarging His Sphere of Usefulness," *New York Times*, 10 April 1874, 8; Eric Shelman and Stephen Lazoritz, *The Mary Ellen Wilson Child Abuse Case and the Beginning of Children's Rights in 19th Century America* (Jefferson, NC: McFarland, 2005).

6. Stuart N. Hart, "From Property to Person Status: Historical Perspective on Children's Rights," *American Psychologist* 46 (1991), 53–59; Douglas Rendleman, "Parens Patriae: From Chancery to the Juvenile Court," *South Carolina Law Review* 23 (1971), 209–227; Lawrence Custer, "The Origins of the Doctrine of *Parens Patriae*," *Emory Law Journal* 27 (1978), 195–208; Mary Ann Mason, *From Father's Property to Children's Rights: The History of Child Custody in the United States* (New York: Columbia University Press, 1994),100–103; David Tanenhaus, "Between Dependency and Liberty: The Conundrum of Children's Rights in the Gilded Age," *Law and History Review* 23 (2005), 351–385.

7. Rendleman, "Parens Patriae," 209; *In re Gault*, 387 U.S. 1 (1967), 16; Neil Howard Cogan, "Juvenile Law, before and after the Entrance of Parens Patriae," *South Carolina Law Review* 22 (1970): 149–181; *Blisset's Case*, 98 Eng. Rep. 900.

8. *Ex parte Crouse*, 4 Whart. 9 (Pa. 1839), 9–12; *Milwaukee Industrial School v. Supervisors of Milwaukee County*, 40 Wisc. 328 (186), 338.

9. "Crimes—Religious Belief as a Lawful Excuse," *Michigan Law Review* 23 (1924–1925), 912–913.

10. Carl H. Esbeck, "Tort Claims against Churches and Ecclesiastical Officers: The First Amendment Considerations," *West Virginia Law Review* 89 (1986–1987): 1–114; Mark A. Weitz, *Clergy Malpractice in America: Nally v. Grace Community Church of the Valley* (Lawrence: University Press of Kansas, 2001).

11. John Alexander Dowie, *The Sermons of John Alexander Dowie: Champion of the Faith* (Shreveport, LA: Voice of Healing, 1951), 22–28; Rolvix Harlan, *John Alexander Dowie and the Christian Catholic Apostolic Church in Zion* (Evansville, WI: Robert M. Antes, 1906); Arthur Newcomb, *Dowie: Anointed of the Lord* (New York: Century, 1930).

12. Baer, "Redeemed Bodies," 735–739, 748–754; Warren Beamn, *From Sect to Cult to Sect: The Christian Catholic Church in Zion* (PhD diss., Iowa State University, 1990), 9–11.

13. Wacker, "Marching to Zion," 496–511; Philip J. Cook, *Zion City, Illinois: Twentieth-Century Utopia* (Syracuse, NY: Syracuse University Press, 1996), ix–xii.

14. Wacker, "Marching to Zion," 496–511; Gordon Lindsay, *John Alexander Dowie: A Life Story of Trials, Tragedies and Triumphs* (Dallas, TX: Christ for the Nations, 1986), 5–6, 114–117.

15. Wacker, "Marching to Zion," 496–511.

16. "Dies in Dowie's Den," *Chicago Daily Tribune*, 27 April 1894, 1.

17. *Chicago Daily Tribune*, 26 October 1899, 1.

18. John Alexander Dowie, *Zion's Holy War Against the Hosts of Hell in Chicago: A Series of Addresses* (Chicago, IL: Zion, 1900), 140–141.

19. Wacker, "Marching to Zion," 500; Lindsay, *John Alexander Dowie*, 116–117.

20. "Two Die While Dr. Dowie Prays," *Chicago Daily Tribune*, 14 May 1901, 1; "Dowie Pictures a Death Scene," *Chicago Daily Tribune*, 17 May 1901, 1.

21. "Law Hits Zion; Dowie Is Held," *Chicago Daily Tribune*, 24 May 1901, 1.

22. "Victim of Fire, Then of Dowie," *Chicago Daily Tribune*, 16 May 1901, 1.

23. "Seeking a Way to Punish Dowie," *Chicago Daily Tribune*, 18 May 1901, 1.

24. "Police Called to Dowie Bank," *Chicago Daily Tribune*, 19 May 1901, 3.

25. "Grand Jury Frees Dowie," *Chicago Daily Tribune*, 2 June 1901, 5.

26. "Dispute about a Child," *New York Times*, 8 May 1901, 2.

27. "Dowie Must Go," *Chicago Daily Tribune*, 18 May 1901, 12; William Jennings Bryan quoted in Cook, *Zion City, Illinois*, 56.

28. "Court Takes Dowieite's Baby," *Chicago Daily Tribune*, 9 May 1901, 16; "To Save Children from Faith Cure," *Chicago Daily Tribune*, 12 June 1901, 9.

29. "Dowie in Towering Rage," *Chicago Daily Tribune*, 17 June 1901, 2.

30. *New York Times*, 20 August 1899, 11.

31. Wacker, "Marching to Zion," 497; Lindsay, *John Alexander Dowie*, 139–140.

32. "Piersons Will Leave Village," *Atlanta Constitution*, 27 May 1901, 3.

33. *People v. Pierson*, 68 N.E. 243 (N.Y. 1903), 244–247; "Faith Curist Convicted," *New York Times*, 22 May 1901, 1.

34. "Faith Curist Convicted," 1.

35. Ibid.

36. "Faith Curist Fined $500," *New York Times*, 23 May 1901, 2.

37. "Faith Curist's Son Dead Now," *New York Times*, 24 May 1901, 6.

38. "Faith Curist's Belief," *New York Times*, 21 November 1902, 2.

39. *People v. Pierson*, 244–247.

40. Ibid.

41. Ibid.

42. "Criminal Faith-Healing," *New York Times*, 14 October 1903, 1.

43. "A Setback for Faith Curists," *American Lawyer* 11 (October 1903), 1.

44. Shirley Nelson, *Fair, Clear and Terrible: The Story of Shiloh, Maine* (Latham, NY: British American, 1989), 41–48.

45. William Charles Hiss, *Shiloh: Frank W. Sandford and the Kingdom, 1893–1948* (PhD diss., Tufts University, 1978), 1–10.

46. Nelson, *Fair, Clear and Terrible*, 86–91.

47. Ibid., 111–115.

48. Ibid., 125–126.

49. *Lisbon Falls Enterprise* quoted in Arnold L. White, *The Almighty and Us: The Inside Story of Shiloh, Maine* (Ft. Lauderdale, FL: self-published, 1979), 169.

50. Nelson, *Fair, Clear and Terrible*, 201–216, 227–242; *State v. Sandford*, 59 A. 597 (Me. 1905), 598–601.

51. Nelson, *Fair, Clear and Terrible*, 201–216, 227–242; *State v. Sandford*, 598–601.

52. Nelson, *Fair, Clear and Terrible*, 201–216, 227–242; *State v. Sandford*, 598–601.

53. Nelson, *Fair, Clear and Terrible*, 201–216, 227–242; *State v. Sandford*, 598–601.

54. *Lewiston Evening Journal* quoted in White, *The Almighty and Us*, 171.

55. Nelson, *Fair, Clear and Terrible*, 201–216, 227–242; *State v. Sandford*, 598–601.

56. Nelson, *Fair, Clear and Terrible*, 201–216, 227–242; *State v. Sandford*, 598–601.

57. Nelson, *Fair, Clear and Terrible*, 201–216, 227–242; *State v. Sandford*, 598–601.

58. Nelson, *Fair, Clear and Terrible*, 201–216, 227–242; *State v. Sandford*, 598–601.

59. Nelson, *Fair, Clear and Terrible*, 201–216, 227–242; *State v. Sandford*, 598–601.

60. *Owens v. State*, 116 P. 345 (Ct. App. OK 1911), 345–348.

61. *State v. Chenoweth*, 71 N.E. 197 (Ind. 1904), 198–201.

62. Ibid.

63. *Bradley v. State*, 84 So. 677 (Fla. 1920), 678–683.

64. Ibid.

65. Ibid.

66. *Beck v. State*, 233 P. 495 (Crim. App. Okla. 1925), 495–496. Although Beck apparently did not raise his religious beliefs as a possible defense at trial, the appeals court considered the issue on appeal.

67. Ibid.; "Recent Important Decisions," *Michigan Law Review* 23 (1924–1925), 912.

68. For more on these cases, see Peters, *Judging Jehovah's Witnesses*; Carolyn Long, *Religious Freedom and Indian Rights: The Case of* Oregon v. Smith (Lawrence: University Press of Kansas, 2000); David M. O'Brien, *Animal Sacrifice and Religious Freedom:* Church of the Lukumi Babalu Aye v. City of Hialeah (Lawrence: University Press of Kansas, 2004).

CHAPTER 5

1. Henry James, *The Bostonians: A Novel* (New York: Penguin, 2000), 73, 277; William Carlos Williams, *The Autobiography of William Carlos Williams* (New York: New Directions, 1951), 160, 167; Willa Cather and Georgine Milmine, *The Life of Mary G. Baker Eddy and the History of Christian Science* (Lincoln: University of Nebraska Press, 1993); Updike quoted in Fraser, *God's Perfect Child*, 122–128.

2. Caroline Fraser, "Suffering Children and the Christian Science Church," *Atlantic Monthly*, April 1995, 105–120; "What They Think of It," *Boston Sunday Globe*, 2 April 1882, 1.

3. Mark Twain, *Christian Science: With Notes Containing Corrections to Date* (New York: Harper, 1907), 66.

4. Ibid.

5. Harold Bloom, *The American Religion: The Emergence of the Post-Christian Nation* (New York: Simon and Schuster, 1992), 133; Fraser, *God's Perfect Child*, 536–540.

6. Catherine Albanese, "Physic and Metaphysic in Nineteenth-Century America: Medical Sectarians and Religious Healing," *Church History* 55 (1986), 489–502.

7. Mary Baker Eddy, *Retrospection and Introspection* (Boston: Trustees Under the Will of Mary Baker G. Eddy, 1920), 24–25.

8. Alfie Kohn, "Mind Over Matter," *New England Monthly*, March 1988, 59–63, 95–97.

9. "Miracles?" *Boston Sunday Globe*, 26 March 1882, 1. The "religious science" referred to here is Christian Science rather than the Religious Science movement later founded by Ernest Holmes.

10. "The Death of Mr. Harold Frederic," *Times* (London), 27 October 1898, 4; Susan Albertine, " 'With Their Tongues Doom Men to Death': Christian Science and the Case of Harold Frederic," *American Literary Realism 1870–1910* 21 (1989): 52–66.

11. "Christian Scientists Held," *New York Times*, 24 May 1899, 1; "Christian Science Arrests," *New York Times*, 25 May 1899, 1.

12. "The Christian Science Case," *New York Times*, 27 May 1899, 4.

13. "Christian Scientists Free," *New York Times*, 29 September 1899, 7; "Christian Scientists Defend Their Faith," *New York Times*, 14 February 1901, 6.

14. "Child Died without Medical Attendance," *New York Times*, 22 October 1902, 16; "How Prayer Failed to Cure Diphtheria," *New York Times*, 23 October 1902, 16; "Christian Scientists Held for Manslaughter," *New York Times*, 24 October 1902, 1.

15. "Child Died without Medical Attendance," 16; "How Prayer Failed to Cure Diphtheria," *New York Times*, 23 October 1902, 16; "Christian Scientists Held for Manslaughter," *New York Times*, 24 October 1902, 1.

16. Rennie B. Schoepflin, *Christian Science on Trial: Religious Healing in America* (Baltimore, MD: Johns Hopkins University Press, 2003), 186–188; "Ready to Aid 'Healer,' " *New York Times*, 25 October 1902, 6.

17. "Christian Scientists Must Stand Trial," *New York Times*, 31 October 1902, 1; Schoepflin, *Christian Science on Trial*, 186–188.

18. "Christian Scientists' Change of Front," *New York Times*, 14 November 1902, 2; Schoepflin, *Christian Science on Trial*, 186–188.

19. *American School of Magnetic Healing v. McAnnulty*, 187 U.S. 94 (1902), 95–111.

20. Schoepflin, *Christian Science on Trial*, 188–189; "Christian Scientists Freed," *New York Times*, 8 August 1905, 7.

21. Margery Fox, "Conflict to Coexistence: Christian Science and Medicine," *Medical Anthropology* 8 (1984), 295–296.

22. W. F. Bynum, *Science and the Practice of Medicine in the Nineteenth Century* (Cambridge: Cambridge University Press, 1994), 222–223; John S. Haller, *American Medicine in Transition, 1840–1910* (Urbana: University of Illinois Press, 1981), 235–238.

23. Harris Livermore Coulter, "Political and Social Aspects of Nineteenth-Century Medicine in the United States: The Formation of the American Medical Association and Its Struggle with Homeopathic and Eclectic Physicians" (PhD diss., Columbia University, 1969), 232–261; James Burrow, *AMA: Voice of American Medicine* (Baltimore, MD: Johns Hopkins University Press, 1963), 2–7.

24. "An Aggressive Delusion," *Journal of the American Medical Association* 33 (1899), 107; Fraser, *God's Perfect Child*, 261–266.

25. Fraser, *God's Perfect Child*, 263; *Dent v. West Virginia*, 129 U.S. 114 (1889), 121–128.

26. Clifford P. Smith, "Christian Science and Legislation," *Christian Science Journal*, October 1905, 405–412; "One of the New 'Laws,'" *Christian Science Journal*, July 1897, 235–236.

27. Irving Campbell, "Christian Science and the Law," *Virginia Law Register* 10 (1904–1905), 285–300; William Purrington, "Manslaughter, Christian Science and the Law," *American Lawyer* 7 (1899), 5–9.

28. William Purrington, "'Christian Science' and Its Legal Aspects," *North American Review*, March 1899, 345–361; *Chicago Tribune* quoted in "Dr. Rausch's Prescription," *Christian Science Journal*, July 1887, 215.

29. "Editor's Table," *Christian Science Journal*, April 1898, 66–75.

30. Ibid.

31. "The Medical Bill at Albany," *Christian Science Journal*, May 1898, 96–102; "Christian Scientists Win," *New York Times*, 17 March 1898, 3.

32. "Hearing at Albany for Christian Scientists," *New York Times*, 31 January 1901, 3; "Protecting Medical Regularity," *New York Times*, 31 March 1901, 22.

33. "Christian Science Wins," *New York Times*, 28 March 1901, 6; "Defense and Advice for Mr. Bell," *New York Times*, 5 April 1901, 8.

34. C. Smith, "Christian Science and Legislation," 405–412.

35. "Mrs. Corner on Trial," *New York Times*, 23 May 1898, 1; "The Christian Scientist Not Indicted," *New York Times*, 10 June 1898; Gillian Gill, *Mary Baker Eddy* (Reading, MA: Perseus Books, 1998), 346–348.

36. "The Buswell Case," *Christian Science Journal*, May 1893, 65–86.

37. Ibid.

38. Ibid.

39. Ibid.

40. *State v. Buswell*, 58 N.W. 728 (Neb. 1894), 728–732.

41. *JAMA* quoted in Thomas Johnsen, "Christian Scientists and the Medical Profession," *Medical Heritage* 2 (1986): 70–78; "Against Scientists," *Lincoln (NE) Evening News*, 18 April 1894, 4; J. Sterling Morton and Albert Watkins, *History of Nebraska: From the Earliest Explorations of the Trans-Mississippi* (Lincoln, NE: Western, 1918), 837–838.

42. Elizabeth Barnaby Kenney, Susan Eyrich Lederer, and Edmond P. Minihan, "Sectarians and Scientists: Alternatives to Orthodox Medicine," in Ronald L. Numbers and Judith Walzer Leavitt, eds., *Wisconsin Medicine: Historical Perspectives* (Madison: University of Wisconsin Press, 1981), 60–61.

43. A. C. Umbreit, ed., *Christian Science and the Practice of Medicine: State of Wisconsin vs. Crecentia Arries and Emma Nichols* (Milwaukee, WI: Keogh, 1900), 55–57.

44. Ibid., 43–45.

45. Ibid., 19–22.

46. Ibid., 130.

47. Ibid., 125–129.

48. Ibid., 132–133.

49. Elliott's ruling is quoted in full in an untitled article in the *Evening Wisconsin*, 15 April 1901, 1.

50. *Kansas City v. Baird*, 92 Mo. App. Rept. 204 (1902), 206–214.

51. Eric Michael Mazur, *The Americanization of Religious Minorities: Confronting the Constitutional Order* (Baltimore, MD: Johns Hopkins University Press, 1999), ix–xiv, 141–143.

CHAPTER 6

1. Arthur Corey, *Behind the Scenes with the Metaphysicians* (Los Angeles: Devorss, 1968), 152–153; Fraser, *God's Perfect Child*, 271–272; "Grieving Dad Shoots Practitioner," *Chicago Daily News*, 30 January 1959, 1A; "Practitioner Shot by Dad of Girl Who Died," *Chicago Tribune*, 31 January 1959, 5.

2. Corey, *Behind the Scenes with the Metaphysicians*, 152–153; Fraser, *God's Perfect Child*, 271–272; "Grieving Dad Shoots Practitioner," 1A; "Practitioner Shot by Dad of Girl Who Died," 5.

3. Fraser, *God's Perfect Child*, 271–272; "Grieving Dad Shoots Practitioner," 1A; "Practitioner Shot by Dad of Girl Who Died," 5.

4. Corey, *Behind the Scenes with the Metaphysicians*, 152–153; "Grieving Dad Shoots Practitioner," 1A; "Practitioner Shot by Dad of Girl Who Died," 5.

5. "Grieving Dad Shoots Practitioner," 1A; "Practitioner Shot by Dad of Girl Who Died," 5.

6. Corey, *Behind the Scenes with the Metaphysicians*, 152–153.

7. Friedman, *American Law in the 20th Century*, 365–367; Friedman, *Total Justice*, 50–53.

8. Peters, *The Yoder Case*, 166–180.

9. Henry J. Abraham, "Religion, Medicine, and the State: Reflections on Some Contemporary Issues," *Journal of Church and State* 22 (1980): 423–436.

10. Ibid.

11. Ibid.

12. Leo Damore, *The "Crime" of Dorothy Sheridan* (New York: Arbor House, 1978), 19.

13. Ibid., 27–29, 105.

14. Ibid., 83–84.

15. *Boston Globe* quoted in Damore, *"Crime" of Dorothy Sheridan*, 136.

16. Damore, *"Crime" of Dorothy Sheridan*, 141, 205, 214, 253.

17. Ibid., 253.

18. Ibid., 259.

19. Ibid., 283.

20. Ibid., 301.

21. Herbert Leman quoted in Steven Schneider, "Christian Science and the Law: Room for Compromise?" *Columbia Journal of Law and Social Problems* 1 (1965): 81–88.

22. Bette Novit Evans, *Interpreting the Free Exercise of Religion: The Constitution and American Pluralism* (Chapel Hill: University of North Carolina Press, 1997), 111; Swan, "On Statutes"; Swan, "When Faith Fails Children," 11–16. Ronald Flowers has questioned Swan's conclusions on this score: "It has been claimed that the Christian Science church was the prime mover in the promulgation of the religious exemption in the regulations of 1974 and vigorously protested its withdrawal in 1983. However, there

is no mention of any representative of the Christian Science church in the list of those who testified at the congressional hearing before the passage of the act in 1974. But a great deal of lobbying and persuasion could have taken place at the agency level, as regulations were hammered out. I have not been able to locate any documentation of that." See Flowers, "Withholding Medical Care for Religious Reasons," *Journal of Religion and Health* 23 (1984): 268–282.

23. *Walker v. State*, 763 P. 2d 852 (Cal. 1988), 855–878.

24. Philip Hager, "Prayer Healing Faces Court Test in Girl's Death," *Los Angeles Times*, 6 March 1988, 1.

25. *Walker v. State*, 194 Cal. App. 3d 1090 (Cal. Ct. App. 1986); *Walker v. State*, 763 P. 2d 852, 855–878; Hager, "Prayer Healing Faces Court Test," 1. For the perspective of the Mother Church on the *Walker* case, see Nathan Talbot, "Spiritual Healing: Still in Court after Eight Decades," *Los Angeles Times*, 1 May 1988, sec. 5, 3.

26. *Walker v. State*, 763 P. 2d 852, 855–878.

27. Evans, *Interpreting the Free Exercise of Religion*, 111; Marci Hamilton, *God vs. the Gavel: Religion and the Rule of Law* (New York: Cambridge University Press, 2005), 36.

28. Edward Egan Smith, "The Criminalization of Belief: When Free Exercise Isn't," *Hastings Law Journal* 42 (1991): 1491–1526; Richard Brenneman, *Deadly Blessings: Faith Healing on Trial* (Buffalo, NY: Prometheus Books, 1990), 49–105; "Couple Is Acquitted in Death of Son in Religious Healing," *New York Times*, 19 February 1990, A14.

29. Brenneman, *Deadly Blessings*, 49–105.

30. Ibid.; "Couple Is Acquitted in Death," A14.

31. Brenneman, *Deadly Blessings*, 49–105; "Couple Is Acquitted in Death," A14.

32. *People v. Rippberger*, 231 Cal. App. 3d 1667 (Cal. Ct. of App.), 1673–1691. For an analysis of the First Amendment arguments employed by Christian Scientists such as Mark Rippberger, see Daniel Vaillant, "The Prosecution of Christian Scientists: A Needed Protection for Children or Insult Added to Injury?" *Cleveland State Law Review* 48 (2000): 479–502.

33. *People v. Rippberger*, 1673–1691.

34. Ibid.

35. Mark Curriden, "Blood, the Bible and the Law," *Barrister Magazine*, Fall 1990, 13–15, 41–42; *People v. Rippberger*, 1673–1691.

36. *People v. Rippberger*, 1673–1691.

37. Curriden, "Blood, the Bible, and the Law," 13–15; *Hermanson v. State*, 604 So. 2d 775 (Fla. 1992), 775–783. For public response to the *Hermanson* ruling, see "Drawing a Line on Child Neglect," *St. Petersburg Times*, 13 July 1992, 8A. For one of the myriad law review articles to have assessed *Hermanson*, see Zaven T. Saroyan, "Spiritual Healing the Free Exercise Clause: An Argument for the Use of Strict Scrutiny," *Boston Public Interest Law Journal* 12 (2003), 368–388.

38. *Commonwealth v. Twitchell*, 617 N.E. 2d 609 (Mass. 1993), 612–621; Doris Sue Wong, "Twitchell Boy May Have Been Dead Hours before Help Arrived, Jury Told," *Boston Globe*, 8 May 1990, 22.

39. *Commonwealth v. Twitchell*, 617 N.E. 2d at 612–621; Doris Sue Wong, "Child's Death Called Preventable 'Catastrophe,' " *Boston Globe*, 16 May 1990, 25.

40. Wong, "Child's Death Called Preventable 'Catastrophe,'" 25; Doris Sue Wong, "Neighbor Calls Twitchell Son's Cries 'Unbearable,'" *Boston Globe*, 24 May 1990, 92.

41. Charles-Edward Anderson, "When Faith Healing Fails," *American Bar Association Journal* 75 (July 1989): 22; Doris Sue Wong, "A Couple's Faith Is Key as Twitchell Trial Opens," *Boston Globe*, 5 May 1990, 21.

42. Anderson, "When Faith Healing Fails," 22; Wong, "Couple's Faith Is Key," 21.

43. Doris Sue Wong, "Twitchell Says with 2d Chance, He'd Seek Doctor for Son's Illness," *Boston Globe*, 5 June 1990, 1.

44. Marcia Chambers, "Deliberating Faith, Law and a Life," *National Law Journal*, 2 July 1990, 13; Wong, "Twitchell Says He'd Seek Doctor," 1; Wong, "Twitchell Cites Faith on Last Day of His Testimony," *Boston Globe*, 6 June 1990, 45.

45. "Boston Jury Convicts 2 Christian Scientists in Death of a Son," *New York Times*, 5 July 1990, A12; Doris Sue Wong, "Christian Science Couple Convicted in Son's Death," *Boston Globe*, 5 July 1990, 1; *Commonwealth v. Twitchell*, 617 N.E. 2d at 612–621.

46. *Commonwealth v. Twitchell*, 617 N.E. 2d at 612–621. For an analysis of Twitchell within the broader context of free-exercise-of-religion claims, see Stanley H. Friedelbaum, "Free Exercise in the States: Belief, Conduct, and Judicial Benchmarks," *Albany Law Review* 63 (2000): 1059, 1091–1093.

47. *Commonwealth v. Twitchell*, 617 N.E. 2d at 612–621; "A Message for Christian Scientists," *Boston Globe*, 13 August 1993, 16.

48. *State v. McKown*, 461 N.W. 2d 720 (Minn. Ct. App. 1990); *State v. McKown*, 475 N.W. 2d 63 (Minn. 1991), 64–71.

49. *Jones v. Czapkay*, 182 Cal. App. 2d 192 (Cal. Ct. App. 1960); Fraser, *God's Perfect Child*, 295–297.

50. Margaret Zack, "Judge Allows Father to Sue in Death of Boy Who Was Denied Medical Care," *Minneapolis Star Tribune*, 6 December 1991, 1A; *Lundman v. McKown*, 530 N.W. 2d 807 (Minn. Ct. App. 1995), 813–834.

51. Margaret Zack, "Religion an Issue as Trial Starts in Boy's Death," *Minneapolis Star Tribune*, 20 July 1993, 6B.

52. Margaret Zack, "Lawyer Says Woman Held Lifelong Belief in Spiritual Healing," *Minneapolis Star Tribune*, 21 July 1993, 3B.

53. Margaret Zack, "Father Testifies in Case of Boy's Death; Mother Had Chosen Spiritual Healing," *Minneapolis Star Tribune*, 31 July 1993, 3B.

54. Hamilton, *God vs. the Gavel*, 36–38; *Lundman v. McKown*, 530 N.W. at 813–834; "Avenging the Death of Ian Lundman," *Minneapolis Star Tribune*, 24 August 1993, 8A.

55. Margaret Zack, "Jury Deliberates without Verdict," *Minneapolis Star Tribune*, 25 August 1993, 3B.

56. *Lundman v. McKown*, 530 N.W. 813–834; Margaret Cronin Fisk, "Christian Scientists Held Liable in Death," *National Law Journal*, 20 September 1993, 9; Hamilton, *God vs. the Gavel*, 36–38.

57. *Lundman v. McKown*, 530 N.W. 813–834.

58. *McKown v. Lundman*, 516 U.S. 1099 (1996).

59. Stephen L. Carter, "The Power of Prayer, Denied," *New York Times*, 31 January 1997, A17.

CHAPTER 7

1. *Epidemiology and Prevention of Vaccine-Preventable Diseases*, 8th ed. (Washington, DC: Centers for Disease Control and Prevention, National Immunization Program), 2005, 115–133.

2. Ibid.

3. Ibid.

4. H. Cody Meissner, Peter M. Strebel, and Walter A. Orenstein, "Measles Vaccines and the Potential for Worldwide Eradication of Measles," *Pediatrics* 114 (October 2004): 1065–1069.

5. *Jacobson v. Massachusetts*, 197 U.S. 11 (1905); Daniel Salmon et al., "Health Consequences of Religious and Philosophical Exemptions from Immunization Laws: Individual and Societal Risk of Measles," *Journal of the American Medical Association* 282 (1999): 47–53.

6. Daniel Feikin et al.,"Individual and Community Risks of Measles and Pertussis Associated with Personal Exemptions to Immunization," *Journal of the American Medical Association* 284 (2000), 3145–3150; Paul Etkind et al., "Pertussis Outbreaks in Groups Claiming Religious Exemptions to Vaccinations," *American Journal of Diseases of Children* 146 (1992), 173–176; Sean Coletti, "Taking Account of Partial Exemptors in Vaccination Law, Policy, and Pratice," *Connecticut Law Review* 36 (2003–2004), 1341–1398.

7. Rosalie Beck and David Hendon, "Notes on Church-State Affairs," *Journal of Church and State* 33 (1991), 379, 404–405; Tamar Lewin, "Measles and Faith Combine in 5 Deaths in Philadelphia," *New York Times*, 16 February 1991, 12.

8. "Measles Outbreak in Philadelphia Runs Its Course," *New York Times*, 17 February 1991, 32.

9. Gifford, "Matter of Faith," 96–101, 154–156.

10. Ibid.

11. Michael E. Ruane, "Church Believes in Healing through Faith," *Philadelphia Inquirer*, 12 February 1991, 1B.

12. *Matter of Vasko*, 238 App. Div. 128 (N.Y. App. Div. 1933); "Infants—Power of Court to Order Operation on Minor Child against Will of Parents," *Tennessee Law Review* 12 (1933–1934), 59–60; *State v. Sisson*, 281 N.Y.S. 559 (N.Y. Sup. Ct. 1935), 559–560.

13. "State Intervenes to Save Child's Leg," *Literary Digest*, 18 August 1934, 30.

14. Ibid.

15. Ibid.

16. Superior Court of Pennsylvania, *Commonwealth v. William Barnhart and Linda Barnhart*, Brief for Appellants (hereafter *Barnhart* Appellants' Brief), 1–29; Superior Court of Pennsylvania, *Commonwealth v. William Barnhart and Linda Barnhart*, Brief for Appellee (hereafter *Barnhart* Appellee's Brief), 2–24.

17. *Barnhart* Appellants' Brief, 1–29; *Barnhart* Appellee's Brief, 2–24.

18. *Barnhart* Appellee's Brief, 2–24; *Commonwealth v. Barnhart*, 497 A.2d. 616 (Pa. Super. Ct. 1985), 620–630.

19. *Commonwealth v. Barnhart*, 497 A.2d. 620–630; National Cancer Institute, "Wilms' Tumor and Other Childhood Kidney Tumors: Treatment," http://www .cancer.gov/cancertopics/pdq/treatment/wilms/patient, accessed on 2 October 2005.

20. *Barnhart* Appellee's Brief, 2–24.

21. *Barnhart* Appellants' Brief, 1–29; *Barnhart* Appellee's Brief, 2–24.

22. Ibid.

23. Appendix to *Barnhart* Appellants' Brief, 1–40.

24. Ibid., 142–151.

25. *Barnhart* Appellants' Brief, 1–29; *Barnhart* Appellee Brief, 2–24.

26. *Commonwealth v. Barnhart*, 497 A.2d. 620–630. For critiques of the *Barnhart* decision, see Daniel J. Kearney, "Parental Failure to Provide Child with Medical Assistance Based on Religious Beliefs Causing Child's Death—Involuntary Manslaughter in Pennsylvania," *Dickinson Law Review* 90 (1985–1986): 861–890 and Kathleen Fischer, "Freedom of Religion and Parental Care," *Journal of Juvenile Law* 11 (1990): 73–79.

27. Desiree Rodgers et al., "High Attack Rates and Case Fatality during a Measles Outbreak in Groups with Religious Exemption to Vaccination," *Pediatric Infectious Disease Journal* 12 (1988): 288–292. These findings echo those of an earlier study of religious exemptors: Thomas Novotny et al., "Measles Outbreaks in Religious Groups Exempt from Immunization Laws," *Public Health Reports* 103 (1988): 49–54.

28. Lewin, "Measles and Faith Combine," 12.

29. "City Shuts School after Two Deaths," *New York Times*, 13 February 1991, B6; Peter Landry, "Measles Kill 2 Church School Pupils," *Philadelphia Inquirer*, 11 February 1991, 1B.

30. Daniel Rubin, "Measles Epidemic Spurs a Rush of Doctor Visits," *Philadelphia Inquirer*, 17 February 2001, 1A; Gifford, "Matter of Faith," 96–101, 154–156.

31. Susan FitzGerald and Daniel Rubin, "Cheltenham Girl, 14, Is Third Measles Victim," *Philadelphia Inquirer*, 15 February 1991, 1B.

32. Steve Lopez, "Of God, Man and Measles," *Philadelphia Inquirer*, 12 March 1991, 1B.

33. Susan FitzGerald, Thomas Gibbons, Jr., and Kristin Holmes, "2 Girls Die; Measles Cited," *Philadelphia Inquirer*, 16 February 1991, 1A.

34. Idris Diaz and Denise-Marie Santiago, "Phila. Compels Hospitalization in Measles Case," *Philadelphia Inquirer*, 18 February 1991, 1B.

35. Robin Clark, "Measles Abating, but City Might Still Seek Inoculations," *Philadelphia Inquirer*, 23 February 1991, 3B.

36. Ibid.

37. Tamar Lewin, "Epidemic in Philadelphia Raises Issue of Religion vs. State's Interest," *New York Times*, 25 February 1991, B8.

38. Henry Goldman, "Measles Ruling Questioned," *Philadelphia Inquirer*, 6 March 1991, 1B.

39. Jennifer Trahan and Susan Wolf, "Rights of State and Family Clash in Forced-Immunization Cases," *National Law Journal*, 13 May 1991, 28.

40. "Sixth Child Dies in Philadelphia; 5 Others Are Given Measles Shots," *New York Times*, 9 March 1991, 10.

41. Ibid.; Henry Goldman, "Church Child Dies; Five Others Vaccinated," *Philadelphia Inquirer*, 9 March 1991, 1A. The citations for the Faith Tabernacle hospitalization and immunization cases are as follows. In family court: *In re W.E.*, 308813-01 (March 4, 1991); *In re K.E.*, 308813-02 (March 4, 1991); *In re R.E.*, 308813-03 (March 4, 1991); *In re E.S.H.*, 308815-01 (March 4,1991); *In re K.J.M.*, 308817-01 (March 4, 1991); *In re J.R.R.*, 308819-01 (March 4, 1991). In superior court: *In re K.E.*, 232 Misc. 16 (March 8, 1991); *In re R.E.*, 233 Misc. 16 (March 8, 1991); *In re K.J.M.*, 234 Misc. 16 (March 8, 1991); *In re W.E.*, 235 Misc. 16 (March 8, 1991); *In re E.S.H.*, 236 Misc. 16 (March 8, 1991). In state supreme court: *In re R.E.*, 45 ED Misc. 1991 (March 8, 1991); *In re K.J.M.*, 46 ED Misc. 1991 (March 8, 1991); *In re E.S.H.*, 47 ED Misc. (March 8, 1991); *In re W.E.*, 48 ED Misc. 1991 (March 8, 1991); *In re K.E.*, 49 ED Misc. 1991 (March 8, 1991).

42. "Children Vaccinated after Court Order Is Upheld," *Los Angeles Times*, 9 March 1991, 18.

43. "Thy Will Be Done?" *60 Minutes*, CBS, 1 February 1998.

44. Ibid.

45. In the Supreme Court of Pennsylvania, Western District, *Commonwealth v. Dennis Nixon and Commonwealth v. Lorie Nixon*, Brief for Appellants (hereafter *Nixon* Appellants' Brief), 5–10; William Dowell, "Her Dying Prayers," *Time*, 5 May 1997, 66.

46. *Nixon* Appellants' Brief, 5–10; Gifford, "Matter of Faith," 96–101, 154–156.

47. "Thy Will Be Done?"

48. J. E. Bevacqua, "Diabetic Ketoacidosis in the Pediatric ICU," *Critical Care Nursing Clinics of North America*, 17 (2005): 341–347; M. S. Agus and J. I. Wolfsdorf, "Diabetic Ketoacidosis in Children," *Pediatric Clinics of North America* 52 (2005): 1147–1163.

49. Gifford, "Matter of Faith," 96–101, 154–156; Dowell, "Her Dying Prayers," 66.

50. *Nixon* Appellants' Brief, 11–31.

51. "Faith-Healing Couple Gets Maximum Sentence—and More," *Pennsylvania Law Weekly*, 16 June 1997, 2.

52. In the Supreme Court of Pennsylvania, Western District, *Commonwealth v. Dennis Nixon and Commonwealth v. Lorie Nixon*, Brief for *Amici Curiae* Children's Healthcare Is a Legal Duty; the American Humane Association, Children's Division; the National Association of Counsel for Children; and the National Exchange Club Foundation, 1–30.

53. *Commonwealth v. Nixon*, 761 A.2d 1151 (Pa. 2000), 1152– 1157; Tom Gibb, "Parents Convicted in Death of Diabetic Daughter," *Pittsburgh Post-Gazette*, 29 November 2000, 1.

54. *Commonwealth v. Foster*, 764 A. 2d 1076 (Pa. Super. Ct. 2000), 1078–1084.

55. Ibid.

56. Meki Cox, "Faith Healer: I'd Do It Again," *Philadelphia Daily News*, 9 May 1998, 6; Linda Loyd, "Sick Boy's Father Sticks by his Beliefs," *Philadelphia Inquirer*, 9 May 1998, B1.

57. Linda Loyd, "Couple Convicted in Refusal to Take Tot to a Doctor," *Philadelphia Inquirer*, 12 May 1998, B1.

58. Robert Moran, "Boy Died of Untreated Cancer," *Philadelphia Inquirer*, 5 February 2003, B4.

CHAPTER 8

1. Tom Farmer and Dave Wedge, "Attleboro Cult Mother's Newborn Taken by DSS," *Boston Herald*, 17 October 2000, 5.

2. *The Early Show*, CBS, 30 August 2000.

3. *Talkback Live*, CNN, 1 September 2000.

4. Farah Stockman and Mac Daniel, "The Sect Led by Father's Religious Zeal, Family Spurned Society's Rules," *Boston Globe*, 26 November 2000, B1.

5. Ruth Tucker, "From the Fringe to the Fold," *Christianity Today*, 15 July 1996, 26–32; Michael McCoy, *Twentieth-Century Shapers of American Popular Religion* (Westport, CT : Greenwood, 1989), 9–14.

6. "A Child Betrayed? Disappearance of Children in Cult Run by Roland Robidoux," *Dateline*, NBC, 23 February 2001.

7. Carol Balizet, *Born in Zion* (Grapevine, TX: Perazim House, 1996), 46–48.

8. "A Child Betrayed?"

9. Ibid.

10. Robert T. Pardon, " 'The Body of Christ': Descent from Benign Bible Study to Destructive Cult," New England Institute of Religious Research, http://people.ne.mediaone.net/neirr/AttleboroHistory.html, accessed on 4 December 2000.

11. Hamilton, *God vs. the Gavel*, 38–39; Shelley Murphy, "Sect Leader Convicted in Starvation of Son," *Boston Globe*, 15 June 2002, A1.

12. "A Child Betrayed?"; Pardon, "The Body of Christ"; Murphy, "Sect Leader Convicted," A1.

13. *Adoption of Fran*, 766 N.E. 2d 91 (Mass. App. Ct. 2002), 93–101.

14. Pardon, "The Body of Christ"; "A Child Betrayed?"

15. *Adoption of Fran*, 766 N.E. 2d 93–101.

16. Ibid.

17. Ibid.

18. Mac Daniel, "3 in Sect Indicted in Boy's Death," *Boston Globe*, 14 November 2000, A1.

19. Ralph Ranalli, "Legal Opinions Vary on Sect Case; Severity of Charge Raises a Question," *Boston Globe*, 19 November 2000, B1.

20. John Ellement, "2 Views of Mother on Trial in Death," *Boston Globe*, 23 January 2004, B1; Dave Wedge, "Cult Mom Acquitted in Baby's Starving Death," *Boston Herald*, 4 February 2004, 4; Dave Wedge, "Cult Mom Fears Worst," *Boston Herald*, 4 March 2004, 5; Hamilton, *God vs. the Gavel*, 38–39.

21. "Unborn Child's Attorney John Rego, . . ." *Good Morning America*, ABC, 22 September 2000; Thomas Fields-Meyer, "Protective Custody," *People*, 25 September 2000, 64.

22. "A Child Betrayed?"; Tom Farmer and Dave Wedge, "Grim Discovery—Cops Find Cult Kids' Burial Site," *Boston Herald*, 25 October 2000, 1.

23. *The Early Show*, CBS, 30 August 2000.

24. Andrew Kaunitz et al., "Perinatal and Maternal Mortality in a Religious Group Avoiding Obstetric Care," *American Journal of Obstetrics and Gynecology* 150 (1984): 826–31; C. Spence et al., "The Faith Assembly: A Follow-up Study of Faith Healing and Mortality," *Indiana Medicine* 80 (1987): 238–40.

25. "Government Steps in to Save Unborn Child," *Morning Edition*, NPR, 1 September 2000.

26. *The Early Show*, CBS, 30 August 2000.

27. Ibid.; *Morning Edition*.

28. *Talkback Live*, 1 September 2000.

29. "Pregnant Woman Being Forced into State Custody," *All Things Considered*, NPR, 14 September 2000; Ellen Goodman, "Just How Far Can the State Go in Protecting an 'Unborn Child'?" *Boston Globe*, 10 September 2000, F7.

30. "Unborn Child's Attorney John Rego"; *Talkback Live*, 1 September 2000; "Pregnant Woman Being Forced"; Adrian Walker, "Strange Ruling, but a Sound One," *Boston Globe*, 9 September 2000, B1.

31. *Morning Edition*.

32. Bob Smletana, "Fatal Revelations," *Christianity Today*, 21 May 2002, 25–27. For perceptive law review articles that address similar issues, see Marilyn Miller, "Fetal Neglect and State Intervention: Preventing Another Attleboro Cult Baby Death," *Cardozo Women's Law Journal* 8 (2001–2002): 71–104; Hedy R. Bower, "How Far Can a State Go to Protect a Fetus—The Rebecca Corneau Story and the Case for Requiring Massachusetts to Follow the U.S. Constitution," *Golden Gate University Law Review* 31 (2001): 123–154; Robin Power Morris, "The Corneau Case, Furthering Trends of Fetal Rights and Religious Freedom," *New England Journal on Criminal and Civil Confinement* 28 (2002): 89–121; and Amy F. Cohen, "The Midwifery Stalemate and Childbirth Choice: Recognizing Mothers-to-Be as the Best Late Pregnancy Decisionmakers," *Indiana Law Journal* 80 (2005): 849–880.

33. *Barbara F. v. Bristol Division of the Juvenile Court*, 735 N.E. 2d 357 (Mass. 2000), 358–359; Dave Wedge, "SJC to Rule on Cult Mother Case," *Boston Herald*, 8 September 2000, 3. Nasif was ridiculed when it was reported that he claimed to have literally heard the fetus speak, but several witnesses said it was clear that the judge spoke figuratively.

34. *Barbara F. v. Bristol Division of the Juvenile Court*, 735 N.E. at 358–359.

35. *Adoption of Darla*, 778 N.E. 2d 985 (Mass. App. Ct. 2002), 986–988; Tom Farmer and Dave Wedge, "Attleboro Cult Mother's Newborn Taken by DSS," *Boston Herald*, 17 October 2000, 5.

36. Corey Dade, "Sect Member Given Court Order," *Boston Globe*, 16 January 2002, B3; Dave Wedge, "DSS Worries about Baby," *Boston Herald*, 3 January 2002, 3.

37. *In the Matter of a Care and Protections Summons*, 770 N.E. 2d 456 (Mass. 2002), 458–469.

38. Corey Dade, "Sect Member Refuses to Answer," *Boston Globe*, 9 January 2002, B2.

39. Dave Wedge, "DSS Worries over Cult Ruling," *Boston Herald*, 1 February 2002, 3; Laurel J. Sweet, "Judge to Cult Couple: Bring in Your Baby or Go to Jail," *Boston Herald*, 5 February 2002, 20.

40. *In the Matter of a Care and Protections Summons*, 770 N.E. 2d 458–469.

41. Dave Wedge, "Defense Attorney Tells Judge Cult Mom Had Miscarriage," *Boston Herald*, 6 February 2002, 2.

42. Corey Dade, "Judge Jails Sect Couple Who Say She Miscarried," *Boston Globe*, 6 February 2002, B1; *In the Matter of a Care and Protections Summons*, 770 N.E. 2d 458–469.

43. Margery Eagan, "What Happened to the Outrage over Injustices against Women?" *Boston Herald*, 24 January 2002, 16; Wendy Kaminer, "Sectual Discrimination," *American Prospect*, 11 March 2002, 9.

44. Michele Kurtz, "Citing Standstill, Judge Releases Jailed Sect Couple," *Boston Globe*, 19 June 2002, B1; Hamilton, *God vs. the Gavel*, 38–39.

45. Joel Stephen Williams, "Ethical Issues in Compulsory Medical Treatment: A Study of Jehovah's Witnesses and Blood Transfusion" (PhD diss., Baylor University, 1987), 44–77; Gretchen Passantino, "Are Jehovah's Witnesses Giving Up on Their Blood Transfusion Ban?" *Christian Research Journal* 23 (2000), 6–9.

46. Williams, "Ethical Issues in Compulsory Medical Treatment," 44–77; Passantino, "Are Jehovah's Witness Witnesses Giving Up?" 6–9.

47. *People ex rel. Wallace v. Labrenz*, 104 N.E.2d 769 (Ill. 1952), 772.

48. *State v. Perricone*, 181 A.2d 751 (N.J. 1962), 753–760.

49. Ibid.

50. Ibid.

51. *In the Matter of the Guardianship of L. S. and H. S.*, 87 P.3d 521 (Nev. 2004), 522–527.

52. *Raleigh Fitkin-Paul Morgan Memorial Hospital v. Anderson*, 201 A.2d 537 (N.J. 1964), 537; Murray Illson, "Pregnant Woman May Not Need Transfusion Ordered by Court," *New York Times*, 21 June 1964, 50.

53. *In the Matter of Jamaica Hospital*, 491 N.Y.S.2d 898 (N.Y. 1985), 898–900.

54. Joelyn Knopf Levy, "Jehovah's Witnesses, Pregnancy, and Blood Transfusions: A Paradigm for Autonomy Rights of All Pregnant Women," *Journal of Law, Medicine and Ethics* 27 (1999), 171–185; *In re Fetus Brown*, 689 N.E.2d 397 (Ill. App. Ct. 1997), 398–406.

55. *Application of the President and Directors of Georgetown College*, 331 F.2d 1000 (D.C. Cir. 1964), 1001–1010.

56. Ibid.

57. *Stamford Hospital v. Vega*, 674 A.2d 821 (Conn. 1995), 823–834.

58. Paul Conkin, *American Originals: Homemade Varieties of Christianity* (Chapel Hill: University of North Carolina Press, 1997); Stephen J. Stein, *Communities of Dissent: A History of Alternative Religions in America* (New York: Oxford University Press, 2000), 2–12. For two thoughtful overviews of "new" religions, see James R. Lewis and Jesper Aagaard Petersen, eds., *Controversial New Religions* (New York: Oxford University Press, 2005) and James R. Lewis, *Legitimating New Religions* (New Brunswick, NJ: Rutgers University Press, 2003).

CHAPTER 9

1. Court of Appeals of the State of Oregon, *State v. Hays*, Appellant's Brief (hereafter *Hays* Brief), 6–13; *State v. Hays*, 964 P.2d 1042 (Or. Ct. App. 1998), 1044–1046.

2. *Hays* Brief, 6–13; *State v. Hays*, 1044–1046.

3. J. Gordon Melton, ed., *Encyclopedia of American Religions*, 6th ed. (Detroit: Gale Research, 1998), 560; *Hays* Brief, 6–8.

4. *Hays* Brief, 6–8.

5. Ibid, 6–13.

6. Mark O'Keefe, "Boy's Death Reinforces Faithful, Splits Town," *Portland Oregonian*, 26 March 1995, A1.

7. Ibid.

8. Ibid.

9. Ellis E. Conklin, "Trial Tested Town's Faith: Oregon Case Pitted Prayer vs. Medicine," *Seattle Post-Intelligencer*, 27 April 1996, A1; Swan quoted in O'Keefe, "Boy's Death Reinforces Faithful," A1.

10. *People v. Arnold*, 426 P.2d 515 (Cal. 1967), 517–525.

11. Ibid.

12. *Northrup v. Superior Court of Modoc County*, 192 Cal. App. 3d 276 (Cal. Ct. App. 1987), 278–281.

13. Ibid.

14. *In re Jensen*, 633 P.2d 1302 (Or. Ct. App. 1981), 1303–1306.

15. Ibid.

16. *Hays* Brief, 6–13; Conklin, "Trial Tested Town's Faith," A1.

17. *Hays* Brief, 6–13; *State v. Hays*, 1044–1046.

18. *Hays* Brief, 6–13; *State v. Hays*, 1044–1046.

19. *Hays* Brief, 6–13; *State v. Hays*, 1044–1046. In addition to reviewing the details of Tony Hays's medical history, I've referred to the Web site operated by the National Marrow Donor Program, accessible at http://www.marrow.org.

20. Mark O'Keefe, "Religion vs. Medicine: A Family's Faith Allows a Boy's Death," *Portland Oregonian*, 22 March 1995, A1.

21. *State v. Hays*, 1044–1046; Conklin, "Trial Tested Town's Faith," A1.

22. Conklin, "Trial Tested Town's Faith," A1; O'Keefe, "Boy's Death Reinforces Faithful," A1.

23. Conklin, "Trial Tested Town's Faith," A1; O'Keefe, "Boy's Death Reinforces Faithful," A1.

24. Conklin, "Trial Tested Town's Faith," A1; O'Keefe, "Boy's Death Reinforces Faithful," A1; Cheryl Martinis, "Man Argues Conviction in Death of His Son," *Portland Oregonian*, 30 May 1998, A1.

25. Conklin, "Trial Tested Town's Faith," A1; O'Keefe, "Boy's Death Reinforces Faithful," A1.

26. Conklin, "Trial Tested Town's Faith," A1; O'Keefe, "Boy's Death Reinforces Faithful," A1.

27. *State v. Hays*, 1044–1046.

28. *State v. Lockhart*, 664 P.2d 1059 (Okla. Crim. App. 1983).

29. Barbara Allen, "Church Has History of Conflict over Medical Care," *Tulsa World*, 6 August 1998.

30. *Funkhouser v. State*, 763 P.2d 695 (Okla. Crim. App. 1988), 696–700.

31. *Hays* Brief, 15–27; *State v. Hays*, 1044–1046.

32. Steve Dunn, "Disappearing into That Dark Attic Alone," *Portland Oregonian*, 21 April 1996.

33. Rob Eure, "Verdict Right but Hard, Jurors Say," *Portland Oregonian*, 23 April 1996.

34. Ibid.

35. *Hays* Brief, Appendix, 1–2.

36. Ibid.

37. *Hays* Brief, 15–26.

38. Ibid., 27–38.

39. As in the case of the Church of the First Born, there is a dearth of reliable scholarly literature about the Followers of Christ. Fragments of the faith's history and doctrines can be pieced together from judicial opinions and newspaper accounts. Here I have relied on the excellent research of reporter Mark Larabee, in particular his stories "Followers' Roots Reveal Numerous Splinters," *Portland Oregonian*, 7 June 1998 and "Doubt, Secrecy Circle Followers of Christ," *Portland Oregonian*, 28 June 1998.

40. Larabee, "Doubt, Secrecy Circle Followers." 1A

41. Ibid.

42. Mark Larabee and Peter Sleeth, "Faith Healing Raises Questions of Law's Duty—Belief or Life?" *Portland Oregonian*, 7 June 1998, 1A.

43. Larabee, "Doubt, Secrecy Circle Followers," 1A.

44. Larabee and Sleeth, "Faith Healing Raises Questions," 1A.

45. "Who Will Save the Children? Taking Faith Healing to the Extreme," *20/20*, ABC, 4 August 1999; Larabee and Sleeth, "Faith Healing Raises Questions," 1A.

46. "Who Will Save the Children?"; David Van Biema, "Faith or Healing?" *Time*, 31 August 1998, 68–69.

47. "Who Will Save the Children?"; Biema, "Faith or Healing?" 68–69.

48. Mark Larabee, "The Battle over Faith Healing," *Portland Oregonian*, 28 November 1998, 1A.

49. "Who Will Save the Children?"; Mark Larabee, "An Oregon Case Shines a Light on the Issue," *Portland Oregonian*, 29 November 1988, 1A.

50. Swan, "On Statutes," 86; "Who Will Save the Children?"; Larabee, "Oregon Case Shines a Light," 1A.

51. "Who Will Save the Children?"; Larabee, "Oregon Case Shines a Light," 1A.

52. *State v. Hays*, 1044–1046.

CHAPTER 10

1. Ramona Cass, "We Let Our Son Die: The Tragic Story of Rita and Doug Swan," *Journal of Christian Nursing*, Spring 1987, 4–8.

2. Fraser, *God's Perfect Child*, 285–296.

3. Cass, "We Let Our Son Die," 4–8; Fraser, *God's Perfect Child*, 285–296.

4. Cass, "We Let Our Son Die," 4–8; Fraser, *God's Perfect Child*, 285–296.

5. Cass, "We Let Our Son Die," 4–8; Fraser, *God's Perfect Child*, 285–296.

6. Fraser, *God's Perfect Child*, 285–296. CHILD's philosophy and activities are outlined in detail on the organization's Web site, http://www.childrenshealthcare.org/.

7. Rita Swan, "The Law Should Protect All Children," *Journal of Christian Nursing*, Spring 1987, 40.

8. James T. Richardson and John DeWitt, "Christian Science Spiritual Healing, the Law, and Public Opinion," *Journal of Church and State* 34 (1992): 549–561.

9. Teresa Hanafin, "Bill Seeks to Eliminate Faith-Healing Shield," *Boston Globe*, 12 December 1991, 63.

10. M. E. Malone, "New Bill Seeks to End Protection for Parents Who Use Faith Healing," *Boston Globe*, 26 March 1991, 29.

11. Don Aucoin, "Bill Aims to Get Tough on Child Abusers," *Boston Globe*, 6 October 1993, 25; Doris Sue Wong and Don Aucoin, "Weld Bid on Law Faulted," *Boston Globe*, 11 December 1993, 15.

12. Wong and Aucoin, "Weld Bid on Law Faulted,"15; Bella English, "Weld Flip-Flop May Risk Lives," *Boston Globe*, 15 December 1993, 33; Doris Sue Wong, "Rebuffed on Abuse Bill, Weld Still Will Sign It," *Boston Globe*, 23 December 1993, 23.

13. Swan, "Moral, Economic, and Social Issues," 73–95; Swan, "When Faith Fails Children," 11–16; Mark Larabee, "One Denomination Lobbies Tirelessly," *Portland Oregonian*, 28 November 1998, A1.

14. Larabee, "One Denomination Lobbies Tirelessly," A1.

15. Mark Larabee, "Shield-Law Bills Face Easy Win in House," *Portland Oregonian*, 5 March 1999, A1.

16. Lisa Grace Lednicer, "House Votes to End Faith-Healing Defense in Child Murder Cases," *Portland Oregonian*, 14 May 1999, B6.

17. Mark Larabee, "Balancing Rights Makes Faith-Healing Bills Thorny," *Portland Oregonian*, 28 June 1999, A1.

18. Ashbel Green, "Panel Revamps Faith-Healing Bill," *Portland Oregonian*, 22 June 1999, E1; "Defend Children First," *Portland Oregonian*, 2 July 1999, D10.

19. Ashbel Green, "Praying Over Ailing Children Won't Be Enough under Bill," *Portland Oregonian*, 23 July 1999, D6; Laura Oppenheimer, "Parents Lose Legal Defense for Using Faith Healing," *Portland Oregonian*, 17 August 1999, A1.

20. Dianna Gordon, "When Faith-Healing Fails," *State Legislatures*, March 2000, 26–27.

21. Nancy Lofholm, "Faith Healing vs. Kids' Rights," *Denver Post*, 10 February 2001, B1.

22. Doug Friednash, "Children of Faith Healers Deserve Protection," *Denver Rocky Mountain News*, 23 February 2001, 47A.

23. Nancy Lofholm, "Couple Get 16 Years' Probation," *Denver Post*, 11 February 2000, B5.

24. Nancy Lofholm, "Clifton Infant's Death Won't Be Ruled Homicide," *Denver Post*, 3 August 2000, A1.

25. Ibid.

26. Julia C. Martinez, "Faith Healing Fails Kids, Mother Tells Lawmakers," *Denver Post*, 14 February 2001, A1.

27. Valerie Richardson, "Faith Healing Vilified in Wake of Colorado Teenager's Death," *Insight on the News*, 21 May 2001, 31.

28. Michael Janofsky, "Colorado Children's Deaths Rekindle Debate on Religion," *New York Times*, 21 February 2001, A10; "Spinning Legislative Wheels," *Denver Rocky Mountain News*, 29 March 2001, 48A; "Faith Gives Way to Hope," *Denver Post*, 29 March 2001, B6; Julia Martinez, "Faith-Healing Bill Gets Owens' Signature," *Denver Post*, 17 April 2001, A8.

29. Milwaukee Police Department Detective Djordie Rankovic, report of interview with Patrice Cooper (conducted 25 August 2003) and Milwaukee Police Department Detective William Beauchene, report of interview with Patrice Cooper (conducted

22 August 2003) (hereafter MPD Cooper Interviews). I am grateful to the Milwaukee Police Department for promptly responding to my public-records request for materials relating to the David and Ray Hemphill case.

30. Milwaukee Police Department Detective Shannon Jones, report of interview with Tamara Tolefree (conducted 22 August 2003) (hereafter MPD Tolefree Interview).

31. Amanda Mantone, "Storefront Churches Are Lifeblood to Urban Poor," *Christian Century*, 20 April 2004, 14; Monica Davey, "Faith Healing Gone Wrong Claims Boy's Life," *New York Times*, 29 August 2003, A12.

32. Derrick Nunnally, "Prosecutors in Boy's Death Allow Choice of Lesser Charge," *Milwaukee Journal Sentinel*, 8 July 2004, 1B.

33. Lisa Sweetingham, "Exorcist's Brother Says God Claimed Autistic Boy's Life, Not Defendant," Court TV.com, 8 July 2004.

34. Milwaukee Police Department Detective Jason Smith, report of interview with Denise Allison (conducted 24 August 2003).

35. MPD Tolefree Interview.

36. MPD Cooper Interviews. In his effort to exorcise Terrance's alleged demons, Hemphill was following in some formidable footsteps. The scholar Paul Hollenbach has written that if the Gospels provide a reliable record, it seems that "exorcisms played a large role in Jesus' career" by furnishing dramatic evidence of his divinity. As Hollenbach has noted, no other single method of healing is cited more frequently in the Gospels' chronicles of Jesus's ministry. See Paul W. Hollenbach, "Jesus, Demoniacs, and Public Authorities: A Socio-Historical Study," *Journal of the American Academy of Religion*, 49 (1981): 567–588.

37. MPD Cooper Interviews; Milwaukee Police Department Detective Tom Casper, report of interview with Monica Tarver (conducted 22 August 2003) (hereafter MPD Tarver Interview).

38. Milwaukee Police Department Detective Mark Walton, report of interview with Alisa Dawkins (conducted 24 August 2003) (hereafter MPD Dawkins Interview).

39. Ibid.; MPD Cooper Interviews.

40. MPD Tolefree Interview.

41. Milwaukee Police Department Detective Mark Walton, report of interview with Cansell Mitchell (conducted 24 August 2003) (hereafter MPD Mitchell Interview).

42. MPD Mitchell Interview; *State of Wisconsin v. Ray Anthony Hemphill*, Criminal Complaint, Circuit Court, Criminal Division, Milwaukee County, WI, 20 August 2003 (hereafter *Hemphill* Criminal Complaint).

43. MPD Cooper Interviews.

44. Jessica McBride, "Minister Banned from Exorcisms," *Milwaukee Journal Sentinel*, 28 August 2003, 1B.

45. Reid Epstein and Allison Smith, "Boy's Death Ruled a Homicide," *Milwaukee Journal Sentinel*, 26 August 2003, 1A.

46. Wis. Stat. Ch. 948 (2005).

47. Lisa Sweetingham, "Minister Faces Five Years in Prison after Killing Boy during Exorcism," Court TV.com, 6 July 2004.

48. Monica Davey, "Faith Healing Gone Wrong Claims Boy's Life," *New York Times*, 29 August 2003, A12; Kelly Wells, "Church Expects Clearance in Boy's Death,"

Milwaukee Journal Sentinel, 25 August 2003, 1B; Laura Dahlke, "Disabled Deserve Justice, Too," *Milwaukee Journal Sentinel*, 7 September 2003, 5J.

49. Hamilton, *God vs. the Gavel*, 40; Freedom From Religion Foundation, "Minister Faces Only Abuse Charge for Boy's Death," press release, 27 August 2003. Materials relating to the foundation's positions on the Hemphill case and myriad other issues are available on the organization's Web site, http://www.ffrf.org.

50. State of Wisconsin Court of Appeals (District 1), *State of Wisconsin v. Ray Anthony Hemphill*, Brief and Appendix for Plaintiff-Respondent (hereafter *Hemphill* Plaintiff Brief), 2–30; Derrick Nunnally, "Preacher Going on Trial in Autistic Boy's Death," *Milwaukee Journal Sentinel*, 6 July 2004, 1B; Derrick Nunnally, "Details of Boy's Death Changed," *Milwaukee Journal Sentinel*, 7 July 2004, 1A; Derrick Nunnally, "Prosecution Rests in Minister's Abuse Trial," *Milwaukee Journal Sentinel*, 8 July 2004, 1B; Derrick Nunnally, "Prosecutors in Boy's Death Allow Choice of Lesser Charge," *Milwaukee Journal Sentinel*, 9 July 2004, 1B; Derrick Nunnally, "Minister Convicted of Felony Child Abuse," *Milwaukee Journal Sentinel*, 10 July 2004, 1A.

51. *Hemphill* Plaintiff Brief, 2–30; Nunnally, "Details of Boy's Death Changed," 1A; Nunnally, "Preacher Going on Trial," 1B; Nunnally, "Prosecution Rests in Abuse Trial," 1B; Nunnally, "Prosecutors Allow Choice of Lesser Charge," 1B; Nunnally, "Minister Convicted of Felony," 1A.

52. *Hemphill* Plaintiff Brief, 2–30; Nunnally, "Details of Boy's Death Changed," 1A; Nunnally, "Preacher Going on Trial," 1B; Nunnally, "Prosecution Rests in Abuse Trial," 1B; Nunnally, "Prosecutors Allow Choice of Lesser Charge," 1B; Nunnally, "Minister Convicted of Felony," 1A.

53. *Hemphill* Plaintiff Brief, 2–30; Nunnally, "Details of Boy's Death Changed," 1A; Nunnally, "Preacher Going on Trial," 1B; Nunnally, "Prosecution Rests in Abuse Trial," 1B; Nunnally, "Prosecutors Allow Choice of Lesser Charge," 1B; Nunnally, "Minister Convicted of Felony," 1A.

54. Hemphill Plaintiff Brief, 2–30; Nunnally, "Details of Boy's Death Changed," 1A; Nunnally, "Preacher Going on Trial," 1B; Nunnally, "Prosecution Rests in Abuse Trial," 1B; Nunnally, "Prosecutors Allow Choice of Lesser Charge," 1B; Nunnally, "Minister Convicted of Felony," 1A.

55. Nunnally, "Minister Convicted of Felony," 1A; Hamilton, *God vs. the Gavel*, 40.

56. *Hemphill* Plaintiff Brief, 2–30; Derrick Nunnally, "Minister Gets 30 Months in Boy's Death," *Milwaukee Journal Sentinel*, 18 August 2004, 1B.

57. Sweetingham, "Minister Faces Five Years"; Freedom From Religion Foundation, "Minister Faces Only Abuse Charge."

58. Harold Berman, *The Interaction of Law and Religion* (Nashville, TN: Abingdon, 1974), 24–31; Mazur, *Americanization of Religious Minorities*, xx–xxi.

59. Kent Greenawalt, *Private Consciences and Public Reasons* (New York: Oxford University Press, 1995), 7–9.

Bibliography

Abraham, Henry J. "Abraham, Isaac and the State: Faith-Healing and Legal Intervention." *University of Richmond Law Review* 27 (1992–1993): 951–988.

———. "Religion, Medicine, and the State: Reflections on Some Contemporary Issues." *Journal of Church and State* 22 (1980): 423–436.

"An Aggressive Delusion." *Journal of the American Medical Association* 33 (1899): 107.

Agus, M. S. and J. I. Wolfsdorf. "Diabetic Ketoacidosis in Children." *Pediatric Clinics of North America* 52 (2005): 1147–1163.

Albanese, Catherine. "Physic and Metaphysic in Nineteenth-Century America: Medical Sectarians and Religious Healing." *Church History* 55 (1986): 489–502.

Albertine, Susan. "'With Their Tongues Doom Men to Death': Christian Science and the Case of Harold Frederic." *American Literary Realism 1870–1910* 21 (1989): 52–66.

Albl, Martin. "'Are Any among You Sick?' The Health Care System in the Letter of James." *Journal of Biblical Literature* 121 (2002): 123–143.

American Academy of Pediatrics Committee on Bioethics. "Religious Exemptions from Child Abuse Statutes." *Pediatrics* 81 (1988): 169–171.

Amundsen, Darrel. "Medicine and Faith in Early Christianity." *Bulletin of the History of Medicine* 56 (1982): 326–350.

Amundsen, Darrel, and Gary Ferngren. "The Early Christian Tradition." In Numbers and Amundsen, *Caring and Curing*, 40–64.

Anderson, Charles-Edward. "When Faith Healing Fails." *American Bar Association Journal* 75 (July 1989): 22.

Asser, Seth, and Rita Swan. "Child Fatalities from Religion-Motivated Medical Neglect." *Pediatrics* 101 (1998): 625–629.

Avalos, Hector. "Can Science Prove That Prayer Works?" *Free Inquiry* 17 (1997): 27–31.

Baer, Johnathan. "Perfectly Empowered Bodies: Divine Healing in Modernizing America." PhD diss., Yale University, 2002.

———. "Redeemed Bodies: The Functions of Divine Healing in Incipient Pentecostalism." *Church History* 70 (2001): 735–771.

Balizet, Carol. *Born in Zion*. Grapevine, TX: Perazim House, 1996.

Barnes, Linda, and Susan Sered, eds. *Religion and Healing in America*. New York: Oxford University Press, 2005.

Barnes, Patricia, et al. "Complementary and Alternative Medicine Use among Adults: United States, 2002." *Advance Data from Vital and Health Statistics* 343 (2004): 1–19.

Beamn, Warren. "From Sect to Cult to Sect: The Christian Catholic Church in Zion." PhD diss., Iowa State University, 1990.

Beck, Rosalie, and David Hendon. "Notes on Church-State Affairs." *Journal of Church and State* 33 (1991): 404–405.

Benson, Herbert, et al. "Study of the Therapeutic Effects of Intercessory Prayer (STEP) in Cardiac Bypass Patients: A Multicenter Randomized Trial of Uncertainty and Certainty of Receiving Intercessory Prayer." *American Heart Journal* 151 (2006): 934–942.

Berman, Harold. *The Interaction of Law and Religion*. Nashville, TN: Abingdon, 1974.

Bevacqua, J. E. "Diabetic Ketoacidosis in the Pediatric ICU." *Critical Care Nursing Clinics of North America* 17 (2005): 341–347.

Black, Tom. "Real Power." *Christian Science Sentinel* (14 June 2004): 8.

Bloom, Harold. *The American Religion: The Emergence of the Post-Christian Nation*. New York: Simon and Schuster, 1992.

Bosworth, F. F. *Christ the Healer*. Grand Rapids, MI: Revell, 1973.

Bottoms, Bette, et al. "In the Name of God: A Profile of Religion-Related Child Abuse." *Journal of Social Issues* 51 (1995): 85–111.

Bower, Hedy R. "How Far Can a State Go to Protect a Fetus—The Rebecca Corneau Story and the Case for Requiring Massachusetts to Follow the U.S. Constitution." *Golden Gate University Law Review* 123 (2001): 123–154.

Bremmer, Robert, ed. *Children and Youth in America: A Documentary History*. Vol. 1. Cambridge, MA: Harvard University Press, 1970.

Brenneman, Richard. *Deadly Blessings: Faith Healing on Trial*. Buffalo, NY: Prometheus Books, 1990.

The Brethren Encyclopedia. Vol. 1. Philadelphia, PA: Brethren Encyclopedia, 1983.

Brown, Candy Gunther. "From Tent Meetings and Store-Front Healing Rooms to Wal-Marts and the Internet: Healing Spaces in the United States, the Americas, and the World, 1906–2006." *Church History* 75 (2006): 631–647.

Burrow, James. *AMA: Voice of American Medicine*. Baltimore, MD: Johns Hopkins University Press, 1963.

"The Buswell Case." *Christian Science Journal* (May 1893): 65–86.

Bynum, W. F. *Science and the Practice of Medicine in the Nineteenth Century*. Cambridge: Cambridge University Press, 1994.

Byrd, Randolph C. "Positive Therapeutic Effects of Intercessory Prayer in a Coronary Care Unit Population." *Southern Medical Journal* 81 (1988): 826–829.

Calvin, John. *Calvin's Commentary on the Epistle of James*. Aberdeen, Scot.: Chalmers, 1797.

Campbell, Irving. "Christian Science and the Law." *Virginia Law Register* 10 (1904–1905): 285–300.

Carroll, John T. "Sickness and Healing in the New Testament Gospels." *Interpretation* 49 (1995): 130–142.

Cass, Ramona. "We Let Our Son Die: The Tragic Story of Rita and Doug Swan." *Journal of Christian Nursing* (Spring 1987): 4–8.

Cather, Willa, and Georgine Milmine. *The Life of Mary G. Baker Eddy and the History of Christian Science*. Lincoln: University of Nebraska Press, 1993.

Cavendish, Richard, ed. *Man, Myth and Magic: An Illustrated Encyclopedia of the Supernatural*. Vol. 16. New York: Cavendish, 1970.

Cawley, C. C. *The Right to Live*. South Brunswick, NJ: Barnes, 1969.

Chambers, Marcia. "Deliberating Faith, Law and a Life." *National Law Journal* (2 July 1990): 13.

Cockburn, J. S., H. P. F. King, and K. G. T. Mc Donnell, eds. *A History of the County of Middlesex: Volume 1: Physique, Archaeology, Domesday, Ecclesiastical Organization, the Jews, Religious Houses, Education of Working Classes to 1870, Private Education from Sixteenth Century*. London: Victoria County History, 1969.

Cogan, Neil Howard. "Juvenile Law, before and after the Entrance of Parens Patriae." *South Carolina Law Review* 22 (1970): 149–181.

Cohen, Amy F. "The Midwifery Stalemate and Childbirth Choice: Recognizing Mothers-to-Be as the Best Late Pregnancy Decisionmakers." *Indiana Law Journal* 80 (2005): 849–880.

Cohn, Jordan. "When God Is the Doctor." *Student Lawyer* (February 1987): 31–36.

Coletti, Sean. "Taking Account of Partial Exemptors in Vaccination Law, Policy, and Pratice." *Connecticut Law Review* 36 (2003–2004): 1341–1398.

Condran, Gretchen, and Rose Cheney. "Mortality Trends in Philadelphia: Age- and Cause-Specific Death Rates 1870–1930." *Demography* 19 (1982): 97–123.

Conkin, Paul. *American Originals: Homemade Varieties of Christianity*. Chapel Hill: University of North Carolina Press, 1997.

"Conscientious Scruples." *Green Bag* 10 (1898): 496.

Cook, Philip J. *Zion City, Illinois: Twentieth-Century Utopia*. Syracuse, NY: Syracuse University Press, 1996.

Corey, Arthur. *Behind the Scenes with the Metaphysicians*. Los Angeles: Devorss, 1968.

Coulter, Harris Livermore. "Political and Social Aspects of Nineteenth-Century Medicine in the United States: The Formation of the American Medical Association and Its Struggle with Homeopathic and Eclectic Physicians." PhD diss., Columbia University, 1969.

"Crimes—Religious Belief as a Lawful Excuse." *Michigan Law Review* 23 (1924–1925): 912–913.

Cullis, Charles. *Faith Cures; or, Answers to Prayer in the Healing of the Sick*. Boston: Willard Tract Repository, 1879.

Cunningham, Raymond J. "From Holiness to Healing: The Faith Cure in America, 1872–1892." *Church History* 43 (1974): 499–513.

Curriden, Mark. "Blood, the Bible and the Law." *Barrister Magazine* (Fall 1990): 13–15, 41–42.

Curtis, Heather D. "The Lord for the Body: Pain, Suffering, and the Practice of Divine Healing in Late-Nineteenth-Century American Protestantism." ThD diss., Harvard University, 2004.

Custer, Lawrence. "The Origins of the Doctrine of *Parens Patriae*." *Emory Law Journal* 27 (1978): 195–208.

Damore, Leo. *The "Crime" of Dorothy Sheridan*. New York: Arbor House, 1978.

Davies, Stevan. *Jesus the Healer: Possession, Trance, and the Origins of Christianity*. New York: Continuum, 1995.

Dayton, Donald. "The Rise of the Evangelical Healing Movement in Nineteenth Century America." *Pneuma: The Journal of the Society for Pentecostal Studies* 4 (1982): 1–18.

Dossey, Larry. *Healing Words: The Power of Prayer and the Practice of Medicine*. San Francisco: HarperSanFrancisco, 1993.

———. *Prayer Is Good Medicine: How to Reap the Healing Benefits of Prayer*. New York: HarperCollins, 1996.

Dowell, William. "Her Dying Prayers." *Time* (5 May 1997): 66.

Dowie, John Alexander. *The Sermons of John Alexander Dowie: Champion of the Faith*. Shreveport, LA: Voice of Healing, 1951.

———. *Zion's Holy War against the Hosts of Hell in Chicago: A Series of Addresses*. Chicago, IL: Zion, 1900.

"Dr. Rausch's Prescription." *Christian Science Journal* (July 1887): 215.

Dwyer, James G. "The Children We Abandon: Religious Exemptions to Child Welfare and Education Laws as Denials of Equal Protection to Children of Religious Objectors." *North Carolina Law Review* 74 (1996): 1321–1478.

———. "Symposium: Spiritual Treatment Exemptions to Child Medical Neglect Laws: What We Outsiders Should Think." *Notre Dame Law Review* 76 (2000): 147–178.

Eddy, Mary Baker. *Retrospection and Introspection*. Boston: Trustees Under the Will of Mary Baker G. Eddy, 1920.

"Editor's Table." *Christian Science Journal* (April 1898): 66–75.

Epidemiology and Prevention of Vaccine-Preventable Diseases. 8th ed. Washington, DC: Centers for Disease Control and Prevention, National Immunization Program, 2005.

Esbeck, Carl H. "Tort Claims against Churches and Ecclesiastical Officers: The First Amendment Considerations." *West Virginia Law Review* 89 (1986–1987): 1–114.

Etkind, Paul, et al. "Pertussis Outbreaks in Groups Claiming Religious Exemptions to Vaccinations." *American Journal of Diseases of Children* 146 (1992): 173–176.

Evans, Bette Novit. *Interpreting the Free Exercise of Religion: The Constitution and American Pluralism*. Chapel Hill: University of North Carolina Press, 1997.

Fadiman, Anne. *The Spirit Catches You and You Fall Down: A Hmong Child, Her American Doctors, and the Collision of Two Cultures*. New York: Farrar, Straus, & Giroux, 1997.

"Faith-Healing Couple Gets Maximum Sentence—and More." *Pennsylvania Law Weekly* (16 June 1997): 2.

Feikin, Daniel, et al. "Individual and Community Risks of Measles and Pertussis Associated with Personal Exemptions to Immunization." *Journal of the American Medical Association* 284 (2000): 3145–3150.

Fields-Meyer, Thomas. "Protective Custody." *People* (25 September 2000): 64.

Fischer, Kathleen. "Freedom of Religion and Parental Care." *Journal of Juvenile Law* 11 (1990): 73–79.

Fisk, Margaret Cronin. "Christian Scientists Held Liable in Death." *National Law Journal* (20 September 1993): 9.

Flamm, Bruce. "Faith Healing Confronts Modern Medicine." *Scientific Review of Medicine* 8 (2003/2004): 9–14.

Flowers, Ronald. *That Godless Court? Supreme Court Decisions on Church-State Relationships.* 2d ed. Louisville, KY: Westminster John Knox, 2005.

———. "Withholding Medical Care for Religious Reasons." *Journal of Religion and Health* 23 (1984): 268–282.

Foote, G. W. *Peculiar People: An Open Letter to Mr. Justice Wills on His Sentencing Thomas George Senior to Four Months' Imprisonment with Hard Labor for Obeying the Bible.* London: Secular Society, 1899.

Fox, George. *Book of Miracles.* Cambridge: Cambridge University Press, 1948.

———. *The Journal of George Fox.* 2 vols. Cambridge: Cambridge University Press, 1911.

Fox, Margery. "Conflict to Coexistence: Christian Science and Medicine." *Medical Anthropology* 8 (1984): 295–296.

Fox, Richard W. *Jesus in America: Personal Savior, Cultural Hero, National Obsession.* New York: HarperCollins, 2005.

Frame, Randy. "Indiana Grand Jury Indicts a Faith-Healing Preacher." *Christianity Today* (23 November 1984): 38–39.

Fraser, Caroline. *God's Perfect Child: Living and Dying in the Christian Science Church.* New York: Henry Holt, 1999.

———. "Suffering Children and the Christian Science Church." *Atlantic Monthly* (April 1995): 105–120.

Friedelbaum, Stanley H. "Free Exercise in the States: Belief, Conduct, and Judicial Benchmarks." *Albany Law Review* 63 (2000): 1059–1100.

Friedman, Lawrence M. *American Law in the 20th Century.* New Haven, CT: Yale University Press, 2002.

———. *Total Justice: What Americans Want from the Legal System and Why.* Boston: Beacon Press, 1985.

Galton, Francis. "Statistical Inquiries into the Efficacy of Prayer." *Fortnightly Review* 12 (1872): 125–135.

Gardyn, Rebecca, ed. "Quackery No More." *American Demographics* (January 2001): 10.

Gifford, Bill. "A Matter of Faith." *Philadelphia Magazine* (September 1997): 96–101, 154–156.

Gill, Gillian. *Mary Baker Eddy.* Reading, MA: Perseus Books, 1998.

Gordon, A. J. *The Ministry of Healing. Healing: The Three Great Classics on Divine Healing.* Ed. Jonathan Graf. Camp Hill, PA: Christian, 1992.

Gordon, Dianna. "When Faith-Healing Fails." *State Legislatures* (March 2000): 26–27.

Gottschalk, Stephen. "Spiritual Healing and the Law: A Dispute." *Christian Century* (19 October 1988): 928–929.

———. "Spiritual Healing on Trial: A Christian Scientist Reports." *Christian Century* (22–29 June 1988): 602–605.

Greenawalt, Kent. *Private Consciences and Public Reasons.* New York: Oxford University Press, 1995.

Haller, John S. *American Medicine in Transition, 1840–1910.* Urbana: University of Illinois Press, 1981.

Hamilton, Marci. *God vs. the Gavel: Religion and the Rule of Law.* New York: Cambridge University Press, 2005.

Hansen, Bert. "New Images of a New Medicine: Visual Evidence for the Widespread Popularity of Therapeutic Discoveries in America after 1885." *Bulletin of the History of Medicine* 73 (1999): 629–678.

Harlan, Rolvix. *John Alexander Dowie and the Christian Catholic Apostolic Church in Zion.* Evansville, WI: Antes, 1906.

Harrell, David Edwin, Jr. *All Things Are Possible: The Healing and Charismatic Revivals in Modern America.* Bloomington: Indiana University Press, 1975.

Hart, Stuart N. "From Property to Person Status: Historical Perspective on Children's Rights." *American Psychologist* 46 (1991): 53–59.

Hayden, Daniel. "Calling the Elders to Pray." *Bibliotheca Sacra* 138 (1981): 258–266.

Hiss, William Charles. "Shiloh: Frank W. Sandford and the Kingdom, 1893–1948." PhD diss., Tufts University, 1978.

Hollenbach, Paul W. "Jesus, Demoniacs, and Public Authorities: A Socio-Historical Study." *Journal of the American Academy of Religion* 49 (1981): 567–588.

The Holy Bible: New Revised Standard Version with Apocrypha. New York: Oxford University Press, 2001.

"Infants—Power of Court to Order Operation on Minor Child against Will of Parents." *Tennessee Law Review* 12 (1933–1934): 59–60.

James, Henry. *The Bostonians: A Novel.* New York: Penguin, 2000.

Jiggens, Fred J. *"Glory Be."* Elms Court, UK: Stockwell, 1978.

Johnsen, Thomas. "Christian Scientists and the Medical Profession." *Medical Heritage* 2 (1986): 70–78.

Johnson, Daniel M., et al. "Religion, Health and Healing: Findings from a Southern City." *Sociological Analysis* 47 (1986): 66–73.

Juhnke, Eric S. *Quacks and Crusaders: The Fabulous Careers of John Brinkley, Norman Baker, and Harry Hoxsey.* Lawrence: University Press of Kansas, 2002.

Kaminer, Wendy. "Sectual Discrimination." *American Prospect* (11 March 2002): 9.

Kaunitz, Andrew, et al. "Perinatal and Maternal Mortality in a Religious Group Avoiding Obstetric Care." *American Journal of Obstetrics and Gynecology* 150 (1984): 826–31.

Kearney, Daniel J. "Parental Failure to Provide Child with Medical Assistance Based on Religious Beliefs Causing Child's Death—Involuntary Manslaughter in Pennsylvania." *Dickinson Law Review* 90 (1985–1986): 861–890.

Kelsey, Morton. *Healing and Christianity: In Ancient Thought and Modern Times.* New York: Harper and Row, 1973.

Kenney, Elizabeth Barnaby, Susan Eyrich Lederer, and Edmond P. Minihan. "Sectarians and Scientists: Alternatives to Orthodox Medicine." In Ronald L. Numbers and Judith Walzer Leavitt, eds., *Wisconsin Medicine: Historical Perspectives*. Madison: University of Wisconsin Press, 1981. 60–61.

Koenig, Harold. *The Healing Power of Faith: Science Explores Medicine's Last Great Frontier*. New York: Simon & Schuster, 1999.

Koenig, Harold, Michael McCullough, and David Larson, eds. *Handbook of Religion and Health*. New York: Oxford University Press, 2001.

Kohn, Alfie. "Mind over Matter." *New England Monthly* (March 1988): 59–63, 95–97.

Kuhlman, Kathryn. *God Can Do It Again*. Englewood Cliffs, NJ: Prentice-Hall, 1969.

———. *I Believe in Miracles*. Englewood Cliffs, NJ: Prentice-Hall, 1962.

Lee, Christine, Erik Berntorp, and W. Keith Hoots, eds. *Textbook of Hemophilia*. Malden, MA: Blackwell, 2004.

Levy, Joelyn Knopf. "Jehovah's Witnesses, Pregnancy, and Blood Transfusions: A Paradigm for Autonomy Rights of All Pregnant Women." *Journal of Law, Medicine and Ethics* 27 (1999): 171–185.

Lewis, James R. *Legitimating New Religions*. New Brunswick, NJ: Rutgers University Press, 2003.

Lewis, James R., and Jesper Aagaard Petersen, eds. *Controversial New Religions*. New York: Oxford University Press, 2005.

Lindsay, Gordon. *John Alexander Dowie: A Life Story of Trials, Tragedies and Triumphs*. Dallas, TX: Christ for the Nations, 1986.

Long, Carolyn. *Religious Freedom and Indian Rights: The Case of* Oregon v. Smith. Lawrence: University Press of Kansas, 2000.

Lutes, Chris. "Former Staff Pastor Says Faith Assembly Is a Cult." *Christianity Today* (7 November 1986): 61–62.

Luther, Martin. *Luther's Works*. Vol. 35. Philadelphia, PA: Muhlenberg Press, 1960.

Mantone, Amanda. "Storefront Churches Are Lifeblood to Urban Poor." *Christian Century* (20 April 2004): 14.

Markel, Howard, and Janet Golden. "Children's Public Health Policy in the United States: How the Past Can Inform the Future." *Health Affairs* 23 (2004): 147–152.

Mason, Mary Ann. *From Father's Property to Children's Rights: The History of Child Custody in the United States*. New York: Columbia University Press, 1994.

Massie, Ann MacLean. "The Religion Clauses and Parental Health Care Decisionmaking for Children: Suggestions for a New Approach." *Hastings Constitutional Law Quarterly* 21 (1994): 725–776.

Matthews, Dale. *The Faith Factor: Proof of the Healing Power of Prayer*. With Connie Clark. New York: Viking, 1998.

Mazur, Eric Michael. *The Americanization of Religious Minorities: Confronting the Constitutional Order*. Baltimore, MD: Johns Hopkins University Press, 1999.

McClendon, James. "Spiritual Healing and Folklore Research: Evaluating the Hypnosis/Placebo Theory." *Alternative Therapies* 3 (January 1997): 61–66.

McCoy, Michael. *Twentieth-Century Shapers of American Popular Religion*. Westport, CT: Greenwood, 1989.

McGuire, Meredith B. *Ritual Healing in Suburban America*. New Brunswick, NJ: Rutgers University Press, 1988.

"The Medical Bill at Albany." *Christian Science Journal* (May 1898): 96–102.

Meissner, H. Cody, Peter M. Strebel, and Walter A. Orenstein. "Measles Vaccines and the Potential for Worldwide Eradication of Measles." *Pediatrics* 114 (October 2004): 1065–1069.

Melton, J. Gordon. *Encyclopedia of American Religions.* 6th ed. Detroit: Gale Research, 1998.

Merrick, Janna C. "Spiritual Healing, Sick Kids and the Law: Inequities in the American Health Care System." *American Journal of Law and Medicine* 29 (2003): 269–300.

Merrill, J. H., ed. *The American and English Encyclopedia of Law.* Vol. 21. Northport, NY: Thompson, 1889.

Miller, Marilyn. "Fetal Neglect and State Intervention: Preventing Another Attleboro Cult Baby Death." *Cardozo Women's Law Journal* 8 (2001–2002): 71–104.

Monopoli, Paula A. "Allocating the Costs of Parental Free Exercise: Striking a New Balance between Sincere Religious Belief and a Child's Right to Medical Treatment." *Pepperdine Law Review* 18 (1991): 319–352.

Montgomery, Carrie Judd. *The Life and Teaching of Carrie Judd Montgomery,* comp. Roberts Liardon. New York: Garland, 1985.

Moore, R. Laurence. *Religious Outsiders and the Making of Americans.* New York: Oxford University Press, 1986.

Morris, Robin Power. "The Corneau Case, Furthering Trends of Fetal Rights and Religious Freedom." *New England Journal on Criminal and Civil Confinement* 28 (2002): 89–121.

Morton, J. Sterling, and Albert Watkins. *History of Nebraska: From the Earliest Explorations of the Trans-Mississippi.* Lincoln, NE: Western, 1918.

Mullin, Robert Bruce. *Miracles and the Modern Religious Imagination.* New Haven, CT: Yale University Press, 1996.

Nelson, Kathleen. "The Curious World of Quacks." *Lancet* 360 (26 October 2002): 1337.

Nelson, Shirley. *Fair, Clear and Terrible: The Story of Shiloh, Maine.* Latham, NY: British American, 1989.

Newcomb, Arthur. *Dowie: Anointed of the Lord.* New York: Century, 1930.

"News from Abroad." *Christian Science Journal* (March 1889): 637–639.

Nickerson, Bruce, ed. "Faith Healing in Indiana and Illinois." *Indiana Folklore* 6 (1973): 33–99.

Nobel, Barry. "Religious Healing in the Courts: The Liberties and Liabilities of Patients, Parents, and Healers." *Puget Sound Law Review* 16 (1993): 599–710.

Nolen, William. *Healing: A Doctor in Search of a Miracle.* New York: Random House, 1974.

Noll, Mark. *The Work We Have to Do: A History of Protestants in America.* New York: Oxford University Press, 2002.

Novotny, Thomas, et al. "Measles Outbreaks in Religious Groups Exempt from Immunization Laws." *Public Health Reports* 103 (1988): 49–54.

Numbers, Ronald, and Darrel Amundsen, eds. *Caring and Curing: Health and Medicine in the Western Religious Traditions.* Baltimore, MD: Johns Hopkins University Press, 1986.

Numbers, Ronald, and Darrel Amundsen. "Introduction." In Numbers and Amundsen, *Caring and Curing*, 1–4.

O'Brien, David. *Animal Sacrifice and Religious Freedom:* Church of the Lukumi Babalu Aye v. City of Hialeah. Lawrence: University Press of Kansas, 2004.

"One of the New 'Laws.'" *Christian Science Journal* (July 1897): 235–236.

Parker, Larry. *Assumptions About Faith and Tradition.* Frederick, MD: PublishAmerica, 2002.

———. *We Let Our Son Die: A Parent's Search for Truth.* Irvine, CA: Harvest House, 1980.

Parker, William R., and Elaine St. Johns. *Prayer Can Change Your Life: Experiments and Techniques in Prayer Therapy.* Carmel, NY: Guideposts, 1957.

Passantino, Gretchen. "Are Jehovah's Witness Witnesses Giving Up on Their Blood Transfusion Ban?" *Christian Research Journal* 23 (2000): 6–9.

Payne, George Henry. *The Child in Human Progress.* New York: Putnam's, 1916.

Peters, Shawn Francis. *Judging Jehovah's Witnesses: Religious Persecution and the Dawn of the Rights Revolution.* Lawrence: University Press of Kansas, 2000.

———. *The* Yoder *Case: Religious Liberty, Education, and Parental Rights,* Lawrence: University Press of Kansas, 2003.

Poloma, Margaret M. "A Comparison of Christian Science and Mainline Christian Healing Ideologies and Practices." *Review of Religious Research* 32 (1991): 337–350.

Porter, Roy. "Before the Fringe: Quack Medicine in Georgian England." *History Today* (November 1986): 16–22.

Porterfield, Amanda. *Healing in the History of Christianity.* New York: Oxford University Press, 2005.

———. "Healing in the History of Christianity: Presidential Address, January 2002, American Society of Church History." *Church History* 72 (June 2002): 227–242.

Purrington, William. "'Christian Science' and Its Legal Aspects." *North American Review* (March 1899): 345–361.

———. "Manslaughter, Christian Science and the Law." *American Lawyer* 7 (1899): 5–9.

Randi, James. *The Faith Healers.* Buffalo, NY: Prometheus Books, 1987.

"Recent Important Decisions." *Michigan Law Review* 23 (1924–1925): 912.

Rendleman, Douglas R. "Parens Patriae: From Chancery to the Juvenile Court." *South Carolina Law Review* 209 (1971): 209–227.

Review of *A History of Crime in England,* vol. 2, by Luke Owen Pike. *Law Magazine and Review* 241 (1876–1877): 261–163.

Richardson, James T., and John DeWitt. "Christian Science Spiritual Healing, the Law, and Public Opinion." *Journal of Church and State* 34 (1992): 549–561.

Rodgers, Desiree, et al. "High Attack Rates and Case Fatality during a Measles Outbreak in Groups with Religious Exemption to Vaccination." *Pediatric Infectious Disease Journal* 12 (1988): 288–292.

Rosato, Jennifer. "Putting Square Pegs in a Round Hole: Procedural Due Process and the Effect of Faith Healing Exemptions on the Prosecution of Faith Healing Parents." *University of South Florida Law Review* 29 (1994): 43–120.

Salmon, Daniel, et al. "Health Consequences of Religious and Philosophical Exemp-
    tions from Immunization Laws: Individual and Societal Risk of Measles." *Journal
    of the American Medical Association* 282 (1999): 47–53.

Saroyan, Zaven T. "Spiritual Healing and the Free Exercise Clause: An Argument
    for the Use of Strict Scrutiny." *Boston Public Interest Law Journal* 12 (2003):
    368–388.

Schally, Gabriel, and Isabel Oliver. "Putting Jenner back in his place." *Lancet* 362 (4
    October 2003): 1092.

Schiederer, Judith. "When Children Die as a Result of Religious Practices." *Ohio State
    Law Journal* 51 (1990): 1429–1446.

Schneider, Steven. "Christian Science and the Law: Room for Compromise?" *Columbia
    Journal of Law and Social Problems* 1 (1965): 81–88.

Schoepflin, Rennie B. *Christian Science on Trial: Religious Healing in America.*
    Baltimore, MD: Johns Hopkins University Press, 2003.

"A Setback for Faith Curists." *American Lawyer* 11 (October 1903): 10.

Shaw, George Bernard. *The Complete Prefaces: Vol. 2: 1914–1929.* London: Penguin,
    1995.

Shelman, Eric, and Stephen Lazoritz. *The Mary Ellen Wilson Child Abuse Case and the
    Beginning of Children's Rights in 19th Century America.* Jefferson, NC: McFarland,
    2005.

Shepard, Suzanne. "Suffer the Little Children." *Redbook* (October 1994): 66, 68, 70,
    72.

Simpson, A. B. *The Gospel of Healing. Healing: The Three Great Classics on Divine
    Healing.* Ed. Jonathan Graf. Camp Hill, PA: Christian Publications, 1992.

Simpson, William Franklin. "Comparative Longevity in a College Cohort of Christian
    Scientists." *Journal of the American Medical Association* 262 (22–29 September
    1989): 1657–1658.

Sloan, R. P., E. Bagiella, and T. Powell. "Religion, Spirituality, and Medicine." *Lancet*
    353 (20 February 1999): 664–667.

Smith, Clifford P. "Christian Science and Legislation." *Christian Science Journal*
    (October 1905): 405–412.

Smith, Edward Egan. "The Criminalization of Belief: When Free Exercise Isn't."
    Hastings Law Journal 42 (1991): 1491–1526.

Smith, Morton. *Jesus the Magician: Charlatan or Son of God?* San Francisco: Harper-
    Collins, 1978.

Smletana, Bob. "Fatal Revelations." *Christianity Today* (21 May 2002): 25–27.

Sorrell, Mark. *The Peculiar People.* Exeter, UK: Paternoster, 1979.

Spence, C., et al. "The Faith Assembly: A Follow-up Study of Faith Healing and
    Mortality." *Indiana Medicine* 80 (1987): 238–40.

Stanfield, Jennifer. "Faith Healing and Religious Treatment Exemptions to Child-
    Endangerment Laws: Should Parents Be Allowed to Refuse Necessary Medical
    Treatment for Their Children Based on Their Religious Beliefs?" *Hamline Journal
    of Public Law and Policy* 22 (2000): 45–86.

Starr, Paul. *The Social Transformation of American Medicine.* New York: Basic Books,
    1982.

"State Intervenes to Save Child's Leg." *Literary Digest* (18 August 1934): 30.

Stein, Stephen J. *Communities of Dissent: A History of Alternative Religions in America.* New York: Oxford University Press, 2000.

Sullivan, Lawrence. "Healing." In *The Encyclopedia of Religion,* ed. Mircea Eliade. Vol. 6. New York: Macmillan, 1987. 226–233.

Swan, Rita. "The Law Should Protect All Children." *Journal of Christian Nursing* (Spring 1987): 40.

———. "On Statutes Depriving a Class of Children of Rights to Medical Care: Can This Discrimination Be Litigated?" *Quinnipiac Health Law Journal* 2 (1998/1999): 73–96.

———. "When Faith Fails Children—Religion-Based Neglect: Pervasive, Deadly . . . and Legal?" *Humanist* (November/December 2000): 11–16.

Szasz, Ferenc. "Francis Schlatter: The Healer of the Southwest." *New Mexico Historical Review* 54 (1979): 89–104.

Tanenhaus, David. "Between Dependency and Liberty: The Conundrum of Children's Rights in the Gilded Age." *Law and History Review* 23 (2005): 351–385.

Thomas, Mason P. "Child Abuse and Neglect, Part I: Historical Overview, Legal Matrix, and Social Perspectives." *North Carolina Law Review* 50 (1972): 293–349.

Trahan, Jennifer, and Susan Wolf. "Rights of State and Family Clash in Forced-Immunization Cases." *National Law Journal* (13 May 1991): 28.

Tucker, Ruth. "From the Fringe to the Fold." *Christianity Today* (15 July 1996): 26–32.

Twain, Mark. *Christian Science: With Notes Containing Corrections to Date.* New York: Harper, 1907.

Umbreit, A. C., ed. *Christian Science and the Practice of Medicine:* State of Wisconsin vs. Crecentia Arries and Emma Nichols. Milwaukee, WI: Keogh, 1900.

Vaillant, Daniel. "The Prosecution of Christian Scientists: A Needed Protection for Children or Insult Added to Injury?" *Cleveland State Law Review* 48 (2000): 479–502.

Van Biema, David. "Faith or Healing?" *Time* (31 August 1998): 68–69.

Wacker, Grant. *Heaven Below: Early Pentecostals and American Culture.* Cambridge, MA: Harvard University Press, 2001.

———. "Marching to Zion: Religion in a Modern Utopian Community." *Church History* 54 (1985): 496–511.

———. "The Pentecostal Tradition." In Numbers and Amundsen, *Caring and Curing,* 514–538.

Waller, John. *The Discovery of the Germ: Twenty Years That Transformed the Way We Think about Disease.* New York: Columbia University Press, 2002.

Warfield, Benjamin. *Counterfeit Miracles.* New York: Scribner's, 1918.

Warner, John Harley. *The Therapeutic Perspective: Medical Practice, Knowledge, and Identity in America, 1820–1885.* Cambridge, MA: Harvard University Press, 1986.

Warner, Wayne. "At the Grass-Roots: Kathryn Kuhlman's Pentecostal-Charismatic Influence on Historic Mainstream Churches." *Pneuma: The Journal of the Society for Pentecostal Studies* 17 (1995): 51–65.

Weaver, C. Douglas. *The Healer-Prophet, William Marrion Branham: A Study in the Prophetic in American Pentecostalism.* Macon, GA: Mercer University Press, 1987.

Weitz, Mark A. *Clergy Malpractice in America:* Nally v. Grace Community Church of the Valley. Lawrence: University Press of Kansas, 2001.

White, Arnold L. *The Almighty and Us: The Inside Story of Shiloh, Maine.* Ft. Lauderdale, FL: self-published, 1979.

Wilkinson, John. *The Bible and Healing: A Medical and Theological Commentary.* Grand Rapids, MI: Eerdmans, 1998.

Williams, Joel Stephen. "Ethical Issues in Compulsory Medical Treatment: A Study of Jehovah's Witnesses and Blood Transfusion." PhD diss., Baylor University, 1987.

Williams, William Carlos. *The Autobiography of William Carlos Williams.* New York: New Directions, 1951.

Wilson, G. E. "Christian Science and Longevity." *Journal of Forensic Science* 1 (1965): 43–60.

Woodworth-Etter, Maria. *Maria Woodworth-Etter: The Complete Collection of Her Life Teachings.* Tulsa, OK: Albury, 2000.

Young, James Harvey. *American Health Quackery: Collected Essays by James Harvey Young.* Princeton, NJ: Princeton University Press, 1992.

——. *Medical Messiahs: A Social History of Health Quackery in Twentieth-Century America.* Princeton, NJ: Princeton University Press, 1967.

Index